ADVANCES IN
RESEARCH ON TEACHING

Volume 2 • 1991

TEACHERS' KNOWLEDGE OF SUBJECT MATTER
AS IT RELATES TO THEIR TEACHING PRACTICE

ADVANCES IN RESEARCH ON TEACHING

A Research Annual

TEACHERS' KNOWLEDGE OF SUBJECT MATTER
AS IT RELATES TO THEIR TEACHING PRACTICE

Editor: JERE BROPHY
College of Education
Michigan State University

VOLUME 2 • 1991

 JAI PRESS INC.

Greenwich, Connecticut   London, England

CONTENTS

LIST OF CONTRIBUTORS

Charles W. Anderson

College of Education
Michigan State University

Deborah Loewenberg Ball

College of Education
Michigan State University

Juliet Baxter

College of Education
University of Oregon

William S. Carlsen

Department of Education
Cornell University

Thomas P. Carpenter

College of Education
University of Wisconsin

Elizabeth Fennema

College of Education
University of Wisconsin

Pamela L. Grossman

College of Education
University of Washington

Sigrun Gudmundsdottir

Pedagogical Institute
University of Trondheim

Robert E. Hollon

College of Education
University of Wisconsin

Gaea Leinhardt

Learning Research and
    Development Center
University of Pittsburgh

Daniel C. Neale   College of Education
                                     University of Delaware

Penelope L. Peterson   College of Education
                                     Michigan State University

Ralph T. Putnam   College of Education
                                     Michigan State University

Kathleen J. Roth   College of Education
                                     Michigan State University

Deborah C. Smith   College of Education
                                     University of Delaware

Mary Kay Stein   Learning Research and
                                        Development Center
                                     University of Pittsburgh

Suzanne M. Wilson   College of Education
                                     Michigan State University

Samuel S. Wineburg   College of Education
                                     University of Washington

INTRODUCTION TO VOLUME 2

This is Volume 2 of the *Advances in Research on Teaching* series, which has been established to provide state-of-the-art conceptualization and analysis of the processes involved in functioning as a classroom teacher. These include not only the behaviors of teachers that can be observed in the classroom, but also the planning, thinking, and decision making that occur before, during, and after interaction with students. Most contributions to the series link information about teaching processes with information about presage variables (especially teacher knowledge and beliefs), context variables, or student outcome variables. Each volume is planned with an eye toward pulling together and providing visibility to emerging trends in research on classroom teaching that appear to be spawning important contributions likely to have lasting value.

The first two volumes reflect complementary aspects of an important trend that characterized research on teaching during the 1980s: a shift in focus from relatively generic aspects of teaching to the specifics involved in teaching particular subject matter at a particular grade level. In order to establish that teachers "make a difference" (i.e., have a significant impact on their students' achievement), researchers of the 1960s and 1970s concentrated on linking measures of teachers' general classroom management effectiveness and time usage patterns to their students' gains on standardized achievement tests. This work showed that student achievement gains were associated with such classroom process variables as *student opportunity to learn/teacher content coverage* (determined by the available classroom time, the percentage of this time that was allocated to academic rather than nonacademic activities, and the degree to which the teacher was successful in keeping the students actively engaged in ongoing academic activities) and *active teaching* (the degree to which teachers actively instructed their students during interactive lessons featuring teacher-student discourse, rather than expecting the students to learn mostly on their own through independent reading and seatwork assignments).

These findings were important for reaffirming the teacher's vital role in stimulating student learning. However, they were limited to the relatively generic aspects of teaching. They provided gross quantitative indicators of the minimal conditions for effective lessons, but did not shed much light on the more subtle and qualitative aspects of good teaching. Aware of these and other limitations of the 1960s and 1970s studies (e.g., reliance on standardized tests that assessed lower-order but not higher-order outcomes), researchers studying teaching during the 1980s developed more qualitative and fine-grained methods. Rather than sampling periodically across a school year, they focused more intensively on particular curriculum units or even individual lessons, taking into account the teacher's instructional objectives and assessing student learning accordingly. This meant knowing what the teacher was trying to accomplish, recording detailed information about classroom processes as they unfolded during the unit or lesson, and assessing learning using criterion-referenced measures keyed to the instructional goals. In addition to or instead of the familiar multiple-choice test, researchers began using more comprehensive assessment procedures involving interviewing students individually at some length to determine the degree to which they could explain concepts or principles in their own words, as well as presenting them with application tasks to determine the degree to which they could apply their learning strategically under realistic problem-solving conditions.

These and other refinements described in the introduction to the first volume in this series (Brophy, 1989) led to the kinds of research described in that volume—studies of the curriculum, instruction, and evaluation practices involved in teaching subject-matter content for meaningful understanding and self-regulated learning by the students. These studies highlighted the importance of such factors as couching the teaching of content within application contexts, emphasizing conceptual understanding of knowledge and self-regulated application of skills, providing explicit explanations and elaborating on these in ways that are responsive to students' questions or learning difficulties, connecting input with students' existing ideas and correcting their misconceptions, and scaffolding their learning efforts by initially providing a good deal of explanation, modeling, and cueing, but gradually fading these supports as the students develop expertise and become capable of more independent and self-regulated learning.

As investigators developed more information about these elements involved in teaching subject matter for understanding and self-regulated learning, they began to note that teachers differed considerably from one another not only in the degree to which they incorporated these elements into their teaching, but also in their knowledge of the subject matter and in their beliefs about what is involved in teaching and learning it. Also, those who mounted intervention studies that called for training teachers in models of good subject-matter teaching found that the teachers' willingness and ability to implement the new models were determined in part by their subject-matter knowledge and beliefs. Some elements of the models apparently could not be implemented effectively unless teachers had sufficiently well-organized and accessible subject-matter knowledge, and some elements were ignored because the teachers did not understand why they were important or were resisted because they conflicted with the teachers' beliefs about what is involved in teaching and learning the subject. Thus, research on the process aspects of good subject-matter teaching (the focus of the first volume in this series) led many investigators to an interest in the teacher knowledge and beliefs that are needed to support such teaching (the focus of this second volume).

Movement toward focus on these same topics also occurred during the 1980s among investigators who had been focusing on the "mental lives" of teachers by studying their planning, thinking, judgment, and decision making. A burgeoning literature (reviewed by Clark & Peterson, 1986) had developed on these topics in the 1970s and early 1980s, in which cognitive activities of teachers were studied either in their own right or in connection with observed classroom behavior. Early efforts relied on highly artificial methods borrowed from psychologists studying human judgment and decision making, but these soon gave way to more valid and informative work based on such methods as asking teachers to think aloud as they planned a lesson (and then interrogating them for elaboration) or viewing teachers' videotaped lessons with them and questioning them about the rationales underlying their behavior at key decision points.

Like the classroom process research on teacher effects on student achievement, this research on teachers' cognitive activities conducted during the 1970s and early 1980s focused on relatively generic aspects of teaching (in this case, management of activities and interactions with students) without delving much into the specifics involved in teaching particular subject matter. The same general trend toward increasing interest in subject matter began to affect this line of research as well, however, so that investigators interested in teachers' cognitive activities began to pay increasing attention to teachers' knowledge of and beliefs about subject matter.

Shulman (1986) provided impetus to this movement in both lines of research by arguing that subject matter had been all but neglected in the research on teaching done in the 1960s and 1970s and calling for systematic attention to it. Drawing on early findings from his own project on how beginning teachers learn to teach, he argued that teachers need to develop several different kinds of knowledge to support effective instruction. In particular, he stressed their need for *pedagogical content knowledge*, which he defined as a special form of professional understanding that is unique to teachers and combines knowledge of the content to be taught with knowledge of what students know or think they know about this content and knowledge of how the content can be represented to the students (through examples, analogies, etc.) in ways that are most likely to be effective for helping them to attain the intended outcomes of instruction. Thus, effective teachers not only know their subject but know what aspects of it to present to particular students and how to represent that content in ways that the students can understand and appreciate.

The contributions to this volume differ from earlier, less productive work on teachers' subject-matter knowledge in large part because they focus on teachers' pedagogical content knowledge (and related beliefs). Instead of merely correlating a broad, indirect measure of teachers' subject-matter knowledge (such as their grade-point average or the number of courses that they have taken in the subject) with some measure of their teaching effectiveness, these studies provide detailed information about the subject-matter goals that teachers pursue with their students, the content selection and representation choices they make in developing their instructional plans, and the pedagogical content knowledge that underlies these decisions. The emphasis is not just on what the teachers know about the subject, but on what they want the students to know, and how they propose to teach them.

Along with teachers' pedagogical *knowledge of* their subject, decisions about what and how to teach are determined by teachers' *beliefs about* the subject. Similar students learning about ostensibly similar content from different teachers may have very different experiences if their teachers have very different beliefs about the nature of the subject matter, about the reasons why it is included in the curriculum and the purposes to be accomplished by teaching it, or about what learning experiences will be most effective for moving students toward the intended outcomes. Given that content is not a goal in itself but is selected as a means to accomplish curricular goals, teachers' beliefs and associated values and attitudes about their subject and what is involved in teaching and learning it are just as important as their pedagogical content knowledge in determining what occurs and how effective it is with their students. It should be noted that I have distinguished teachers' *beliefs about* subject matter from their *knowledge of* subject matter in order to call attention to the fact that the scope of this volume is broader than what is ordinarily implied by the term "subject-matter knowledge," and also to introduce some issues that are addressed in more detail by Ball in Chapter 1. In contrasting the two terms, I do not wish to imply sharp conceptual distinctions or to take a firm position on underlying philosophical issues. Given that the development of knowledge is a dynamic process that features both construction and deconstruction in response to experience and situational demands, and given that much of what is commonly called knowledge has never been directly verified by the knower, one cannot construe knowledge as static or distinguish it unambiguously from beliefs. Furthermore, certain aspects of teachers' subject-matter related cognitions such as their perspectives on the nature of their discipline would be difficult to classify as either knowledge or beliefs. Thus, although it is useful to draw contrasts between *knowledge of* and *beliefs about* a subject for purposes of analysis, readers should bear in mind that these contrasts are relative rather than absolute.

The research described in various chapters in this volume encompasses a variety of school subjects (mathematics, science, English literature, and history), grade levels (most of the K-12 range), and methodologies, and it conveys a wealth of detail about teachers' knowledge and beliefs concerning the teaching of particular content in particular contexts. Yet, as in Volume 1, the different contributions also address many common issues and report mostly complementary and mutually supportive findings. Here, the findings deal with such issues as the differences between the subject-matter knowledge and beliefs of novice teachers and those of experienced teachers, changes that occur as novice teachers gain experience or as experienced teachers participate in inservice programs, relationships between teachers' knowledge and beliefs about teaching a subject and the ways that they actually teach it to their students, and contrasts between how teachers teach content about which they are highly knowledgeable and how they teach content about which they are less knowledgeable.

The volume begins with three chapters on teachers' knowledge and beliefs concerning elementary mathematics instruction. In Chapter 1, Deborah Ball provides an overview of this topic and then illustrates several themes using case studies of three teachers who contrast with one another in their knowledge, beliefs, and instructional practices. In Chapter 2, Penelope Peterson, Elizabeth Fennema, and Thomas Carpenter describe the nature and effects of their Cognitively Guided Instruction inservice program for elementary teachers. The program successfully changed the teachers' beliefs about and knowledge of children's mathematical learning, leading to changes in instructional methods that resulted in improved accomplishment of higher order outcomes without any reduction in accomplishment of lower order outcomes. In Chapter 3, Gaea Leinhardt, Ralph Putnam, Mary Kay Stein, and Juliet Baxter illustrate the role of subject-matter knowledge by comparing novice with expert teachers concerning: (1) their general agendas describing the major purposes and strategies for the lesson as a whole, (2) the curriculum scripts that represent their goals and actions for teaching particular topics within the lesson, (3) their explanations of particular mathematical content, and (4) their representations of particular concepts, meanings, or procedures. In each of these areas, the experts' knowledge tends to be both better differentiated and better organized, as well as more accessible for use when needed and more adaptable to the particular circumstances that arise as a lesson develops.

The next three chapters concern teachers' knowledge and beliefs related to science teaching. Chapter 4 focuses on the conceptual change orientation to this topic. In this chapter, William Carlsen describes some of the reasons why movement from more typical orientations toward a conceptual change orientation is likely to be slow, uneven, and dependent on the specific teaching context. He illustrates the latter point with data indicating that the same teachers are likely to be more effective in several respects when teaching content about which they are highly knowledgeable than when teaching other content. In Chapter 5, Robert Hollon, Kathleen Roth, and Charles Anderson argue that the most effective teachers of science construe science learning as a process of inducing conceptual change in their students (not merely providing them with information) and of instructing the students in such a way that they not only can pass tests on the knowledge but can use it to describe, explain, make predictions about, or exert control over their world. They also describe the teacher knowledge and beliefs that support this kind of science teaching and contrast these with alternatives that are associated with less effective science teaching. In Chapter 6, Deborah Smith and Daniel Neale present case studies of five teachers who participated in an inservice program designed to help them become the kind of conceptual change teachers described by Hollon, Roth, and Anderson. The case studies illustrate that the degree to which different teachers made progress toward the goals of the inservice program was determined in part by the content knowledge and especially the orientations to teaching and learning science that the teachers had developed prior to their involvement in the program.

Along with Chapter 4, the studies reported in Chapters 7 through 9 are related in that they all were done as part of the program of research on how teachers learn to teach that was initiated by Lee Shulman at Stanford University.

Chapters 7 though 9 concern instruction in secondary English literature and history. In Chapter 7, Pamela Grossman describes different orientations that teachers can take to the teaching of literature and provides case studies illustrating that teachers with contrasting orientations pursue different goals and plan different lessons and activities. In Chapter 8, Sigrun Gudmundsdottir continues with this same theme, presenting case material from two English literature teachers and two history teachers to illustrate that similarities and differences in the ways that they taught their subjects were related to similarities and differences in the pedagogical models that they had developed to guide their instructional planning. Finally, in Chapter 9, Samuel Wineburg and Suzanne Wilson present extended case examples from the teaching of two history teachers who had been identified as outstanding. They first describe the teachers' instruction in detail and then reflect on the ways that this instruction was informed by rich networks of pedagogical content knowledge and beliefs.

Following most of the chapters is a brief cross-talk section in which the authors respond to questions and comments raised by myself or by other chapter authors. Then, in a concluding section, I describe some of the points of agreement and disagreement between chapter authors and identify additional issues needing research attention.

Jere Brophy
Editor

REFERENCES

Brophy, J. (Ed.). (1989). *Advances in research on teaching, Vol. 1.* Greenwich CT: JAI Press.

Clark, C., & Peterson, P. (1986). Teachers' thought processes. In M.C. Wittrock (Ed.), *Handbook of research on teaching* (3rd ed., pp. 255-296). New York: Macmillan.

Shulman, L. (1986). Paradigms and research programs in the study of teaching: A contemporary perspective. In M.C. Wittrock (Ed.), *Handbook of research on teaching* (3rd ed., pp. 3-36). New York: Macmillan.

ACKNOWLEDGMENTS

The editor wishes to thank Pamela Grossman, Suzanne Wilson, and Samuel Wineburg for their comments on earlier versions of the introductory and concluding material, and June Smith for her assistance in manuscript preparation.

The editor's contributions have been supported in part by the Institute for Research on Teaching, College of Education, Michigan State University. The Institute for Research on Teaching is funded from a variety of federal, state, and private sources including the United States Department of Education and Michigan State University. The opinions expressed in this publication do not necessarily reflect the position, policy, or endorsement of the funding agencies.

Jere Brophy
Editor

RESEARCH ON TEACHING MATHEMATICS:

MAKING SUBJECT-MATTER KNOWLEDGE
PART OF THE EQUATION

Deborah Loewenberg Ball

INTRODUCTION

Subject-matter understanding and its role in teaching mathematics are the focus of this paper. Although few would disagree with the assertion that, in order to teach mathematics effectively, teachers must understand mathematics themselves, past efforts to show the relationship of teachers' mathematical knowledge to their teaching of mathematics have been largely unsuccessful. How can this be? My purpose here is to unravel this intuitively indisputable yet empirically unvalidated requirement of teaching by revisiting what it means to "understand mathematics" and the role played by such understanding in teaching.

The thesis of this paper is that teachers' subject matter knowledge interacts with their assumptions and explicit beliefs about teaching and learning, about

Advances in Research on Teaching, Volume 2, pages 1-48.
ISBN: 1-55938-034-9

students, and about context to shape the ways in which they teach mathematics to students. There are three parts to the development of this argument. First, I briefly analyze past investigations of the role of teachers' subject-matter knowledge in teaching mathematics. Next, I unpack the concept of subject-matter knowledge for teaching mathematics and illustrate what is entailed in finding out what teachers know. In the last section, I present three cases of teaching multiplication and analyze how each teacher's understanding of mathematics figures in her teaching.

To provide a context, I begin by tracing briefly the history of efforts to identify and understand the critical variables in effective mathematics teaching. This history is inevitably nested within the larger story of research on teaching, for it is only recently that many researchers have begun to think about teaching as subject-matter specific.

RESEARCH ON TEACHING MATHEMATICS: COMING FULL CIRCLE ON SUBJECT-MATTER KNOWLEDGE

Through three phases of research on teaching, teachers' subject matter knowledge has figured, faded, and reappeared as a key influence on the teaching of mathematics. Driven by common sense and conventional wisdom about teaching, the earliest research compiled characteristics of teachers whom others perceived as effective (Medley, 1979). The second phase of research attempted to establish connections between what teachers do and what their students learn. In the most recent phase, researchers have investigated teacher thinking.

What Are Effective Teachers Like?

Researchers began by collating the characteristics of good teachers. Based on pupils' assessments of their best teachers, these studies reported that good teachers were enthusiastic, helpful, and strict. Students also said that the best teachers knew the subject matter better (e.g., Hart, 1934). Although such findings seemed intuitively valid, the early studies did not empirically test the influence of "good" teachers' characteristics on what they did or what their students actually learned.

Recognizing the weakness of such claims, researchers began defining "effective teaching" as teaching that results in measurable student learning. In the most ambitious effort to identify teacher characteristics associated with student achievement in mathematics, the National Longitudinal Study of Mathematical Abilities followed 112,000 students from over 1500 schools in 40 states during the 1960s. Twenty teacher characteristics were studied, including years of teaching experience, credits in mathematics, having a major or minor in mathematics, personal enjoyment of mathematics, and philosophical orientation to learning. Overall, neither teacher background characteristics nor teacher attitudes were strongly related to student learning; significant positive relationships were found in fewer than 30 percent of the possible cases. No single teacher characteristic proved to be "consistently and significantly correlated with student achievement" (Begle & Geeslin, 1972). Begle (1979, p. 54) concluded from these results that many widely held beliefs about good teaching "are false, or at the very best rest on shaky foundations."

One of these beliefs was the notion that the more one knows about one's subject, the more effective one can be as a teacher. "The empirical literature suggests that this belief needs drastic modification," wrote Begle (1979, p. 51). The analyses showed that students whose teachers had majored or minored in mathematics scored significantly higher in only 20 percent of the cases. The number of teacher credits in college mathematics was actually *negatively* associated with student achievement in 15 percent of the cases. Convinced by these results that "the effects of a teacher's subject matter knowledge and attitudes on student learning seem to be far less powerful than many of us assumed," Begle argued that researchers should focus their inquiries elsewhere (p.53).

Begle's (1979) conclusion was counterintuitive. Teaching is fundamentally tied up with knowledge and the growth of knowledge (Buchmann, 1984). What sense does it make to say that what teachers know about mathematics is not a significant influence on what their students learn? Yet, in spite of the weight of common sense, the empirical results were discouraging. Few questioned the assumptions underlying the research or offered alternative interpretations. No one asked whether the the number of courses in college-level mathematics was a reasonable proxy for teachers' mathematical knowledge. No one wondered what is acquired through majoring in mathematics in terms of disciplinary understandings or ideas about pedagogy. In fact, some of what is gained through sitting in upper-level mathematics courses may serve as counterproductive preparation for teaching (Kline, 1977).

What Do Effective Teachers Do?

Instead of critically appraising underlying assumptions, operational definitions, or design of these disappointing studies of teacher characteristics, researchers began a new search for factors that influence effective teaching. The field turned from the investigation of teacher characteristics to study generic teacher behaviors such as pacing, questioning, explanation, and praise, as well as qualities such as clarity, directness, and enthusiasm. Medley (1979, p. 13) explained the basis for this shift, arguing that "it is what the teacher *does* rather than what a teacher *is* that matters." Most of the new studies chose to focus on elementary school teaching of mathematics and reading, because achievement in these subjects in the early grades was considered central and outcomes thought to be unambiguous to measure. Subject matter was part of the context, not the focus of the research.

Rosenshine (1979, p. 47) summarizes the picture of effective instruction that emerged from this work:

> Large groups, decision making by the teacher, limited choice of materials and activities by students, orderliness, factual questions, limited exploration of ideas, drill,and high percentages of correct answers.

He argued that, although this picture appeared grim, such orderly, business-like classrooms need not be cold nor humorless. Furthermore, these findings, he suggested, were primarily applicable to instruction in basic skills—reading, writing, and mathematics—and that looser approaches ("messing around") might be perfectly appropriate in other subjects. While some feared that students would enjoy school less in such tightly supervised, teacher-controlled settings, studies indicated that there was little difference on such "affective outcomes" (Peterson, 1979). Some researchers even concluded that students were more anxious in informal classrooms (Bennett, 1976; Wright, 1975).

Critical to understanding this phase of research on effective teaching are its assumptions about mathematics and the goals of teaching and learning mathematics. Taking the prevalent school curriculum as given, it assumed that elementary school mathematics consists of a body of skills to be mastered through drill and practice. Carefully disclaiming the assumption that learning meant accumulating facts and principles, researchers nevertheless talked about students' mathematics learning in terms of "gains." It was not surprising that within this set of assumptions researchers found that students "learned" the most from direct explanations, seatwork, and frequent quizzes in time-efficient, quiet settings.

As they spent more time in classrooms and analyzed complicated data, many researchers became increasingly appreciative of the complexity of classrooms and of the job of teaching. They saw that teachers work with a broad range of students who come with different understandings and attitudes and who do not learn in the same ways. Teachers are also responsible for a variety of educational outcomes that require different approaches. In light of these features of the job, it was simplistic to seek a single most effective teaching approach (Clark & Yinger, 1979; Peterson, 1979).

How Do Teachers Understand Their Work and Decide What to Do?

Several years earlier, Gage (1977, p. 15) had cautioned that "no one can ever prescribe successfully all the twists and turns to be taken as the classroom teacher uses judgment, sudden insight, sensitivity, and agility to promote learning." In a third significant shift in research on teaching, researchers increasingly turned away from their focus on teacher behaviors and began examining teachers' thoughts and decisions. Writing in 1979, Clark and Yinger observed that this

> new approach to the study of teaching assumes that what teachers do is affected by what they think. This approach, which emphasizes the processing of cognitive information, is concerned with the teachers' judgment, decision making, and planning. The study of the thinking processes of teachers—how they gather, organize, and interpret, and evaluate information—is expected to lead to understandings of the uniquely human processes that guide and determine their behavior (p. 231).

In search of what makes some teachers more effective than others, researchers were hot on a new trail by redefining teaching as an activity of both thought *and* action. How do teachers decide on content and goals, select materials and approaches, in order to help different students learn a variety of concepts and skills?

It was in studying teacher thinking and decision making that teachers' knowledge and beliefs about subject matter began to reappear as potentially significant variables. For example, Shroyer (1981) studied how junior high mathematics teachers coped with student difficulties or unusual responses and found that the teachers with weaker mathematics backgrounds had more difficulty generating alternative responses to these critical moments. And, in a study of fourth-grade teachers' curricular decisions, Kuhs (1980) concluded that their conceptions of mathematics and recognition of topics influenced both what the teachers taught and how they modified curriculum materials.

Thompson (1984) investigated the influence of teachers' conceptions of mathematics on their teaching. Her findings further substantiated the notion that what teachers know about math affects what they do. One of the teachers in her study, Lynn, described mathematics as "cut and dried": a process of following procedures and producing right answers. Lynn did not provide opportunities for her students to explore or engage in creative work; instead she emphasized memorizing and using specified procedures. In contrast, Kay, who saw mathematics as a "subject of ideas and mental processes," not a "subject of facts," emphasized problem solving and encouraged her students to make and pursue their own mathematical conjectures (Thompson, 1984, pp. 112-113).

Alerted by these and other similar findings, some researchers have returned to an emphasis on subject matter as a critical variable in teaching mathematics. However, "subject-matter knowledge" in current studies is a concept of varied definition, a fact that threatens to muddy our progress in learning about the role of teachers' mathematical understanding in their teaching. The next section takes up the question of what researchers should mean by "knowledge of mathematics" in the new research on mathematics teaching.

BREAKING THE CIRCLE:
MOVING AWAY FROM PAST ERRORS

Philosophical arguments (e.g., Buchmann, 1984), as well as common sense, have already persuaded us that teachers' knowledge of mathematics influences their teaching of mathematics. In the most extreme case, teachers cannot help children learn things they themselves do not understand. More subtle, and less well understood, are the ways in which teachers' understandings shape their students' opportunities to learn. The dead end of earlier attempts to investigate the relationship of teachers' understandings to teachers' effectiveness was a consequence of the ways in which both "subject-matter knowledge" and "effectiveness" were defined. With different definitions and approaches, the new research on teacher knowledge has already begun to corroborate our tenacious conviction that teachers' subject-matter understanding does, after all, play a significant role in the teaching of mathematics. However, if we are to move beyond what we already believe, if this research is to help us to understand the subtler effects and to improve mathematics teaching and learning, then significant conceptual issues—about what we mean by "subject matter knowledge" or by its "role" in teaching mathematics—must be addressed.

SUBJECT-MATTER KNOWLEDGE IN MATHEMATICS

Although most researchers have moved away from the earlier use of course lists or credits earned as a proxy for teachers' knowledge, how they conceptualize and study "subject matter" varies. Some researchers examine teachers' *conceptions of* or *beliefs about mathematics* (e.g., Blaire, 1981; Ernest, 1988; Ferrini-Mundy, 1986; Kuhs, 1980; Lerman, 1983; Peterson, Fennema, Carpenter, & Loef, 1988; Thompson, 1984). These researchers use a variety of methods to identify teachers' conceptions, including interviews, questionnaires, and inferences based on teachers' practices. These studies generally highlight the influence of teachers' assumptions *about* mathematics on their teaching of the subject.

Other researchers focus on teachers' *understanding of mathematical concepts and procedures* (e.g., Ball, 1988a; Ball & McDiarmid, 1988; Leinhardt & Smith, 1985; Owens, 1987; Post, Behr, Harel, & Lesh, 1988; Steinberg, Haymore, & Marks, 1985). Using interviews and structured tasks, they explore how teachers think about their mathematical knowledge and how they understand (or *mis*understand) specific ideas. What counts, according to these researchers, is the way teachers organize the field and how they understand and think about concepts (as opposed to just whether they can give "right" answers).

What does it mean to "know" mathematics? Does "knowing mathematics" mean being able do it oneself? Does it mean being able to explain it to someone else? Is subject-matter knowledge a question of "knowledge structures"—that is, a function of the richness of the connections among mathematical concepts and principles? What is the relationship among "attitudes," "conceptions," and "knowledge" of mathematics?

Mathematical Understanding: Interweaving Ideas *Of* and *About* the Subject

Understanding mathematics involves *substantive knowledge*—knowledge *of* the substance of the domain—and a mélange of ideas about and dispositions *about* the subject. What I call substantive knowledge includes propositional and procedural knowledge of mathematics: understandings of particular topics (e.g., fractions and trigonometry), procedures (e.g., long division and factoring quadratic equations), and concepts (e.g., quadrilaterals and infinity). Mathematical structures and connections, the relationships among these topics, procedures, and concepts, are also part of the substantive knowledge of mathematics. Substantive knowledge is what is most easily recognized by others as "subject-matter knowledge."

Another critical dimension of understanding mathematics consists of what I call knowledge about the nature and discourse of mathematics.[1] This includes understandings about the nature of mathematical knowledge and activity: what is entailed in doing mathematics and how truth is established in the domain. What counts as a solution in mathematics? How are solutions justified and conjectures disproved? Which ideas are arbitrary or conventional and which are necessary or logical? Knowledge about mathematics entails understanding the role of mathematical tools and accepted knowledge in the pursuit of new ideas, generalizations, and procedures. Rarely are these aspects of mathematical knowledge part of the explicit curriculum in school or college. Rarely do math students learn about the evolution of mathematical ideas or ways of thinking.

Nevertheless, students develop assumptions about the nature of mathematical knowledge and activity from their experiences in mathematics classes. If the teacher's guide is the source of right answers, for example, this suggests that the basis for epistemic authority in mathematics does not rest within the knower. Teachers communicate ideas about mathematics in the tasks they give students, from the kinds of uncertainties that emerge in their classes and the ways in which they respond to those uncertainties, as well as from messages about why pupils should learn particular bits of content or study mathematics in general.

Finally, in addition to knowledge of and about mathematics, people's understanding of mathematics is colored by their emotional responses to the subject and their inclinations and sense of self in relation to it.

Interviews with prospective and experienced teachers[2] illustrate how mathematical understanding is a product of an interweaving of substantive mathematical knowledge with ideas and feelings about the subject. Asked how she would respond to a student who asked what seven divided by zero is, Laura, a prospective elementary teacher, responded:

> Zero is such a *stupid* number! It's just one of those you wonder why it's there sometimes. I'd just say, "Anything divided by zero is zero. That's just a rule, you just *know* it." . . . You know, it's empty, it's nothing. Anything multiplied by zero is zero. I'd just say, "That's something that you have to learn, you have to know." I think that's how I was told. You just *know* it. . . . I'd just say, you know if they were older and they asked me "Why?" I'd just have to start mumbling about something, I don't know. . . . I don't know what. I'd just tell them "Because!" (laughs) That's just the way it is, it's just one of those rules, like in English— sometimes the C sounds like K—you just have to *learn* it. I before E except after C—it's one of those things, in my view.

Laura's answer reveals that she understands division by zero in terms of a rule. She thinks of it as something one must remember, not something one can reason about. Like rules of thumb in spelling, what to do when one divides by zero is something one just must know. In addition, Laura is impatient about the number zero. She describes it as "stupid": useless and empty. Furthermore, the rule she invokes—"Anything divided by zero is zero"—is also false. In other parts of her interview as well, Laura repeatedly refers to rules that she remembers and some that she has forgotten. She talks about hating math and not being good at it. In this tiny snapshot of Laura's understanding of mathematics, we see that what she does not know in this case is framed by her beliefs about mathematical knowledge and her feelings about its senselessness. Abby, a prospective secondary teacher, also thought of mathematics in terms of rules and arbitrary facts. Unlike Laura, however, Abby was comfortable with the rules: She could remember them and felt safe within their structure and certainty. When asked about division by zero, she said emphatically:

> I'd just say . . . "It's undefined," and I'd tell them that this is a rule that you should *never* forget that anytime you divide by zero you *can't*. You just can't do it. It's undefined, so . . . you just can't. They should know that anytime you get a number divided by zero, then you did something wrong before. It's just something to remember.

Abby added that dividing by zero is "something that you won't ever be able to do in mathematics, even in calculus." Unlike Laura, Abby's rule was correct—division by zero is "undefined"—but, like Laura, her understanding was nested within her larger view of mathematics as a collection of rules to remember. She did not try to make meaning out of the "fact" that division by zero is undefined but simply emphasized that it is not permitted.

MATHEMATICAL UNDERSTANDING: EXAMINING WHAT TEACHERS KNOW

Next, in order to illustrate the kind of analysis needed in studying teachers' subject-matter knowledge, a closer look will be taken at some prospective elementary and secondary teachers' understanding of place value in multiplying large numbers (Ball, 1988a). Later, this topic will be revisited in discussing the role of subject-matter knowledge in teaching mathematics. The following discussion is based on data on one question in a series of interviews conducted with teacher education students, half of whom were mathematics majors intending to teach secondary school and half of whom were prospective elementary teachers with no academic major. Analysis of the topic, place value, and of the interview question itself, is followed by a discussion of the results. These results highlight the danger of assuming what teachers understand about the mathematics they teach.

Background: Place Value and Numeration

The question discussed deals with the concept of place value and its role in the algorithm for multiplying large numbers. Some background is necessary to understand the question and the analysis of teachers' responses. The base 10 positional numeration system is part of the working knowledge of most members of our culture. That is, adults read, write, and make sense of written numerals. They know that "56" does not mean $5 + 6$ or 11. They know that "04" represents the same quantity as "4" but that "40" does not.

Still, children do not automatically understand this and the way they learn arithmetic may be a hindrance rather than a help to understanding. In fact, some research suggests that place value is particularly difficult for children to learn. Elementary school students may write 365 as 300605, for example, which represents the way the number *sounds* rather than place value. Kamii (1985) argues that traditional math instruction actually forces young children to operate with numerals without understanding what they represent. We have all heard children performing addition calculations reciting, "5 plus 7 is 12, put down the 2, carry the *1*," or doing long division calculations such as 8945 divided by 43 by saying, "43 goes into 89 twice, put up the 2, 2 times 43 is 86" and so on. These "algorithm rhymes"[3] which pupils learn interfere with paying attention to the essence of the numeration system—that numerals have different values depending on their place. The "1" in the addition rhyme actually means 10. The "89" in the division chant actually means 89 hundred and the "2" represents the fact that there are 2 hundred groups of 43 in 8945.

Place Value in Multiplication Computation

What is the nature of adult working knowledge of place value and numeration? How does it equip teachers to help pupils make sense of written numerals and procedures with numbers? I designed the following question to elicit teachers' understanding of place value in use:

> Some eighth-grade teachers noticed that several of their students were making the same mistake in multiplying large numbers. In trying to calculate

$$
\begin{array}{r}
123 \\
\times\ 645 \\
\hline
\end{array}
$$

> the students seemed to be forgetting to "move the numbers" (i.e., the partial products) over on each line. They were doing this:

$$
\begin{array}{r}
123 \\
\times\ 645 \\
\hline
615 \\
492 \\
738 \\
\hline
1845
\end{array}
$$

instead of this:

$$
\begin{array}{r}
123 \\
\times\ 645 \\
\hline
615 \\
492 \\
738 \\
\hline
79335
\end{array}
$$

> While these teachers agreed that this was a problem, they did not agree on what to do about it. *What would you do if you were teaching eighth grade and you noticed that several of your students were doing this?*

Discussion of Item

The algorithm for multiplying large numbers is derived from the process of decomposing numbers into "expanded form" and multiplying them in parts. To understand this, one must understand decimal numerals as representations of numbers in terms of hundreds, tens, and ones, that is, in the numeral 123, the 1 represents 1 *hundred*, the 2 represents 2 *tens*, and the 3 represents 3 *ones*. In the following example, 123 × 645, first one multiplies 5 × 123:

$$
\begin{array}{r}
123 \\
\times \quad 5 \\
\hline
615
\end{array}
$$

then *40* × 123:

$$
\begin{array}{r}
123 \\
\times \quad 40 \\
\hline
4920
\end{array}
$$

and then *600* × 123:

$$
\begin{array}{r}
123 \\
\times \quad 600 \\
\hline
73800
\end{array}
$$

In the final step, one adds the results of these three products.

$$
\begin{array}{r}
123 \\
\times \quad 645 \\
\hline
615 \\
4920 \\
73800
\end{array}
$$

In effect, one is putting the "parts" of the number back together—that is, 645 × 123 = (600 × 123) + (40 × 123) + (5 × 123).

Many people do not write their computation out this way, but rather "shortcut" it by writing:

$$
\begin{array}{r}
123 \\
\times \quad 645 \\
\hline
615 \\
492 \\
738
\end{array}
$$

This shortcut, in effect, hides the conceptual base of the procedure. Because its logic depends on place value and the distributive property of multiplication over addition, the multiplication algorithm affords a strategic site for investigating the nature of people's mathematical understandings.

Analyzing Teachers' Knowledge of Place Value

In this section, the results of this interview question are discussed, focusing on four issues: the interpretation of what people say when they talk about mathematics, the role of explicitness in understanding mathematics for teaching, the connectedness of mathematical understanding, and the interweaving of knowledge of and about mathematics.[4]

Place Value or "Places"?

Some of the prospective teachers' responses were relatively easy to interpret because they focused explicitly either on the role of place value in the algorithm or on the steps of the procedure. For example, Mike, an elementary major, said that he would "have to explain about that not being 123×4. That it's 123×40." In contrast, Tara, a prospective elementary teacher focused on the steps:

> I would show them how to line them up correctly. I would do what I still do, which is once I multiply out the first number and then I start to do the second line, put a zero there. That's how I was taught to do it and that's how I still, when I have big numbers to multiply, I do, because otherwise I'd get them too mixed up, probably. It helps to keep everything in line, like after the first line, you do one zero and then you do two zeroes to shift things over.

Mike's answer showed that he understood that "moving the numbers over" is not just a rule to remember, but reflects that 123×4 is 4,920, not 492. Tara's understanding was wholly procedural: the numbers must be lined up and the zeroes help you to remember to "shift things over." There was no hint in her answer that she saw any meaningful basis for the procedure.

While these responses were explicit and unambiguous, some prospective teachers' responses were much harder to interpret because they used conceptual language—for example, "the tens place"—to describe procedures, or procedural language—for example, "add a zero"—to (perhaps) refer to concepts. Rhonda's response was an example of this ambiguity:

> You would take the last number and multiply it by all three of the top numbers and you put those underneath and then you start with the next one. You'd want to put it underneath the number that you are using. They aren't understanding that they need to be underneath of that instead of just down in one straight row.

So far this seemed like an answer focused on the rules of the multiplication algorithm. Rhonda was talking only about where to put the numbers and what to do next. But then she said that the students would "probably need to know about places":

> You know, the hundreds, the thousands, you know, whatever. If they don't understand that there is a difference in placing, that could also lead to this if they don't remember. . . . They need to understand that there is a difference in the placing, too.

What did Rhonda mean when she said "placing"? She may have been talking about where to write the numbers—where to place them—or she may have been talking about the difference in the value of a number depending on its placing. To probe how she understood "places," I asked her why this mattered. She replied:

> Because of the fact that you are working with such a large number, like your second and third numbers are not going to be ones. . . . Your numbers get larger and larger and since you are working with such a large sum, you have to know how to work in the thousands, you know, to keep your numbers that way. I guess it all goes back to them understanding why the numbers should be underneath of what you are multiplying.

She added that she was not sure "how that affects the placing."

Rhonda's response was not as clear as Mike's or Tara's. She seemed to focus on lining up the numbers correctly, but then she talked about "places," too. Was her reference to "placing" and "places" conceptual—that is, addressing the *values* of different places within a numeral? Or was Rhonda just talking about "placing" the numbers in the right *place*—so that they would be lined up correctly?

Zero As a "Placeholder"

Also ambiguous were the responses of several prospective teachers who talked about the importance of writing in zeros in the partial products. Joanie, a secondary candidate and mathematics major, said she would get her students to focus on putting the numbers "in the right places" and would "encourage them to use zero as a placeholder" and Karen, another math major, commented, "We were taught to put a zero here, and a zero there, to represent the places." Chris, an elementary major, tried to explain the role of zero:

> I don't exactly know how to explain it, but something having to do with this first column . . . is the ones, and the next column is the tens, and maybe something like there's a zero, you know, the tens there's always one zero, and so you have— God, I don't know. Like to make it balance out for the tens you'd have to add the zero and for the hundreds you'd have to add two zeros. Something to that effect. I don't know.

In some of these cases, interpreting what the prospective teachers understood about place value was difficult. Although their answers focused on how to write the partial products, it is not clear what that meant to them. People could talk about the importance of zero as a "placeholder" and mean simply that using zeros helps one remember to get the numbers lined up correctly.

Some prospective teachers who talked about zeros did elaborate their answers very explicitly and their responses reveal different kinds of thinking that can underlie answers focused on "putting down zeros." The responses of Patty and Mike, both elementary teacher candidates, illustrate such differences in thinking. Patty said she would show pupils to "physically put a zero every time you moved down a line." She explained that "zero doesn't add anything more to the problem. It's just empty. But instead of having an empty space, you have something to fill in the space so that you can use it as a guideline."

Mike also said he would "make it mandatory that the zeros start showing up" on his pupils' papers. But he explained it differently. He said he would "have to explain about that not being 123×4. That's 123×40, which is a multiple of 10—which has that zero on the right side which is why the zero has to be there."

Both Patty and Mike would have their pupils put the zeros down, yet their explanations revealed strikingly different understandings of the role of zero in our decimal positional numeration system. Patty saw the zero as useful for keeping the columns of numbers lined up but says that zero "adds nothing" to the number. Her statement suggested that she confused "adding zero" *to* a number ($78 + 0 = 78$) with the role of zero in a *numeral* (e.g., 78*0*). Mike knew that 123 is multiplied by 5, 40, and 600. He said the zeros "have to be there" because the products are "a multiple of 10 off." Still, his response did not show what he understood about the zeros in place value numeration. Was it a rule he had memorized—that multiples of 10 have one zero, multiples of 100 have two zeros, and so forth? Or did he understand why putting a zero "on the right side" produces a number that is ten times the original?

Partial and Inexplicit Understanding

Those who mentioned "places" and "ones, tens, and hundreds" may have had a partial, fuzzy, understanding of the underlying concepts of place value. Some students figured it out in the course of answering the question. Becky, a post-B.A. student with an undergraduate mathematics major, was one of these. She began her answer much as many others did, focusing on "moving over" from column to column:

> You start in the units column and you multiply that, and then you start in your tens column and so you have to start in your tens column of the next one and you multiply 4 x 123 and then you move over into your hundreds column over here where you're taking 6×123.

Then she talked about how she was taught to "put the zeros there because it helped me line up my columns." She pondered this aloud:

> A lot of the time you say, "Well, put a zero here, put a zero there, and zero there, and you put a zero here, and a zero there," and you get into the *method* of it and you know that you put a zero here, but they don't really understand *why*. And I think it goes back to the units and tens and hundreds and all that. And that might be an easier way to take a look at it. Cause you're going to take 5 times that, and you take 40, and then 600, and you can see where those zeros come from.

She still was not entirely clear about this, though. She said that "when you take the 4 or the 40, you're gonna want to start in, understand that you're working with tens now, so you want to move into the tens column." Becky stopped suddenly and said, "God, I don't know any other way that I'd be able to describe it than, I'd have to think about it." She paused and looked at the problem. Suddenly she realized that 123×40 "is going to be the same as this (492) with a zero on it!" She talked to herself under her breath and then a few moments later looked up and said, "Wow, I haven't even thought about it that way before! . . . *that's* where those zeros come from, *oh! Wow*, okay."

Although Becky could multiply correctly, she did not know the mathematical principles underlying the procedure. She was, however, able to put different pieces of understanding together and figure it out as she talked. Others who lacked explicit understanding also seemed to realize that there was more to know than just procedures, but could not always uncover the deeper levels. Sarah, an elementary major, struggled and then gave up. Her answer seemed to focus on the rules of lining up the numbers:

> I would explain that every time you move over this isn't ones, this is tens, so it's ten more, so you have to have an extra ten there, you have to put the zero there to hold it in place. Does that make sense?

I asked if it made sense to her. She replied, "Oh, I know what I'm saying, I know what I'm thinking, I just, I don't know if I can explain it. . . .I guess it's because the stuff is so basic to me." What Sarah could say was that "you have to put the zero there to hold it in place." Moreover, her explanation that in the tens place "it's ten *more*" misrepresents the fact that the value of the tens place is ten *times* more. Still, her comment that she knew what she was thinking but does not know if she can explain it is worth pondering. Sarah seemed to have part of the idea, that something about the value of the places mattered, but was unable to pull it together.

Tacit Versus Explicit Ways of Knowing

The assumption that people have conceptual knowledge of procedures which they have learned to perform is a fallacy (Hatano, 1982). As one of the math majors reflected when he tried to explain the basis for the multiplication procedure, "I absolutely do it [multiplication] by the rote process—I would have to think about it." Certainly many children and adults go through mathematical motions without ever understanding the underlying principles or meaning. For example, while most people can divide fractions using the rule to "invert and multiply," very few are able to connect any meaning to the procedure (Ball, 1988a; 1990).[5]

Still, mathematical understanding may also be tacit. Successful mathematicians can unravel perplexing problems without being able to articulate all of what they know. Not unrelated to Schon's (1983) "knowing-in-action," the mathematicians' work reflects both tacit understanding and intuitive and habituated actions. Experts in all domains, while able to perform skillfully, may not always be able to specify the components of or bases for their actions. Their activity nevertheless implies knowledge. Similarly, in everyday life, people understand things which they cannot articulate. For instance, a woman may find her way around the town she grew up in, identifying friends' homes and old hangouts, yet not be able to give directions to a visitor. A man may use colloquial French expressions in speaking French but be unable to explain their meaning to a fellow American.

Polanyi (1958) describes what he calls the "ineffable domain"—those things about which our tacit understanding far exceeds our capacity to articulate what we know. He argues further that "nothing we know can be said precisely, and so what I call 'ineffable' may simply mean something I know and can describe even less precisely than usual, or even only very vaguely" (Polanyi, p. 88). It is unclear whether we would want to say that the woman understands her way around less well than someone who can give directions, or that the man understands French less well than someone who can translate. Clumsy attempts to articulate understanding may reflect an area in which, according to Polanyi (1958), the tacit predominates.

In contrast, apparent clumsiness in expression may not be clumsy or inarticulate at all, but rather may reflect how the speaker actually understands what he or she is talking about. Orr (1987) argues that teachers often "fill in" the gaps in what their pupils say, assuming they know what the pupils "mean." She said that when her high school geometry students would talk about distances as locations and locations as distances, she thought these were careless mistakes or awkward wording. Suddenly it occurred to her that these nonstandard ways of talking might actually represent nonstandard understandings of the relationship between location and distance. She began asking some different questions of her students to try to elicit what they understood—asking them to construct diagrams showing where certain cities were located and the distances among them, for example. She discovered in case after case that her students' explanations were accurate reflections of how they were thinking.

Just like mathematicians, ordinary people do things in mathematics—and do them correctly—which they cannot explain. The prospective teachers whom I interviewed all clearly knew the steps of the traditional procedure for multiplying large numbers and could calculate the answer correctly. Yet very few had examined this habituated procedure. Almost no one was able to talk about *why* the numbers "move over" in the partial products, except to say that the product of 123×4 must be "lined up under the 4 because that's what you're multiplying by." This raises two issues critical for research on teacher knowledge: one methodological and one theoretical.

What Do Teachers Understand? Problems of Inference

Analyzing teachers' knowledge is complicated by the extent to which they are able to talk or otherwise represent that knowledge. If someone talks about "lining up the numbers," one cannot fairly assume that the person has no understanding of the role of place value in the multiplication algorithm. At a tacit level, the person may understand that 123×4 is really 123×40, but may never explicitly consider this in performing or thinking about the procedure. This issue clearly presents methodological problems of inference in studies of teachers' subject matter knowledge. A second consideration, however, affords a way out of this methodological tangle.

What Do Teachers Need to Know?

Tacit knowledge, whatever its role in independent mathematical activity, is inadequate for teaching. In order to help someone else understand and do mathematics, being able to "do it" oneself is not sufficient. A necessary level of knowledge for teaching involves being able to talk about mathematics, not just describing the steps for following an algorithm, but also about the judgments made and the meanings and reasons for certain relationships or procedures.[6] Explicit knowledge of mathematics entails more than saying the words of mathematical statements or formulas; rather, it must include language that goes beyond the surface mathematical representation. Explicit knowledge involves reasons and relationships: being able to explain why, as well as being able to relate particular ideas or procedures to others within mathematics.[7]

THE DEGREE OF CONNECTEDNESS WITHIN TEACHERS' SUBSTANTIVE KNOWLEDGE OF MATHEMATICS

However explicitly articulated or carefully memorized, mathematical knowledge is not a collection of separate topics, nor a laundry list of rules and definitions. Addition is fundamentally connected to multiplication, algebra is a first cousin of arithmetic, and the measurement of irregular shapes is akin to integration in calculus. The standard school mathematics curriculum to which most prospective teachers have been subjected, however, treats mathematics as a collection of discrete bits of procedural knowledge.

Not only does this tendency to compartmentalize mathematical knowledge seriously misrepresent the logic and conceptual organization of the discipline to students, but it also substantially increases the cognitive load required to "do" or "know" mathematics. Each idea or procedure seems to be a separate case. Each requires a different rule, all of which must be individually memorized and accessed. "Knowing" mathematics is easily reduced to a senseless activity. If teachers are to break away from this common approach to teaching and learning mathematics, they must have connected rather than compartmentalized knowledge of mathematics themselves.

To investigate the degree to which teachers' knowledge of place value is connected across contexts, the elementary teacher candidates' understanding of place value was explored in a structured exercise focused on teaching subtraction with regrouping (another procedure dependent on concepts of place value). In this exercise, which was longer than the rest, the teacher candidates were asked to examine a section from a second-grade math book. This section (two pages) dealt with subtracting two-digit numbers with regrouping. The teacher candidates were asked to appraise the section, to talk about what they perceived as its strengths and weaknesses, and then to describe how they might go about helping second graders to learn "this." I did not specify what "this" was because I wanted to see what they would focus on. I also asked them what they thought pupils would need to know before they could learn this, and what they would use as evidence that their pupils were "getting it." Finally they examined an actual second grader's work on one of the pages, and were asked to talk about what they thought she understood and what they would do next with her.

In their responses, almost all of the teacher candidates focused explicitly on concepts of place value. Their responses showed that they were aware that "tens and ones" played some sort of role in teaching subtraction with regrouping (which they all referred to as "borrowing"). For some, this awareness of tens and ones was at the surface, readily accessible. For example, Tara described what she would say:

I would say, you know, obviously these numbers, you can't subtract in your head. Alright, you have to cross out one of the tens from the top. And put it over in the ones column on the top, so you are able to subtract the two numbers. And then when you cross that tens number, change it, like subtract 1 from it. So you change, like if it was 64, change it to uh, you know, the 6 to a 5, and the 4 to a 14. And maybe I would show them, like 64, like maybe I would write 64 on the board. And then put that it equals 50 plus 14, so they see it is still the same amount.

$$
\begin{array}{r}
5\ \ 14 \\
\not6\ \not4 \\
-\quad 4\ 6 \\
\hline
\end{array}
$$

Tara, in the midst of a procedural description ("change the 6 to a 5"), explicitly added an important piece of conceptual understanding: that 64 equals 50 plus 14 and so the crossing out has not changed the value of the number.

This use of "conceptual" language creates significant problems of interpretation. In the multiplication question, discussed above, many of the teacher candidates mentioned "places" and yet did not necessarily seem to focus on place *value*. In the subtraction task, most of the prospective teachers did seem to be talking about place value—tens and ones. On one hand, this suggests that they did have some explicit understanding of the decimal numeration system. On the other hand, unlike the steps of the multiplication algorithm, the steps of the "borrowing rhyme" refer explicitly to tens and ones (e.g., "borrow one from the tens, move it to the ones"). This may explain why teacher candidates seemed to focus more on place value when they talked about subtraction with regrouping.

Mention of "tens and ones" may be more procedural than conceptual, however. "Borrow one from the tens" is an ambiguous statement. In the quote from Tara above, it may mean, literally, take 1 away from the number in the tens *place*—that is, cross out the 6 and make it a 5. Or it may mean take 1 ten away from 6 tens, leaving 5 tens. Several responses suggested that referring to ones and tens is possible without engaging the concept of grouping (and regrouping) by tens, just as reference to *places* in the multiplication algorithm may not signal attention to place *value*.

Almost all the teacher candidates were more explicit about place value when talking about subtraction with regrouping than they were when they discussed the multiplication algorithm. With multiplication, for instance, Tara focused on "lining up the numbers" and "shifting things over" on each line. She did not seem to understand that the partial product written as 492 was really 4920 ("adding the zero just keeps everything in line"). Yet, in talking about subtraction with regrouping, Tara talked explicitly about 50 + 14 being "the same amount" as 64.

The teacher candidates seemed to understand the role of "tens and ones," or place value, in "borrowing" but did not connect that understanding with the multiplication algorithm. Their understanding of place value was compartmentalized within specific contexts (e.g., borrowing), and not readily accessible in other relevant ones (e.g., multiplication computation). Similar evidence of fragmented understandings emerged within other topics examined in the interviews—division, for example. Prospective teachers did not connect the concept of division across different division contexts: division of fractions, division by zero, and division in algebra. Instead, they treated each as a specific case, for which they had to invoke a particular rule or procedure. These results point to the importance of investigating the connections within teachers' substantive understanding of mathematics. In seeking to examine what teachers know, researchers should create opportunities to explore teachers' knowledge of particular concepts across different contexts or from a variety of perspectives.

The Interaction of Knowledge *Of* and *About* Mathematics

In addition to the explicitness and connectedness of teachers' knowledge of concepts and procedures, another critical area of inquiry and analysis is the way in which their ideas *about* mathematics influence their representations of mathematics. What do they emphasize? What stands out to them about the mathematical issues they confront?

The prospective teachers tended to focus on the procedures of multiplication for reasons that also went beyond the nature of their substantive understanding of place value and had more to do with their ideas *about* mathematics. Some of the predominant assumptions included the following:

- Doing mathematics means following set procedures step-by-step to arrive at answers.
- Knowing mathematics means knowing "how to do it."
- Mathematics is largely an arbitrary collection of facts and rules.
- A primary reason to learn mathematics is to progress to the next level in school.
- Another main purpose for learning math is to be able to calculate prices at the store.
- Most mathematical ideas have little or no relationship to real objects and therefore can be represented only symbolically.

The prospective teachers' assumptions about the nature of mathematical knowledge and about what it means to know something in mathematics formed the boundaries of what they considered to be a response on all of the interview questions. In talking about the multiplication question, for example, one commented that "you just have to move the number over a place value every time—it's just knowing how to do something." Several others vowed that they would "enforce" or "make mandatory" that pupils use "placeholders" in order to remember to move the numbers over on each row. No one suggested using objects, pictures, or real situations to model the procedure.

Obviously the prospective teachers' ideas about mathematics do not exist separately from their substantive understandings of particular concepts or procedures. Most of them did not have access to any explicit understanding of why the multiplication algorithm works. As such, they could do nothing but respond in terms of rules and procedures. Still, at the same time, many were emphatic about the importance of teaching students to follow the steps correctly and they tried to think of ways to "embed" those steps into students' heads, rather than seeking to figure out the underlying ideas.

Although people have many ideas about the nature of mathematics, these ideas are generally implicit, built up out of years of experience in math classrooms and from living in a culture in which mathematics is both revered and reviled. While such ideas influenced the ways in which they experienced mathematics, the prospective teachers seemed to take their assumptions about mathematics for granted. Unlike their understandings of the *substance* of mathematics, which some of them wished to increase or deepen, the teacher candidates did not focus on their understandings about mathematics. They did not seem dissatisfied with them, nor did they even seem to think explicitly about them.

THE ROLE OF SUBJECT-MATTER KNOWLEDGE IN TEACHING MATHEMATICS

The discussion thus far shows that examining teachers' knowledge of mathematics is a complicated endeavor. Another sticking point in the pursuit of understanding the role of subject-matter knowledge in teaching mathematics, however, lies in the nonlinear relationship between knowledge of mathematics and teaching. In teaching, teachers' understandings and beliefs about mathematics *interact with* their ideas about the teaching and learning of mathematics and their ideas about pupils, teachers, and the context of classrooms.

To make this assertion more concrete, put yourself in a mathematics teacher's shoes. Imagine you are teaching first grade and you are teaching your students to identify geometric shapes. One little girl points to a blue wooden square and says that it's a rectangle. Then another child tilts the square and says that now it is a diamond. How would you respond? Or suppose you teach high school. Bored and frustrated, the students in your fifth-period geometry class demand to know why they have to learn proofs. What would you say? Before reading further, take a moment to consider what you would do or say next.

Now consider your responses. The choices you made in each of these situations was based on what you interpreted it to be *about*. In other words, teaching is as much a process of *problem setting* as it one of *problem solving*. Your interpretation of each situation, perhaps implicit, was shaped by two main factors: your knowledge about pupils of different ages and your understanding of the mathematics involved. For instance, did you think that either of the children in the first example had said something either incorrect or insightful? Can a square be correctly labeled a rectangle or a diamond? Is a diamond a mathematical term? What is the effect of changing the orientation of a geometric shape? How does one answer such questions in mathematics? Are these issues things that first graders can or need to understand? Would exploring the hierarchical relationship between rectangles and squares be confusing for the rest of the class?

In the second example, why did you think these high school students were bored and frustrated? Maybe you hated proofs in high school, too, and you sympathized with them. Maybe you thought the pupils were just trying to get you off on a tangent. Why *do* you think you are teaching proofs? These questions, and others like them, played a role in the way you interpreted and defined each situation.

Having framed each situation, your response—what you think you would do—was then nested within your assumptions about good math teaching. These assumptions are grounded in your ideas about how pupils of particular ages learn, what you believe about the teacher's role, what you think is important to learn in math and what you know about the school mathematics curriculum, as well as your ideas about the context of classroom learning. Your own understanding of mathematics is a critical factor in this interplay of interpretation and response in teaching mathematics.

The examples illustrate that the role of subject-matter knowledge in teaching can be more complicated than whether or not you can define a rectangle. But, what matters about your knowledge of mathematics depends on a host of other factors which, taken together, comprise your view of mathematics teaching. It is a cycle: What you need to understand about shapes or proofs depends on what you think the point of teaching geometry is, which is in turn connected to your larger understanding of mathematics in general, and geometry in particular. Unanimity about good math teaching does not exist among mathematics educators, researchers, or teachers; to gloss over such differences of view is to doom current research efforts to a new set of failures.

To establish this argument, three cases of the teaching of long multiplication in fourth grade are presented. The three teachers are all teaching the same topic, to the same age students, and, in the vignettes, are at similar points in their work on this topic. However, because of what these three teachers understand about mathematics, what they believe about teaching and learning mathematics, about pupils, and about the context of classroom teaching, they approach the teaching of multiplication in distinctly different ways. The purpose of examining these cases is to highlight the role of subject-matter knowledge in teaching mathematics, showing the ways in which subject-matter knowledge interacts with other kinds of knowledge in teaching mathematics. After each case, each teacher's approach and the factors that seem to shape that approach are summarized. Following the three cases is an analytic discussion of the three cases and what they demonstrate about the interaction of subject matter knowledge in teaching mathematics.

Bridget Smith[8]

Bridget Smith teaches in a small suburban community of white middle-class families. She has been teaching for over 20 years. Her preferred approach to teaching math is to "individualize"—allowing the pupils to proceed at their own pace through the text material and, when necessary, "going over and reteaching with them skills that they either had forgotten or had never been taught." Sometimes she works with the whole group if she wants to "expose all of them" to something they have not yet done—such as long division or multiplying by two numbers—or if the pupils are unable to work well alone, which is the case with this year's group.

Smith believes that some of her pupils are naturally good at math while others have personalities that make it difficult for them to comprehend mathematics at all. She describes one of her best students:

> He is capable of listening to a direction and following it and catching on very quickly. He has got, he has just got real good math sense. Very bright boy . . . he just has a real uncanny sense of just listening and it all makes sense to him. It just makes sense.

She thinks "it is just something about him" that enables him to be successful in doing math. In contrast, her struggling students

> always have to be reminded that they have to borrow in subtracting. They know how to do it but to give them a problem if they have not been working in subtracting, they just take the smallest number away from the largest number and cannot understand why it is wrong. They have to be reminded to move, if they multiply by a second number, to go over one place. And in dividing by two numbers, they just cannot handle that at all.

Smith believes that if researchers could figure out "what kinds of personalities are like that," she might better be able to help these kinds of pupils "catch on."

Smith's goal in teaching math is to teach for mastery of the procedures required in fourth grade: adding, subtracting, multiplying, and dividing. She explains, "What I am after is the answer." This is important to her because the pupils' computational skills determine their placements into groups in fifth grade. She finds that, for many of her students, it is just a matter of remembering what to do. For example, on Mondays, they often have forgotten the steps of the procedures and need to be reminded. Then their papers are better on Tuesday.

To help them remember, Smith gives her students mnemonic aids. For example, to remind them what to do in long division, she wrote the following on the board:

bring down

To check division:
× ans by number outside
and + remainder R

This mnemonic represented the steps of the division algorithm—"divide, multiply, subtract, bring down" and the process by which division solutions can be "checked."

I presented Smith with the place value in multiplication question discussed in the last section. It was a familiar problem to her because she teaches multiplication. She said she would try to

> get the students to see that when they multiply, well, 3 × 5, and that would come under the 5. And then because we have used that, that becomes a zero and they could hold that place with a zero if they want to. And then when they multiply 3 × 4, it would come in the same column as the 4. And when you multiply 3 times 6, it is in the same column as the 6.

$$
\begin{array}{r}
123 \\
\times\ 645 \\
\hline
615 \\
492\ \ \\
738\ \ \ \\
\hline
79335 \\
\end{array}
$$

She explained that, although the second partial product is 4,920 and that is why the zero makes sense, she gives her pupils "the option" about putting the zeros in because some students get "very confused about the zero." Although

Smith knows why the 492 is shifted over (i.e., because it is really 4,920), she said she does not talk with her students about the meaning of the procedure. Her concern is to get the students to be able to perform the computation and so she emphasizes using the zero only to help them "hold the place" and to remember to move one column over on each line.

Teaching Multiplication

Smith's approach to helping her students learn to multiply large numbers is to provide reminders, practice, and feedback. One day she starts class by distributing a ditto with multiplication problems. She has been working on multiplication with her class for a while, but does not think they have entirely mastered it. Without comment or question, the 20 students begin the computations; the room is absolutely silent. Smith has written a reminder on the board:

signifying the steps for multiplying large numbers—multiply, multiply, then add. Smith walks around, looking over pupils' shoulders at their work. She pats one of the girls on the shoulder, smiles, and comments quietly, "Good job!" She circulates to other students, placing her hand on their shoulders as she pauses to glance at their papers.

After about 15 minutes everyone has completed the ditto and they have turned them into the basket of finished assignments. Smith announces that the class will now go over the problems together on the board so that "you can see if you were on the right track." She writes the first five problems on the board and calls five pupils up to do them in front of the class. Since they have turned their papers in, they are doing these from scratch, not copying their own work. When they are done, Smith checks each one against her answer sheet, and marks a large C above each one that is correct. Discovering two that are incorrect, she clucks: "Uh-uh-uh-uh-uh! We're doing *multiplication* here." She has those two children return to the board to redo their problems.

By now, the noise level is high and few children are looking at the board. Smith erases the first five, and writes three more problems on the board. She calls students to come up to do them, including the "bonus problem," a 3-digit by 3-digit multiplication, something she said they had not yet been taught. She picks Jon, her best student, to do the bonus problem.

$$\begin{array}{r} 223 \\ \times\ 417 \\ \hline \end{array}$$

Smith checks over the students' work on the board and then asks, "Anybody have any questions about the more difficult problems? How many of you feel you had the bonus question right?" She walks them through it: "How many of you *remember*—when you multiply by the 7, you put it here [under the 7], when you multiply by the 1, you put a zero? Then when you multiply by *another* number, you put *two* zeroes here." She asks again if anyone has any questions. No one does. She reminds them of their social studies homework for tomorrow and the class is dismissed.

Smith's Approach

Ms. Smith thinks it is most important for students to become proficient in the multiplication algorithm, to be able to put together the steps in order to produce the right answer. Her eye is fixed on her students' future in school, that is, on their placement level in middle school. What she emphasizes derives from this concentration. Although she understands the conceptual basis for the rule to "shift the numbers over," she does not feel this is important for her students to understand: No one will expect them to know that in fifth grade (or ever). Her assessment of her students' ability also reflects her conception of mathematics as a set of rules to remember and follow: The better students listen well and follow directions; the weaker ones have to be reminded all the time.

Overall, correct answers are Smith's goal and she is the source of these answers in her class. She checks the students' written work and grades it. When she has pupils do problems in front of the class, she herself marks them right or wrong. Smith's purpose in going over the assigned problems is so that students can see the right answers, not to discuss the reasonableness of the answers or the process by which they were obtained. When two students got wrong answers at the board, Smith had them redo the problems; she did not ask the others to try to figure out where the errors lay.

Interestingly, she did offer them a problem which they have not been taught to do (a 3-digit times 3-digit multiplication). In keeping with her belief that math just makes sense to some students, though, she picks her best student to do this one at the board. When he gets it right, she does not choose to engage the class in a discussion of what he did or why it made sense. Instead, she tells them the steps of the procedure and asks if anyone has any questions.

Finally, Smith's approach is based on her belief that students learn mathematics by independently practicing examples in a quiet setting until they remember the steps. Her role is to give them structured opportunities to practice, provide them with helpful mnemonic aids to reduce their tendency to forget parts of the procedures, and confirm the accuracy of their work. The next teacher seems in some ways to take a similar approach, yet some significant differences in emphasis and rationale are apparent, reflecting a different interaction among subject matter knowledge, ideas about teaching and learning, about learners, and about the context of the classroom.

Belinda Rosen

A teacher for over ten years, Belinda Rosen teaches in a white middle-class suburban community. Her school regroups children across classes for mathematics and reading instruction, and Belinda receives the weakest students in the fourth grade. She uses a whole group approach to teaching math and focuses heavily on computational skills. She is, however, very torn about the appropriateness of this focus, wondering how much time she should spend on computational skills on one hand and problem solving on the other. She realizes that "math is not just computation and the books are written as if math were just computation." This pulls her to do "a variety of things," such as "time, money, graphs, and Cuisenaire rods." At the same time, she acknowledges that her pupils will "have to be able to subtract if they are going to have a checkbook" or buy wallpaper. In addition, they must know how to add, subtract, multiply, and divide for fifth grade.

Rosen's goals are shaped by her ideas about her pupils. Because they are weak, she believes she should emphasize following directions and understanding math vocabulary: "To really get that clear when you say *product*, what does that mean, what does that word key, you know?—That it should be multiplication." She said she tries to "inculcate" them with some of the essential material, so that "when and if something clicks," they'll have had exposure to it before. Rosen also wants the students to develop more confidence that they can figure things out for themselves and to enjoy math class. She thinks variety is important just to help her pupils feel happy about coming to class, and she gives little rewards to encourage them.

Rosen thinks that some students are perhaps "math disabled." They may have "great reasoning ability," but they cannot remember what they have been taught from one day to the next: Every day is "a *brand* new day." While she cares about finding ways to help these students and believes she can "get to them *eventually*," she thinks some approaches would not work with her class because they would not be able to handle them. "Discipline" is her least favorite part of teaching, and she thinks that these weaker students tend to be more distractible and have more behavior problems.

When I presented Rosen with the place value in multiplication question she thought that teaching the students to "do a placeholder" would help. She said she would emphasize the sequence of steps and show them that "the first line down is one placeholder, second one down is two placeholders." Her strategy would be to do several problems together with them, starting with easy ones that "didn't have regrouping or hard math facts" so that she could emphasize "the process."

Rosen also suggested a couple of other strategies that she thought would help. She said she has the students put an asterisk inside the placeholder (the zero) so that they don't "get confused with other zeros":

> If the first one that they had to multiply in that row was, say, 5 × 8, and they are going to put down another zero, I don't want them to get confused about whether they had actually already put their placeholder down.

$$
\begin{array}{r}
375 \\
\times\ \ 83 \\
\hline
1125 \\
\Theta
\end{array}
$$

She said that, with her students, she would also emphasize writing neatly because poor penmanship is often the root of errors in lining the numbers up correctly. She said she sometimes uses graph paper to help them keep the numbers lined up.

Teaching Multiplication

Rosen has been working on multiplication with her pupils for several days. One day she asks a pupil to distribute chalk to the others, all of whom have individual slates at their desks, and says that they are going to work on 3-digit times 2-digit multiplication. She announces that she will give a sticker to everyone who works on multiplication if she doesn't have to talk to them about their behavior. The following series illustrates the detail with which Rosen proceeded to "work on" multiplication with her class. She writes the following on the board and asks what the first step is:

$$
\begin{array}{r}
243 \\
\times\ \ 22 \\
\hline
\end{array}
$$

Ronnie:	3 × 2.
Rosen:	We're going to take the number that's in the ones column and we're going to multiply it, and 3 × 2, Karen?
Karen:	6
Rosen:	And what's our next step?
S:	2 × 4
Rosen:	2 × 4. And Darrell, what are you going to say for 2 × 4?
Darrell:	(pause, being silly with a silly voice) 4
Rosen:	4? 1 × 4 is 4. What's 2 × 4?
Darrell:	2 × 4? . . . 8

(Several other students applaud.)

Rosen:	And then?

S: 2×2
Rosen: And what's our next step?
S: Put the placeholder down.

Rosen repeats, "Put the placeholder down," and writes a zero with an asterisk inside under the ones column in the second row.

$$
\begin{array}{r}
243 \\
\times\ \ 22 \\
\hline
486 \\
\Theta
\end{array}
$$

Rosen: We're going to multiply the number in the tens column by 3.
S: 6

The pupils and teacher continue in this manner until they have finished multiplying. She reminds them to put a plus sign down.

$$
\begin{array}{r}
243 \\
\times\ \ 22 \\
\hline
486 \\
+\ \ \ 486\Theta
\end{array}
$$

Rosen: $6 + 0$? Karen?
Karen: 6
Rosen: And then?
S: 14
                                (Rosen writes the 4 down and carries the 1.)
Rosen: Darrell, take over?
Darrell: $8 \times 4 \ldots$
Rosen: (breaks in) "We're going to *add*, remember, Darrell? Remember about *adding*?"
Darrell: $8 + 4$ is 12.

They finish the problem together. Rosen says she is going to give each of them a problem, "but before I do, let's review the steps. What's our first step?"

S: Multiply?
Rosen: We're going to multiply by the number in the ones place. (She writes "mult $\times$ ν1's place.") Jim, what's our next step?
Jim: Placeholder.
Rosen: Then we're going to do placeholder. (She writes "placeholder.") What are we going to do next?
S: Multiply.

Rosen: We're going to multiply by the number in the tens place.
         (She writes "mult × #10 place.")
Rosen: Next step? Lynn?
Lynn: Add

         (Rosen writes "add.")

         1. Mult × #1's place
         2. Placeholder
         3. Mult × #10's place
         4. Add

The teacher writes another problem on the board and the children proceed to do it on their slates. She walks around helping kids, mostly reminding them about the placeholder step and urging them to work slowly and carefully. Rosen talks one girl through adding up the products. When everyone is done, Rosen goes through the problem, step by step, on the board. She gives the pupils a few more problems to do; the last one requires regrouping (none of the others have). Before class ends, they go over this last one together. Rosen walks them through the steps, asking different pupils to calculate each step as before. Rosen passes out a ditto with more multiplication problems and assigns the first two rows for seatwork.

Rosen's Approach

Ms. Rosen is driven by her concern for her weak pupils and her ideas about what they need. She wants them to be successful in the school curriculum, but knows that this has been very difficult for them. She tries to offer them as much support as possible to enable them to do multiplication correctly. She not only spells out the steps in detail and reviews them several times, she also carefully walks the class through many problems together.

Rosen is aware of many little things that go wrong in her pupils' use of the algorithm—such as forgetting whether the zero that one has written down is a "placeholder" or part of the next computational step—and she tries to build in safeguards, such as the asterisk, to ensure that pupils will not fall into these traps. One of these pitfalls is that students forget to add the partial products and multiply them instead. Rosen tells the students to put an asterisk inside the placeholder zero and to write down a plus sign in order to help them remember what to do. For Rosen, learning the steps *is* what there is to know about multiplication. The help she provides is designed to enable these students, who have trouble learning math, to be successful.

The students are kept active in Rosen's class—with paper and pencil tasks, with slates, or by being called upon to provide answers—because she thinks they are very distractible and that she must keep their attention in order to help them learn. She even offers stickers to encourage them to stay on task.

On some days, Rosen provides a break from computation by doing "time, money, graphs, or Cuisenaire rods." This list reflects a conception of worthwhile mathematics curriculum shaped by beliefs about pupils, grounded more in utility and fun than in mathematical significance. Time and money are mathematical topics in school only; Cuisenaire rods are a representational tool, not content.

Rosen is the one with the answers, the source of validation in her classroom. She leads them skillfully through the steps ("And what do we do next? What's our next step?") When they say something wrong—for example, when Darrell says that 2×4 is 4—she corrects them. She does not wait to see if other students object or if the student who has made the error catches it. Rosen says she wants her students to be able to "figure things out for themselves"; what she means is that she wants them to be able to follow the procedures without guidance. Although she might not argue with such a goal, she is not focusing on developing conceptual autonomy or epistemic power.

The third teacher approaches the teaching of multiplication in an entirely different way than either Smith or Rosen. Her approach, driven by a view of mathematics as a discipline, reflects a different pattern of interaction among subject matter, teaching and learning, learners, and the classroom context.

Magdalene Lampert[9]

Magdalene Lampert teaches mathematics in a heterogeneous elementary school in which over a third of the students speak English as a second language. An elementary teacher with over ten years of experience, Lampert is also a university professor and researcher, who draws on her classroom teaching in her research and writing. Her students' mathematical skills range broadly, from those who do not add or subtract accurately to those who can add, subtract, multiply, and divide with whole numbers. In Lampert's approach to teaching mathematics, learning what mathematics is and how one engages in it are goals purposefully coequal and interconnected with acquiring the "stuff"—concepts and procedures—of mathematics. Lampert's goal is to help students acquire the mathematical skills and understanding necessary to judge the validity of their own and others' ideas and results, to develop mathematical power (National Council of Teachers of Mathematics, 1989).

Lampert's pedagogy subtly blends goal and process. For example, when students give answers or make assertions, Lampert almost always comes back with, "Why do you think that?" or "How did you figure that out?" She explains that this strategy helps her to understand how her students are thinking, critical information for subsequent pedagogical decisions. Yet she also uses this strategy because it contributes to her goal of fostering "a habit of discourse in the classroom in which work in mathematics is referred back to the knower to answer questions of reasonability" (Lampert, 1986, p. 317).

In her teaching, Lampert tries to balance her pedagogical responsibility to make sure students learn the "stuff" of mathematics with her commitment to helping students invent and construct mathematical ideas and procedures. She, for example, chooses the tasks on which students work. Their solutions, however, form the basis for the class discussion and further work. Lampert also introduces various representational systems, such as coins and the number line, which are not ends in themselves but with which students can explore mathematical problems. She models mathematical thinking and activity, and asks questions that push students to examine and articulate their ideas.

She leads class discussion but its substance grows out of students' ideas and proposals for strategies. Perhaps most critical in this approach is her role in guiding the direction, balance, and rhythm of classroom discourse by deciding which points the group should pursue, which questions to play down, which issues to table for the moment. This leads to inevitable dilemmas about when and how much to intervene in their puzzlements. For example, she describes an occasion in her class when a heated debate arose about whether decimal numbers are actually negative. She pondered what she should do:

> Should my first priority in the second lesson be simply to tell these students that decimals are definitely *not* negative numbers? My wish to present mathematics as a subject in which legitimate conclusions are based on reasoning, rather than acquiescing to teacherly authority, led me away from this approach (Lampert, 1989, p. 237).

Lampert believes that all her students are capable of learning and engaging in significant mathematics and she corroborates that conviction frequently, noting with pleasure when her pupils become embroiled with the meaning of negative numbers or the infinity of numbers between zero and one (Lampert, in press). She also assumes that elementary school students can be absorbed in abstract work as well as in problems centered in interesting real-life contexts. Sometimes she constructs problems that draw on familiar knowledge, such as money; at other times, she sets tasks which are wholly separate from her pupils' everyday experience.

Lampert, in preparing to teach her students to multiply large numbers, analyzed what it means to understand multiplication. Knowledge of multiplication, she decided, could be of four kinds: intuitive, computational, principled, or concrete (Lampert, 1986). Intuitive knowledge of multiplication is reflected in people's informal reasoning in solving real-world multiplication problems, independent of formal knowledge about multiplication. Computational knowledge refers to the traditional procedural knowledge taught in school; principled knowledge is the *why* of computational knowledge—for example, knowing that 23×5 can be calculated by decomposing 23 into $20 + 3$, multiplying 20×5 and 3×5, and adding the resulting products. Concrete knowledge is being able to represent a problem with objects in order to solve it. Based on her analysis of the content, Lampert (1986, p. 314) determined that what she wanted was to provide experiences that would enable her students to strengthen their competence in each of these four ways of knowing about multiplication and to help them to build connections among them.

Teaching Multiplication

In Lampert's (1986) series of lessons on multiplication she reached a point comparable with Smith and Rosen—midway in helping students learn about multiplication. She had decided to engage her fourth-grade students in telling and illustrating multiplication stories. After a couple of lessons in which the class constructed stories and pictures to represent multiplications like 12 × 4, she introduced 2-digit by 2-digit problems. By now the pupils were familiar with this mode of representation and she felt they were ready to take on this more complex challenge.

Lampert asks her pupils to come up with a story for 28 × 65. Colleen suggests 28 glasses with 65 drops of water in each glass. Lampert accepts this proposal, but says she does not want to draw 28 glasses on the board so she will draw big jugs that hold the equivalent of 10 glasses. She asks the class how many jugs and how many glasses she needs in order to represent Colleen's 28 glasses. They tell her: 2 jugs and 8 glasses. As she draws big jugs and glasses on the chalkboard, she queries again: How many drops of water in each glass and in each jug? Once again, students reply. Each time a student answers, Lampert asks the student to explain his or her answer. The chalkboard drawing looks like this now:

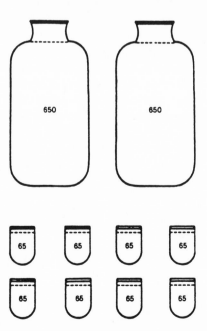

Figure 1. Jugs and Glasses to Represent 28 × 65

Next Lampert asks the class how they can find out how many drops of water there are altogether. They say that they should add the jugs and glasses together. The pupils understand readily that the two jugs contain a total of 1,300 drops. Lampert then proceeds to teach them a "trick" that makes it easier to add the 8 glasses together: She suggests that they could take 5 drops of water out of each glass and put them in another container, leaving 60 drops in each glass. She asks the class how many drops would there be in all the glasses then. Someone explains that it would be 480 with just 40 drops in the other container. Combining those yields 520 drops, and adding those to the 1,300 equals 1,820.

Lampert points out that by using "clever groupings" they have figured out 28×65 without doing any paper-pencil computation. Just as she thinks they have finished this problem and is ready to move on, however, one of her girls, Ko, says she has come up with "another way of thinking about it." Lampert, listening intently, writes Ko's explanation on the board "so as to give it equal weight in the eyes of the class" (Lampert, 1986, p. 329).

Ko proposes that they could have thought about three jugs. Two jugs would hold 1,300 drops, but the third would have 2 glasses, or 130 drops, too much water. She explains that if you remove the 130 drops from the third jug, you are left with 520 drops (650 − 130), which, added to the other two jugs yields a total of 1,820 drops of water. Lampert draws a picture of Ko's idea on the board and together the class explores why it made sense mathematically.

Lampert spent a few more days using students' stories to draw pictures and examine the ways in which the numbers could be decomposed, multiplied in parts, and recombined. Next she constructed assignments which required the students to make up and illustrate stories, as well as write the numerical representations. Sometimes she asked them to decompose and recombine the quantities in more than one way. They presented and defended their solutions to other class members. Lampert moved on from this to work with her class on the meanings of the steps in paper-pencil computation, using alternative algorithms (i.e., "no-carry" method) as well as the traditional one.

In writing about this work, Lampert (1986, p. 330) reflected on the contributions of this series of lessons to her overall goals in teaching multiplication:

> They were using the language and drawings we had practiced to build a bridge between their intuitive knowledge about how concrete knowledge can be grouped for counting and the meaning of arithmetic procedures using arithmetic symbols. By rewarding them for inventing reasonable procedures rather than for simply finding the correct answer, I was able to communicate a broader view of what it means to know mathematics and learn something from what they were doing about how they would use mathematical procedures in a concrete context.

She observed also that her students were gaining in their ability to substantiate their claims using reasons "that came very close to the steps of a mathematical proof as well as inventing "legitimate variations on both concrete and computational procedures" (Lampert, 1986, p. 337).

Lampert's Approach

Lampert draws the strategy and rationale for her approach from the discipline of mathematics itself: The goal is to help students develop mathematical power and to become active participants in mathematics as a system of human thought. To do this, pupils must learn to make sense of and use concepts and procedures that others have invented—the "body" of accumulated knowledge in the discipline—but they also must have experience in developing and pursuing mathematical hunches themselves, inventing mathematics, and learning to make mathematical arguments for their ideas. Good mathematics teaching, according to this perspective, should result in meaningful understandings of concepts and procedures, but also in explicit and appropriate understandings *about* mathematics: what it means to "do" mathematics and how one establishes the validity of answers, for instance.

While exploring the mathematical foundations of multiplication, Lampert's students were also encountering some strong and intentional messages about what it means to "do" and to "know" mathematics. Lampert consciously tried to ensure that students would have to turn back upon themselves and upon their mathematical knowledge in order to validate their answers and strategies. She explains that the essence of her approach is to teach her pupils

> to use representational tools to reason about numerical relationships. In the public discourse of the classroom, such reasoning occurs as argument among peers and between students and teacher. *It is the ability to participate in such arguments that is the mark of mathematics learning* (1989, p. 233, emphasis added).

Lampert's approach thereby fuses assumptions about how learning occurs with a view of what it means to do and to know mathematics. Both entail and depend upon discussion and argument, pursued within a community of shared standards and interests. In the interest of learning, Lampert strives to create a classroom culture in which this kind of intellectual activity is the norm (different from the traditional context of classroom life); within this culture she simultaneously constructs an explicit curriculum of mathematical activity.

Smith, Rosen, and Lampert: What is Mathematics?

Whether they do it consciously or not, teachers represent the subject to students through their teaching. With the tasks that they select, the explanations that they provide, and the kinds of things that they emphasize, teachers convey messages to their students about both the *substance* and the *nature* of mathematical knowledge (McDiarmid, Ball, & Anderson, 1989).

Looking at substance first, how do Smith, Rosen, and Lampert represent multiplication to their students? Smith and Rosen use the symbolic form only, without connection to concrete or real-world objects. Neither do they use visual representations. Multiplication is represented as symbolic manipulation and shorthand language is provided to summarize the procedure so that students will remember the steps and their order.

Lampert represents multiplication using drawings. While the objects (containers and water drops) were proposed by a student, Lampert chose the specific pictorial representation of the student's idea to represent an essential conceptual component of the procedure: grouping by tens. Instead of drawing 28 glasses, each with 65 drops of water, she feigned laziness and suggested drawing jugs that hold the equivalent of 10 glasses. This move allowed her to represent the decomposition of numbers that underlies the reasonableness of the multiplication algorithm. At the same time, she was incorporating student ideas into the process of constructing and using representational tools in doing mathematics.[11]

The ways in which Smith, Rosen, and Lampert approach the teaching of multiplication also reflect and portray to students different views of what counts as "mathematics"—that is, what students are supposed to learn, what matters about learning mathematics, what it means to know and to do mathematics, and where the authority for truth lies. In both Smith's and Rosen's classes, learning multiplication means learning to calculate; mathematics is thereby synonymous with computation. Students are taught the computational algorithm which they practice so that they will memorize the procedure and increase their speed and accuracy in using it. Neither the meaning of the concepts nor the principles underlying the procedure are addressed. In this kind of teaching, knowing mathematics means remembering definitions, rules, and formulas and doing mathematics is portrayed as a straightforward step-by-step process. The goals derive from the school curriculum and what students need in order to move on. Epistemic authority rests with the teacher, who gives explanations and evaluates the correctness of students' answers.

In Lampert's classroom, students encounter a different view of mathematics. While she teaches the required fourth-grade curriculum, the ways in which she approaches it are colored by what she thinks is central to knowing mathematics. On one hand, she emphasizes meaningful understanding. Students are helped to acquire knowledge of concepts and procedures, the relationships among them, and why they work. Although she is teaching the same common fourth-grade topic as Smith and Rosen, her goals are different. Learning about multiplication is valued more for what students can learn about numbers, numeration, and operations with numbers than as an end in itself.

On the other hand, she also explicitly emphasizes the nature and epistemology of mathematics. Just as central as understanding mathematical concepts and procedures is understanding what it means to do mathematics, being able to validate one's own answers, having opportunities to engage in mathematical argument, and seeing value in mathematics beyond its utility in familiar everyday settings. Lampert (1989) discusses how the substantive and epistemological dimensions of mathematical knowledge go hand in hand in this view of mathematics. She explains that she tries to

> shift the locus of authority in the classroom—*away from* the teacher as a judge and the textbook as a standard for judgment and *toward* the teacher and students as inquirers who have the power to use mathematical tools to decide whether an answer or a procedure is reasonable (Lampert, 1989, p. 224).

But, she adds, students can do this only if they have meaningful control of the ideas:

> Students will not reason in mathematically appropriate ways about objects that have no meaning to them; in order for them to learn to reason about assertions involving such abstract symbols and operations as .000056 and $a^2 + b^3$, they need to connect these symbols and operations to a domain in which they are competent to "make sense" (p. 224).

Teaching Mathematics: An Interaction Among Subject Matter Understandings, Views of Teaching, Learning, Learners, and Context

These three examples of teaching differ not only in what counts as knowledge of mathematics, but also in their assumptions about the teaching and learning of mathematics: about pupils, teachers, and the context of classrooms. What each of these teachers does is a function of the interactions among these understandings, assumptions, and beliefs. Smith's eye is on the fourth-grade curriculum; she feels responsible for her students' mastering the required material in order to go on to the next grade. For Smith, knowing math means *remembering* procedures and her teaching approach is based on the assumption that mathematics is learned through repeated practice and drill. She sees her role as showing pupils how to do the procedures, assigning and carefully monitoring their practice, and remediating individual students who have difficulty.

Like Smith, Rosen also believes that learning mathematics requires repeated practice. For both teachers, teaching multiplication begins with explanation and demonstration; the rest of the unit consists of practicing the procedure. Rosen, however, is more influenced by her view of her students than is Smith. Because Rosen believes her students to be weak, even "math disabled," she takes a more directive role throughout the practice phase than does Smith. This includes giving pupils tricks, mnemonics, and shortcuts, as well as walking them through the procedures over and over. Smith's classroom is very quiet; she assumes that pupils are engaged, and worries less than Rosen about keeping them in contact with the content. Rosen, who believes her students to be highly distractible and prone to behavior problems, plans activities which control her pupils' engagement with the subject matter. In both classes, pupils are expected to absorb and retain what they have been shown.

Lampert makes assumptions very different from either Smith or Rosen about what there is to be learned and why, as well as about how fourth graders can learn mathematics. She assumes that students must be actively involved in constructing their own understandings and meanings both individually and in groups. Practice takes on an entirely different meaning in this approach than in either of the other two approaches. Here, instead of a learning view of practice—that is, practicing mathematics by doing repeated examples of the skill being taught—students engage in a disciplinary view of practice: the practice *of* mathematics. Class activities are designed to involve the students in what it means to think about and do mathematics as mathematicians do (Collins, Brown, & Newman, in press; Lave, 1987).

Lampert's view of her role appears to grow out of the interaction of her constructivist assumptions about learning and her disciplinary focus. With the goal of involving students in a mathematical community, she must strive for a balance between helping students acquire established mathematical knowledge and encouraging them to invent and construct ideas themselves. Lampert believes, therefore, that the teacher has a critical role to play in facilitating students' mathematical learning. She introduces a variety of representational systems which can be used to reason about mathematics, models mathematical thinking and activity, and asks questions that push students to examine and articulate their ideas.

However, perhaps most significant in the classroom context is her role in guiding the direction, balance, and rhythm of classroom discourse by deciding which points the group should pursue, which questions to play down, which issues to table for the moment, decisions she makes based on her knowledge of mathematics. The classroom group is critical in Lampert's approach for it represents the mathematical community within which students must establish their claims. In Smith's and Rosen's classes, learning mathematics is considered an individual matter; the group is a feature of the classroom context to be managed in fostering individual learning. Smith, in fact, prefers to "individualize" rather than to work as a group.

SUBJECT-MATTER KNOWLEDGE:
A TERM IN THE PEDAGOGICAL EQUATION

Teachers' understandings of mathematics is a critical part of the resources available which comprise the realm of *pedagogical possibility* in teaching mathematics. Teachers cannot explain to their students the principles underlying the multiplication algorithm if they do not explicitly understand those principles themselves. The representations they choose may be mathematically misleading or may even fail to correspond at all. Yet teachers who do understand the role of place value and the distributive property in multiplying large numbers will not necessarily draw upon this understanding in their teaching, if their ideas about learners or about learning intervene.

Teachers who think, for example, that fourth graders will not profit from such knowledge, or that procedural competence should precede conceptual understanding in learning mathematics, may choose to emphasize memorization of the algorithm. Two teachers who have similar understandings of place value and numeration may teach very differently based on differences in their assumptions about the teacher's role. One may talk directly about place value and explicitly show pupils what the digits in each place of a numeral represent. The other may engage students in a counting task which is designed to help them discover the power of grouping. These differences are a function of different assumptions about the teaching and learning of mathematics.

Still, a teacher who lacks Lampert's disciplinary knowledge of mathematics will not be able to teach as she does, for her approach to teaching is not possible without that kind of understanding of and about mathematics. Making the judgments about which student suggestions to pursue, developing the tasks that encourage certain kinds of exploration, and conducting fruitful class discussions—all these tasks depend heavily on the teacher's subject matter knowledge.

Questions to Pursue About the Role of Subject-Matter Knowledge in Teaching Mathematics

Are all these domains—subject matter, teaching and learning, learners, and context—coequally influential in teaching mathematics? Or does one domain tend to drive and shape a particular teacher's approach? Rosen, for example, seems to start from her ideas about her pupils. Her knowledge of mathematics, her view of her role, and her assumptions about learning all appear to be shaped by that starting point. Lampert's approach, however, seems clearly rooted in the subject matter; the pedagogy follows. In order to understand the role of subject-matter knowledge in teaching mathematics, we need to explore the balance and interaction among the critical domains in different teachers' teaching of mathematics. This includes closely examining teachers' knowledge of and about mathematics as well as how that knowledge shapes or is shaped by their other ideas and assumptions.

The other side of the pedagogical equation is student learning. Studying the whole equation—from teacher knowledge to teacher thinking to teacher actions to student learning—is an agenda to which we must return. Research currently underway tends to focus on only part of the equation. This is appropriate, for in order to understand the subtle relationships among the terms, we need better ways of thinking about and studying each part of the equation. Past efforts often came up short as a result of unexamined or simplistic assumptions about subject-matter knowledge, teaching, or student learning, or about the relationship among them. Still, we must keep our eye on the whole equation, for it is in studying these relationships that we will better understand what goes into teaching mathematics effectively.

We also need to pursue similar questions in research on teacher learning if teacher education is to be a more effective intervention in preparing people to teach mathematics well (Ball, 1988b). What do prospective teachers bring with them to teacher education? How do the ideas and understandings across these domains grow and change over time? We need to investigate the relative contributions of teachers' own schooling in mathematics, formal teacher education, and teaching experience to their subject-matter knowledge and their approaches to teaching mathematics.

This paper ends with the reflection from a prospective teacher who, in trying to teach the concept of permutations, had abruptly discovered that he needed to revise his assumptions about learning to teach mathematics:

> When I decided to be a teacher, I knew there were a lot of things I had to learn about teaching, but I felt I knew everything there was to teach my students. During the permutation activities, I found I was as much a learner of subject matter as I was a learner of the art of teaching. My education in the future will not be limited to "how to teach," but also what it is I'm teaching. My knowledge of math must improve drastically if I am to teach effectively (Ball, 1988b).

Like many people, he had taken subject-matter knowledge for granted in teaching mathematics. Our reconsideration of the role of subject matter calls this assumption sharply into question. First, learning to do mathematics in school, given the ways in which it is typically taught, may not equip even the successful student with adequate or appropriate knowledge of *or* about mathematics. Second, knowing mathematics for oneself may not be the same as knowing it in order to teach it. While tacit knowledge may serve one well personally, explicit understanding is necessary for teaching. Finally, subject-matter knowledge does not exist separately in teaching, but shapes and is shaped by other kinds of knowledge and beliefs.

ACKNOWLEDGMENTS

The author gratefully acknowledges the comments of Mary Kennedy, G. W. McDiarmid, Magdalene Lampert, and Suzanne Wilson on an earlier draft of this chapter. This work was sponsored in part by the National Center for Research on Teacher Education, College of Education, Michigan State University. The National

Center for Research on Teacher Education is funded primarily by the Office of Educational Research and Improvement, United States Department of Education.

NOTES

1. "Knowledge *about*" mathematics deals in part with what Schwab calls the "syntax" of a discipline.

2. The results in this section are drawn from my dissertation research and all names used are pseudonyms. In this study, 19 prospective elementary and secondary teachers were interviewed in depth at their point of entry into formal teacher education. Interviews focused on their knowledge and beliefs about mathematics, about teaching and learning mathematics, about students, and about learning to teach. The goal of the research was to learn about the knowledge and beliefs of the participants as well as to contribute to the development of a theoretical framework for the question, "What do prospective teachers bring with them to teacher education that is likely to affect their learning to teach mathematics?" (See Ball, 1988a).

3. I borrow the term "algorithm rhyme" from Blake and Verhille, 1985.

4. A provocative finding was the lack of difference by level between the responses of secondary teacher candidates, who are math majors, and of elementary teacher candidates, who are not. This issue and its implications are taken up in Ball (1988a).

5. Researchers are currently pursuing critical questions about the relationship between conceptual and procedural knowledge in mathematics. See, for example, Hiebert and Lefevre (1986).

6. This requirement of explicit understanding holds even for teachers who do not choose to teach by telling. Facilitating students' construction of mathematical understanding, for instance, involves selecting fruitful tasks, asking good questions, and encouraging helpfully. In order to do this well, teachers must know what there is to be learned.

7. The distinction between tacit and explicit ways of knowing is not intended as a dichotomy, but rather as a qualitative dimension along which understanding varies.

8. The data about this teacher and the next one are part of the Teacher Education and Teacher Learning Study currently being conducted by the National Center for Research on Teacher Education. For more information about the study and, in particular, about the theoretical framework and instrumentation of the research, see Ball and McDiarmid (1988) or National Center for Research on Teacher Education (1988).

9. Magdalene Lampert is her real name. The material in this section is drawn from her own writing about her teaching (Lampert, 1986, 1989).

10. This provides a striking contrast with the way in which many prospective teachers choose representations. They tend to focus more on using media which will appeal to students (e.g., candies) and often neglect to consider the mathematical appropriateness of the representation or its helpfulness in teaching.

REFERENCES

Ball, D. L. (1988a). *Knowledge and reasoning in mathematical pedagogy: Examining what prospective teachers bring to teacher education.* Unpublished doctoral dissertation, Michigan State University, East Lansing.

Ball, D. L. (1988b). Unlearning to teach mathematics. *For the Learning of Mathematics*, 8(1), 40-48.

Ball, D. L. (1988c). *The subject matter preparation of prospective mathematics teachers: Challenging the myths* (Research Report 88-1). East Lansing: Michigan State University, National Center for Research on Teacher Education.

Ball, D. L. (1990). The mathematical understandings that prospective teachers bring to teacher education. *Elementary School Journal, 90,* 449-466.

Ball, D. L. (in press). Teaching mathematics for understanding: What do teachers need to know about the subject matter? In M. Kennedy (Ed.), *Teaching academic subjects to diverse learners.* New York: Teachers College Press.

Ball, D. L., & McDiarmid, G. (1988). Research on teacher learning: Studying how teachers' knowledge changes. *Action in Teacher Education,* 10(2), 14-21.

Ball, D. L., & McDiarmid, G. W. (1990). The subject matter preparation of teachers. In W. R. Houston (Ed.), *Handbook for research on teacher education* (pp. 437-449). New York: Macmillan.

Begle, E. G. (1979). *Critical variables in mathematics education: Findings from a survey of empirical literature.* Washington, DC: Mathematics Association of America and the National Council of Teachers of Mathematics.

Begle E. G., & Geeslin, W. (1972). *Teacher effectiveness in mathematics instruction* (National Longitudinal Study of Mathematical Abilities Reports: No. 28). Washington, DC: Mathematical Association of America and National Council of Teachers of Mathematics.

Bennett, N. (1976). *Teaching styles and pupil progress.* Cambridge, MA: Harvard University Press.

Blaire, E. (1981). Philosophies of mathematics and perspectives of mathematics teaching. *International Journal of Mathematics Education in Science and Technology,* 12, 147-153.

Blake, R., & Verhille, C. (1985). The story of 0. *For the Learning of Mathematics,* 5(3), 35-46.

Bruner, J. (1970). Some theorems on instruction illustrated with reference to mathematics. In E. Begle (Ed.), *Mathematics education* (69th yearbook of the National Society for the Study of Education, pp. 306-335). Chicago: University of Chicago Press.

Buchmann, M. (1984). The priority of knowledge and understanding in teaching. In J. Raths and L. Katz (Eds.), *Advances in teacher education* (Vol. 1, pp. 29-48). Norwood, NJ: Ablex.

Clark, C., & Yinger, R. (1979). Teachers' thinking. In P. L. Peterson & H. Walberg (Eds.), *Research on teaching: Concepts, findings, and implications* (pp. 231-263). Berkeley, CA: McCutchan.

Collins, A., Brown, J., & Newman, S. (in press). The new apprenticeship: Teaching students the craft of reading, writing, and mathematics. In L. B. Resnick (Ed.), *Knowledge and learning.* Hillsdale, NJ: Erlbaum.

Ernest, P. (1988). *The knowledge, beliefs, and attitudes of the mathematics teacher: A model.* Unpublished manuscript, University of Exeter, School of Education, England.

Ferrini-Mundy, J. (1986, April). *Mathematics teachers' attitudes and beliefs: Implications for inservice education.* Paper presented at the annual meeting of the American Educational Research Association, San Francisco, CA.

Fey, J. (1978). Change in mathematics education since the later 1950s: Ideas and realisation, U.S.A. *Educational Studies in Mathematics, 9,* 339-353.

Gage, N. (1977). *The scientific basis of the art of teaching.* New York: Teachers College Press.

Hart, F. (1934). *Teachers and teaching: By ten thousand high school seniors.* New York: Macmillan.

Hatano, G. (1982). Cognitive consequences of practice in culture-specific procedural skills. *The Quarterly Newsletter of the Laboratory of Comparative Human Cognition,* 4(1), 15-18.

Hiebert, J., & Lefevre, P. (1986). Conceptual and procedural knowledge. In J. Hiebert (Ed.), *Conceptual and procedural knowledge: The case of mathematics* (pp. 1-27). Hillsdale, NJ: Erlbaum.

Kamii, C. (1985). *Young children reinvent arithmetic: Implications of Piaget's theory.* New York: Teachers College Press.

Kline, M. (1970). Logic versus pedagogy. *American Mathematical Monthly, 77,* 264-282.

Kline, M. (1977). *Why the professor can't teach: Mathematics and the dilemma of university education.* New York: St. Martin's Press.

Kuhs, T. (1980). *Elementary school teachers' conceptions of mathematics content as a potential influence on classroom instruction.* Unpublished doctoral dissertation, Michigan State University, East Lansing.

Lakatos, I. (1976). *Proofs and refutations: The logic of mathematical discovery.* Cambridge: University of Cambridge Press.

Lampert, M. (1986). Knowing, doing, and teaching multiplication. *Cognition and Instruction, 3,* 305-342.

Lampert, M. (1989). Choosing and using mathematical tools in classroom discourse. In J. Brophy (Ed.), *Advances in research on teaching (Vol. I): Teaching for meaningful understanding and self-regulated learning* (pp. 223-264). Greenwich, CT: JAI Press.

Lave, J. (1987, April). *The trouble with math: A view from everyday practice.* Paper presented at the annual meeting of the American Educational Research Association, Washington, DC.

Leinhardt, G., & Smith, D. (1985). Expertise in mathematics instruction: Subject matter knowledge. *Journal of Educational Psychology, 77,* 247-271.

Lerman, S. (1983). Problem-solving or knowledge-centred: The influence of philosophy on mathematics teaching. *International Journal of Mathematics, Education, Science, and Technology, 14*(1), 59-66.

McDiarmid, G. W., Ball, D., & Anderson, C. (1989). Why staying ahead one chapter just won't work: Subject-specific pedagogy. In M. Reynolds (Ed.), *Knowledge base for beginning teachers* (pp. 193-205). Washington, DC: American Association of Colleges of Education.

Medley, D. (1979). The effectiveness of teachers. In P. L. Peterson and H. Walberg (Eds.), *Research on teaching: Concepts, findings, and implications* (pp. 11-26). Berkeley, CA: McCutchan.

National Center for Research on Teacher Education (NCRTE). (1988). Teacher education and learning to teach: A research agenda. *Journal of Teacher Education, 32*(6), 27-32.

National Council of Teachers of Mathematics (NCTM). (1989). *Curriculum and Evaluation Standards for School Mathematics.* Reston, VA: National Council of Teachers of Mathematics.

National Research Council (NRC). (1989). *Everybody Counts: A report on the future of mathematics education.* Washington, DC: National Academy Press.

Orr, E. W. (1987). *Twice as less: Black English and the performance of black students in mathematics and science.* New York: Norton.

Owens, J. E. (1987). *A study of four preservice secondary mathematics teachers' constructs of mathematics and mathematics teaching.* Unpublished dissertation, University of Georgia, Athens.

Peterson, P. (1979). Direct instruction reconsidered. In P. L. Peterson and H. Walberg (Eds.), *Research on teaching: Concepts, findings, and implications* (pp. 57-69). Berkeley: McCutchan.

Peterson, P., Fennema, E., Carpenter, T., & Loef, M. (1988). Teachers' pedagogical content beliefs in mathematics. *Cognition and Instruction, 6,* 1-40.

Polanyi, M. (1958). *Personal knowledge: Towards a post-critical philosophy.* Chicago: University of Chicago Press.

Post, T., Behr, M., Harel, G., & Lesh, R. (1988). *A potpourri from the Rational Number Project.* Paper prepared for the National Center for Research in Mathematical Sciences Education, University of Wisconsin, Madison.

Rosenshine, B. (1979). Content, time, and direct instruction. In P. L. Peterson & H. Walberg (Eds.), *Research on teaching: Concepts, findings, and implications,* (pp. 28-56). Berkeley, CA: McCutchan.

Schon, D. (1983). *The reflective practitioner: How professionals think in action.* New York: Basic
Books.
Schwab, J. (1978). Education and the structure of the disciplines. In I. Westbury & N. Wilkof
(Eds.), *Science, curriculum, and liberal education: Selected essays* (pp. 229-272). Chicago:
University of Chicago Press. (Original work published 1961)
Shroyer, J. (1981). *Critical moments in the teaching of mathematics: What makes teaching difficult?*
Unpublished doctoral dissertation, Michigan State University.
Shulman, L. S. (1970). Psychology and mathematics education. In E. Begle (Ed.), *Mathematics
education* (69th yearbook of the National Society for the Study of Education, pp. 23-71).
Chicago: University of Chicago Press.
Steinberg, R., Haymore, J., & Marks, R. (1985, April). *Teachers' knowledge and content
structuring in mathematics.* Paper presented at the annual meeting of the American
Educational Research Association, Chicago.
Thompson, A. (1984). The relationship of teachers' conceptions of mathematics and mathematics
teaching to instructional practice. *Educational Studies in Mathematics, 15,* 105-127.
Wright, R. (1975). The affective and cognitive consequences of an open education elementary
school. *American Educational Research Journal, 12,* 449-468.

*   *   *

CROSS-TALK

Is knowledge about mathematics analagous to "orientations" toward the teaching of a subject (e.g., English or science)?

Smith and Neale commented that my category of "knowledge *about* mathematics" seemed similar to the categories they and others have used to understand differences in science teachers' orientations to teaching science. Grossman, too, wondered about the resemblance with what she calls "orientations" in her work on English teachers' knowledge. In references to my chapter in others' writing, I have noticed that "knowledge about mathematics" is often interpreted as a set of pedagogical orientations to teaching the subject. To cite Grossman's definition, "an orientation includes beliefs about the purposes for learning a subject, beliefs about how one comes to know a subject, and beliefs about the locus of authority for knowing."

Knowledge about mathematics is not, in my mind, equivalent to orientations. The notion of teachers' orientations seems broader than what I am talking about. By knowledge about mathematics, I mean a dimension of *subject-matter knowledge*, not necessarily tied to pedagogy. Understanding mathematics, I argue, entails both knowledge of its substance (concepts, procedures, and connections among them) and of its nature and discourse. It is this latter—knowledge of the nature and discourse of mathematics—that I call knowledge *about* mathematics. It entails ideas about what is involved in doing mathematics and how truth or validity is established in the domain.

No single or correct position exists on these issues; mathematicians and philosophers differ on the role of proof, the adequacy of different approaches to proof in different contexts, and the role of community in the development of mathematics and mathematical activity, for example. Still, perspectives on the nature of mathematics are intertwined with understanding mathematical ideas and processes.

Although teachers' ideas about mathematics affect their pedagogical choices—their orientations to teaching mathematics—knowledge about mathematics is a component of subject-matter knowledge for both teachers and non-teachers (including students). In Lampert's classroom, for example, helping students develop particular understandings about mathematics and mathematical activity is as much a part of her goals for her students as is helping them develop understandings of multiplication or place value, aspects of the substance of mathematics. She engages her students in arguing about alternative mathematical hypotheses. They learn that their solutions are subject to the scrutiny of their classmates as well as of their teacher. They develop the idea that that part of doing mathematics entails looking for patterns, trying to reach generalizations, challenging old assumptions and formulating new ideas. Rather than letting their ideas about mathematics develop by default (and often to misleading conclusions) as they do in most classrooms, Lampert explicitly intertwines knowledge of and about mathematics in her classroom. Learning about mathematics—about the generation and justification of mathematical knowledge by looking for patterns, formulating conjectures, constructing mathematical arguments, and revising hypotheses in light of the challenges of one's peers—is part of *what* students are supposed to learn, part of the development of their subject-matter knowledge.

What are the implications of the claim that college-level mathematics study may be counterproductive preparation for teaching?

Carlsen and Brophy both raised questions about this claim, which was briefly made earlier. This claim represents a comment on the current state of college-level mathematics study, presently under at least as much fire as is K-12 mathematics education. I do not mean to suggest here that teachers should not study mathematics beyond the high school level or that they should have only courses especially designed for prospective teachers. Quite the contrary. To teach mathematics in ways that help students engage in authentic mathematical activity, as suggested by the National Council of Teachers of Mathematics' *Curriculum and Evaluation for School Mathematics* (1989), demands a depth and breadth of mathematical understanding not easily acquired in either precollege or college-level mathematics study under present conditions. I have begun to develop these ideas elsewhere (Ball, in press; Ball & McDiarmid, 1990); they are complicated and entail difficult conceptual and empirical questions as well as dilemmas in the structural arrangements for preparing mathematics teachers.

A mathematically based pedagogy and the discipline of mathematics: In what sense is Lampert being more faithful to the discipline of mathematics than Smith or Rosen? And is the goal of a mathematical pedagogy to make children into "little mathematicians"? How does this relate to the "new math" of the 1960s?

Anderson suggested that Lampert is perhaps no more faithful to the discipline of mathematics in her teaching than are either of the other two teachers, that she deliberately chooses not to represent mathematics "accurately." Smith and Neale also asked about the role of "the discipline" in Lampert's approach to teaching mathematics.

Rather than saying that she deliberately chooses not to represent mathematics accurately, it would be more correct to say that Lampert chooses to represent the discipline using a *particular perspective* on the nature of mathematical knowledge and activity. (I discuss this in more depth in Ball [1988a.]) Lampert's representation of mathematics—as a discourse community concerned with common questions and engaged collaboratively in pursuing and assessing mathematical ideas and in which more than traditional formal proof counts—may not match the traditional picture of formal mathematics. It may be seen as "toooooo democratic," as one mathematican recently observed. But the view of mathematics on which Lampert bases her pedagogy is rooted in a particular perspective on mathematical knowledge and activity, one most similar to the view advanced by Imre Lakatos in *Proofs and Refutations* (1976).

Lakatos represents mathematics as a domain in which new knowledge is developed via conjectures which are strengthened or discarded using counterexemplary cases. The process of conjecture and refutation, as Lakatos describes it, fuses discovery and justification; that is, ideas are refined via efforts to disprove them. In the more conventional view, mathematicans discover (or propose) ideas and then set out to prove them. In this view, proofs can be inspected and judged on the basis of logic alone, rather than on their persuasiveness to other members of the mathematical community. Lakatos contrasts this classic deductivist representation of mathematics with his view, arguing that the former presents a misleading picture of mathematics as an "ever-increasing set of eternal, immutable truths."

> Deductivist style hides the struggle, hides the adventure. The whole story vanishes, the successive tentative formulations of the theorem in the course of the proof-procedure are doomed to oblivion while the end result is exalted into sacred infallibility (Lakatos, 1976, p. 142).

Kline (1970) makes a similar argument that the view of mathematical activity as smooth, abstract, and deductive misrepresents the evolution of mathematical knowledge and, as such, serves poorly as the foundation for pedagogy. Both Lakatos and Kline find themselves simultaneously criticizing this view of mathematics and its traditional pedagogy; the emphasis in their perspective on mathematics, they argue, has positive implications for improving the way in which mathematics is taught and learned. A mathematically based pedagogy such as Lampert's (as opposed to a pedagogy founded on a particular theory of learning, for example) needs to be based either on one defensible view of the discipline or in a plurality of views. In her case, her teaching is rooted in a perspective that, although not the traditional one, has intellectual merit as a foundation for pedagogy. As children develop their ideas—whether about multiplication, fractions, or quadrilaterals—they hit sticking points and encounter instances that challenge their assumptions. Sometimes they develop ideas that are later refuted (e.g., the common second-grade belief that "you cannot take a larger number away from a smaller one") and they find they must revise or discard ideas. What

Lampert's mathematically-based pedagogy aims to do is to engage children in authentic mathematical activity as a context for their mathematical development. That it is not rooted in a traditional view of mathematics is less the point than that its epistemological foundation is mathematical.

Smith and Neale also asked how a mathematical pedagogy such as Lampert's compares with the trends in mathematics education in the 1950s and 1960s, when the emphasis also appeared to be discipline-based: discovery teaching and the "new mathematics." Discovery teaching did emphasize process, but a kind of process in which standards of justification and verification of mathematical validity were much less explicitly (if at all) the focus. The "new math" focused on "the" unifying concepts and structures of the discipline, and, by default, represented a formalist view of mathematics (see Bruner, 1970; Fey, 1978; Shulman, 1970), one quite different from the view discussed briefly above.

Smith and Neale also ask how the goals of a mathematical-based pedagogy such as Lampert's relate to those of the new math: Is the goal to make children into "little mathematicians?" Making children into "little mathematicians" has often had a pejorative ring to it—and yet, without compunction, we expect school to help children develop as authors and literary critics. If being a mathematician includes having the power to use and appraise quantitative information, having the ability to use mathematical methods effectively to frame and solve problems, being able and inclined to inspect and evaluate mathematical claims, and to appreciate the value and beauty of mathematics, then I think that helping children develop into "little mathematicians" seems a reasonable aim. These goals are no more than what is spelled out in all the current reform documents—the National Council of Teachers of Mathematics *Curriculum and Evaluation Standards* (1989), for example, or the National Research Council's *Everybody Counts* (1989).

Whether students are in fact learning these things is an empirical question, one that I suggest (near the end of my chapter) warrants intensive and innovative pursuit. Most research on student learning has separated knowledge of mathematics from knowledge about mathematics, and most often has entirely ignored the latter. We need new conceptual frames and approaches for studying what all students learn under these broader visions and goals. We will need ways of assessing how students inspect and respond to a mathematical argument about perimeter and area, how they construe the process of establishing the truth of an assertion about probability, how they approach persuading others of a generalization they form about fractions. And, if mathematics is seen as a contextualized practice, then the contexts of assessment need reexamination for their possibilities and limits.

Is there "one best way" to teach mathematics? And how do elementary teachers' approaches to teaching mathematics correspond with their approaches to teaching social studies, science, or language arts?

Several readers became intrigued with the case of Lampert's teaching: Does her case suggest that there is one best way to teach mathematics? First, it is critical to note that the justification for such a mathematically based pedagogy is logical; questions about its success are empirical and deserve intensive pursuit, as my earlier comments suggest.

However, examining what is at the core of her teaching suggests that it is not her "approach" that is key, but the underlying orientations toward knowledge. It is not that there is "one best way," but that, on logical grounds, what is crucial is a stance toward knowledge and knowing that makes the knower's activity central, that views knowledge as changing, and that places the currently accepted ideas of the domain as critical tools for engaging in the doing. This view of knowledge and knowing wraps conventional mathematical knowledge into mathematical activity and transfers the determination of truth from the personal (the teacher or the individual student) to the discipline (standards for mathematical reasoning). However, what is important here is that this epistemological core may provide a foundation for a set of pedagogical variations whose surface structures differ. That is, whether students work in small groups or use concrete objects to reason about mathematics may be less the point than whether their engagement in mathematical tasks affords them opportunities to learn to think mathematically.

This suggests that views of knowledge and of knowing may be significant in underpinning elementary teachers' approaches to teaching different subjects. Do teachers hold similar views about the nature of scientific knowlege as they do about historical knowledge? How do their assumptions about science and history affect how they teach those subjects, and how do either of those compare with their perspectives on mathematics? In addition to exploring such questions about teaching, researchers should examine related teacher education questions: Can teachers' approaches to teaching mathematics, for example, be affected by helping them learn to consider the nature of knowledge and knowing in another subject area? Can explicit attention to teachers' assumptions about knowledge help to make teacher education more effective? And how do teacher educators' assumptions about the nature of knowledge in teaching affect the curriculum and outcomes of teacher education?

The chapters in this volume help to raise issues about the role of subject-matter knowledge in research and practice in both teaching and teacher education. The cross-talk conversations are but a starting point for our collective and related work and our discourse on making subject-matter knowledge one important part of the pedagogical equation.

TEACHERS' KNOWLEDGE OF STUDENTS' MATHEMATICS PROBLEM-SOLVING KNOWLEDGE

Penelope L. Peterson, Elizabeth Fennema,

and Thomas P. Carpenter

Over the past decade, researchers studying children's learning and cognition have shown that problem solving, comprehension, and meaningful learning by a student are based on knowledge and that people "continually try to understand and think about the new in terms of what they already know" (Glaser, 1984, p. 100). Moreover, researchers have shown that specific content knowledge plays a central role in the learner's thinking and learning. Researchers have focused on the knowledge that students bring to instruction, how this knowledge influences what and how students learn, and how it changes as a result of instruction (Resnick, 1985).

Only recently have researchers begun to recognize that just as knowledge is central to a student's learning in the classroom, knowledge is also central to teachers' thinking and teaching in the classroom, as well as to a teacher's

Advances in Research on Teaching, Volume 2, pages 49-86.
Copyright © 1991 by JAI Press Inc.
All rights of reproduction in any form reserved.
ISBN: 1-55938-034-9

professional growth and development (see, for example, Leinhardt & Smith, 1985; Shulman, 1986, 1987). Moreover researchers studying teachers have only begun to analyze and conceptualize the knowledge base that *teachers* bring to their instruction, how this knowledge influences what and how teachers teach, and how it changes as a result of both their instruction of their students and their own education.

In this chapter we report on a series of studies with a group of first-grade teachers in which we conducted such analyses. Our studies with this group of teachers represent our beginning attempt to think about and to understand a specific kind of teacher's knowledge, to trace the influence of this knowledge on mathematics instruction over the course of a school year, and to examine the effects both on teaching and on students' mathematics learning. The focus of our investigations was on teachers' knowledge of their students' knowledge about addition and subtraction problem solving. Lampert (1984) described this knowledge as the teacher's understanding of the student's intuitive knowledge, ways of thinking, and understanding. Shulman (1986) has referred to this type of knowledge as *pedagogical content knowledge*, and Peterson (1988a) referred to it as *content-specific cognitional knowledge*. We selected this specific knowledge as the focus of study both because addition and subtraction is the primary focus of mathematics instruction in the primary grades and also because researchers have provided detailed knowledge of young children's thinking and problem solving in addition and subtraction. (For reviews of this research, see Carpenter & Moser, 1983; Riley, Greeno, & Heller; 1983, Riley & Greeno, 1988.)

Researchers have described the general levels that children pass through in acquiring the concepts and procedures in addition and subtraction, the processes that children use to solve different problems at each level, and the nature of children's knowledge that underlies these processes. Further, researchers have distinguished between different classes of verbal problems in addition and subtraction based on semantic characteristics of the problems shown in Table 1. These distinctions between problem types have been shown to be reflected in children's solutions at different levels as children acquire knowledge and expertise in addition and subtraction problem solving. In sum, researchers have provided detailed research-based knowledge of children's knowledge in addition and subtraction problem solving that constitutes a base against which teachers' knowledge might be compared and examined. Thus, we decided to begin our research by attempting to determine to what extent first-grade teachers have this kind of knowledge of their students' mathematical knowledge (Carpenter, Fennema, Peterson, & Carey, 1988).

Table 1. Classification of Word Problems

Problem Type	Result Unknown	Change Unknown	Start Unknown
Join	1. Connie had 5 marbles. Jim gave her 8 more marbles. How many does Connie have altogether?	2. Connie has 5 marbles. How many more marbles does she need to win to have 13 marbles altogether?	3. Connie had some marbles. Jim gave her 5 more marbles. Now she has 13 marbles. How many marbles did Connie have to start with?
Separate	4. Connie had 13 marbles. She gave 5 marbles to Jim. How many marbles does she have left?	5. Connie had 13 marbles. She gave some to Jim. Now she has 5 marbles. How many did Connie give to Jim?	6. Connie had some marbles. She gave 5 to Jim. Now she has 8 marbles. How many marbles did Connie have to start with?
Combine	7. Connie has 5 red marbles and 8 blue marbles. How many marbles does she have?		8. Connie has 13 marbles. Five are red and the rest are blue. How many blue marbles does Connie have?
Compare	9. Connie has 13 marbles. Jim has 5 marbles. How many more marbles does Connie have than Jim?	10. Jim has 5 marbles. Connie has 8 more than Jim. How many marbles does Connie have?	11. Connie has 13 marbles. She has 5 more marbles than Jim. How many marbles does Jim have?

TEACHERS' KNOWLEDGE OF CHILDREN'S PROBLEM-SOLVING KNOWLEDGE: INITIAL STUDIES

The teachers whom we studied taught first-grade mathematics in 27 different schools, including 3 Catholic schools and 24 public schools, located either in Madison, Wisconsin, or in one of four small rural communities near Madison. All the teachers had agreed to participate in this initial study as well as to participate in the follow-up experimental study that would involve a month-long inservice program. (See Carpenter, Fennema, Peterson & Carey, 1988, for a complete description of the study.)

Structured Measures of Teachers' Knowledge

Our measures of teachers' knowledge included specific, structured questions that focused on teachers' knowledge of distinctions between addition and subtraction problem types; teachers' knowledge of the strategies that children use to solve different addition and subtraction problems; teachers' knowledge of their own students' knowledge as measured by their ability to predict individual performance on different problems; and general, open-ended questions about what children knew and how the knowledge was used.

For one test, we asked the teachers to write six word problems that best represent six given number sentences: $(5 + 7 = ?, 6 + ? = 11, ? + 4 = 12, 13 - 4 = ?, 15 - ? = 9,$ and $? - 3 = 9)$. Although the numbers in the problems are different, these number sentences correspond to the six join-and-separate problem types presented in Table 1. We scored the test by assigning two points to appropriate word problems that corresponded to the given number sentence and one point to word problems that did not match directly the given number sentence but had the same answer. We gave no points for word problems written by teachers that had different answers, were incomplete, or made no sense.

On this test the teachers scored an average score of 11 out of 12 possible. Twenty-three of the 40 teachers had perfect scores. All but one teacher wrote valid result-unknown word problems when given the corresponding number sentences. However, 9 errors were made by teachers on the two change-unknown problems, and 17 errors occurred on the two start-unknown problems. Thus, while some teachers were more knowledgeable about result-unknown problems than about change-unknown or start-unknown problems, most teachers could write appropriate word problems that corresponded to different addition or subtraction number sentences.

For the Relative Problem Difficulty test teachers were given 16 pairs of word problems and asked to identify which of the two problems would be more difficult for first-grade children. The teachers were told to assume that the problems were read aloud and that the children had counters available to help them solve the problems. In 4 of the pairs, the problems were of the same type with relatively minor changes in context and wording. The other 12 items consisted of pairs of problems for which there is a well-established hierarchy of problem difficulty (Carpenter & Moser, 1983; Riley et al., 1983). Six pairs included a separate-result-unknown problem (Table 1, Problem 4), and 6 included a join-change-unknown problem (Table 1, Problem 2). These problems were each paired with a more difficult combine, compare, or separate-start-unknown problem. Within each pair the same number combinations were used, and problem length and other factors that might affect problem difficulty were held constant. After the teachers had responded to all 16 pairs, they were asked to explain their responses for 5 of the pairs selected in advance to represent different relationships between problems.

On the Relative Problem Difficulty test, teachers were very accurate in identifying the same types of problems as equal in difficulty (an average of 3.67 out of 4 comparisons correct). They were also extremely accurate (an average of 5.40 out of 6 comparisons correct) in identifying a separate-result-unknown problem as easier for a first-grade child to solve than a more difficult compare, combine, or separate-start-unknown problem, respectively. However, teachers were much less knowledgeable about how difficult a join-change-unknown problem was for a first-grade child to solve. Indeed, teachers consistently *overestimated* the difficulty of join-change-unknown problems, and the teachers' average score was only 2.13 out of the 6 possible comparisons. Teachers consistently judged join-change-unknown problems to be more difficult for first-grade children to solve than compare, combine, or separate-start-unknown problems.

Many first-grade children would solve a join-change-unknown problem by directly modeling the action in the problem as illustrated by the following protocol.

Interviewer: Joshua had 8 pennies. His mom gave him some more. Now he has 13 pennies. How many pennies did Joshua's mom give him?

The child counts out 8 pennies. Then he counts out more pennies until he has 13. Then he counts how many pennies he added, "1, 2, 3, 4, 5."

Many of the first-grade teachers in this study did not seem to recognize the general principle that problems that can be directly modeled are easier for children than problems that cannot. When the teachers were asked to explain why they judged a given problem to be more difficult than another, they rarely focused on the semantics of the problems that are reflected in children's solutions. Teachers tended to focus on syntactic features of the word problems such as key words like "how many more". Even when teachers focused on the semantics of the problem, they seldom related the semantic structure of the problem to children's solution strategies when they judged and discussed the relative difficulty of types of word problems. For example, in explaining the relative difficulty of start-unknown problems, 18 of the 40 teachers referred specifically to the fact that the unknown appeared at the beginning of the problem, but only 8 teachers related the difficulty of the problem to the difficulty of directly representing or modeling the problem. Thus, the teachers seemed to judge the difficulty of word problems based on how they think about and solve the problem not how the children might think about and solve the problem.

Teachers' General Knowledge of Children's Strategies

To determine whether or not teachers did know how children think about and solve word problems, we showed them videotapes of first-grade children solving different problems and asked the teachers to describe how these children would solve related problems. Almost all teachers could characterize the direct modeling strategies and could associate the strategies with appropriate problems. The teachers were somewhat less successful on counting strategies. In particular, the teachers were generally successful in identifying the counting strategies they observed on the tape but had difficulty in identifying how counting strategies could be used with different problems. When derived facts were used by the children on the videotape, most teachers recognized that the child was using some sort of derived fact strategy, but many of them did not identify doubles as the basis for the derived facts. This test of general knowledge of childrens' strategies showed that teachers recognized the distinction among the different strategies they observed, but they had more difficulty extrapolating to related strategies that they had not observed.

Knowledge of Their Own Students' Problem-Solving Knowledge and Strategies

To test teachers' knowledge of their own students, we asked each teacher to demonstrate how each of six students, selected randomly from the teacher's class, would solve six different addition and subtraction word problems. The target students had solved the same problems in individual interviews that took place 1 or 2 days before the teacher interview. The analysis was based on the match between a teacher's predictions about each student's performance for a given item and the student's actual performance on the item.

Two scores were generated from the interviews. A Knowledge of Students' Correct Answers score was based on the teacher's success in predicting whether a student solved a given problem correctly irrespective of whether the teacher correctly predicted the strategy the student used. A Knowledge of Students' Strategies score was based on the teacher's success in predicting accurately the strategy the student used to solve the problem.

Results of this test showed that teachers were moderately knowledgeable about their students' ability to solve particular problems. Seventy-five percent of the time, they accurately predicted whether their students could solve a variety of addition and subtraction word problems. About half of the time, they accurately predicted the strategy that students would use.

When we examined teachers' knowledge of the particular kinds of strategies they thought their children would use to solve addition/subtraction word problems, we found some interesting differences. Teachers consistently overestimated their students' use of direct modeling and recall of number facts as strategies to solve problems. They seemed to think that children would use either physical modeling with concrete objects to directly model the solution to the word problem or memorization of number facts to solve the problems. They consistently underestimated the extent to which their children would use counting strategies to solve word problems.

Open-Ended Questions about Teachers' Knowledge

As part of a larger interview (Peterson, Fennema, Carpenter, & Loef, 1989), teachers were asked several questions that focused directly on relevant aspects of teachers' knowledge. These included the following:

1. What do most children in your classroom know about addition when they start the school year?
2. Where do children get this knowledge?
3. Children have different abilities and knowledge about addition. How do you find out about these differences?
4. Do you use this knowledge in planning instruction?
5. Are there certain kinds of word problems in addition that you believe all children should learn to solve? If so, what are they?
6. Why did you decide that these kinds of word problems are important for all children to learn to solve?

Most revealing were teachers' responses to the question, "What do most children in your classroom know about addition when they start the school year?" Eight of the 40 teachers stated that children knew "not much" or "very little." Illustrative of these teachers' responses was the following response from teacher 21: "Many of them [the children] think they know how to add, but as far as the concept itself and being able to apply it, they don't." An additional seven teachers answered by responding that "it varied from child to child," and one teacher remarked that "it varied from year to year." The most frequent response (made by 19 of the teachers) was that at the beginning of the year most children know the "concept of addition." The following teachers' responses were typical:

Teacher 53: The majority do have the idea of putting together.
Teacher 11: They already know what it's all about. They don't know how you do it; most of them don't know how you do it on a piece of paper."
Teacher 66: [They know that if you] have a number and add one more, it's going to get a little bigger."
Teacher 63: Most children know that if you get more, you are going to end up with a bigger number.
Teacher 62: Most of them know how to put together small numbers.

For these teachers the question of what their children know about addition at the beginning of the year seems to have been interpreted by them to mean, "What do your children know about the meaning of addition?" or "What addition facts do your children know?" When teachers were more specific in describing the knowledge of their children, they tended to focus on children's knowledge of number facts. Ten teachers commented that some of their children "knew some of their basic number facts." This emphasis is in keeping with the existing picture of school mathematics in our culture in which the teachers and students perceive knowing mathematics to mean knowing the symbolic algorithms to solve computational problems (e.g., Stigler & Baranes, 1988). Five teachers indicated that some of their children knew the double number facts such as $1 + 1 = 2; 2 + 2 = 4;$ or $5 + 5 = 10$. These five teachers seemed to show some greater awareness of which specific number facts are learned first by children.

Teachers did not talk spontaneously about children's knowledge of addition and subtraction in terms of the kinds of word problems or story problems that their children could solve at the beginning of the year. The closest that a teacher got to such a description was teacher 55 who indicated that her children had "pretty good concepts as far as words like "how many."

Later in the interview, teachers were asked, "Are there certain kinds of word problems in addition that you believe all children should learn to solve, and if so, what are they?" The majority of the teachers mentioned only simple join and combine addition problems. As one teacher put it, "How many altogether? How many in all?. . . these are probably the easiest and most concrete and most basic word problems." Another teacher responded similarly but with a concrete example: "John has three cards, and Joe has four. How many cards do they have altogether? I teach them the most common addition story problem."

Thus, where teachers were asked explicit questions about distinctions among word problems and how children might solve different problems, they exhibited quite a bit of knowlege about problems and ways they might be solved. However, this knowledge was not well integrated into a coherent network that related distinctions among problems, children's strategies for solving them, and problem difficulty. Furthermore, the responses to the open-ended questions suggest that most teachers do not relate what they know about problems and children's natural strategies for solving them to instruction in arithmetic. They tend to think about addition and subtraction in terms of manipulations of symbols, and even though they knew about different problem types and they knew that many children could solve them, they described a limited range of problems appropriate for instruction in first grade. When they thought in general terms about what was appropriate for instruction, they did not seem to draw on their explicit knowledge about the range of problems children could solve.

TEACHERS' BELIEFS ABOUT CHILDREN'S MATHEMATICAL KNOWLEDGE

In a second but related study with the same teachers, we examined teachers' pedagogical content beliefs in addition and subtraction (see Peterson et al.,

1989). In particular, we were interested in teachers' beliefs about children's knowledge of addition and subtraction and the extent to which teachers believed that mathematics instruction should be organized to facilitate children's construction of knowledge.

A Framework for Analyzing Teachers' Pedagogical Content Beliefs

From our review of the scholarly research, we derived four separate but interrelated constructs that represent fundamental assumptions underlying much of the contemporary cognitive research on children's learning (see, for example, Case, 1983; Cobb, 1988; Resnick, 1981; Resnick & Ford, 1981).

1. Children construct their own mathematics knowledge. Cognitive science researchers have shown that children develop informal systems of mathematics outside of the classroom. Children do not simply absorb what they are taught; they structure and interpret the presented mathematics curriculum and instruction in light of their existing knowledge. (See, for example, Cobb, 1988; and Resnick & Ford, 1981.) The proposition might be represented as a continuum with the notion that "children actively construct their own knowledge" at one end and the notion that "children receive mathematical knowledge from the teacher or others" at the other end. While other theoretical conceptions of learning and the learner might support the latter proposition, cognitive theory and research generally would not.

2. Mathematics instruction should be organized to facilitate children's construction of knowledge. A second proposition that is related to the first one is the notion that mathematics instruction should be organized to facilitate children's construction of knowledge. A contrasting proposition might be that mathematics instruction should be organized to facilitate the teacher's clear presentation of knowledge. Attempts to draw instructional implications from recent cognitive research on children's learning of mathematics favor the former proposition. (See, for example, Cobb, 1988; Confrey, 1986.)

3. Children's development of mathematical ideas should provide the basis for sequencing topics for instruction. A third proposition that is related to the first two propositions is the notion that children's development of mathematical ideas should provide the basis for sequencing topics for instruction. (See, for example, Case, 1983; Case & Bereiter, 1982.) A contrasting proposition would be that the structure of mathematics should provide the basis for sequencing topics for instruction. Recent findings from cognitive research on children's mathematics learning provide evidence for the former proposition. For example, although young children develop reasonably sophisticated processes for analyzing and solving addition and subtraction word problems, they have difficulty relating this new knowledge to the formal mathematical procedures that they learn in school (see, for example, Romberg & Carpenter, 1986). If the structure of mathematics were to provide the basis for sequencing topics for instruction, it might follow that instruction would begin immediately with teaching the formal mathematical symbolism and formal mathematical procedures. However, the findings from cognitive research suggest that children progress through different developmental strategies and use direct modeling strategies and counting strategies before they can come to understand and use the more abstract number facts and written symbolism that accompany number facts.

The three propositions discussed thus far imply that a major goal of mathematics instruction is to facilitate students' understanding of mathematics and their construction of meaning and knowledge. The fourth proposition deals more specifically with the goals of mathematics instruction and the relationship between these goals.

4.   Mathematical skills should be taught in relation to understanding and problem solving.   The fourth proposition states that mathematics skills should be taught in relation to understanding and problem solving. A contrasting perspective would be that mathematical skills should be taught in isolation from or as separate from understanding and problem solving. Both perspectives assume that the learning of mathematics skills, understanding, and problem solving are all important goals of mathematics instruction. However, the two propositions make very different statements both about the relationship between these goals and about the most effective ways to achieve these goals.

The proposition that mathematical skills should be taught in relation to understanding and problem solving is based on underlying theoretical notions of memory and understanding. Most cognitive theorists assume that performance of mathematical skills with understanding requires that links exist in an individual's cognitive structures among mathematics problem information, specific mathematics procedures, and general concepts in mathematics (Davis, 1983; Greeno, 1978; Riley, Greeno, & Heller, 1983). For example, Greeno (1978) has proposed that performance with understanding occurs when an individual connects problem knowledge with conceptual and procedural knowledge. In addition, in order for new information to be learned and understood, this information somehow must be integrated into the set of meaningfully connected propositions, including problem knowledge and procedural knowledge.

Using these four constructs as subscales, we constructed a questionnaire consisting of 48 items, 12 for each subscale (see Peterson et al., 1989, for a complete description). Teachers responded to each item on a 5-point Likert scale by indicating, strongly agree, agree, undecided, disagree, or strongly disagree. Scores were summed across items. A high score indicated a cognitively based perspective.

Teachers With Cognitively Based Beliefs

In examining teachers' scores on the belief questionnaire, we found that our 40 teachers varied significantly in the degree to which their beliefs about children's knowledge, mathematics instruction, the teacher, and the learner, reflected a cognitively based perspective. (see Peterson et al., 1989.) To gain further insight into how teachers' cognitively based beliefs were reflected in their knowledge about instruction and their views of their own instruction, the learner, and the goals of mathematics instruction, we selected a group of seven teachers who were most cognitively based (CB) in their perspectives and compared them to a group of seven teachers who were least cognitively based (LCB). When we did this, we found some interesting differences between CB teachers and LCB teachers in their views of children's mathematics learning and the development of children's knowledge in addition and subtraction.

Teaching Mathematics for Understanding

One teacher, Ms. Wallaby (teacher 2), consistently scored the highest of all teachers on three of the constructs above (1, 2, and 4). Wallaby also was the second most knowledgeable of all the teachers about her individual children's abilities to solve different kinds of word problems as measured by the knowledge of students' knowledge interview described earlier. Her students also were the highest in their actual problem-solving knowledge and number fact knowledge. In an interview, Ms. Wallaby responded to a question about the concepts in addition and subtraction that she tried to teach and why she thought these concepts were important. Ms. Wallaby provided the following insightful view of teaching mathematics for understanding:

> I think the more we (teachers) work for understanding, the better it is. I think nothing turns children off more than facing 36 problems and not knowing why they are doing them and not really understanding them. It is just simply a procedure. There is no relation to real life, and what they are doing. So, I guess, I try and go for understanding . . . .I find that many of the children that come to me (maybe it's probably a bigger problem here at this school because of the economic class of the children). But I find many of the children have been exposed to addition and subtraction, but just as, "Let's do $1 + 1$, $2 + 2$, $3 + 3$ and so and $3 + 2$." If the little girl or the little guy can tell them (the parents) the answer in two seconds, [then the parent thinks] "Wow, my child is good at math!" The same with subtraction. And it has gotten to be quite a big ego thing if, "Oh, my child is doing multiplication by 7 years of age!" Some parents have even resorted to giving them [the children] math problems at home just so they [the children] can memorize. But they [the children] don't relate it to anything. I can't stop what's being done at home, but I do have control over what is being done in the classroom, so I do spend most of the time in math really with the understanding part, working for understanding.

Interestingly, although Wallaby's view of teaching mathematics for understanding may have derived from years of experience and her "accumulated wisdom of practice," (Shulman, 1987), her view of understanding corresponds remarkably well to the views of contemporary mathematics educators and cognitive researchers who agree that children can and do learn mathematics symbols and procedures for computing and manipulating those symbols without having an understanding of the quantities or mathematical ideas represented by the symbols and without acquiring the knowledge of how and when to use the procedures when needed. (See, for example, reviews by Romberg & Carpenter, 1986; Putnam, Lampert, & Peterson, 1990.) For example, cognitive researchers have focused on the need for the learner to make connections between *procedural* and *conceptual* knowledge in mathematics (Hiebert & Lefevre, 1986; Greeno, Riley, & Gillman, 1984; Nesher, 1986). In her description of the need to teach addition and subtraction for understanding, Wallaby seems to have tacit knowledge that not only is it possible, but also probable, that children in her class are learning addition and subtraction number facts by rote, without any real understanding. She realizes that these children are then unable to apply the knowledge as a result. Thus, Wallaby sees the need to link conceptual and procedural knowledge—a need that has also been pointed out by cognitive researchers.

Cognitively Based Teachers' Thoughts About Instruction

In general, we noted the following themes in CB teachers' thoughts about instruction in addition and subtraction when we compared them with LCB teachers (Peterson et al., 1989):

- early emphasis and use of word problems in teaching addition and subtraction;
- a belief that children are able to solve word problems if presented orally;
- least emphasis on memorization of number facts and most emphasis on teaching problem-solving and teaching for understanding;
- a conception of the learner as cognitively active, not passively receiving information;
- a conception of teaching as facilitating learning as opposed to a conception of teaching as "telling";
- assessment of children's knowledge by observing informally and by listening to children in problem solving situations rather than by relying on tests or using formal written assessments.

Because we have discussed these findings elsewhere, we will not elaborate upon them here. In reading the interview protocols we were struck both by the influences of teachers' knowledge on teachers' thinking about instruction, learning, and assessment as well as by the pervasive influence of teachers' beliefs about students' knowledge; by the way in which teachers' thinking was influenced both by their beliefs and by their knowledge; and by the interconnections that seemed to exist between knowledge and beliefs in teachers' minds. The quantitative data also showed some relationships between teachers' beliefs and knowledge. For example, teachers' general knowledge of children's strategies was significantly related to teachers' beliefs. CB teachers had significantly greater knowledge of children's strategies than LCB teachers, scoring more than one standard deviation higher.

THE INTERCONNECTEDNESS OF TEACHERS' KNOWLEDGE AND BELIEFS

One important conclusion that we drew from our initial study was that teachers' pedagogical content beliefs and knowledge in addition and subtraction, particularly knowledge of children's cognitions and learning, exist as a delicate web of interconnections. The interconnectedness of teachers' knowledge and beliefs raises questions about researchers' distinctions between knowledge and beliefs.

Researchers should consider seriously where teachers' knowledge ends and beliefs take over. In our study, we defined belief constructs as propositions based on research-based knowledge gleaned from cognitive research on children's mathematical learning. The extent to which teachers agreed with these constructs we defined as beliefs. However, the extent to which these cognitive research-based propositions can be defined as truth determines the extent to which teachers' beliefs in this initial study might be considered knowledge (Peterson, Fennema, Carpenter, & Loef, 1987). Cobb, Yackel, and Wood (1988, p. 106) suggest the following interconnections between knowledge and beliefs:

> Knowledge has traditionally been defined as true belief. This, of course, merely leads to the question of what we mean by truth. From the anthropological perspective, knowledge can be defined as institutionalized belief. . . . In this regard, research into students' arithmetical word problem-solving provides a clear example of the process of institutionalization. The various systematically distinct types of word problems are classified as pedagogical knowledge because they have been negotiated and institutionalized by the mathematics education research community. It is doubtful that these problem types could be considered knowledge without debate even five years ago. Conversely, certain tenets of constructivism are pedagogical beliefs because they have not been institutionalized. In short, the distinction between knowledge and belief is relative to the practices of a community.

Cobb et al.'s (1988) remarks underscore the need for more and different kinds of evidence both about teachers' cognitive/constructivist beliefs and about teachers' knowledge that will enlighten the dialogue between researchers on teaching who espouse a scientific view, asking "Where are the data?" (Brophy, 1986); researchers in mathematics education and cognitive researchers who view learning as the active construction of knowledge (Resnick, 1987; Romberg & Carpenter, 1986); and more radical constructivists in mathematics education who reject empiricism and argue that the external world can never be known and that reality and meaning depend, ultimately, on the individual (Cobb, 1986; Confrey, 1986; Steffe, 1988). In our studies of teachers' knowledge of children's knowledge we wanted to provide evidence that would be helpful as well as useful to researchers within each of the above discourse communities as well as to provide information and descriptions that might promote dialogue across researchers and across different communities of scholars. To this end, we collected and have reported here both quantitative data from structured measures of teachers' knowledge as well as more descriptive data in teachers' own words from our interviews with them. We also collected achievement data on children's problem-solving and number fact knowledge in the 40 teachers' classes, and we examined the relationship between teachers' knowledge, teachers' beliefs, and children's achievement in addition and subtraction.

Teachers' Knowledge, Teachers' Beliefs, and Problem-Solving Achievement

We wondered whether teachers who were more knowledgeable about their children's problem-solving knowledge were more effective in facilitating children's problem-solving achievement in addition and subtraction. We were interested particularly in whether teachers' knowledge of their children's mathematics problem-solving abilities would be related similarly to children's achievement on number facts and problem-solving. Although Leinhardt and her colleagues have provided detailed information on expert teachers' knowledge in elementary mathematics, she has defined her teachers as expert practitioners because they "had students who were highly proficient in performing mathematical computations and procedures" and were "moderately proficient in coping with a variety of extension and higher-order mathematics tasks" (Leinhardt, 1988, p. 47). We wanted to find out about the knowledge of teachers who are highly proficient in facilitating children's mathematics problem-solving and understanding as well as highly proficient in facilitating children's knowledge of number facts and computational skills. We also wanted to investigate how teachers' beliefs are related to children's problem-solving achievement.

We expected that teachers' general knowledge of children's problem-solving strategies, teachers' specific knowledge of their own students' problem-solving strategies, and teachers' general knowledge of word problem difficulty might be significantly positively related to their children's problem-solving achievement. We assessed students' achievement on a number facts test and a problem-solving test. The number facts test consisted of 20 addition and subtraction basic number facts. The problem-solving test consisted of 17 word problems, each of which included numbers less than 20. Nine problems were addition and subtraction problems that represented the range of problems shown in Table 1. Four problems involved several operations or included extraneous numbers, and four problems involved grouping and partitioning.

The only measure of teachers' knowledge that we found to be significantly related to students' performance was teachers' ability to predict their students' success in solving different word problems. Teachers' knowledge of their own students' problem-solving was significantly positively correlated with their students' performance on the problem-solving test ($r = .31$) and with students' performance on the number fact test ($r = .32$). These findings are similar to those from the Beginning Teacher Evaluation Study (Fisher, Berliner, Filby, Marliave, Cahen, and Dishaw, 1980) that showed that teachers' ability to predict their students' mathematics achievement scores was significantly positively related to their students' mathematics achievement. But our findings are also different because we defined problem-solving knowledge more precisely according to type of addition and subtraction word problems that could or could not be solved by individual children.

When we examined the relationship between teachers' beliefs and students' performance, we found results similar to those above. We found that teachers' scores on the belief questionnaire were significantly positively related to children's number fact knowledge ($r = .48$) as well as to children's problem-solving achievement in addition and subtraction ($r = .32$). A similar pattern emerged when we compared children's problem-solving achievement in the classes of CB teachers with children's problem-solving achievement in the classes of LCB teachers. Children in CB teachers' classes scored significantly higher on problem-solving achievement than did children in LCB teachers' classes. However, CB and LCB classes did not differ significantly in their number fact knowledge. These findings were intriguing because they raised the possibility that somehow cognitively based teachers were effective at facilitating their children's problem-solving achievement in addition to or not at the expense of facilitating children's knowledge of number facts and computational procedures. This finding is important in light of the fact that some researchers have argued that we need to find teachers who "enrich the students' concepts, concrete experience, and extended problem-solving capabilities while not abandoning the computational aspects of arithmetic education that society seems to value" (Leinhardt, 1988, p. 65).

Because the data in our initial study were correlational and were collected at one point in time, we were unable to determine the relationship between teachers' beliefs, teachers' knowledge, and their children's problem-solving achievement or to trace the development of the processes over time. Thus, cognitively based teachers might have had children who were higher in problem solving achievement and, as a result, came to believe that all children and/ or that their children, in particular, have a lot of problem-solving knowledge. Alternatively, cognitively based teachers may have used word problems more frequently than less cognitively based teachers, and as a result their children may have learned to solve addition and subtraction word problems better than children in LCB teachers' classes. Rather than having the expectation that skill in computation should precede solving word problems, cognitively based teachers believed that experience with problems helped develop children's ability to compute and to understand addition and subtraction. Thus, the number fact knowledge of children in cognitive-based teachers' classes may have emerged from the children's experience with solving word problems.

The relationships among teachers' beliefs, teachers' knowledge of their children's knowledge and their children's problem-solving achievement are undoubtedly complex, involving recursive relationships between teachers' beliefs, teachers' knowledge and student's problem solving and computation achievement. Such relationships might depend on the kinds of interactions that occur between teachers and students in the classroom about mathematics, the way the teacher thinks about, represents, and presents the mathematics content of addition and subtraction, the kinds of thinking that the teacher has children do about addition and subtraction in her classroom, and the kinds of addition and subtraction activities in which the children tend to be cognitively engaged (Cobb et al., 1988). We attempted to explore further these multiple relationships and influences between teachers' beliefs, teachers' knowledge, and children's problem solving in an experimental study (Carpenter, Fennema, Peterson, Chiang, and Loef, 1989).

AN EXPERIMENTAL STUDY OF TEACHERS' KNOWLEDGE AND BELIEFS

From our initial sample of 40 teachers we selected randomly 20 teachers to participate in an experimental (Cognitively Guided Instruction) workshop and 20 teachers to serve as a control group. Control teachers participated in a half-day workshop on nonroutine problem-solving. We provided the experimental teachers with knowledge derived from recent cognitive research in children's problem solving in addition and subtraction. We gave teachers access to this knowledge through a four-week workshop on Cognitively Guided Instruction (CGI).

We then studied the effects of provision of this knowledge on: (a) teachers' knowledge of children's knowledge; (b) teachers' beliefs about children's knowledge; (c) teachers' actual teaching of addition and subtraction over the school year; and (d) their children's problem-solving and computation achievement. Although we have discussed some of this research-based knowledge in earlier parts of the paper, we summarize here the knowledge base from which we derived the principles that we used in working with teachers.

The Knowledge Base in Recent Research on Children's Mathematics Learning

Recent cognitive research in mathematics on addition and subtraction has shown that contrary to popular notions, young children are relatively successful at analyzing and solving simple addition and subtraction word problems. Before receiving formal instruction in addition and subtraction, most young children invent informal modeling and counting strategies for successfully solving addition and subtraction problems (Carpenter, Hiebert, & Moser, 1981; Carpenter & Moser, 1983; Riley & Greeno, 1988; Riley, Greeno, & Heller, 1983). The modeling and counting strategies that children exhibit when they enter school continue to develop throughout the first few years of school, becoming increasingly efficient and flexible (Carpenter & Moser, 1984). This informal knowledge could provide a basis for the student to develop both mathematics concepts and skills and also a meaningful understanding of mathematics. However, the traditional mathematics curriculum does not build systematically on children's informal knowledge or support its development. The curriculum has been based on the assumption that computational skills must be learned before children are taught to solve even simple word problems. The use of direct instruction by teachers in the early grades to teach mathematical algorithms and procedures may result in children rotely learning the mathematics algorithms but not acquiring a true mathematical understanding. Children may not see the connection between their informal knowledge and the formal mathematics they are taught in school. This may result in the formal mathematics being reduced to meaningless symbol manipulation.

Giving Teachers Access to Knowledge about Children's Mathematics Learning

The first objective of the workshop was to help teachers understand children's thinking by becoming familiar with research findings on children's solution of addition and subtraction problems. They learned to classify addition and subtraction word problems and to identify the processes that children usually use to solve these problems. This knowledge provided the basis for everything that followed. Principles for applying this knowledge to classroom instruction were: (a) teachers should assess not only whether a child can solve a particular word problem but also how the child solves the problem, and they should analyze children's thinking by asking appropriate questions and listening to children's responses; (b) teachers should use the knowledge that they derive from assessment and diagnosis of the children to plan appropriate instruction; (c) teachers should organize instruction to involve children so that they actively construct their own knowledge with understanding; and (d) teachers should insure that elementary mathematics instruction stresses relationships between mathematics concepts, skills, and problem solving, with a greater emphasis on problem solving than exists in most instructional programs.

We provided the above knowledge through a 4-week inservice course on Cognitively Guided Instruction (CGI). Fennema and Carpenter provided teachers with information, curriculum, and materials that built on the CGI principles described above. CGI teachers were *not* trained in specific techniques for altering their classrooms and curricula. Thus, as researchers and teacher educators, we employed a CGI approach to educating the teachers and working with them as thoughtful professionals who construct their own knowledge and understanding. Our view of teachers as problem solvers (Carpenter, 1987) and individuals actively constructing their own knowledge was consistent with our view of children as actively constructing their own knowledge.

Although instructional practices were not prescribed, the broad principles of instruction presented above were discussed. Specific questions were identified that teachers needed to address in planning their instruction, but teachers were not told how they should answer them. These questions included the following: (a) how should instruction build initially upon the informal and counting strategies that children use to solve simple word problems when they enter first grade?; (b) should specific strategies like counting on be taught explicitly?; and (c) how should symbols be linked to the informal knowledge of addition and subtraction that children exhibit in their modeling and counting solutions of word problems?

Format of the CGI Workshop

The workshop was taught by Professors Carpenter and Fennema with the assistance of three graduate students, two mathematics supervisors from the Madison Metropolitan School District, and one curriculum supervisor from the Watertown, Wisconsin, Unified School District. The workshop involved five hours of participation each day, four days a week for four weeks. Although teachers were told that they could complete all work during the 20 workshop hours each week, some teachers did take work home with them.

Teachers were provided with readings written for the workshop that presented the problem type taxonomy, synthesized the results of research on children's solutions of addition and subtraction word problems, and discussed how these findings might be applied in the classroom. A number of videotapes of children solving problems was used to illustrate children's solution strategies, and teachers had the opportunity to interview one or two young children. A variety of instructional materials was also available for the teachers to review including textbooks, manipulatives, and enrichment materials.

A typical day included an hour presentation/discussion led by Carpenter or Fennema. During the first six days, these discussions focused on the findings from research on addition and subtraction. Discussions during the next four days explored ways that these findings might be implemented in the classroom. In the remaining sessions, the topics discussed included general problem solving, time on task, and equity issues. Each day the teachers could also participate in a small group session led by one of the graduate students. The purpose of these sessions was to examine different curricula or enrichment materials and to discuss how these materials might be used to facilitate children's problem solving following principles of CGI. During the rest of the time, teachers were free to read; to plan the following year's instruction; to study videotapes of children solving problems; to talk with other participants and the staff; and to examine textbooks, manipulatives, or enrichment materials.

Teachers monitored their own progress and selected and worked on activities that facilitated their own learning. Although they were given no specific written assignments, teachers were asked to plan a unit to teach during the following year, as well as a year-long plan for instruction based on principles of CGI. Each week teachers met with one of the staff to discuss their progress for the week and to clarify their ideas about their plans. Teachers worked either alone or with others as they desired.

Because we hypothesized that the teacher's knowledge about each of her student's thinking about addition and subtraction would develop during the instructional year, we conceptualized the treatment as including the following instructional year. However, after the workshop, our formal contact with the CGI teachers was limited. We met one time with them in October when teachers discussed with us what they had done to that point with CGI. One of the staff also served as a resource person and responded to any questions that CGI teachers posed to her throughout the year.

Changes in Teachers' Knowledge of and Beliefs about Children's Knowledge

At the end of the school year in May, we interviewed teachers about their knowledge of and beliefs about children's knowledge using the same kinds of questions and measures that we had used in the initial study (see Carpenter et al., 1989). In contrast to teachers in the control group, CGI teachers were more knowledgeable about the strategies that individual children in their classes actually used to solve word problems and number facts. In addition, CGI teachers were significantly more cognitively based in their beliefs about children's knowledge as measured by their scores on the same belief questionnaire used in the initial study. Interestingly, non-CGI teachers were much more likely to overestimate their students' knowledge of number facts at a recall level by a factor of three to one. CGI teachers' predictions for whether or not a particular student knew a particular number fact at the recall level did not differ by more than 10 to 20 percent from the actual level of use.

Differences in Students' Actual Problem-Solving and Number Fact Knowledge

Although non-CGI teachers predicted higher levels of recall of number facts for their students, students in CGI teachers' classes actually recalled significantly more number facts than students in non-CGI teachers' classes. Thus, students in CGI teachers' classes knew number facts significantly better than students in non-CGI teachers' classes even though systematic observational data showed that non-CGI teachers taught number facts about 1 1/2 times as much as did CGI teachers (Carpenter et al., 1989). On a test of complex addition and subtraction problems, students in CGI teachers' classes outperformed students in non-CGI teachers' classes. Moreover, on a problem-solving interview, students in CGI classes used strategies that led to a correct answer significantly more often than did students in control classes.

Making Thinking Explicit, Assessing Thinking, and Building Upon Knowledge

We found that, in contrast to non-CGI teachers, CGI teachers' knowledge, beliefs, and instructional practices were more consistent with the principle that it is important to assess children's knowledge and thinking (Carpenter et al., 1989). Observation data showed that CGI teachers posed problems and listened to the processes that students used to solve word problems significantly more often than did non-CGI teachers. CGI teachers also encouraged students to use a variety of strategies to solve a particular problem more frequently than did non-CGI teachers. Moreover, classroom observations of the engagement of individual students showed differences in the lesson context within which students worked on and solved problems. Control students worked on word problems significantly more often as individual seatwork while CGI students solved word problems more often as part of a group lesson directed by the teacher.

CGI teachers often conducted problem-solving lessons with the whole class or with a small group of students in which the teacher presented a word problem to the students, gave students time to figure out a solution, and then called on individual students to say and show how they thought about and solved the problem (Fennema, Carpenter & Peterson, 1989).

There are two ways that CGI teachers' lessons may have enhanced the development of children's problem solving. First, the teachers did not instruct children in a particular strategy. They were given the opportunity to use their informal strategies to solve problems. They were given the opportunity to construct solutions that were meaningful to them. This may have helped children to consolidate their informal knowledge and connect it to a variety of problem situations. By encouraging children to talk about how they solved problems, the strategies may have become more overt and objects of reflection for the children. This perspective focuses on how CGI instruction may build upon individual children's construction of knowledge. From another perspective, discussion of alternative strategies may have made the thinking processes of individual students explicit and learnable for other students in the class. This perspective suggests that the CGI approach shares certain elements with the reciprocal teaching method of Palincsar and Brown (1989). In CGI classes, however, the teacher played a much less central role in modeling explicit strategies herself than the role described in other models of apprenticeship instruction for real world tasks (Brown, Collins, & Duguid, 1989; Gott, 1988; Greeno, 1988).

The CGI approach has other parallels with recent cognitive analyses of learning. Brown et al. (1989), Gott (1988), Greeno (1988), and others propose that "Learning is *situated* in the functional context of problem solving" and thus "knowledge is acquired in its applied form, that is, tied to its intended use" (Gott, 1988, p. 163). Thus, students in CGI teachers' classes may have learned to solve word problems better than students in non-CGI teachers' classes because their learning of addition and subtraction was situated within the context of story problems that had meaning for them.

Both posing problems and listening to process provided the opportunity for teachers to assess students' knowledge. By allowing a student to use any strategy that the student chose, the teacher was able to assess how each student was thinking about the problem rather than requiring the student to imitate one strategy that the teacher taught. This approach also was more consistent with the belief expressed by CGI teachers that instruction should facilitate children's construction of knowledge rather than present information and procedures to children. This approach is represented in the following words of two teachers, Donaldson and Jennings, who each talked about a typical lesson on addition and subtraction in their classes:

> Donaldson: I'll make up a story problem and say, "OK, who can put that on the board how they would solve it?" If they [the children] couldn't do it in their head, or if they could do it in their head, [I say] "Show us how you do it on the board. Can you explain another way of doing it? Can anyone else explain another way to do it?" Then ask somebody else to make up a problem. Tell a story, and I'm doing more of telling stories. Get a story involved in it . . . . I discovered that many children are doing things many different ways, and I think it's exciting for them to share if they're doing it in a little bit different way they can see and explain to us why they did it that way. I really

believe that children can learn more from each other than they do from the teacher. The more I get children involved and complimenting. You know, saying, "Boy that's a great way. I haven't thought of that. Tell us about it." So, the rest of the children will feel comfortable thinking, "Hey I can get up there, and they will do something, [and they won't think] if it's not right or the way the book shows it.

Jennings: And then the other part is giving different combinations of numbers and saying, you know, like say if we are working with the number ten, "Ok, what's one way of saying ten? What's another of saying ten? What's another way?" And that takes time, yes, another way? Or even when they are doing the word problems." Ok, Erica figured it out this way. Who knows another way of figuring out this problem? Who knows another way?" So, we take time just to listen to each other—how each person is figuring it out, and someone says, "Oh, yes, I'm doing that."

Because when they are figuring out the word problems, they don't figure them all out the same way, and even when they are thinking about adding numbers, some of them don't figure it out the same way. Like say, three plus four. Some kids might go "three plus three plus one more". Many of them know that there are options to figuring out the same problem. I'll even ask. I'll say, "Who's right?" "Oh, nobody." "That's right, nobody is right. Nobody is wrong. This is how you have figured it out at this particular time."

In their descriptions, Jennings and Donaldson showed a knowledge that individual students have different strategies for solving problems and knowledge of how to solve problems. These two examples also illustrate that the teachers focused on *how* and *why* the students got the answer to the problem, not on the correctness or incorrectness of the answer. Donaldson's words also suggest the notion of children serving as models of expertise in thinking and problem solving by making their thinking processes explicit.

In a subsequent correlational analysis of the data on the 20 CGI teachers we found that teachers who engaged more in this kind of questioning were more knowledgeable about their students' problem-solving knowledge, and more knowledgeable teachers had students who did better on problem solving than did less knowledgeable teachers (Peterson, Carpenter, & Fennema, 1989). Teachers who explained the problem-solving process to students and who engaged in nonverbal checking and monitoring had students who did less well on problem-solving achievement. Thus, more knowledgeable teachers seemed to get their knowledge of students' knowledge and thinking by posing problems to students, questioning students about their problem-solving, and listening to students solving the problem. In contrast, less knowledgeable teachers relied on observing students' nonverbal responses or solutions, and explained the problem-solving process to students, thus doing the thinking for students. Profiles of the knowledge and behavior of an expert teacher, Miller, and a less expert teacher, Hardy provided additional support for these two conclusions.

We selected Miller as an expert CGI teacher because her class had the highest adjusted achievement scores on the word problem subtest of the Iowa Test of Basic Skills (ITBS) as well as the highest mean score on simple word problems, complex word problems, and advanced word problems. We selected Hardy, as a less expert CGI teacher because her class had the lowest score of the 20 classes on the word problem subtest of the ITBS, the lowest score on the complex problems, and the second to the lowest score on advanced problems. Interestingly, Hardy's class performed above the mean on the test of simple word problems that consisted of word problems involving simple joining and separating situations with the result unknown.

Although we selected Miller and Hardy because they were the more and less effective, respectively, in facilitating their students' complex problem solving, we also examined their effectiveness in facilitating students' computational skills. Interestingly, in addition to excelling on the ITBS problem-solving test, Miller's class was second highest in achievement on the ITBS computational subtest, performing 1.4 standard deviation above the mean of all teachers' classes. In contrast, Hardy's class performed only slightly above the mean on the ITBS computation subtest. Thus, although Hardy's students had the lowest scores for complex problem solving, she was not ineffective in teaching computational skills. We hypothesize that an important difference between the achievement of the two teachers' classes may be that students in Miller's class attained high levels of both procedural and conceptual knowledge of addition and subtraction, as shown by their high scores on the ITBS computation and problem-solving tests. Moreover, Miller's students were able to use and apply this knowledge to new problems (e.g., solving problems on the Advanced Problems Subscale). In contrast, although students in Hardy's class had some procedural knowledge as indicated by their average score on the ITBS computation subtest, they may have lacked the conceptual understanding of addition and subtraction which would have facilitated their solving more complex addition and subtraction word problems and new kinds of word problems that required new procedures, such as grouping, partitioning, or identifying irrelevant information.

These two teachers' responses to the same interview question illustrate how these teachers act and think very differently in the same problem solving situation with students.

Interviewer: Would you describe a specific example in which you are teaching children to solve addition and subtraction word problems?

Hardy: Ok, well they would all be at their seats. I found that better than sitting on the floor, because they get "antsy" on the floor—at their seats with their counters, and I would read a problem: "If there were five children in the lunch room and four more came, how many were there in all?" And I would make them put them in groups in front of them, so that I could walk around the room and make sure that everybody had the answer and everybody would, I would give them think time to make sure that everybody, at least seventy-five percent of the class had the problem solved and in front of them and then call on someone. They give the answer and then I would see, ask how many had it right. Then if somebody didn't have it right, or I couldn't do it, then I would stop and say, "Ok, this is how we do it."

In contrast, the most expert teacher, Ms. Miller, described a very different scenario in response to the same question by the interviewer.

Miller: Ok, I would have them in groups so that the ones [—students—would be together that] I would hope would come up with the answer at about the same time and then I would ask, "How do you know that?" And then I might ask, "Has anybody figured out a different way?"

The above descriptions by the teachers are consistent with actual observations of these teachers in the classroom. In her teaching, Hardy tended to focus on the correct answer rather than on the process. She seemed to judge students' knowledge and understanding by monitoring and checking to see if they had the correct answer. Her monitoring was very directive and focused on a correct procedure. She would often say, "Good" if the student appeared to have the right answer. She made directive comments such as the following when students did not have the correct answers: "Put 'take away' here, then a line, then your answer." The other kind of directive help that Hardy sometimes gave was to have students focus on key words in the problem. For example, for one problem she said to a student: "Look at the problem, 4 more *came*. What sign do you need?" Similarly, for a join result unknown problem, she said, "Its says how many in all. So what sign do you think you should use? 'In all'—You tell me if it is adding or subtracting."

Other examples also show how she directed the students' problem solving. For example, for a given separate start unknown problem, she had the student read the problem twice. She then had the student give the correct number sentence which was: $? - 4 = 8$. Hardy then said, "So how many did she have to start with?" "Make two piles of the numbers that you know and find out how many she had to start with. Then copy the sentence from the board." To another student working on the same problem she said, "What numbers do you know? Make a pile of 4, and a pile of 8, and find the answer."

For Hardy, students' knowledge was represented by the correct answer or correct procedure. Thus, checking for students' understanding seemed to mean checking to see if the student had written the correct answer or made the correct number of piles. Rather than attempting to elicit students' own thinking by asking "Why?" or "How?", she often asked yes/no or fact questions to make the student go step-by-step through her predetermined procedure. Alternatively, she showed the student how to do the problem or explained the procedure. Thus, Hardy never really found out what the student actually knew about the process for solving the problem or how the student would represent the problem for himself or herself.

Hardy's conception of the role of the learner and the teacher was consistent with her representation of students' understanding as passive reception of knowledge. As she put it, the role of learners is to "stay on task and try their best to do their work accurately . . . and that they understand the concepts presented. And if they don't, to ask for extra help, and then I would work individually one-to-one to help them understand." Consistent with this notion of the learner as passive recipient of knowledge, Hardy viewed the role of the teacher as "to teach the strategies, the concepts."

Miller's concept of the teacher was very different than Hardy's concept. She said that the teacher's role in introducing addition and subtraction was to give students problems, provide students with lots of opportunities to solve problems, pick up where students are, and to keep the pace going that's right for the youngsters. She saw the learner's role as "trying." The descriptions provided by Miller and Hardy of their students' knowledge at the end of the year also provide some insight into their conceptions of children's knowledge.

Knowledge of Children's Knowledge at Year's End

In an interview in May, teachers were asked to describe the knowledge that their children had now—at the end of the school year—about addition and subtraction. The two teachers replied as follows:

Miller: They know you can use it for more than just finding out how many there are in joining sets or how many are left. They can see how you use it to compare and how to find unknown quantities. Um, I guess it's [the knowledge is] more usable. We use it during lunch count. We use it during attendance. We use it. We have so many sheets to do, and [we ask] "How many of you have done the work?" They use it during the course of the day. Not just during math time.

Hardy: Most of them have a good grasp and understanding of it. There are few that still struggle just because I have taken the counting blocks away from everybody. And they—the lower ability children—have difficulty without them [the blocks].

In her description of children's knowledge at the end of the year, Hardy focused on students' lack of knowledge while Miller described how much her students knew about addition and subtraction and how well they were able to access and use their knowledge in actual problem solving situations. Here she seemed to be emphasizing the interrelationship of mathematical skills, problem solving, and understanding. In her response, Miller used the typology of word problems in her descriptions of what her children knew and thus, her description of children's knowledge was both more explicit and more complex than Hardy's. In contrast, Hardy gave a rather vague description of her children's knowledge as a "good grasp and understanding." These differences in explicitness between the two teachers are consistent with findings of Leinhardt (1988), who has shown that expert traditional teachers tend to have more precise and differentiated subject matter knowledge. Miller's focus on the usability of knowledge sounds very much like recent writings of cognitive researchers who view teaching as facilitating the use of knowledge (e.g., Brown, Collins, & Duguid, 1989; Resnick, 1987).

These portraits of Miller and Hardy place in stark relief the fact that even though both teachers had access to the same principled knowledge or representations of the taxonomy of problems and the developmental sequence of students' strategies in the CGI workshop, at the end of the school year, these two teachers differed not only in how knowledgeable they were about their students' knowledge and strategies, but also in their representations of students' knowledge, the way they thought about students' understanding, and the way they thought about instruction in relationship to students' knowledge. Despite her participation in the CGI workshop in which students' learning was portrayed as the active construction of knowledge, Hardy's conception of students' knowledge and understanding still seemed to reflect a behavioral view of knowledge so that to judge students' understanding, she focused on written answers which were observable and on what the student did. She did not make an effort to get inside students' heads by having students verbalize their thinking processes. Because she did not have students verbalize their strategies or think aloud, neither she nor students in the class had access to students' knowledge, thinking, and alternative ways of representing problems. Thus, Hardy did not have accurate knowledge of her students' thinking and ability to solve different types of word problems, and students in her class did not know how other children—both more and less expert children—were solving the problems. In contrast to Hardy's students, Miller's students may have excelled on the ITBS word problem subtest because they had access to these multiple strategies for solving a wide variety of word problems as modeled and made explicit by the thinking aloud of their peers in response to the teacher's posing of problems and asking questions such as, "How did you get that answer?" and "Why do you think that?"

IMPLICATIONS

In light of the numerous calls for reform of the curriculum for school mathematics (Mathematical Sciences Education Board, 1989; National Commission on Excellence in Education, 1983; National Science Board Commission, 1983), new visions of elementary school mathematics are being put forth. One such vision is that of the National Council of Teachers of Mathematics (1989) as proposed in their *Curriculum and Evaluation Standards for School Mathematics*. As an overall curriculum goal for kindergarten through fourth grade curriculum, the *Standards* emphasize the need for a developmentally appropriate curriculum that "capitalizes on children's intuitive insights and language in selecting and teaching mathematical ideas and skills. . . . It incorporates real-world contexts, children's experiences, and children's language in developing ideas. It looks beyond what children appear to know to determine how they think about ideas" (National Council of Teachers of Mathematics, 1989, p. 16). A second overall goal emphasizes "the development of mathematical understandings and relationships" and that "skills can be acquired in ways that make sense to children and in ways that result in more effective learning" (p. 17). These and other statements in the *Standards* suggest that to teach this new elementary curriculum in mathematics, elementary teachers will need to have extensive knowledge and understanding of children's mathematical knowledge and understanding and of the development of that mathematical understanding. Further, teachers' knowledge and understanding of children's knowledge will need to encompass the qualitative aspects of children's mathematical understanding, not simply children's knowledge of mathematical skills.

Within the context of the curriculum domain of the present study and the knowledge and understanding that we gained about teachers' knowledge, we consider a series of questions that occurred to us as we attempted to envision a scenario of elementary teachers implementing the new elementary curriculum suggested by the *Standards*. These questions are: What might elementary teachers need to know about children's knowledge? How might teachers get this knowledge? And finally, how do teachers use this knowledge?

What Might Elementary Teachers Need to Know about Children's Knowledge?

What might elementary teachers need to know about children's mathematics knowledge and learning in order to be able to teach this new curriculum? Our research suggests that the following knowledge may play a critical role in implementing the primary school curriculum of the *Standards*:

1.   knowledge that children have informal knowledge and strategies for solving mathematics problems and that children can solve some kinds of word problems when they enter first grade;

2. knowledge of the ways in which children's knowledge and thinking about math problems develop, including explicit knowledge of the strategies that children typically use to solve a given kind of math problem and the ways that children typically represent mathematics to themselves; and
3. knowledge of their own children's knowledge and strategies for solving different types of problems.

To understand what is really meant by the new mathematics curriculum, teachers must understand the first idea in the list because it provides an underlying rationale for much of the curriculum as outlined. Thus, teachers will need to know and believe that children have informal knowledge and strategies for solving mathematics problems, that children bring this knowledge with them to any new mathematics problem-solving situation, and that children come to understand new mathematics in terms of what they already know. Teachers also will need to understand that children's knowledge and strategies are often different from theirs and from other adults who may, for example, represent a math problem differently than a child or who may use shortcuts or algorithms developed through repeated practice.

Children's developing mathematical knowledge and understanding are consistent with the ways that they try to represent and understand mathematical ideas. With knowledge of the general ways that children come to know and think about mathematics problems and ideas, the teacher has a representation (Wilson, Shulman, & Richert, 1987) or cognitive map of the territory of children's mathematics knowledge and thinking (cf., Lampert, 1988). In our study the principled knowledge or ways of representing children's knowledge that teachers developed as a result of the CGI workshop and as a result of testing and trying out ideas in their classrooms during the school year gave the teachers such a map. The teachers then used this knowledge in several ways: (a) to understand children's responses and strategies that children verbalized to solve problems; (b) to guide their own thinking and decision making as they planned and interacted with children; and (c) to facilitate children's problem solving.

The knowledge that teachers developed of their own children's knowledge and strategies for solving word problems gave them an even more specific map or representation of the thinking and knowledge of individual students in their class. It is not clear what level of detail and explicitness of knowledge a teacher will need of the knowledge and thinking of individual children in her class. Research currently being conducted by us as well as others should provide further information on this point (see, for example, Cobb, et. al., 1988; Lampert, 1989, Putnam, 1987; Carpenter and Fennema, in press). However, teachers will need to have enough knowledge of how individual children are thinking and representing mathematics problems and ideas, both to understand each child's mathematical understanding or misunderstanding and to facilitate the development of children's mathematical understanding. In our study, the more knowledgeable and expert teachers were those who were more accurate in their knowledge of the problem-solving knowledge of individual students in their class. CGI teachers were significantly more knowledgeable than non-CGI teachers about the exact strategies that individual children in their class would use to solve specific kinds of word problems. Within the CGI group more expert teachers were more knowledgeable about the kinds of word problems that an individual child could solve and the kinds of word problems that an individual child could not solve.

How Might Teachers Get this Knowledge?

A second question that follows from the first is, if the above knowledge is important, then how might teachers get this knowledge? From our research we gained some insights that may be useful in thinking about this question. During the CGI workshop, teachers viewed videotapes of actual individual children solving word problems in addition and subtraction. Then each teacher interviewed a child, gave the child different types of word problems, and then asked the child how he or she solved the problem. Thus, beginning in the workshop the teachers gathered evidence and tested for themselves the assertion that children entering first grade do have knowledge and strategies for solving word problems. When teachers began teaching addition and subtraction to their own classes, they further tested out these ideas with their own children. They found out that the children that they had seen on the videotape in the workshop were not exceptional and that their children had knowledge and strategies for solving word problems too, just as did the videotaped children. When teachers came to see that children can solve different problems by counting on or modeling, this knowledge served as a hook into expanding teachers' understanding of children's informal and formal mathematical knowledge and thinking. It also served as a hook into expanding teachers' conceptions and thinking about their own mathematical understanding and problem solving (Peterson, 1988b).

In viewing the videotapes, teachers saw examples of children's knowledge and understanding. They gained additional evidence of this when they interviewed children themselves. However, teachers' beliefs about children's knowledge changed most fundamentally as a result of asking kids to solve word problems aloud during class and then listening to the strategies that children used to solve those problems.

Principled Knowledge or Representations of Children's Problem-Solving Knowledge

The taxonomy of word problem types presented to the teachers in the CGI workshop gave teachers a conceptual framework for thinking about the mathematics domain of addition and subtraction problem solving in a broader way. The information on the development of children's strategies gave teachers a cognitive map (e.g., Lampert, 1988), for thinking about their children's thinking or a way of representing children's problem-solving knowledge to themselves. Teachers were then able to access and use these representations to help them in thinking about their children's problem-solving and about the development of their children's knowledge in addition and subtraction over the course of the year. As one teacher, Taylor, put it when she was asked at the end of the year to describe the major changes in her children's knowledge about addition and subtraction over the course of the year and the major stages that children went through:

> I think that different children went through different stages at different times and in different orders, to some degree, and they are all at different stages right now. I think that despite the idea that certain problems seem more conceptually difficult, certain children can visualize, understand, or have had an experience with compare problems, for instance, and they just don't understand the change-unknown type problem. But they can understand a comparison type problem. So, I think that there is no definite set way that you can describe the levels. Basically, because the majority of children fit this pattern, they go through the stages that we talked about. The idea that those result-unknown type problems were the simplest for them, the change-unknowns came next. The start-unknowns were more difficult. The compares were more difficult. But for some children, they really "bounced around" and so I would say for half of them to three-quarters of them, they fit the general "growing" [developmental] mold that we had thought was true—that the CGI had presented to us. But then there is a quarter to a little bit more of the kids who bounced around in their own unique mold.

Taylor developed her representation of children's knowledge from the two major knowledge taxonomies presented in the CGI workshop—the taxonomy of word problem types and the developmental framework of strategies that children use to solve addition and subtraction word problems.

A similarly insightful answer to the question of "How?" was provided by Jennings who, like Miller, was among the most knowledgeable teachers, as measured by her ability to predict her students' knowledge and strategies in word-problem solving. She was also the second highest teacher in her agreement with cognitively based beliefs on the questionnaire. Our observations of and interviews with Jennings suggest that she had adopted a personal and active view of the learning process in which she redefined her work as a teacher "to include on-the-spot clinical research into the way a learner thinks about something" (Lampert, 1984, p. 1). In an interview, Jennings gave an almost up-to-the-minute description of the knowledge of a particular child in her class:

That's interesting. I was working with Cheryl the other day, and she had twelve cubes in her hand. The problem was Riva had twelve carrots, and she made three carrot cakes. She needed to divide them equally into each cake. And you know, Cheryl had these cubes, and go, go, go—she snapped it off real quick. I said, "How did you get that so quickly?" And she goes, "Oh, you know the numbers, you know—First there were three. If you put three cakes, three carrots in each cake, and then I had nine. But if I add one more, that would be four." So they [the children] are thinking. It's just so *sophisticated*. It just seems to come together for them.

Although we did not collect systematic information that would allow us to diagram or map teachers' representations of problem types and children's strategies at the end of the year, from our observations and interviews we suspect that teachers differed substantially in the representations of children's knowledge that they had developed. For example, teachers probably differed in how and whether they integrated their knowledge of word problem types with their knowledge of children's strategies and how they made connections between children's strategies and the problem types. An important question for further investigation is how such representations of children's knowledge in specific context domains are developed by teachers and how these representations of children's knowledge, in general, are related to teachers' representations of the knowledge of individual children, in particular.

Knowledge of Individual Children's Knowledge and Strategies

For the CGI teachers, the representations of word problem types and children's strategies for solving word problems gave them a framework for thinking about and assessing the problem solving knowledge and strategies of individual children in their classes. They obtained knowledge of individual students' problem-solving by posing problems and asking questions that resulted in individual students verbalizing aloud the processes that they used to solve problems. Thus, teachers listened and observed how children solved addition and subtraction problems. Both in the initial study and in the experimental study, teachers who were less knowledgeable of their students' problem-solving knowledge tended to rely on students' written answers. Interestingly, the results of our initial study suggest that there exist teachers, who like the most expert CGI teachers in our study, are expert at facilitating their students' problem solving. They are also more knowledgeable than other teachers of individual students' problem solving knowledge, and they obtain this knowledge by posing problems, asking "How?" and "Why?" questions of students as students solve the problems. They consistently listen to and observe students' problem-solving strategies and ways of representing the problem. Although these teachers have developed their expertise through their own learning and teaching experience, such expert teachers have knowledge that is no less valid and indeed, is strikingly similar to the knowledge and beliefs developed by teachers in this study using the research-based knowledge provided to them in the CGI workshop.

How Do Teachers Use this Knowledge?

A final question is: If teachers have the above kinds of knowledge, how do they use this knowledge? Although our teachers varied considerably in how they used their knowledge of children's knowledge, just as they varied in their actual knowledge of children's knowledge, their use and nonuse of children's knowledge suggest alternative explanations that deserve further thought and research.

The major way in which teachers used their knowledge that children have informal knowledge was to organize their teaching of addition and subtraction around word problems. At the end of the year, CGI teachers reported that they had done more problem solving in addition and subtraction than they had the previous year. Further, they posed word problems to children at the beginning of the year and throughout the year. They assumed that their children would be able to use a variety of informal strategies to solve these problems even before children had memorized addition and subtraction number facts. Classroom observations documented this emphasis on word problems and showed that CGI teachers spent significantly more time on word problems than did non-CGI teachers. However, students' problem-solving achievement was not a direct linear function of time spent by the teacher and students on problem solving compared to number facts because, in contrast to control students, CGI students achieved significantly more on tests of word problem solving, but also had significantly greater knowledge of addition and subtraction number facts at a recall level. Alternative explanations for these findings are possible. These include the possibility that CGI students learned number facts better because their knowledge of addition and subtraction was within the context of real-world solving of problems. Alternatively or additionally, CGI students may have learned addition and subtraction better than their counterparts because their teachers built instruction on students' informal knowledge. Children naturally think about and use addition and subtraction to solve real-world problems expressed in words or as stories. The in-class instruction built upon children's informal knowledge and naturally developing strategies for solving these problems.

Teachers who experienced the CGI workshop differed in the extent to which they knew and believed that children have their own knowledge. Some teachers like Jennings, Donaldson, Taylor, Miller, and Pruitt clearly knew and believed that children have their own knowledge. For example, Pruitt referred specifically to children's knowledge as "their own," and Jennings described the sophistication of her children's own knowledge. In describing children's knowledge, Taylor commented on how children "bounced around in their own unique mold." Donaldson noted how listening and observing children's problem-solving strategies made her "realize how many children can do these things [problem solving] in different ways" and that "We were trying to mold them into one way of doing that. It's exciting to see what they [children] can do without us molding."

These five teachers were also the highest among the CGI teachers in their cognitively based beliefs about children's knowledge. However, even these teachers, who were the most constructivist in their beliefs about children's knowledge, varied in the extent to which they were constructivist in classroom practice. CGI teachers were significantly higher than non-CGI teachers in listening to processes that their students used to solve problems (Carpenter et al., in press). The average for these five teachers was 2.4 standard deviations above the mean of non-CGI teachers and .34 standard deviations above the mean for CGI teachers in "listening to processes" that their students were using to solve problems. These data indicated that teachers were taking seriously the processes that children use to solve problems and attending to the knowledge that children have. Moreover, Jennings, the teacher who was highest in amount of time spent listening to process (5.54 standard deviations above the mean for non-CGI teachers), was also the most constructivist teacher in her classroom practice. She clearly listened to determine the knowledge of mathematics that her children had, and then she used that information to decide what to teach, given where the child was in his or her thinking. The following excerpt captures Jennings' approach:

> Some first graders don't need to be introduced to addition. I think teachers do kids injustice when they drill on things that kids already know, because kids get bored. I found my kids a lot more exciting. I was more excited, and I tried to give things to them and really listen to them, . . . Before the holidays one kid said, "five times five is twenty-five take away twenty is five," and my mouth dropped open. And I said, "Oh, they are ready for multiplication." And not everybody was, but some kids were, and so then it was my challenge to find out which kids were ready for it.

Teachers used the taxonomy of word problem types from the CGI workshop to expand their use of types of word problems from the two types that they typically taught to include the 11 categories of word problems in the taxonomy. This also led the teachers to think about additional types of problems that they might pose in math class. Thus, CGI teachers tended to pose many more types of problems to their children than are typically included in the first-grade curriculum.

Teachers also used their knowledge of the general developmental sequence of children's strategies for solving addition and subtraction problems. Observations of the teachers showed that in contrast to non-CGI teachers, CGI teachers more frequently expected their students to use different strategies to solve addition and subtraction problems. CGI teachers were aware that children in their classes were at different places in the development of their understanding of addition and subtraction problems. As a result, they expected and encouraged children to represent the problems in different ways and to use different strategies to solve addition and subtraction word problems.

Using their knowledge of word problem types, their knowledge of the strategies that children generally develop to solve these problems, and their knowledge of their children's problem-solving knowledge, teachers adapted their addition and subtraction instruction. A most significant way in which teachers changed was in their assessment procedures for children's mathematics learning. This change is summed up by Pruitt's response to the question, "Did your assessment procedures differ from what you used last year and if so, how?" Pruitt replied, "I guess rather drastically. . . . I knew kids could solve problems in different ways, but I really didn't realize how many different ways. Now I pretty much can diagnose if they [the children] understand the concept or not." Clearly, CGI teachers used their knowledge of their children's problem solving knowledge to inform their own thinking and teaching. Thus, although a highly diagnostic view of children's knowledge and teaching has not been typical of experienced or expert teachers (Leinhardt & Greeno, 1986; Putnam, 1987; Putnam & Leinhardt, 1986), such a view by the teacher is possible and may be necessary to the development of children's mathematical knowledge and understanding within the context of the elementary classroom.

In general, CGI teachers differed in the ways they adapted instruction to fit what they knew about students. For example, Jennings continuously asked individual children whether a given problem was hard or easy for them and then used that information to pose problems that she perceived would be slightly more difficult for individual children based on her knowledge of problem types and children's strategy development. Thus, she attempted to match the difficulty of the type of word problem she presented to the problem-solving knowledge and strategies of her own children. In contrast, Miller made extensive use of small groups that changed over the school year. She grouped children together who were using similar strategies to solve similar types of problems.

SUMMARY

In sum, our research represents a beginning attempt to understand the kinds of knowledge that teachers have, how teachers' knowledge is influenced by new knowledge, how teachers use knowledge of children's problem-solving knowledge in their own teaching, and how this knowledge might be related to students' actual knowledge and problem-solving performance. Our studies represent a beginning attempt to delineate a small part of the research base for reform of elementary school mathematics—the part that deals with teachers' knowledge of children's problem-solving knowledge. As such, our efforts contribute not only "to the growing base of scientific knowledge about mathematics teaching and learning" but also complement and inform "the efforts of mathematics educators to reform curricular, pedagogical, and assessment practices" (Silver, 1988, p. 343).

REFERENCES

Brophy, J.E. (1986). Teaching and learning mathematics: Where research should be going. *Journal for Research in Mathematics Education, 17*, 323-346.

Brown, J.S., Collins, A., & Duguid, A. (1989). Cognitive apprenticeship, situated cognition, and social interaction. *Educational Researcher, 18*(1), 32-42.

Carpenter, T. (1987, January). *Teaching as problem solving.* Paper presented at the Conference on Teaching and Evaluation of Problem Solving, San Diego, CA.

Carpenter, T.P., & Fennema, E. (in press). Cognitively-guided instruction: Building on the knowledge of students and teachers. *International Journal of Educational Research.*

Carpenter, T.P., Fennema, E., Peterson, P.L., & Carey, D. (1988). Teachers' pedagogical content knowledge of students' problem solving in mathematics. *Journal for Research in Mathematics Education, 19*, 385-401.

Carpenter, T.P., Fennema, E., Peterson, P.L., Chiang, C., & Loef, M. (1989). Using knowledge of children's mathematics thinking in classroom teaching: An experimental study. *American Educational Research Journal, 26*, 499-531.

Carpenter, T.P., Hiebert, J., & Moser, J.M. (1981). Problem structure and first-grade children's initial solution process for simple addition and subtraction problems. *Journal for Research in Mathematics Education, 12*, 27-39.

Carpenter, T.P., & Moser, J.M. (1983). The acquisition of addition and subtraction concepts. In R. Lesh & M. Landau (Eds.), *The acquisition of mathematical concepts and processes* (pp. 7-14). New York: Academic.

Carpenter, T.P., & Moser, J.M. (1984). The acquisition of addition and subtraction concepts in grades one through three. *Journal for Research in Mathematics Education, 15*, 179-202.

Case, R. (1983). *Intellectual development: A systematic reinterpretation.* New York: Academic.

Case, R., & Bereiter, C. (1982). *From behaviorism to cognitive behaviorism: Steps in the evolution of instructional design.* Paper presented at the Conference for Educational Psychologists, Caracus, Venezuela.

Cobb, P. (1986). Making mathematics: Children's learning and the constructivist tradition [Review of *Young children reinvent arithmetic* and *Learning from children*]. *Harvard Educational Review, 56*, 301-306.

Cobb, P. (1988). The tension between theories of learning and theories of instruction in mathematics education. *Educational Psychologist, 23*(2), 87-104.

Cobb, P., Yackel, E., & Wood, T. (1988). Curriculum and teacher development: Psychological and anthropological perspectives. In E. Fennema, T. Carpenter, & S.J. Lamon (Eds.), *Integrating research on teaching and learning mathematics* (pp. 92-131). Madison: University of Wisconsin, National Center for Research in Mathematical Sciences Education.

Confrey, J. (1986). A critique of teacher effectiveness research in mathematics education. *Journal of Research in Mathematics Education, 17*, 347-360.

Davis, R.B. (1983). Complex mathematical cognition. In H.P. Ginsburg (Ed.), *The development of mathematical thinking.* New York: Academic.

Fennema, E., Carpenter, T., & Peterson, P.L. (1989). Learning mathematics with understanding: Cognitively guided instruction. In J.E. Brophy (Ed.), *Advances in research on teaching: Vol. 1. Teaching for meaningful understanding and self-regulated learning.* (pp. 195-221). Greenwich, CT: JAI Press.

Fisher, C.W., Berliner, D.C., Filby, N.N., Marliave, R., Cahen, L.S., & Dishaw, M.M. (1980). Teaching behaviors, academic learning time, and student achievement: An overview. In C. Denham & A. Lieberman (Eds.), *Time to learn* (pp. 7-32). Washington, D.C.: United States Department of Education.

Glaser, R. (1984). Education and thinking: The role of knowledge. *American Psychologist, 39,* 93-104.

Gott, S.P. (1988). Apprenticeship Instruction for Real-World Tasks: The Coordination of Procedures, Mental Models, and Strategies. In E.Z. Rothkopf (Ed.), *Review of research in education* (pp. 97-170). Washington, DC: American Educational Research Association.

Greeno, J. (1978). Understanding and procedural knowledge in mathematics instruction. *Educational Psychologist, 12,* 262-283.

Greeno, J.G. (1988, November). *The situated activities of learning and knowing mathematics.* Invited address presented at the meeting of the North American Chapter of the International Group for the Psychology of Mathematics, DeKalb, IL.

Greeno, J. G., Riley, M. S., & Gelman, R. (1984). Conceptual competence and children's counting. *Cognitive Psychology, 16,* 94-134.

Hiebert, J., & Lefevre, P. (1986). Conceptual and procedural knowledge in mathematics: An introductory analysis. In J. Hiebert (Ed.), *Conceptual and procedural knowledge: The case of mathematics* (pp. 1-27). Hillsdale, NJ: Erlbaum.

Lampert, M. (1984). Teaching about thinking and thinking about teaching. *Curriculum Studies, 16*(1), 1-18.

Lampert, M. (1988). Connecting mathematics teaching and learning. In E. Fennema, T. Carpenter, and S. Lamon (Eds.), *Integrating research on teaching and learning of mathematics* (pp. 132-167). Madison: University of Wisconsin, National Center for Research in Mathematical Sciences Education.

Lampert, M. (1989). Choosing and using mathematical tools in classroom discourse. In J.E. Brophy (Ed.), *Advances in research on teaching: Vol. 1. Teaching for meaningful understanding and self-regulated learning* (pp. 223-264). Greenwich, CT: JAI Press.

Leinhardt, G. (1988). Expertise in instructional lessons: An example from fractions. In D.A. Grouws & T.J. Cooney (Eds.), *Perspectives on research on effective mathematics teaching* (pp. 47-66). Reston, VA: The National Council of Teachers of Mathematics.

Leinhardt, G., & Greeno, J.G. (1986). The cognitive skill of teaching. *Journal of Educational Psychology, 78,* 75-95.

Leinhardt, G., & Smith, D. (1985). Expertise in mathematics instruction: Subject matter knowledge. *Journal of Educational Psychology, 77,* 247-271.

Mathematical Sciences Education Board. (1989). *Everybody counts: A report to the nation on the future of mathematics education.* Washington, DC: National Academy Press.

National Commission on Excellence in Education. (1983). *A nation at risk: The imperative for educational reform.* Washington, DC: U.S. Government Printing Office.

National Council of Teachers of Mathematics. (1989). *Curriculum and evaluation standards for school mathematics.* Reston, VA: Author.

National Science Board Commission on Precollege Education in Mathematics, Science and Technology. (1983). *Educating Americans for the 21st century: A plan of action for improving the mathematics, science and technology education for all American elementary and secondary students so that their achievement is the best in the world by 1995.* Washington, DC: National Science Foundation.

Nesher, P. (1986). Learning mathematics: A cognitive perspective. *American Psychologist, 41*, 1114-1122.

Palincsar, A., & Brown, A. (1989). Classroom dialogue to promote self-regulated composition. In J.E. Brophy (Ed.), *Advances in research on teaching: Vol. 1. Teaching for meaningful understanding and self-regulated learning.* Greenwich, CT: JAI Press.

Peterson, P.L. (1988a). Teachers' and students' cognitional knowledge for classroom teaching and learning. *Educational Researcher, 17*(5), 5-14.

Peterson, P.L. (1988b, April). *New roles and classroom practice.* Paper presented at the annual meeting of the American Educational Research Association, New Orleans, LA.

Peterson, P.L., Carpenter, T.C., & Fennema, E. (1989). Teachers' knowledge of students' knowledge and cognitions in mathematics problem solving. *Journal of Educational Psychology, 81*, 558-569.

Peterson, P.L., Fennema, E., Carpenter, T., & Loef, M. (1987, April). *Teachers' pedagogical content beliefs in mathematics.* Paper presented at the annual meeting of the American Educational Research Association, Washington, DC.

Peterson, P.L., Fennema, E., Carpenter, T., & Loef, M. (1989). Teachers' pedagogical content beliefs in mathematics. *Cognition and Instruction, 6*, 1-40.

Putnam, R. T. (1987). Structuring and adjusting content for students: A study of live and simulated tutoring of addition. *American Educational Research Journal, 24*, 13-48.

Putnam, R.T., Lampert, M., & Peterson, P.L. (1990). Alternative perspectives on knowing mathematics. In C. Cazden (Ed.), *Review of research in education,* (Vol. 16, pp. 57-150). Washington, DC: American Educational Research Association.

Putnam, R. T., & Leinhardt, G. (1986, April). *Curriculum scripts and the adjustment of content in mathematics lessons.* Paper presented at the annual meeting of the American Educational Research Association, San Francisco, CA.

Resnick, L.B. (1981). Instructional psychology. *Annual Review of Psychology, 32*, 659-704.

Resnick, L.B. (1985). Cognition and instruction: Recent theories of human competence. In B.L. Hammonds (Ed.), *Master lecture series: Vol. 4. psychology and learning* (pp. 123-186). Washington, DC: American Psychological Association.

Resnick, L.B. (1987). Learning in school and out. *Educational Researcher, 16*(9), 13-20.

Resnick, L.B., & Ford,W.W. (1981). *The psychology of mathematics for instruction.* Hillsdale, NJ: Lawrence Erlbaum.

Riley, M.S., & Greeno, J.G. (1988). Developmental analysis of understanding language about quantities and of solving problems. *Cognition and Instruction, 5*, 49-101.

Riley, M. S., Greeno, J. G., & Heller, J. I. (1983). Development of children's problem-solving ability in arithmetic. In H. P. Ginsburg (Ed.), *The development of mathematical thinking* (pp. 153-196). New York: Academic.

Romberg, T.A., & Carpenter, T.C. (1986). Research on teaching and learning mathematics: Two disciplines of scientific inquiry. In M.C. Wittrock (Ed.), *Handbook of research on teaching* (3rd ed., pp. 850-873). New York: Macmillan.

Shulman, L.S. (1986). Those who understand: Knowledge growth in teaching. *Educational Researcher, 15*(2), 4-14.

Shulman, L. S. (1987). Knowledge and teaching: Foundations of the new reform. *Harvard Educational Review, 57*(1), 1-22.

Silver, E.A. (1988). NCTM curriculum and evaluation standards for school mathematics: Responses from the research community. *Journal for Research in Mathematics Education, 19*, 338-344.

Steffe, L. (1988, July). *Principles of mathematics curriculum design: A constructivist perspective.* Paper presented at the Sixth International Congress on Mathematics Education, Budapest.

Stigler, J.W., & Baranes, R. (1988). Culture and mathematics learning. In E.Z. Rothkopf (Ed.), *Review of research in education* (Vol. 15, pp. 253-306). Washington, DC: American Educational Research Association.

Wilson, S.M., Shulman, L.S., & Richert, A.E. (1987). "150 different ways" of knowing: Representations of knowledge in teaching. In J. Calderhead (Ed.), *Exploring teachers' thinking* (pp. 104-124). London, Cassell.

WHERE SUBJECT KNOWLEDGE MATTERS

Gaea Leinhardt, Ralph T. Putnam, Mary Kay Stein,
and Juliet Baxter

Teaching is a highly complex activity that draws on many kinds of knowledge. In this chapter we focus on teachers' subject-matter knowledge and how the nature and organization of a teacher's subject-matter knowledge influences his or her teaching. For illustration, we focus on the domain of mathematics.

We frame our consideration of subject-matter knowledge from a perspective of teaching as a complex cognitive skill occurring in a relatively ill-structured, dynamic environment (Leinhardt & Greeno, 1986). As expertise in other complex tasks, such as medical diagnosis (Johnson et al., 1981; Lesgold, Glaser, Feltovich, & Wang, 1981; Pople, 1982), chess (Chase & Simon, 1973; Wilkins, 1980), and writing (Hayes & Flower, 1980), expertise in teaching is dependent on flexible access to highly organized systems of knowledge (Glaser, 1984). We believe that there exist many knowledge systems that are fundamental to teaching, for example, knowledge of student thinking and learning, and knowledge of social dynamics and group structure. Two important areas are knowledge of *lesson structure* and knowledge of *subject matter*. The first consists of the knowledge necessary for conducting lessons, including general routines for interacting with students, for coordinating lesson segments, and

Advances in Research on Teaching, Volume 2, pages 87-113.
Copyright © 1991 by JAI Press Inc.
All rights of reproduction in any form reserved.
ISBN: 1-55938-034-9

for fitting lessons together within a day (across subject areas) and within a unit (across days). The second, subject-matter knowledge, supports lesson-structure knowledge by providing the subject-matter content to be taught. This subject-matter knowledge is accessed both during lesson formulation and during the course of instruction. The focus of this chapter is on the relationship between the subject-matter knowledge in elementary mathematics and aspects of lesson formulation and instruction.

By subject-matter knowledge we mean the knowledge that a teacher needs to have or uses in the course of teaching a particular school-level curriculum in mathematics. We do not mean the knowledge of advanced topics that a mathematician might have. The point here is that a teacher will not become a better teacher *simply* by taking increasingly more advanced math courses in topics such as Chaos (although this might go a long way toward increasing love of mathematics), but will become better if the depth of knowledge about a particular school topic such as integers, rational numbers, or functions is enriched. This deep knowledge includes knowledge about ways of representing and presenting content in order to foster student learning or construction of meaningful understanding. It also includes knowledge of what the students bring to the learning situation, knowledge that might be either facilitative or dysfunctional for the particular learning task at hand. This knowledge of students includes their strategies, prior conceptions (both "naive" and instructionally produced), misconceptions students are likely to have about a particular domain, and potential misapplications of prior knowledge.

Expert teachers use many complex cognitive skills, weaving together elegant lesson that are made up of many smaller lesson segments. These segments, in turn, depend on small socially scripted pieces of behavior called routines, which teachers teach, participate in, and use extensively. Expert teachers also have a rich repertoire of instructional scripts that are updated and revised throughout their personal history of teaching. Teachers are flexible, precise, and parsimonious planners. That is, they plan what they need to but not what they already know and do automatically. Experts plan better than novices in the sense of efficiency and in terms of the mental outline from which they operate and that they can report verbally to others. From that more global plan—usually of a unit of material—they select an agenda for a lesson. The key elements of the agenda are available as mental notes the teacher has before teaching. The agenda serves not only to set up and coordinate the lesson segments but also to lay out the strategy for actually explaining the mathematical topic under consideration. The ensuing explanations are developed from a system of goals and actions that the teacher has for ensuring that the students understand the particular piece of mathematics.

In examining how teachers use their subject-matter knowledge, we will focus on several key sites in the instructional processes of teachers, namely *agendas, curriculum scripts, explanations, and representations.* These terms will be defined briefly here and described in more detail in the sections that follow. The agenda is the teacher's dynamic plan for a lesson. It is a mental plan that contains the goals and actions for the lesson. The function of the agenda is that of a map or chart for the flow and landscape markers of the lesson; it lays out the lesson segments and the strategy for explaining the mathematical topic to be taught. It is not, however, a static lesson plan. Rather, it is a dynamic plan in which elements are modified in the course of instruction.

A curriculum script (Putnam, 1985, 1987b; Putnam & Leinhardt, 1986) is an important part of the agenda that provides the overall goal structure for the content presentation for a particular lesson. It consists of a loosely ordered set of goals and actions that a teacher has built up over time for teaching a particular topic. It contains layers of accumulated knowledge about how to teach the topic, including sequences of ideas or steps to be introduced, representatons to be used, and markers for concepts or procedures that are likely to cause student difficulties. The curriculum script often contains a sketch of the primary explanation to be given. Thus the curriculum script provides the structure for the content in a lesson. Unlike the agenda, however, whose elements may change during a lesson, the curriculum script is relatively stable during a given lesson and is revised or updated in a cumulative way over time. Teachers have a rich repertoire of these scripts developed over their personal history of teaching. Because the agenda and curriculum script reflect the subject-matter content of lessons, they serve as important sites in our examinations of teacher subject-matter knowledge and its effects.

An explanation is an activity in which teachers communicate subject-matter content to students. From our perspective, an explanation is not only what a teacher says or shows to the student, but also includes the systematic arrangement of experiences so that the student can construct a meaningful understanding of a concept or procedure. Explanations are one set of techniques used by teachers to address the content goals of a curriculum script (explanation is one way agendas and curriculum scripts are instantiated). While explanations are both short in duration and not a daily occurrence, they are crucial elements in the process of instruction and learning. They are the heart of what is usually meant by teaching. Like the agenda and the curriculum script, explanations offer a window into teachers' subject-matter knowledge. The ways in which teachers design explanations—the examples they select, the demonstrations they perform—reflect knowledge of subject matter and knowledge of how to teach subject matter.

In constructing explanations, teachers draw on various representations of the target information. Representations are physical or conceptual objects or systems of objects that embody mathematical entities or ideas (operators), for example using Diene's place-value blocks to teach subtraction with regrouping or shaded diagrams to teach fractions. Understanding when particular representations are appropriate and being aware of the more subtle aspects of each representation are specific instances of teacher subject-matter knowledge.

As we examine agendas, curriculum scripts, explanations, and representations, we draw on a variety of classroom lessons. One important dimension along which classrooms vary is the degree to which the teacher directs the course of lessons. At one extreme are lessons that are completely teacher directed (i.e., lectures). At the other extreme are lessons in which students decide what they want to do next, with the teacher serving primarily as a facilitator and resource person. The lessons we examine here are teacher led. These teacher-led lessons include both lessons in which the teacher has a clear pre-specified agenda and more inquiry-oriented lessons in which student contributions play a major role but in which the teacher still plays a directive role of moving the lesson toward a target.

AGENDAS

A teacher's agenda for a lesson is a mental plan that includes both the objectives or goals for segments, or parts, of the lesson, and the actions that can be used to achieve these goals. As the teacher's own mental note pad for the lesson, the agenda includes the major action schemas that will be used (Leinhardt & Greeno, 1986; Sacerdoti, 1977), along with markers for points in the lesson to obtain specific information about students. Because these agendas exist as teachers' mental representations of lessons, they are not visible in written plans. They can, however, be tapped by interviewing teachers immediately prior to their lessons, asking them what they are going to do and what they expect will happen.

In general, when teachers describe what they are going to do in a lesson, they give a relatively brief list of topic and action segments—the important events or divisions within a lesson. Actions are sometimes described in terms of what the teacher will do, sometimes in terms of what students will do. The list may contain references to check points or "tests" at certain points in the lesson that will help the teacher decide whether to continue.

Because the verbal description of a teacher's agenda sketches the content to be taught in the lesson, it provides an important site for examining the nature of subject-matter knowledge used by teachers. We have examined the reported agendas of novice and expert teachers[1] teaching various topics in mathematics, including subtraction with regrouping and rational numbers (Leinhardt, 1988, 1989). Striking contrasts appear between the reported agendas of novice teachers and those of experts. The reported agendas of experts are richer and more detailed than novices' agendas. This richness is evidenced in the sheer amount of talk teachers produce in describing lessons they are about to teach, as in a comparison of agendas for lessons on rational numbers (fractions) by novice and expert teachers (Leinhardt, 1989), where the experts produced on average twice as many lines of response as the novices.

This richness is also evidenced by the differing nature and amount of mathematical content described in the agendas of experts and novices. In reporting their agendas, both novice and expert teachers generally report a topic or lesson title, for example, "fractions and fractional parts," "review equivalent fractions," "problem-solving skills," or "word problems on time and money." But experts report more separate mathematical instructional actions within these topics, again indicating a richer plan organized around the mathematical content to be taught.

Experts also make more explicit references to student actions and to test points within lessons. In our study of agendas, experts referred to student actions twice as often as did novices (Leinhardt, 1989). The mention of a student action suggested that the teacher maintained parallel plans, one for the teacher's sequence of goals and actions, and one for the students'. This parallel planning is a difficult but necessary part of being an effective teacher. It also indicates a linkage on the part of the expert teachers of knowledge of the content to be taught with actions to be taken by the students. Expert teachers also mentioned *tests* or checks on lesson progress more frequently than did novices. Most of these tests involved checking on students' understanding or performance, with some indication that this check would influence a decision about whether to move on to the next instructional segment. The reporting of these tests in the agendas of experts suggests an awareness on their part of critical points in the learning of content that must be reached by students. Experts also provide a sense of instructional logic or flow along some dimension, such as moving from more concrete to abstract representations or the weaving of prior information into the current topic; instructional flow constitutes the markers for the presentational structure. Novices, on the other hand, describe the content to be taught in much more general terms and without highlighting critical points for the students' acquisition or construction of knowledge and skill.

The following excerpts from novice and expert agendas (some of which are taken from Leinhardt, 1989), reported before teaching lessons, illustrate these differences. The protocols include coding for instructional actions, student actions, tests, and statements that indicate instructional logic and flow. A novice is first:

> Novice: Okay, today I'm planning on introducing geometry.
> Interviewer: Mmm-hmm.
> Novice: Uh, just basically. I'll introduce square, rectangle, ah—cylinder. [instructional action]
> [Coding: one instructional action, no student action, no test, no instructional logic]

This novice reports only that the lesson topic is geometry. There is no description of how ideas or skills to be presented fit together, either within the lesson or in relation to other lessons. There is also no mention of student actions or test points during the lesson. A second novice agenda is similarly sparse:

> Novice: Okay, today, I'm planning on going over the homework that I gave yesterday on fractions. I'm planning on going-, on going over it on the board, okay? [first instructional action]
> It'd probably be good for this class and I don't know how many I'm going to go over. There are 36 problems on the homework page, but I'm gonna see how it goes. If they're all getting them very quickly, then we'll move on. [test]
>
> [Coding: one instructional action, one test]

Again, the novice appears not to have much of a mental representation of a lesson from which to work. In this case there is a test point, but there is no mention of the mathematical content of the lesson aside from the topic, "fractions." The following expert agenda provides a contrast:

> Expert: We're going to begin adding fractions. [first instructional action]
> Yesterday we compared fractions, so we'll kind of review that after I introduce adding fractions. [first instructional logic]
> After we do some at the board, then we'll bring in what we did yesterday, comparison fractions . . . [second instructional action]
> And I found out yesterday we can only do those if we draw objects. [second instructional logic]
> It's hard for the children to see three fourths is greater than or less than one fourth. So if they draw the object . . . [third instructional action, student action]
> it's much easier. So we'll be doing some of that today, just review. They don't compare fractions too much in fourth grade. But I'll review it so the better ones will know it pretty well. Then we'll continue with adding fractions at the board. [fourth instructional action]
> And then we'll go into the textbook.
>
> [Coding: four instructional actions, two instructional logic, one student action, no test]

This expert's agenda was far richer and more detailed than those of the novices. There were more references to instructional actions, student actions, and instructional logic or justification. Another expert's agenda is similarly detailed:

Expert: Okay, now first of all, yesterday we used at the end of the period, we used a feltboard.

Interviewer: Mmm-hmm.

Expert: . . . to show us, tens and ones and then to change a ten to ones.

Interviewer: Mmm-hmm.

Expert: Okay, so we're going to continue with that . . . [first instructional action]

Interviewer: Okay.

Expert: and the kids will be recording some of the information on a piece of paper that they saved from yesterday. [second instructional action, student action]

Interviewer: Mmm.

Expert: And then I'm going to uh, write that on the board in long form, renaming 5 tens and 2 ones as 4 tens and 12 ones. [third instructional action]

Interviewer: Right.

Expert: Okay, and then I'm going to wean them away from the regular name like 5 tens and 2 ones and just go to the one line . . . [fourth instructional action, first instructional logic]

Interviewer: Mmm.

Expert: Just rename it, and then I'm going to, uh, just putting the number on the board and showing them how to cross out. [fifth instructional action]

Interviewer: Mmm.

Expert: . . . And narrow it down. And then I'm going to go to uh, uh, their fooler problem. [sixth instructional action]

Interviewer: Mmm.

Expert: And show them how they can rename the top number and then subtract.

Interviewer: Mmm.

Expert: So, that's the logical way I want to do it. [second instructional logic (content: move away from expanded language and toward algorithm)]

Interviewer: Yeah, okay.

Expert: And I'll go at the pace they let me go at. [test]
[Coding: six instructional actions, one student action, one test, two instructional logic]

Each of these experts laid out the logical sequence for an entire lesson and how it built on previous lessons. The topical segments were clearly differentiated and noted, in terms of both goals and student actions. The experts also had a specific overarching goal that ordered the actions so that the lessons moved from the broad, general procedures to the more focused algorithm. This meant that not only was there a more complete action list for the lesson, with each action supported by sub-goals and routines (Leinhardt & Greeno, 1986), but there was a conceptual road map to keep the lesson flowing in a particular direction, "weaning away" and "narrowing it down"—a focusing on the concepts and procedures of regrouping.

To the extent that these conceptual road maps are previously known, and the teacher can access a fully scripted set of mental notes for explaining a particular piece of the curriculum, we refer to them as curriculum scripts. These experts are familiar with the subject-matter content they are teaching, and the context in which they are teaching them. Over time they have developed curriculum scripts for particular topics.

CURRICULUM SCRIPTS

A curriculum script refers to the goals and actions for teaching a particular topic (Putnam, 1985; 1987b; Putnam & Leinhardt, 1986). The curriculum script concept emerged from Putnam's (1985; 1987b) research examining the ways in which teachers presented content and responded to student errors while tutoring. Putnam found each teacher to engage in a limited set of teaching actions or moves. These actions included recycling through explanations and constructing settings for student moves, but did not involve building detailed models about how an individual student was thinking about a problem. The point here is that the teachers focused their energy on altering and adjusting their own behaviors rather than on designing hypotheses about why the students did what they did.

One might ask why these teachers did not build the student-as-learner models we might expect them as diagnosticians to build (Brown & Burton, 1978). The teachers did build models, but these models focused on their teaching and its cycle rather than on the mental representation of an individual student. Teachers seemed to have markers which signaled material that was likely to cause difficulty as it is learned, and to build up a script of actions and representations that "work" for teaching the topic—a curriculum script. We use the term *script* in the sense that Schank & Abelson (1977) use the term—as a knowledge structure, similar to a schema, that provides expectancies and structures for interpreting situations and acting in them. In this case the situation is a lesson on a particular topic. A major goal of teaching a lesson appears to be to move through such a curriculum script, making modest adjustments during instruction in response to individual student needs. Thus, a lesson given by an effective teacher who has been teaching for many years contains layers of accumulated knowledge about the topic and how to teach it. The curriculum script constitutes an important part of a teacher's knowledge for teaching in a form that is highly accessible because it is organized as it will be used in the teaching of lessons.

Teachers' reliance on curriculum scripts does not imply that their teaching is rigid and inflexible. Rather, curriculum scripts provide a cohesiveness to lessons by providing a structure (often a sequence) of ideas to be presented and actions to be taken to help students construct the desired knowledge structure. The structure provides cohesiveness, much like the sequence of ideas in a book or a play that build an argument or create a particular impression. What makes classroom teaching different from a book or a formal lecture, however, is its interactive quality. While moving through the sequence provided by the curriculum script, the teacher continually monitors students' performance to see whether the target concepts or understandings are being developed as they are needed for a particular point in the lesson. If students are not producing the expected responses (i.e., have not comprehended the point to be made or have not learned the correct procedure being presented) the teacher makes modest adjustments by re-presenting or elaborating. Without the curriculum script to provide cohesiveness, teachers may be drawn off their focus to follow particular students in ways that are not helpful for the rest of the class, and may fail to anticipate crucial features or dimensions of what is important or difficult about learning a topic.

Curriculum scripts vary in their flexibility and the extent to which they incorporate alternative routes for content presentation or directions the lesson might take based on student input—sometimes in terms of their performance and sometimes in terms of more affective responses during the lesson. Whereas some scripts may be quite rigid in terms of style, progression, and content, others appear "looser," capitalizing on specific issues so that unique points can be raised. A teacher who has rich and flexible knowledge of a particular domain may have a curriculum script whose overall goals are clear but whose sub-goals and actions are much more loosely ordered. Goals may be organized as a network, rather than as a more linear sequence. Such a script permits following up on various inputs and ideas by students. Because of the uncertainty in where the lesson will go, however, this kind of script requires considerably more accessible content knowledge on the part of the teacher.

The importance of having a well-developed curriculum script can be illustrated by its absence in the lesson of a novice teacher teaching relatively unfamiliar content. (The following example is taken from Putnam & Leinhardt [1986], and Leinhardt, [1989]).

Ms. Benny was a student teacher in a third-grade classroom. She had been teaching a series of lessons on the basic multiplication combinations. In general, her lessons were well planned and made fairly consistent use of two representation systems to present multiplication: arrays of circular plastic counters and a numberline. In other words, Ms. Benny had at least the beginnings of a workable curriculum script and representations for teaching multiplication. Two significant problems arose, however, in one of the lessons that we observed and videotaped. Ms. Benny's main goal for the lesson was to present multiplying by 9. She began the lesson by using an array of 9 by 9 counters displayed on the overhead projector. To show 3×9 in this representation she created 3 sets of 9 by placing strings on the array, as in the top of Figure 1.

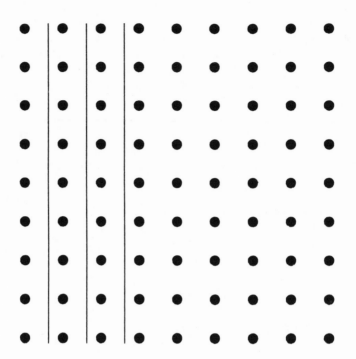

Ms. Benny's actual display of 3 x 9

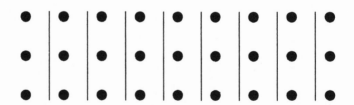

(presumed) Ms. Benny's intended display of 9 x 3

Figure 1.   Displays of Chips to Demostrate Multiplication

This representation is consistent with the way she had presented combinations in an earlier lesson. Ms. Benny ran into difficulty, however, when she asked a student to illustrate 9×3 as 9 groups of 3 on the 9 by 9 array:

Teacher: (writes $3 \times 9 = 27$ on board) We have 3 times 9 equals 27. What do you think is another equation we can write that will equal 27?

John: 9 times 3.

Teacher: 9 times 3. Let's see if it works. (writes $9 \times 3 = \_\_$ on the board) John, go up there and change those strings to show me 9×3.

At this point, Ms. Benny realized that showing nine groups of three on the display could not easily be done. Presumably she had intended the student to show a representation like that in the bottom of Figure 1. Ms. Benny tried to correct the tactical error she had just made by not letting the student finish his task, but the student insisted:

John: (comes to overhead projector to move the strings)

Teacher: I don't know if you can do that.

John: Yeah, I can do it.

Teacher: No, I don't know if you can do it with these strings.

John: Yeah, I can do it.

Ms. Benny and John then spent a full 60 seconds (quite a long time in a lesson) trying to display 9×3. Ms. Benny ended up having John pull 9 separate groups of 3 away from the array. The resulting display did not clearly show 9×3 and did nothing to show the equivalence of 9×3 and 3×9. By this time, the other students in the class had lost interest and the noise level had risen. Ms. Benny went on with the lesson, but had lost valuable instructional time and had difficulty getting the students back with her.

Ms. Benny's goal was for her students to understand the equivalence of 9×3 and 3×9, but she was unable to illustrate this equivalence because an important detail of her curriculum script had not been worked out. The problematic aspect of the script in this case was the representation Ms. Benny was using to teach multiplication (compounded by her lack of a secure and flexible knowledge of lesson structure and routines). Concrete representations can be powerful tools for helping students construct understanding of mathematical concepts, but using them effectively is deceptively complex. It is critical in using a particular representation that the features of the representation being used provide a good match to the target concept or procedure (commutativity of multiplication in this case). We discuss this and related issues in the effective use of representations later in this chapter. The important point here is that, given richer knowledge of the representation embedded in a curriculum script, Ms. Benny would probably have avoided the confusion in this lesson.

Later in the same lesson, Ms. Benny ran into serious difficulty by introducing a trick for multiplying by 9 that her supervising teacher taught her. She was thus using new material that she had not worked into a curriculum script; she was *borrowing* someone else's script without integrating it into her own knowledge. Here is the way the trick was *supposed* to work for 6 × 9: First, take the number that's one less than 6 and write that down (write down a 5). Then think what number you'd have to add to 5 to get 9 and write that number next to the 5 (write a 4 next to the 5 to make 54). Ms. Benny got hopelessly confused in presenting the "trick;" she could not even remember all of the steps in it. The supervising teacher, who was at the back of the room, had to lead Ms. Benny through the steps during the lesson. The steps of this new procedure were never made clear in the lesson, nor was there any discussion or justification for why the trick might work.

Again, the difficulty Ms. Benny had in teaching this procedure illustrates a poorly formed curriculum script. Ms. Benny did not have or was unable to access during the lesson knowledge of how to carry out the procedure herself, how to *present* the procedure for her students to learn it, and how this procedure fit within the context of the larger lesson (i.e., she had no way to tie this procedure to the chips representation and activities that preceded it). Also missing were clear goals for the lesson. These are important aspects of a teacher's subject-matter knowledge; the curriculum scripts of expert teachers integrate this knowledge in a form that can be accessed during the teaching of lessons.

Curriculum scripts can be seen as an overall game plan for the presentation of content in a particular lesson. One place in which the curriculum script is "played out" is in the explanation of the to-be-learned concepts or procedures. Although explanations are only one component of a curriculum script, they represent the core of most teaching episodes. We turn now to discussion of instructional explanations.

EXPLANATIONS

Explanations can range from didactic and direct to discovery-based and indirect. For example, some teachers design circumstances that lead a child to have insights about a particular concept or problem, while other teachers take a more direct teaching stance, explicitly stating information to be learned. Regardless of which type of teaching one is describing, explanations are fundamental to the teaching process.

Based on work with expert elementary mathematics teachers, a theoretical model of an effective explanation has been developed. This model was initially described by Leinhardt and Greeno (1986) and was later expanded when studying lessons in subtraction with regrouping (Leinhardt, 1987). We have continued to develop the model using explanations of equivalent fractions, functions and graphing, and computer programming (Baxter, 1987, 1988; Leinhardt, 1988a). The model includes different levels of goals to be achieved in an adequate explanation and the associated action schemas that lead to each goal state.

Teachers and students construct explanations in order to instruct and learn new material. The new material may be in the form of new concepts or principles or it may be new procedures or actions or both. Explanation is a complex action that occurs in response to several overarching goals. For example, one might explain the base-ten notation (place value) system because one was teaching regrouping in subtaction and it was "time" to "run through" the part about columns and value. Or one might offer the same explanation because a student or group of students simply did not seem to understand how *to do* the procedure. Or, one might offer this same explanation because of a student error or uncertainty. It is important to note that a teacher might offer one explanation both to review a procedure *and* to clear up a student misconception. Thus, an explanation is a complex action that can occur in response to several different goals.

Regardless of the purpose for which an explanation is offered, certain elements are common to good explanations. We describe these elements as goal states that must be achieved before or during an explanation. The specific goals and their relationship to action sequences have been detailed in Leinhardt (1987; 1988; 1989).

1. Component Elements and Sub-Skills Available. Explanations often incorporate component elements (e.g., trading base-ten blocks) and sub-skills (e.g., addition facts for a lesson on carrying) that must be known by the student if the explanation is to succeed. If a teacher attempts to explain a new concept by using a new representation that must also be learned, then the explanation has little chance of benefiting the hapless student who will likely lose sight of the principal objective. However, if sub-skills have already been taught, then the teacher can make these sub-skills available to the student merely by asking for them—taking them out of cold storage, so to speak. By performing one or more of these retrieving actions before or during an explanation, the teacher can meet the goal of having component elements and sub-skills available. For example, when explaining decimal numbers, one teacher began with a review of place value for whole numbers. The place value of whole numbers operated as a sub-skill in this lesson on decimals, so through the review the teacher helped students access their knowledge of this sub-skill. In another lesson on reducing fractions, the sub-skills used were factoring, knowing multiplication and division facts, knowing fractions terminology, and knowing the syntax of the particular representation being used.

2. Problem Identified. The particular problem or issue that is being dealt with must be identified clearly enough so that students can see what is being explained. This may involve locating a particular contradiction that requires a solution, or generating attributes or features of a phenomenon. This can be done by setting up actions that constrain the solution path so students "bump into" the problem. For example, to begin an explanation of negative numbers, one teacher asked students to solve the problem $50 - 70$. The students were familiar with subtraction, but they had thus far only worked subtraction problems that yielded positive numbers. Many students claimed that $50 - 70$ was impossible to solve. By using an "impossible" problem, the teacher helped the students realize that another type of number (i.e., negative) was needed to solve certain problems.

3. Completion. Explanations are not always complete, in some specific ways. Sometimes they simply are not finished; sometimes mappings between representation systems are not exhaustive; and sometimes there are not enough markers for students to follow the logical flow. Usually, explanations include both a verbal and a physical part, both of which are used to support the numerical/symbolic aspects of an explanation and the concrete aspects. Although it is theoretically possible to present an example with little or no verbal accompaniment, it is rarely done. Likewise, although it is possible to merely talk through a description without any demonstration, it would be unusual. If a teacher uses two or more systems (numerical and concrete, for example) during an explanation, appropriate links need to be established in order to show the correspondences between the systems as well as to complete all the portions. Thus, one would expect to observe language that labels and describes all of the aspects and key moves. We have found that expert teachers tend both to make clearer connections among their representations and to complete their demonstrations more often than do novices. Because it is a somewhat complex task to move through an explanation juggling these different aspects, expert explanations often include markers of progress towards completion. These markers help the student keep the goal in view and help the teacher reach a complete explanation (see Leinhardt & Putnam, 1987, for a more detailed discussion).

4. Conditions of Use Specified. The conditions under which the concept is relevant or under which the procedure is to be used need to be highlighted in an explanation. That is, a procedure needs to be signaled if it is one which does not get used all the time but only under some specific circumstances. In the course of an explanation on subtraction with regrouping, for example, one teacher had students note problems that did require regrouping and those that did not require regrouping. Thus, regrouping is used for subtraction in some cases. Similarly, the part/whole interpretation of fractions is appropriate in some, but not all, situations. Signaling when a concept or procedure is relevant helps to connect the new information to the old or familiar situation and to distinguish it at the same time. Often, but not always, an explanation sketches out the type of error or misconception associated with the new idea—pointing out where the pitfalls are, so to speak. Within an explanation a teacher might deliberately include errors of misapplication or overgeneralization in order to highlight them. The intentional production of errors is often a key move in an explanation—it is an action that can be used to accomplish the subgoal of identifying principles of use. For example, during an explanation on graphing simple linear functions, one teacher intentionally misplotted an ordered pair. The students quickly noted that the misplotted point did not line up with the other points. Guided by the teacher, the students came to realize the principle that ordered pairs from a particular kind of function produce a linear graph.

5. Principles Identified. Finally, the principles which undergird the explanation need to be presented in a way that legitimizes the new concept. This can be done by cross checks with other systems, compelling logic, or a search for ways in which previous principles have been violated or adhered to.

Not all explanations contain all of these elements, but for each math topic a competent teacher is able to access a specific set of actions that support these subgoals to a greater or lesser degree. The following analysis of two teachers' explanations illustrates the contrast between expert and novice explanations. We continue the discussion of the novice teacher who was teaching a lesson on multiplying by 9 and contrast it with the expert whose agenda for a lesson teaching subtraction with regrouping was presented in the first section of this chapter. This expert lesson on subtraction was chosen because of its display of virtually all the idealized subgoals for an explanation.

As part of the analysis of these explanations, we constructed semantic net diagrams of the first major portions of one novice and one expert explanation (see Figures 2 and 3). The nodes in the diagrams show the concepts that were presented and the lines between nodes show how the concepts were connected and organized. In Figure 2, the novice's explanation is shown with numbers that indicate the order of presentation of each information cluster. The novice started directly with the statement that the lesson would be about the "last two one-digit numbers that you're gonna learn to multiply by, 8 and 9. Nine is the harder of the two, so we're going to work with 9 a little more." The novice then turned on an overhead projector that was crammed with a 9 by 9 array of 81 chips. A child interrupted and said he knew the answer, to which the novice replied that that was impossible because there had not been a question. One might presume that the student assumed that the "question" was either what is 9 times 9 or what is 9 times 8, depending on how the opening statement was interpreted. However, the student's reaction to the display was treated as wrong.

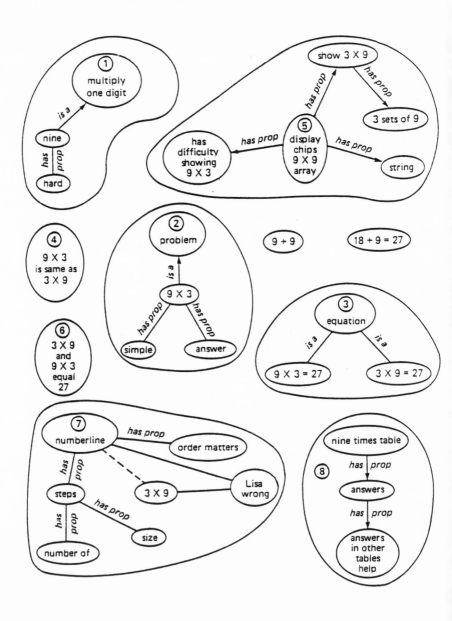

Figure 2. Semantic Net for a Novice Teacher's Explanation of Multiplication

The novice's next statement was that she would start with a "simple" problem, 3 times 9. In 60 seconds of dialogue, the novice had mentioned the numbers 2, 1, 8, 9, 9 by 9, 1, 2, 3, 4, 5, 9, 9, and then 3 times 9, with six different meanings (one-digit, last two numbers of the times table, 9 by 9 array, counting 1 to 5, skipping to 9, and the "problem" 3 times 9). She then introduced sets as a label and talked while standing at the overhead, having one child rope off 3 groups of 9 chips while she simultaneously got another student to verbally answer 3 times 9 as an addition problem. Here is the dialogue:

Teacher: That means we have 1, 2, and 3 (columns of 9). What's the answer, Robin?
Student: (No response.)
Teacher: If there's 3 sets of 9, what's the answer?
Student: What?
Teacher: All right, Robin, what is 9 plus 9?
Student: (Inaudible response.)
Teacher: No, what is 9 plus 9?
Student: (No response.)
Teacher: What's 18 plus 9?
Student: (Inaudible response.)
Teacher: Twenty-five?
Student: Fifty?
Teacher: How much, Tom?
Student: Twenty-seven.

During this exchange, the display was abandoned as a possible source for the answer. The novice then proceeded to an "equation" to show the equivalence of 3 times 9 and 9 times 3, but could not show it on the overhead (see previous discussion under curriculum scripts). At this point she called on students to demonstrate 3 times 9 and 9 times 3 by drawing "steps" (arcs) on a number line that was on the chalkboard. In this demonstration one of the three students was told that her display was incorrect although a subsequent identical drawing by another student was lauded as correct. As shown by the separate clusters in Figure 2, each piece of the novice's explanation lacked a connection to any other piece and was often at odds with it. For example, the chips display and the number line showed the *difference* between 3 times 9 and 9 times 3, whereas the equations and problem solutions showed the equality of both expressions. Of course, these two attributes are both correct, but showing both and making a clear distinction between them is difficult and was not accomplished.

Figure 3 shows a semantic net of the expert's lesson on subtraction with regrouping in which she introduced the regrouping concept and procedure. The first and most noticeable feature of the diagram is the degree to which everything is connected; the lesson worked as an integrated whole. The second

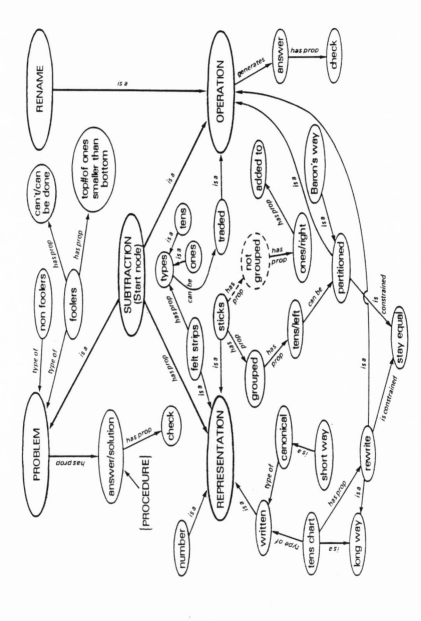

Figure 3. Semantic Net for an Expert Teacher's Explanation of Subtraction

feature to note is the set of three parallel strands of smaller nets extending from the representation node. The expert presented three iterations of the same notion of regrouping with different procedures—one using sticks, another using felt strips, and a third using numerals with two versions of a written procedure. The sticks were "regrouped" by unbanding, the felt was "regrouped" by trading, and the numerals were regrouped by rewriting in expanded form. Although the expert did not choose to connect the representations explicitly (e.g., by saying, "This one stick is like this one felt square"), the parallelism of the presentations highlighted the connections. A third feature to note is the degree to which the expert's explanation was denser or richer than the novice's. Although the lengths of these two analyzed explanations were not identical, the novice was clearly covering less content in a less integrated way than the expert. (If the analyzed portion of the novice's explanation had been extended to equal the length of the expert's, the addition would have consisted of only a prolonged erroneous piece of explanation in which the novice attempted to teach the "rule" of digits summing to 9, but forgot it in midlesson.)

An additional comment on the difference between the expert and novice explanations concerns what they were each trying to explain. The expert was trying to explain the procedure, concept, and legitimacy of trading or regrouping tens in order to calculate the answers to a specific set of subtraction problems. The novice was trying simultaneously to explain the relationship between 3 times 9 and 9 times 3, and to teach the 9s multiplication facts. The novice's explanations were to some extent incompatible. It seemed as though one part of the lesson had nothing to do with the other, but that the novice was trying to make it appear that it did.

In describing agendas, scripts, and explanations we have emphasized the clarity and connectedness of the expert's knowledge. There is also, of course, an intended sense of depth and completeness. When the teacher has deep knowledge about a particular content topic, such as equivalent fractions or graphing or regrouping, she or he knows how to keep the lesson moving in a desirable direction by building on opportunities and heading away from blind alleys. She or he also knows when, where, and, perhaps, why confusions and misconceptions are likely to occur. Another image that might be helpful in considering the expert's knowledge is a strand, or thread, of actions that can be accessed to teach a concept or procedure. Each action is well supported by a rich knowledge base of subject matter, including, for example, knowledge of part-whole versus ordered-pair interpretations of fractions, of the inconsistency of fractions greater than one with the part-whole interpretation, or of the notion of bounded infinite subdivisions. Each action is also supported by knowledge of student acquisitional difficulties, such as students' logical tendency to add numerators and denominators or the fact that students find reducing fractions much harder than the seemingly parallel process of raising fractions. The strand is thus richly supported and intricate, but it is a strand that follows a mostly predetermined path. A second image is one in which the extremely competent teacher's knowledge consists of multiple strands (embroidery floss comes to mind). Given an action on any one of these strands the teacher is capable of jumping from one approach to another, emphasizing different things and warning against different pitfalls—weaving a lesson or a series of lessons as she or he goes. Doing this requires a tremendous amount of flexibility and knowledge.

One instance in which we can clearly see this flexibility is in the use of multiple representations. Both teachers and students gain in their knowledge as they both extend the single representation and add new ones. In the next section we describe in some detail the meaning and role of representations in instructional explanations.

REPRESENTATIONS

One's understanding of mathematics is greatly enhanced by the ability to work both within and among various representations of mathematical ideas and operations (Kaput, 1987). In this chapter, we use the term *representation* to refer to the entity used to explain something (usually an analogy, picture, or manipulative) and we use the term *target* to refer to the concept, meaning, or procedure being explained.

As with agendas, curriculum scripts, and explanations, the representations used by teachers offer windows into their subject-matter knowledge. However, the "representations window" can be seen as a window made of magnifying glass. By this we mean that teachers' use of representations lends insight into very detailed and subtle aspects of how they understand a particular mathematical topic. As we shall see, there is much more than meets the eye in the expert use of well-chosen representations. On the surface, the content and flow of the representational portion of the explanation may seem straightforward. Nevertheless, the kind and level of subject-matter knowledge needed to "back up" the accurate, fluid, and effective use of representations is substantial.

We view the use of representations from a particular perspective, that is, within the framework suggested by teachers' agendas, curriculum scripts, and explanations. Representations are one of the important components of explanations and, as such, can be seen as embedded in and contextualized by the overall instructional explanation. Thus the goals and associated action sequences of an explanation will influence the particular representation a teacher chooses and how she or he uses it. Representations can also be seen as part of a teacher's curriculum script. For example, a given teacher's "game plan" for teaching subtraction with regrouping may include the use of Diene's place-value blocks or popsicle sticks. The manner in which the teacher uses the place-value blocks and popsicle sticks (as well as his or her initial choice of those representations) will be influenced by the goals of the curriculum script. Similarly, a teacher's agenda may influence how, when, and what representations are used. This view of representations is important because it does not treat representations as isolated pieces of instruction but rather views them within the larger picture of teachers' goals, plans, and actions.

We will begin our discussion of representations with an example of Ms. Konrad, an expert fourth-grade teacher, teaching a lesson on equivalent fractions. (See Leinhardt & Smith [1985] for a more extensive discussion.) The goals of Ms. Konrad's lesson were (1) to show that two "different" fractions can be used to show the same amount (e.g., $1/2 = 2/4$); and (2) to demonstrate how to operate on a given fraction in order to produce an equivalent fraction (i.e., multiply or divide by a fractional equivalent of one). During the lesson, Ms. Konrad moved through three different representations of fractions: number lines, regions of figures drawn on the blackboard, and sets. In the numberline representation, Ms. Konrad drew several number lines on the blackboard, each number line being divided into different fractional parts. (There was a number line divided into halves, one into thirds, one into fourths, etc.) The number lines were arranged vertically (i.e., one on top of the other) with equivalent fractions aligned. Ms. Konrad went to great lengths to show that when a particular fraction from one number line was in alignment with a fraction from another number line, the two fractions were equivalent (e.g., $1/2 = 2/4 = 3/6 = 4/8$). What is interesting about this particular representation is that it totally fails to capture the process of transformation—how one gets from one number line to another—but, on the other hand, it emphasizes the bidirectionality of equivalence, something that tends to be masked by the numerical procedures of multiplication and division.

Using a different version of alignment, Ms. Konrad also explored a regional representation of equivalence. Two equal-sized rectangles were drawn on the blackboard, one divided and shaded to show $1/2$ and the other divided and shaded to show $3/6$. Students were invited to compare them and (hopefully) discover that the same amount of area is covered in each figure.[2] Finally, Ms. Konrad went on to a set representation that rather cleverly built on the shapes chosen for the regional representation. She concluded the lesson with a fairly elaborate proof from a symbolic (numeric) point of view.

The point of this example is that Ms. Konrad enriched the basic explanation by making use of several representations. The various representations benefit the teaching act by providing students with multiple hooks with which to connect into critical concepts and to analyze basic procedures. Ohlsson (1987) has suggested that such familiarity with multiple representations may not result in improved accuracy on a test, but it may foster considerable flexibility, especially when the problem space changes or becomes more constrained.

In addition to being aware of the benefits to be gained from multiple representations, teachers must also consider the suitability of *particular* representations for *particular* purposes. It is not possible for any one representation to capture all of the salient components of the target material (Ohlsson, 1987). However, certain representations will take an instructor farther in his or her attempts to explain the to-be-learned material and still remain consistent and useful. It is crucial that teachers know the general robustness of a given representation as well as understand when a particular representation system has outlived its usefulness.

The choice of an effective representation for a particular purpose is not a trivial matter. Consider the case of fractions. Kieren (1976) has identified six different ways in which fractions can be conceptualized: a part-to-whole comparison, a decimal, a ratio, an indicated division (quotient), an operator, and a measure of continuous or discrete quantities. These six different ways of conceptualizing fractions are differentially useful in various problem situations. For example, thinking of fractions as ratios is effective when converting a fraction to a percentage but it is not useful in the multiplication of fractions. Before teachers entertain the question of representations, they first need to be aware of which conceptualization best suits a particular problem. Teachers then need to be knowledgeable regarding which representation(s) best conveys each of the above conceptualizations. For example, the shaded region representation is a reasonable model for the "part-to-whole comparison" conceptualization but is not effective when thinking of fractions as an indicated division. A circle with 3/4 shaded tells one nothing related to 3 divided by 4.

We turn now to an example from the domain of graphing. The teacher is Mr. Gene, an experienced fifth-grade math teacher.[3] The target material in these lessons was the set of conventions for setting up and moving within a four-quadrant Cartesian coordinate system. Because Mr. Gene's students were already familiar with the conventions of a one-quadrant Cartesian coordinate system, the goal of Mr. Gene's lesson was to introduce and to locate the negative coordinates.

The textbook had provided one representation of a four-quadrant Cartesian coordinate system, a map of "Graph City." Graph City consisted of a system of streets and avenues with the streets running vertically and the avenues running horizontally. The streets to the left of a centrally located "Zero Street" were consecutively numbered and labeled "east" while the streets to the right of "Zero Street" were numbered and labeled "west." Similarly, the avenues above a centrally located "Zero Avenue" were labeled "north" while the avenues below "Zero Avenue" were labeled "south." After explaining the Graph City representation, Mr. Gene introduced a second representation, Wishville, the town in which the elementary school was located. He asked the students if the town of Wishville also had directional labels for its streets and avenues. For an example, he asked for the name of the roadway on which the elementary school was located. A student replied with the name, "West 18th Street." Technically, the answer was incorrect because the name of the roadway was "West 18th Avenue." Mr. Gene, however, chose not to highlight the distinction between avenue and street in Wishville but instead focused on the directional label of West.

The above example illustrates a teacher focusing on relevant components of a representation and "playing down" irrelevant components. The distinction between streets and avenues (in either the Graph City or the Wishville representation) is not crucial for the target goal of locating negative numbers on the Cartesian coordinate system. Rather the crucial distinction is east versus west and north versus south because these directional labels correspond to positive and negative numbers on the Cartesian coordinate system.

When using a representation, a teacher needs to be aware of the fact that all components of the representation may not (probably will not) be salient to understanding the target material. In fact, some components, if attended to, could potentially provide distracting or confusing information. Schoenfeld (1986) has suggested that representations (he refers to them as "reference worlds") have a dual nature: the real-world meanings that individuals naturally attach to them and a symbolic meaning that corresponds to mathematical ideas and operations. Although the real-world meanings contribute to the attractiveness of representations as teaching tools, certain aspects of these meanings may not coincide with or may be irrelevant to understanding the to-be-learned material. In the above example, the goal was the introduction and location of negative coordinates; the real-world distinction between streets and avenues was not relevant to learning this goal.

Another lesson involving Graph City provides a second example of the subtleties of using representations effectively. In this lesson, Mr. Gene's goal was to teach students how to plot points on a Cartesian coordinate system. Mr. Gene wanted to make sure that the students were plotting their points at the intersection of lines rather than in the spaces between lines. When a few students placed points in spaces instead of at the intersection of lines, Mr. Gene corrected them with a reminder about Graph City: "Remember the cars have to travel along the streets; they cannot ride in the middle of the block." Whereas a mapping from Graph City's streets to the Cartesian coordinate system's lines served Mr. Gene's immediate purpose, mapping from the movement of cars on Graph City's streets to the plotting of points on the Cartesian coordinate system may have been stretching the representation too far. Mapping this feature may cause problems in the future. Many times it is necessary not to plot points at the intersection of two lines (when, for example, one is plotting [2.5, 2.5] on a Cartesian coordinate system scaled with whole numbers in units of one). If, however, students remember Graph City and the fact that cars must stay on the streets, they may be reluctant to plot the points in the spaces.

This example illustrates the precision required when drawing parallels between moves in the target material and moves in the representation. A teacher must focus on the mathematically relevant components of a representation in a dynamic sense as well as in a definitional sense. In other words, when discussing moves in the target material and appealing to the representation for justification of those moves, the teacher needs to be aware of what kinds of moves are parallel between the two systems and what kinds of moves are not parallel.

In summary, the effective use of appropriate representations requires that teachers deeply understand the topics they are teaching. The example of Ms. Konrad illustrates the usefulness of multiple representations while the examples of Mr. Gene illustrate the subtleties involved in the expert use of representations. Compared to work on agendas, curriculum scripts, and explanations, investigations into the role of representations in expert instruction are in their infancy. Nevertheless, the study of how teachers choose and use representations holds the potential to reveal much about teachers, their knowledge bases, and the subject matters they teach.

SUMMARY AND CONCLUSION

We have provided a sampling of places in the instructional process where teacher subject-matter knowledge plays a critical role. Our choice of sites has been guided by findings from classroom-based studies that focused on detailed observations of experts and novices as they taught various topics in the elementary mathematics curriculum. As such, our delineation of where teacher subject-matter knowledge makes a difference begins to tighten the evolving conceptualization of the intricate relationship between subject-matter knowledge and actual classroom instruction.

We have suggested four locations where teachers' knowledge of the subjects they teach matters. Our work has shown that teachers' mental plans, or agendas, for lessons vary from skeletal to detailed depending, in large part, on their familiarity with the content to be taught. In addition, teachers' curriculum scripts provide an especially fruitful site for exploring teacher subject-matter knowledge because they represent the transformation of teachers' knowledge of the content into a form that is accessed during the teaching of lessons. Similarly, the explanations that teachers offer to their students can be seen as a reflection of the content and structure of their subject-matter knowledge. Finally, we have suggested that more in-depth study of how teachers choose and use representations has the potential to shed light on the interface between very detailed aspects of teacher subject-matter knowledge and their classroom instruction. Recent work in the area of cognitive learning suggests yet a fifth location where teacher subject-matter knowledge matters:

teachers' responses to students' comments and questions as they are engaged in the process of learning. It should be noted that the analyses in this chapter have focused on teachers who use a teacher-led, didactic style. Although our experts have been shown to be responsive and supportive of student efforts to learn key concepts and procedures, the content, method, and direction of their lessons are situated primarily with the teacher. Cognitively based learning theories, however, suggest that it is pedagogically sound and cognitively necessary for students to have a role in determining the method and direction of their own learning (Collins, Brown, & Newman, 1989; Putnam, Lampert, & Peterson, 1990; Resnick, 1987; Schoenfeld, 1985). Such a shift in participant roles changes significantly the task and problem space for the teacher, who must somehow juggle the active participation of 20 to 30 students with the need to address particular content. Doing this requires that the teacher be able to keep active simultaneously a broad and deep conceptualization of the subject matter content and a highly focused understanding of an individual student's reasoning. We are beginning to explore the nature and organization of the subject-matter knowledge teachers use in this kind of teaching. Such explorations will be based on the study of the subject-matter knowledge of teachers who focus on student understanding (Putnam, 1987a) and on a more in-depth examination of various types of instructional explanations including the role of representations in them (Leinhardt & Odoroff, 1988). A key feature of these studies will be the distinction between explanations that are essentially designed by teachers in advance, and those in which students play an active role in constructing during classroom dialogue.

In closing, we want to point out that our investigation into where teacher subject-matter knowledge impacts instruction has been based on analyses of *instances* of particularly good and particularly poor pieces of instruction. As such, it as only a beginning. It does not offer a theory of the role of teacher subject-matter knowledge in classroom instruction nor does it provide detailed specification of the mechanisms by which teacher subject-matter knowledge influences instruction. Needed are further investigations and theorizing into what kinds of subject-matter knowledge are particularly salient and how subject-matter knowledge is accessed and used during the course of instruction.

NOTES

1. Throughout this chapter we will refer to studies in which novice and expert teachers are compared. In these studies, novice teachers are teachers in their last year of training who are teaching in classrooms with a supervising teacher. In most cases the cooperating teacher was not present and, in all cases, the novices had complete control over the instructional portion of the lessons. Experts refer to teachers who were chosen because of their positive performance according to several criteria: consistent student growth on standard tests over several years, consistent student achievement on standardized tests, and supervisor and peer nomination. Further follow up on

the teachers over time indicated that these experts were often selected for district-level committees on text selection, test development, and teacher coordination.

2. This representation actually works better as a mental overlay procedure in which the *same* unit is divided in two different ways and the two ways are shown to cover the same area of the figure if they are superimposed one over the other. The problem is, of course, that on a chalk board there are usually two separate figures and it is not always clear if the unit is one or two regions large (e.g., the base drawing for 1 3/4 is identical to the drawing for the equivalence between 1/2 and 2/4).

3. Mr. Gene was not identified as an expert through the procedures described earlier. We studied his lessons because of his reputation as a good math teacher and our judgment of him as expert. References to Mr. Gene's work can be found in Baxter, Stein, and Leinhardt (1991); Leinhardt, Stein, and Baxter (1988); and Stein, Baxter, and Leinhardt (1990).

REFERENCES

Baxter, J. (1987). *Teacher explanations in computer programming: A study, of knowledge transformations.* Unpublished doctoral dissertation, Stanford University, Stanford, CA.

Baxter, J.A., Stein, M.K., & Leinhardt, G. (1991). *The role of instructional representations in teaching.* Unpublished manuscript. University of Oregon, Eugene, OR.

Brown, J. S., & Burton, R. R. (1978). Diagnostic models for procedural bugs in basic mathematical skills. *Cognitive Science, 2,* 155-192.

Chase, W., & Simon, H. (1973). The mind's eye in chess. In W. G. Chase (Ed.), *Visual information processing* (pp. 215-281). New York: Academic.

Collins, A., Brown, J.S., & Newman, S.E. (1989). Cognitive apprenticeship: Teaching the craft of reading, writing, and mathematics. In L.B. Resnick (Ed.), *Knowing, learning, and instruction: Essays in honor of Robert Glaser* (pp. 453-494). Hillsdale, NJ: Erlbaum.

Glaser, R. (1984). Education and thinking: The role of knowledge. *American Psychologist, 39,* 93-104.

Hayes, J. R., & Flower, L. (1980). The dynamics of composing: Making plans and juggling constraints. In L. W. Gregg & E. R. Steinberg (Eds.), *Cognitive processes in writing* (pp. 31-50). Hillsdale, NJ: Erlbaum.

Johnson, P. E., Duran, A.S., Hassebrock, F., Moller, J., Prietula, M., Feltovich, P. J., & Swanson, D. B. (1981). Expertise and error in diagnostic reasoning. *Cognitive Science, 5,* 235-283.

Kaput, J.J. (1987). Representation systems and mathematics. In C. Janvier (Ed.), *Problems of representation in the teaching and learning of mathematics* (pp. 19-26). Hillsdale, NJ: Erlbaum.

Kieren, T.E. (1976). Perspectives on rational numbers. In R.A. Lesh & D.A. Bradbard (Eds.), *Number and measurement* (pp. 101-144). Columbus, OH: ERIC/SMEAC.

Leinhardt, G. (1987). The development of an expert explanation: An analysis of a sequence of subtraction lessons. *Cognition and Instruction, 4*(4), 225-282.

Leinhardt, G. (1988). Expertise in instructional lessons: An example from fractions. In D. A. Grouws & R. J. Cooney (Eds.), *Perspectives on research on effective mathematics teaching* (Vol.1 in a series of monographs from conferences of the National Council of Teachers of Mathematics, pp. 47-66). Hillsdale, NJ: Erlbaum.

Leinhardt, G., Stein, M., & Baxter, J. (1988, April). *What a difference a class makes.* Paper presented at the annual meeting of the American Educational Research Association, New Orlean, LA.

Leinhardt, G. (1989). Math lessons: A contrast of novice and expert competence. *Journal for Research in Mathematics Education, 20*(1), 52-75.

Leinhardt, G., & Greeno, J. G. (1986). The cognitive skill of teaching. *Journal of Educational Psychology, 78*(2), 75-95.

Leinhardt, G., & Odoroff, E. (1988). *Instructional Explanations Project year end report to the McDonnell Foundation.* Unpublished manuscript. University of Pittsburgh, Learning Research and Development Center, Pittsburgh, PA.

Leinhardt, G., & Putnam, R.T. (1987). The skill of learning from classroom lessons. *American Educational Research Journal, 24*(4), 557-587.

Leinhardt, G., & Smith, D.A. (1985). Expertise in mathematics instruction: Subject matter knowledge. *Journal of Educational Psychology, 77*(3), 247-271.

Lesgold, A., Glaser, R., Feltovich, R., & Wang, Y. (1981, April). *Radiological expertise.* Paper presented at the annual meeting of the American Educational Research Association, Los Angeles.

Ohlsson, S. (1987). Sense and reference in the design of interactive illustrations for rational numbers. In R. Lawler & M. Yazdani (Eds.), *Artificial intelligence and education* (Vol. 1, pp. 307-344). Norwood, NJ: Ablex.

Pople, H. E. (1982). Heuristic methods for imposing structure on ill-structured problems: The structuring of medical diagnostics. In P. Szolovits (Ed.), *Artificial intelligence in medicine* (pp.119-185). Boulder, CO: Westview.

Putnam, R. T. (1985). Teacher thoughts and actions in live and simulated tutoring of addition. (Doctoral dissertation, Stanford University, 1985.) *Dissertation Abstracts International, 46,* 933A-934A.

Putnam, R. T. (1987a). *Spencer fellowship project description: Expert teaching of mathematics for understanding.* Unpublished proposal to the National Academy of Education.

Putnam, R. T. (1987b). Structuring and adjusting content for students: A study of live and simulated tutoring of addition. *American Educational Research Journal, 24*(1), 13-28.

Putnam, R. T., Lampert, M., & Peterson, P. L. (1990). Alternative perspectives on knowing mathematics in elementary schools. In C. Cazden (Ed.,), *Review of research in education* (Vol. 16, pp. 57-150). Washington, DC: American Educational Research Association.

Putnam, R. T., & Leinhardt, G. (1986, April). *Curriculum scripts and adjustment of content in mathematics lessons.* Paper presented at the annual meeting of the American Educational Research Association, San Francisco.

Resnick, L.B. (1987). Learning in school and out. *Educational Researcher, 16*(9), 13-20.

Sacerdoti, E. D. (1977). *A structure for plans and behavior.* New York: Elsevier-North Holland.

Schank, R. C., & Abelson, R. P. (1977). *Scripts, plans, goals and understanding: An inquiry into human knowledge structures.* Hillsdale, NJ: Erlbaum.

Schoenfeld, A.S. (1985). *Mathematical problem solving.* New York: Academic.

Schoenfeld, A.S. (1986). On having and using geometric knowledge. In J. Hiebert (Ed.), *Conceptual and procedural knowledge: The case of mathematics* (pp. 225-264). Hillsdale, NJ: Erlbaum.

Stein, M. K., Baxter, J. A., & Leinhardt, G. (1990). Subject-matter knowledge and elementary instruction: A case from functions and graphing. *American Educational Research Journal, 27,* 639-663.

Wilkins, D. (1980). Patterns and plans in chess. *Artificial Intelligence, 14,* 165-203.

SUBJECT-MATTER KNOWLEDGE
AND SCIENCE TEACHING:
A PRAGMATIC PERSPECTIVE

William S. Carlsen

American educational researchers have put out an All-Points Bulletin for the "missing paradigm" in research on teaching: subject matter. Where is the school subject matter in studies of teacher planning, instruction, and evaluation? The call to search for the missing paradigm was first broadcast at the 1985 meeting of the American Educational Research Association (see Shulman, 1986), but the historical record of research on teacher thinking and the subjects taught in schools indicates that a search actually began earlier (e.g., Buchmann, 1984; Elbaz, 1983; Leinhardt & Greeno, 1986).

As evidenced by the chapters in this book, the quest for the missing paradigm is beginning to locate the subject matter of teaching, but so far, no one has called off the search. There are good reasons to continue it. For example, we recognize that the interplay between teacher subject-matter knowledge and teaching practice is dynamic and complex. Understanding the effects of subject-matter knowledge on the act of teaching and the act of teaching on teacher

Advances in Research on Teaching, Volume 2, pages 115-143.
Copyright © 1991 by JAI Press Inc.
All rights of reproduction in any form reserved.
ISBN: 1-55938-034-9

subject-matter knowledge are challenging tasks that will require careful, and probably longitudinal, study (Shulman, Sykes, & Phillips, 1983).

Some of the logistical problems in mounting a search for subject matter in teaching are especially troublesome for researchers of science education. Three of these problems will be discussed in this chapter. These three problems concern distinguishing science from other subject matters and describing it in ways that are meaningful to science educators. In discussing the three problems, I will review research concerned with teaching and science subject-matter knowledge, describe some models that have been proposed to describe science knowledge, and propose a model of subject-matter knowledge which draws on work in psychology, philosophy and linguistics. According to this model, science teachers hold multiple views of scientific concepts, and, in their teaching, choose representations based on their understanding of the context of instruction. Just as speakers use and make sense of language in context-specific ways—the focus of semiotic pragmatics—teachers and other users of scientific knowledge think and talk about science in context-specific ways.

PROBLEM ONE: THERE ARE A NUMBER OF SUBJECT MATTERS MISSING

The first logistical challenge in the search for the missing paradigm is that there are not one, but several subject matters missing from research on teaching: science, social studies, English, art, physical education, and so on. Furthermore, some of these subject matters can be subdivided: science at the secondary level often includes biology, earth and space science, chemistry and physics. To stretch the search analogy, we are not out looking for a missing person; we're looking for an entire Scout troop, and we are not too sure how many Scouts there are. To make things worse, the Scouts are all doing different things: one may be near the pond watching frogs; another may have wandered into town to visit city hall. We need to locate an undetermined number of missing subject matters, each with its own concerns, each warranting a different search strategy. It is unlikely that techniques that reveal teacher cognitions about teaching writing will be helpful in studying teacher cognitions about laboratory science.

Questions concerning the nature and number of subject matters have been debated for centuries, and some of the most influential recent participants in the debate have had special interests in the sciences. I want to avoid entering the probably irresolvable debate about the number of subject matters, but will attempt to point out some of the important epistemological arguments which underlie that debate. Defining subject-matter knowledge is predicated on understanding what a subject matter is.

In his often-quoted paper, "Structure of the disciplines: Meanings and significances," Joseph Schwab (1964) argued that two types of knowledge structures distinguish the disciplines from one another. *Substantive structures* are the conceptual tools, models, and principles that guide inquiry in a discipline. Like Kuhn (1970), Schwab recognized that substantive structures are human constructs: they are created by human inquiry, not truths which "emerge from data." Substantive structures guide inquiry conceptually. A second aspect of knowledge, its syntax, guides inquiry methodologically. *Syntactical structures*, in Schwab's formulation, include a discipline's canons of evidence and proof, and rules concerning how they are applied.

To Schwab, unique combinations of substantive and syntactical structures served both to define the sciences as unique disciplines and to describe the knowledge of scientists. Although Schwab was primarily concerned with the definition of disciplines, he used the word "knowledge" interchangeably in referring to the structure of the discipline in the scientific community and in the mind of an individual person.

Since Schwab, many authors have chosen to distinguish between disciplinary knowledge and the knowledge of individuals. West, Fensham, and Garrard (1985), for example, speak of "public knowledge" and "private understandings." *Public knowledge* of science is comparatively static and visible. Examples of public knowledge include propositions, images, and algorithms published in textbooks and scientific papers. *Private understandings* are comparatively dynamic and idiosyncratic. Whereas public knowledge is a function of the community practice of science and teaching, private understandings are a function of the cognitive structures of individuals. The public knowledge represented in a high school physics class is the same for all students, yet each student in the class develops his or her own private understandings.

In studying the cognitive structures of students in a chemistry course, West et al. (1985) compared propositional representations (or "skeletons") of public knowledge (gleaned from lectures, handouts, and other materials) with representations of students' science understanding. Their research suggests that it may be possible to represent public knowledge and private understandings with a common grammar, and thereby simplify the task of describing how one is transformed into the other.

Representation using a common grammar had a cost, however. By transforming a lecturer's words into propositional representations, West et al. captured some features of the substantive and syntactic content of public knowledge. The context of those words, however, was irretrievably lost. For example, what was studied before this lesson? How credible as a scientist was the instructor to the students? Did the instructor communicate only dry facts, or did affect creep into his voice (skepticism, enthusiasm, passion, or dismay)? The answers to each of these questions have repercussions for the formation of private understandings in students, by affecting the context of public knowledge. Propositional representation of the scientific concepts (substantive structures) and reasons (syntactic structures) in a lesson provides an incomplete picture of the subject matter, both from the perspective of the discipline and from the perspective of the learner.

There are ways of representing science knowledge which go beyond the substantive and syntactic dimensions. For example, Posner, Strike, Hewson, and Gertzog (1982), in a study of conceptual change learning, defined seven dimensions of an individual's cognitive resources or "conceptual ecology." These include anomalies, analogies and metaphors, exemplars and images, past experiences, epistemological commitments, metaphysical beliefs and concepts, and other related knowledge. One advantage of this formulation over many other representations of cognitive structure is that it broadens the definition of an individual's knowledge base to include, for example, past history and general views about the character of knowledge. Although Posner et al. (1982) restricted their use of this explanatory framework to describing an individual's knowledge, one might utilize a similar template to describe the subject matter of a discipline or a lesson.

These three models of science knowledge differ in orientation and complexity. Schwab (1964) was primarily concerned with distinguishing between the conceptual and methodological features of a discipline. West et al. (1985) added the important distinction between public knowledge and private understandings. Posner et al. (1982) focused on describing the many features of an individual's conceptual structure. The three models also vary in scope: Schwab was chiefly concerned with the structure of subject matter in the scientific community; Posner and his colleagues were chiefly concerned with describing the knowledge of the individual person. Of the three models, only West's was explicitly concerned with mapping knowledge between science as discipline and science as an individual's knowledge base.

A framework for describing the subject matter of science might combine the best features of each of the three perspectives. This framework should make clear what a subject matter is: what makes science distinct from mathematics, and what makes physics distinct from chemistry. This function—clearly one of Schwab's primary concerns—would be useful in guiding decision-making about science curricula and teacher education.

A framework for describing the subject matter of science should also facilitate mapping between the structures of the scientific disciplines and the knowledge of individuals. Such mapping is what occurs when a person's knowledge is tested. The recent growth of interest in teacher testing (e.g., Haney, Madaus, & Kreitzer, 1988) does not follow the development of a well-defined research base relating the important features of subject matters and the cognitions of teachers. Consequently, researchers trying to develop subject-matter specific assessment technologies must simultaneously work to develop testing methods and conduct research relating the subject-matters to the knowledge of teachers (e.g., Shulman & Sykes, 1986).

Unfortunately, the task of relating disciplinary knowledge to an individual's cognitive structure is fraught with philosophical problems. Phillips (1987) pointed out two of these. First, disciplinary structure and cognitive structure are not the same thing. If learning a discipline were simply the process of internalizing disciplinary knowledge, we would have no need to speak of cognitive structure! There may be very little match between the field of chemistry and the organization of knowledge in the mind of an expert chemistry teacher, and therefore little need for conceptualizations which use a common language. Furthermore, it may be impossible, using current methods, to determine what an individual's cognitive structures are. Phillips exemplified this second point by posing a thought problem: if a student of Russian provides a coherent Russian response to a question delivered in that language, can one infer that she is *thinking* in Russian? Phillips' answer was "no"; one can infer very little about unobservable cognitive structures from a person's behavior. A model for relating disciplinary and teacher knowledge about science will have to address concerns like these.

A model of subject-matter knowledge will have to strike a balance between conciseness and scope. Before attempting to apply frameworks like conceptual ecology to new domains, one needs to acknowledge that each new domain may make the model more complex. The problem of ballooning complexity is troublesome because science teaching is concerned with more than two locations for knowledge. Gilbert, Watts, & Osborne (1985), for example, note that science education deals with five domains of science: scientists' science, teachers' science, curricular science, students' science, and children's science. Each of these distinct domains may require its own description. Even if such descriptions can be limited to the seven features used by Posner et al. (and these features are far from exhaustive when one considers instructional context), the sheer weight of conceptual categories—to say nothing of the details described therein—will become ponderous.

Solving the first logistical problem in locating the missing subject matter in research on teaching—the fact that there are many subject matters missing—will require more than simply distinguishing between social studies and science, or between biology and physics. A distinction must also be made between the different versions of the subject matters which exist in the discipline-at-large and in the cognitions of teachers. To do this, researchers of teaching will need models of subject matter that both acknowledge the unique knowledge structures of the disciplines and also facilitate the process of mapping between the different places subject-matter knowledge exists. The development of such a model in science is complicated, however, by a second logistical problem: the missing subject matter is on the move.

PROBLEM 2: SCIENCE MOVES

The second logistical problem in the search for subject matter in research on teaching is one which is especially troublesome for the subject matter of science. In four important ways, science is a discipline characterized by movement. Three of these prompt periodic revision of the secondary science curriculum. The fourth aspect of movement in science concerns the ways concepts are altered in the scientific community and in the minds of students and teachers. In our search for the subject matter of science in teaching, movement presents a logistical problem: the subject matter is sometimes difficult to find because it refuses to stay in one place.

The first way in which science moves is common to all disciplines. Like the other subject matters, the important concepts and methods of scientific inquiry change with time. Scientific research today is more likely to center on invisible subatomic particles than on invisible phlogiston. As the subject matters of science change, so too does the nature of secondary education and the knowledge that teachers need.

Second, science moves because it is a "growth" subject matter, both in society and in the schools. Evidence for this claim can be seen in large governmental outlays for research in science and in recent increased science requirements for secondary school graduation. Our society invests a great deal of its material and intellectual resources in science and expects much in return. As Mayr (1982) points out, the return in recent years has included an exponential increase in the published output of scientific research programs; it is now difficult for scientists to keep up-to-date in their fields. The task for science teachers, whose subject matters are much broader, is even more challenging.

A third aspect of movement in science concerns the scope of science education. In recent years some educators have called for broadening science education to include topics such as the relationship between science, technology, and society (Hofstein & Yager, 1982; Hurd, 1975). America's leading science teachers' organization now requires study of these issues for its voluntary science teacher certification program (National Science Teachers Association, 1984); some state curriculum guides show a similar reorientation (e.g., California State Department of Education, 1984).

A fourth aspect of movement in the subject matter of science is found in contemporary philosophy and psychology: the history of science and the learning of science can be characterized as a process of conceptual change. This process has been described for entire scientific disciplines (Kuhn, 1970) and scientific research programs (Lakatos, 1970). It has also been a powerful idea in describing the growth of science knowledge in students (Champagne, Gunstone & Klopfer, 1985; Hewson & Hewson, 1983; Novak, 1987) and teachers (Roth, 1987). In fact, it has been argued that the process of conceptual change is the single most important feature distinguishing science learning from other types of learning (Wittrock, 1985).

Although science education may not have an exclusive claim to conceptual change as a powerful explanatory structure (cf., Confrey, 1981), science education has been the origin to date of much of the most important work in conceptual change research (see West & Pines, 1985). Furthermore, several researchers currently investigating science teacher knowledge begin with a conceptual change orientation (Hashweh, 1985; Roth, 1987; Smith & Neale, 1987). Before turning to the third and last logistical problem in the search for the missing paradigm, I will review some of the lessons and challenges of conceptual change research on teacher knowledge. How can a conceptual change perspective help us to interpret research on teaching and teacher knowledge about science? What are the limitations of this perspective?

Conceptual Change

Science learning can be viewed as a process in which an individual integrates new knowledge about science into an existing cognitive structure. Two types of such integration have been described (Posner, Strike, Hewson, & Gertzog, 1982); they correspond roughly with Kuhn's (1970) descriptions of normal and revolutionary progress in scientific disciplines. *Assimilation* (the analogue to "normal science") occurs when students are able to incorporate new knowledge into their old knowledge using existing concepts. A second form of cognitive change, *accommodation* (the analogue to Kuhn's "revolutionary science"), occurs when students are unable to incorporate new knowledge into old cognitive structures, and are forced to replace or reorganize old beliefs.

Most conceptual change research to date has focused on the more radical of these two types of change: accommodation. Researchers studying accommodation in science education have noted two interesting phenomena that have implications for our current discussion. First, accommodation is not an easy process to stimulate in learners. Aristotelian views of science, for example, characteristic of students who have never studied physics, persist even in students who have studied college physics (Chi, Feltovich, & Glaser, 1981). Second, even when accommodation has apparently occurred, if the surface features of a problem are changed, students will often return to their original (scientifically inaccurate) conceptions (Viennot, 1979). Rather than replace a faulty conception, they may compartmentalize their understanding. Students may even go as far as to argue that different explanations for the same phenomena apply in and out of the classroom.

Posner et al. (1982) have proposed a general theory of accommodation which may explain the first of these two phenomena. According to that theory, accommodation only occurs when a learner is dissatisfied with existing conceptions, has a preliminary understanding of a new conception, recognizes that the new conception is plausible, and is convinced that the new conception will have explanatory power with future problems. If correct, this theory of accommodation can be used to explain the reluctance of learners to adopt a new conception: for example, they may be satisfied with their old (scientifically inaccurate) conception or they may fail to grasp the power of a new idea in explaining other problems. The general theory of accommodation, however, does not explain the compartmentalization phenomenon. How is it that a learner is able to demonstrate commitment to a new conception in one context but not in another?

Conceptual Change and Science Teacher Subject-Matter Knowledge

Some evidence for the two phenomena described above—reluctance to adopt a new conception and sporadic use of an accommodated conception—can be seen in research reported in this volume in the chapters by Smith and Neale, and by Hollon, Roth, and Anderson. Elsewhere, Roth (1987) reported other details about the latter research program which are salient to this discussion. Thirteen experienced junior-high life science teachers were introduced to conceptual change strategies for teaching science, and a series of observations and interviews focused on their teaching of three instructional units. The study was designed to investigate how teacher knowledge about science influenced acquisition of conceptual change teaching strategies. In effect, it was a conceptual change study about conceptual change teaching.

Some of the teachers in Roth's sample were unwilling to adopt the new instructional strategies. Like learners in other settings, they were reluctant to integrate a new conception with their old models of instruction. Roth (1987, p. 9) called this group "fact acquisition" teachers:

> They viewed science learning per se as less central and placed more emphasis on issues of motivation, management, and students' personal development. Their teaching exposed students to information or facts as defined by the textbook or district science curriculum. They did not treat the monitoring of students' scientific understanding as central to their role as teachers; thus, they knew less than the other teachers about their students' thinking and misconceptions. *These teachers also tended to have a less rich understanding of science and the topics being taught. Most of them were reassigned teachers with college majors other than science.* Because of their lack of knowledge about their students' ways of learning and understanding and because of weaknesses in their subject matter knowledge, these teachers had a difficult time making sense of conceptual change ideas and using them in effective ways (emphasis added).

The experiences of the "fact acquisition" group can be explained using models of subject-matter knowledge discussed thus far. Having had little formal education in the sciences, these teachers had, relative to other teachers in the study, inadequate knowledge about the substantive and syntactic structures of biology. Deficiencies in their understandings of science and their understandings of their students' preconceptions about science characterized their conceptual ecologies. The necessary preconditions for conceptual change did not exist for these teachers.

Roth described two other groups of teachers in her study. In contrast to the fact acquisition group, the "conceptual development" teachers "were very receptive to the training sessions and to the experimental materials, and they were often successful in using the suggested conceptual change strategies" (Roth, 1987, p. 9). Apparently, this group underwent the process of accommodation easily. As with the first group, conceptual change theory seems adequate to explain the second group's adoption of conceptual change teaching strategies.

Roth focused most of her analysis on a third group: "content understanding" teachers. This group consisted of teachers who were knowledgeable about science and students, but had trouble using conceptual change strategies. In a detailed analysis of two of these teachers, Roth (1987, p. 10) noted:

> They had the topic specific knowledge about the content and about their students' misconceptions that we felt was necessary for effective conceptual change teaching. And these teachers introduced into their teaching a fairly frequent use of the conceptual change teaching strategies recommended to them in either training workshops or in the curriculum materials we supplied. However, student learning in these classrooms was not as high as expected . . . Analysis of the interactions between the teachers' knowledge and how they actually taught the three units revealed that both teachers were using the conceptual change teaching strategies in unintended ways. Their use of the strategy is best described as an "empty" use, because it did not engage students in making sense and constructing meaning of the concepts.

Roth pointed out that for these teachers, knowledge about the subject matter of science and familiarity with students' common scientific misconceptions were necessary but insufficient to change their conceptions about science teaching. She concluded that in addition to having knowledge about science and misconceptions, teachers need to be convinced that students will not learn the subject matter unless they can overcome their misconceptions. Her analysis is generally consistent with conceptual change theory. The "content understanding" teachers may have been satisfied with their old conceptions of science teaching, and hence unwilling to change them.

An alternative explanation is possible, however. Roth noted that the content understanding teachers were inconsistent in their use of conceptual change teaching strategies. One teacher, for example, began a unit on respiration by "brainstorming" to elicit student conceptions with a series of questions in everyday language: "Why do we eat? Why do we need food? Why do we breathe?" (Roth, 1987, p. 24). Following that activity, however, she led the students laboriously through an explanation of respiration which was devoid of the everyday language used in the brainstorming activity. Although the first part of the lesson was a model of conceptual change teaching, the second part was a fact-centered exposition.

Intermittent use of intended teaching strategies by the content understanding group in Roth's study is similar to intermittent use of science conceptions by science students. Why would a teacher who "put a great deal of thought and effort into incorporating conceptual change teaching into her lessons" switch back and forth between an intended teaching strategy and an older strategy, despite a good understanding of student misconceptions and training in using conceptual change teaching? (Roth, 1987, p. 21). Possibly, teachers like this know the *concepts* and *strategies* of conceptual change teaching. What they are unable to do is to integrate the two in the context of a particular set of student misconceptions and a particular subject matter. In effect, they have a new conception, but their knowledge is compartmentalized. Sometimes their teaching appears to be guided by the new conception. At other times, they rely on a previous conception of teaching. An all-or-nothing view of the process of accommodation is unable to account for this phenomenon.

A recent dissertation by Hashweh (1985; see also Hashweh, 1987) complements Roth's study in many ways. Hashweh conducted a series of clinical interviews with three experienced physics teachers and three experienced biology teachers in an effort to define subject-matter knowledge and explore its implications in teaching science. Using these interviews, which included free recall tasks, concept-mapping tasks, unit planning, and simulated teaching, Hashweh identified four relatively independent dimensions of subject-matter knowledge related to specific topics (simple machines and photosynthesis). These included: (1) knowledge of details about the topic, (2) knowledge about other topics in the discipline (simple concepts, principles, and relations), (3) knowledge about the discipline's important higher-order principles or conceptual schemes, and (4) knowledge of instructional approaches for relating the topic to other topics, concepts, principles, and conceptual schemes.

Hashweh's design analyzed teacher subject-matter knowledge and its effects on simulated planning, teaching, and evaluation. The teachers were given two sets of tasks, one on a topic that they had often taught and one on a topic that they had rarely, if ever, taught. For example, the physics teachers each planned one instructional unit in physics and one in biology. Consequently, Hashweh's principal comparisons were within-subject. He identified a number of effects of subject-matter knowledge, summarized below.

Planning for Instruction

Each of Hashweh's teachers was provided with textbooks to use in the instructional planning tasks. In doing their planning, knowledgeable teachers were more likely to add related concepts and delete unrelated concepts from the information in these textbooks. Knowledgeable teachers extensively modified activities included in the textbook; unknowledgeable teachers made few modifications. Both groups of teachers planned a variety of methods for representing subject-matter knowledge to students, but unknowledgeable teachers' representations reflected a greater number of teacher misunderstandings about the topic. Similar findings regarding the relationship between teacher knowledge and use of curriculum materials have been reported by Lantz and Kass (1987).

Simulated Teaching

Hashweh simulated one aspect of teaching using critical incidents: instructional vignettes that presented the teacher with a student insight, question or other problem. He noted a knowledge effect in teacher responses: "Knowledgeable teachers were more likely to detect student preconceptions, to exploit opportunities for fruitful 'digressions,' to deal effectively with general class difficulties, and to interpret correctly students' insightful comments" (Hashweh, 1985, p. 246) Some of the unknowledgeable teachers even went as far as reinforcing student misconceptions.

Planning for Evaluation

Hashweh asked the teachers to plan questions that could be used to assess student understanding after instruction. The teachers produced questions that tended to reflect their own misunderstandings about the topic. In addition, questions asked by the unknowledgeable teachers emphasized recall of facts contained in the textbook; questions asked by the knowledgeable teachers required supplemental knowledge (added by the teacher during instructional planning) or synthesis of concepts in the textbook. These findings are similar to those of Dobey and Schafer (1984).

An important contribution of Hashweh's (1985, pp. 297-298) work was his suggestion that the notion of subject-matter knowledge should be broadened to include an instructional dimension:

> The findings . . . indicate that as a result of planning, teaching, and reflection on planning and teaching, experienced teachers develop a category of topic-specific knowledge which we called subject-matter pedagogical knowledge. The category consists of a repertoire of approaches to "how to teach" the topic. It includes the possible levels of treatment of the topic, the prerequisite knowledge needed for understanding the topic, the specific knowledge that the students usually bring to the topic, the difficulties students have with the topic and how to deal with them, the lesson type or types that can be used in teaching the topic, the representations and other "tools" that can be used in teaching it, and the utility of the topic.

Hashweh's description of topic-specific subject-matter pedagogical knowledge complements Roth's (1987) analysis by suggesting that in addition to knowledge about science and knowledge about teaching, experienced science teachers may have a well-developed knowledge base which integrates the two. Biology pedagogical knowledge, for example, might include knowledge about common student misconceptions about photosynthesis and possible alternative ways of describing the process of photosynthesis.

Hashweh noted that it was possible for a teacher to be knowledgeable on one of the four dimensions (e.g., topic details) but not on others, and that this was reflected in teaching performance:

> It is not expected that teachers with a few courses in the discipline can develop such rich knowledge on each of the four dimensions. Most of the teachers in the present study had taken a few courses in the discipline which were not within their area of expertise. Yet their knowledge of that discipline proved to be quite poor. It is also not expected that teachers develop this knowledge just through teaching. One of the biology teachers, for example, had taught general science for a few years. He had rich knowledge on only one dimension: topic details. This knowledge alone was not adequate for effective planning and teaching . . . Knowledge of other discipline entities, of conceptual schemes and approaches, results from a strong disciplinary background. It was found that that knowledge was essential for adequate understanding of a topic and for adequate planning . . . and teaching. The implications for teacher education are clear: a strong background in the subject matter is needed for teaching at the secondary school level (Hashweh, 1985, pp. 305-306).

Although Hashweh suggested that subject-matter pedagogical knowledge includes rules that enable teachers to match specific student misconceptions with appropriate instructional strategies, his analysis did not probe this aspect of teaching in detail. Furthermore, although his study detailed some interesting findings concerning conceptual change teaching, Hashweh was unable to relate conceptual change strategies to subject-matter knowledge.[1] Consequently, some questions were left unanswered concerning the ways teachers match subject-matter concepts and teaching strategies in specific instructional settings.

The studies by Roth and Hashweh illustrate the problematic nature of "movement" in conceptual change teaching. The process of conceptual change involves movement from one conception to another. As Roth pointed out, successful teaching in this fashion requires that the nature of instruction—the particular teaching strategies that a science educator uses—must be tailored to the specifics of students' prior conceptions. It is not sufficient to assess students' preinstructional conceptions, teach by "telling," and then reassess student conceptions. This constitutes an "empty" use of the method, and is unlikely to produce the desired results.

Hashweh's study proposed a model of subject-matter knowledge which included information about students' prior conceptions and strategies for teaching the same scientific content in different ways. Furthermore, Hashweh suggested that this integrated knowledge of subject matter and pedagogy matches students' preinstructional conceptions with teaching strategies. However, a key part of the model was left undescribed. How does this matching occur? Are we to infer that a given preconception maps onto one and only one remedial teaching strategy? Clearly not: like Roth, Hashweh noted that teachers' conceptions of the learner influenced their instructional decisions. It is not clear, however, what additional dimensions of a teaching event affect a teacher's choice of instructional strategy for any given student conception. Consequently, we are faced with the same dilemma we encountered earlier in reviewing substantive and syntactic knowledge structures: do the terms "concept" and "teaching strategy" have universal meaning independent of a particular instructional context? If so, "movement" in conceptual change teaching becomes simply a process of matching student conception to teaching strategy, and educating science teachers for conceptual change teaching could be reducible to looking things up in a handbook.

If, on the other hand, the process of matching student concepts to teaching strategies is more complex and context-dependent than a one-to-one mapping, we will require a model of subject-matter knowledge that is more powerful than those we have heretofore considered. Developing such a model is the third and last logistical problem in the search for the subject-matter of science in teaching.

PROBLEM 3: DESCRIBING THE SUBJECT-MATTER KNOWLEDGE OF SCIENCE TEACHERS

A search is most likely to succeed if those who are searching have a good description of the thing that is missing. One of the problems that has accompanied research on the relationship between science teacher subject-matter knowledge and teaching has been an inadequate model of science subject-matter knowledge. Consequently, the meager research literature on the subject contains perplexing inconsistencies.[2]

For example, a meta-analysis of research on science education by Druva and Anderson (1983) disclosed a pattern of positive (although weak) correlations between teacher subject-matter knowledge and student outcomes (science achievement, science process skills and affect toward science) and between teacher subject-matter knowledge and a set of "effective" teaching behaviors. In contrast, a study by Lederman (Lederman & Druger, 1985; Lederman & Zeidler, 1987) on science teachers' understandings of the nature of scientific knowledge disclosed no relationship between teacher understanding and teaching behaviors, nor between teacher understanding and student understanding of the nature of scientific knowledge (a relationship was found, however, between certain teacher *behaviors* and student outcomes). In some ways, the two studies contradict each other. Druva and Anderson (1983) suggested that teaching effectiveness and teaching behaviors are related to teacher knowledge about science. Lederman's study suggested that the effects of teacher knowledge on science teaching may be overstated.[3] Research using a well-defined model of subject-matter knowledge might resolve some of these inconsistencies.

A conceptual framework for describing teacher subject-matter knowledge proposed by Grossman, Wilson, and Shulman (1989) addresses some of the concerns I have raised in this chapter. In describing the subject-matter knowledge of beginning teachers, the authors propose four categories of knowledge: *substantive knowledge, syntactic knowledge, content knowledge, and beliefs about the subject matter.* The first two categories are similar to those defined by Schwab (1964), although Grossman et al. (1989, p. 27) use content knowledge to describe "factual information, organizing principles [and] central concepts," and restrict the meaning of substantive knowledge to "the explanatory frameworks or paradigms that are used both to guide inquiry in the field and to make sense of data" (p. 29). The authors retain Schwab's definition of syntactic knowledge (canons of evidence used to guide inquiry), and add beliefs about the subject matter, which are characterized by their affective and disputable nature.

Although the 4-part framework proposed by Grossman, Wilson, and Shulman has the virtue of flexibility (the authors developed it while studying teacher knowledge in a number of subject matters), two factors lead me to reject it as a model of subject-matter knowledge in science. First, as Phillips (1987) has pointed out, in science it is often difficult to clearly distinguish between substantive and syntactic knowledge structures. As an example in astronomy, Phillips cites "red shift." As a rule, light arriving from distant stars tends to appear redder than light arriving from nearby stars. This phenomenon is attributed to the Doppler effect: the wavelength of light from distant stars is increased due to the rapid movement of these stars away from us on earth. Red shift is both an important concept in physics and an important scientific tool. Its existence prompted the development of theories about an expanding universe, helped to validate Einstein's general theory of relativity, and provided a method for measuring distances between stars (Hubble's law). Red shift, like many other scientific ideas, has both substantive and syntactic merit. This substantive/syntactic fuzziness does not make Schwab's distinction obsolete— it is often very easy to distinguish between substantive and syntactic structures—but it does suggest a test to apply to proposed additions to Schwab's model. How much overlap exists between "different" categories of knowledge?

In the specific case of the subject matters of science, both of the categories added by Grossman et al. overlap considerably with Schwab's categories. For example, the authors use knowledge "about theories of evolution and heredity" as examples of content knowledge (Grossman et al., 1989, p. 27), yet these could also serve as good examples of substantive structures in biology. Similarly, "beliefs about the subject-matter" overlap with Schwab's syntactic dimension; the writings of Kuhn (1970), Lakatos (1970), and Toulmin (1972) suggest that scientists often make judgments using evidence which is affective and disputable.

My second reason for not adopting the 4-part framework relates to the view that science education is a process of conceptual change. A comprehensive model of subject-matter knowledge should be consistent with research on conceptual change in science students and science teachers. For example, the model should be able to account for the compartmentalization phenomenon described earlier, where an individual is able to know something in more than one way (i.e., to rely on Newtonian explanations in the physics classroom and Aristotelian explanations outside the classroom).

Although categorical taxonomies of knowledge (ones in which categories are mutually exclusive) are useful in describing knowledge in a static fashion, they are inconsistent with a conceptual change view of science. In describing the subject-matter knowledge of a science teacher, we are interested in more than the organization of scientific concepts and principles in the teacher's mind. We are also interested in that teacher's *ability to understand the subject matter in different ways,* depending on the situation. Teaching is more than simply presenting substantive and syntactic knowledge to students. It requires skill in matching concepts and explanations with instructional setting. To accomplish this matching, the teacher may have to switch back and forth between alternative conceptions of the subject matter: the students' conceptions, the textbook's conception, the disciplinary (or scientist's) conception, and so on (cf. Gilbert et al.'s [1985] five types of science).

Sometimes, teaching science may be a matter of reconciling alternative views, an assimilatory process. At other times, teaching science may require leading students to reject their conceptions. In either case, the teacher must be able to know the subject matter in different ways. It is not enough to acknowledge that different views exist. Using conceptual change arguments in teaching requires understanding and beginning with the learner's prior conceptions. For example, while teaching an introductory lesson on genetics, I recently asked a high school biology class to name a human characteristic which is inherited. One student suggested "AIDS." With further probing, it became clear that although his response was *genetically* incorrect, he possessed a model for infant acquisition of venereal disease that was scientifically sound: babies are sometimes infected as they move through the birth canal during childbirth. As the teacher, my unspoken initial evaluation of his answer ("incorrect") had to be modified. The instructional problem was not that this student incorrectly believed that AIDS is genetically transmitted, but that he was interpreting the term "inherit" in a non-genetic fashion (as in, "The girl inherited the property of her parents.").

For the teacher, identifying student conceptions and responding to them appropriately can be extremely difficult. How does one make public a student's private understanding and reconcile it with the curriculum, without confusing the 30 other students in the classroom, who may have other mental models of inheritance? Minimally, it must begin with a teacher who is knowledgeable enough to recognize the scientific merits of an unexpected student comment, flexible enough to shift between different views of the subject matter, and sufficiently skillful at managing discourse to encourage students to share their reasons as well as their answers.[4]

Finally, among the applicators of scientific knowledge, teachers are not alone in their need to understand science in contextually appropriate ways. If, on different occasions, a physician discussed measles with her child, a patient, a public health official, a medical school student, and a mathematician, variations in audience might lead her to "understand" measles as a problem of etiquette ("Cover your mouth when you sneeze."), diagnosis ("Have you ever had measles before?"), economics ("What is the current wholesale cost of the vaccine?"), immunity, even chaos.[5] Similarly, in talking about a bridge, an engineer might describe a physical structure, a sculpture, a traffic bottleneck, a resource for human migration, a financial commitment, or a set of mathematical equations, depending on his audience and the task at hand. The successful application of science in a social world appears to require flexibility in matching scientific knowledge with interactional context. Successful science teachers, physicians, and engineers monitor their settings and filter the public representations of their knowledge through an understanding of context. The goal of their talk may or may not be to teach (it may be to achieve better personal understanding of measles or to build a better bridge). When their goals are pedagogical, it may be useful to discuss "science-specific pedagogical knowledge." A model of science knowledge must recognize, however, that the process of matching scientific knowledge and context transcends pedagogy and appears in other types of human interaction.

A MODEL FOR DESCRIBING SCIENCE SUBJECT-MATTER KNOWLEDGE

Although Schwab's distinction between the substantive and syntactic structures of knowledge has proven useful for describing the knowledge of teachers (hence its appearance in much of the research discussed in this chapter), it cannot provide a comprehensive description. In teaching for conceptual change, the expert science teacher may need to juggle more than one set of conceptions about a topic simultaneously. For example, in guiding students to an understanding of photosynthesis, she may need to consider her students' prior conceptions (e.g., "plants get their food from their roots"), the textbook's description (e.g., "plants make their food from carbon dioxide and water using sunlight"), and a realistic student target conception (e.g., "plants make food using sunlight, water, air, and minerals"). Furthermore, the nature of the teaching setting determines the sophistication of the concepts and arguments the teacher must understand. Consequently, the *context* of instruction is a key dimension of the subject matter in the mind of the teacher. A physicist teaching mechanics to second graders must understand her subject in a different way than when she is teaching it to undergraduate physics majors. The concepts (substantive structures) and arguments (syntactic structures) she can use to induce conceptual change will vary between the two settings.

A simple modification to Schwab's (1964) description of the knowledge structures of a discipline addresses many of the problems outlined in this chapter. To the substantive and syntactic structures, I propose we add a third structure, the *pragmatic*. The term is borrowed from linguistic semiotics. Semiotics, the science of signs, was first outlined by the philosopher Charles Morris (1938), and contains three branches: semantics, syntactics, and pragmatics. Semantics can be roughly described as the study of words and their meanings, syntactics can be described as the study of the rules governing how words are combined to form sentences, and pragmatics can be described as the study of how users of a language make sense of words and sentences in a given context.

There are similarities between the categories of Morris (1938) and Schwab (1964). Semiotic semantics is concerned with words; Schwab's substantive structures are concerned with concepts. Semiotic syntactics is concerned with the rules governing how words are used in sentences; Schwab's syntactic structures concern how concepts are used in scientific inquiry. Finally, semiotic pragmatics is concerned with how people make sense of words and sentences in a given speech context; in studying subject-matter knowledge, the term "pragmatics" could be used to describe how people make sense of concepts and scientific arguments in a given context.

Obvious differences exist between semiotics and the study of science knowledge, and there are limits to the utility of a linguistic concept in our search for the missing paradigm in educational research. Nevertheless, the lessons of linguistic pragmatics suggest some possible resolutions to the logistical problems outlined in this chapter. These can be expressed as hypotheses for future research on science subject-matter knowledge:

1. The meaning of a scientific concept (a substantive structure) is context-dependent. To induce conceptual change, a teacher must be able to understand scientific concepts in context-appropriate ways. In explaining a concept, a teacher minimally needs to consider the following aspects of context: the learners, the school setting and the curriculum.

2. The form of a scientific argument (a syntactic structure) is context-dependent. There are no universal canons of evidence: understanding science in a way that permits conceptual change teaching means identifying canons of evidence that are appropriate to a given context.

3. Science as a subject matter for teaching is characterized by substance and syntax bound to particular contexts by people. These three components (substantive, syntactic, and pragmatic) are interrelated and mutually dependent—parts of a subject-matter ecology.

4. Teachers are concerned with many different types of science. Since each version of science is context-dependent (e.g., curricular science is dependent on the context of the textbook), representations of teacher subject-matter knowledge must include specification of the context of instruction.

5. Expertise in conceptual change teaching depends on a teacher's knowledge of the relationships between the substantive, syntactic, and pragmatic dimensions of the subject matter. This ability to match concepts, arguments and context constitutes subject-matter pedagogical knowledge. According to this hypothesis, the substantive knowledge of a teacher may include a number of alternative representations of a scientific concept. The teacher's capacity to choose a representation appropriate to a particular teaching situation is what characterizes subject-specific pedagogy.

In short, subject-matter pragmatics can be viewed as the study of how teachers and students make sense of the substantive and syntactic knowledge structures of science in specific settings. This view acknowledges that a teacher may hold multiple conceptions of a scientific concept. Some of these conceptions may be highly abstract and sophisticated, useful primarily as "private understandings." Others may be simplified to the point of being scientifically inaccurate, but may have instructional utility as temporary analogies in, for example, a long public explanation to students.

Understanding science knowledge from a pragmatic perspective dictates two lines of research. First, it requires the collection of baseline data in science classrooms on scientific concepts, scientific arguments, and instructional settings. These data come from a variety of sources and research perspectives. For example, Lemke (1982) has described many common communicative arrangements in science classrooms; his analysis provides a useful description of ways of describing the sociolinguistic context of science instruction.

A second line of research that a pragmatic perspective requires is study of the *interrelationships* between science content, argument, and context. This has been one goal of my research on discourse in the classrooms of secondary science teachers during the induction year to teaching. While supervising two groups of beginning teachers, I have monitored teacher planning, instruction, and evaluation as it relates to teacher subject-matter knowledge. This research underscores the strong three-way relationship between science teachers' knowledge of the substance, the syntax, and the context of instruction.

Specification of Context

No single, simple definition of context exists, even when analysis is restricted to a single research perspective. For example, Ochs (1979, p. 5) points out that sociolinguistic context "includes minimally, language users' beliefs and assumptions about temporal, spatial, and social settings; prior, ongoing, and future actions (verbal, non-verbal), and the state of knowledge and attentiveness of those participating in the social interaction in hand." Clearly, complete specification of such a broad view of context in a study of a teacher knowledge would be impossible. Consequently, the researcher of subject-matter pragmatics is faced with the difficult task of choosing an imperfect but serviceable definition of the context of instruction.

One way to deal with this problem is to collect and interpret data on science teaching using multiple definitions of context. For example, data analysis in my research is done at three different analytic levels. These levels are the long-term plans of teachers (the *curriculum* level), the interactive discourse in a science lesson (the *conversation* level), and the individual utterances in a lesson (the *speech act* level). When the unit of analysis is a teacher's *question* directed at a single student in lab (the speech act level), context includes a teacher and a student (and, perhaps, any other student within earshot). When the unit of analysis is a *lecture* on the human digestive system (the conversation level), context includes all potential and actual speech participants: minimally, the teacher and all students in the classroom. Finally, when the unit of analysis is a *unit plan* (the curriculum level), context includes individuals who may not even enter the classroom, such as a department chairperson who insists that all teachers use the same unit examinations.

The use of multiple, mutually inclusive definitions of context permits the researcher to study relationships between teacher knowledge and instructional context without committing to a single definition of context. In the absence of a well-integrated knowledge base on subject-matter pragmatics, this is an important advantage. Furthermore, multiple-level analysis provides a way of triangulating research findings: by asking related research questions at different levels of analysis, one is potentially better able to understand the generalizability of findings.

AN EXAMPLE OF PRAGMATIC RESEARCH ON TEACHER KNOWLEDGE

In two related studies, I have been documenting the effects of teacher subject-matter knowledge on discourse in biology teachers' classrooms (Carlsen, 1987,

1988). In the more recent of these two studies, analysis focused on a year's lesson plans (the curriculum level), transcripts of eight science lessons divided between teachers' high-knowledge topics and low-knowledge topics (the conversation level), and statistics on individual teacher and student utterances (the speech act level), for each of four beginning biology teachers. The primary contrasts in this study were within-teacher, examining individual differences in instruction on high-knowledge and low-knowledge topics while holding teacher, school, academic course, and student group constant.[6] Across these three levels, each using different units of analysis and definitions of context, a relationship was found between teacher subject-matter knowledge and classroom discourse. When the teachers understood well the topics they were teaching, their actions encouraged student questions and other student participation in discourse. When the teachers taught unfamiliar topics, they tended to discourage student participation in discourse. The precise *definitions* of context used in the study were important only insofar as they dictated appropriate research methods at each level of analysis.

Although the relationship between teacher knowledge and discourse was not sensitive to context-*definition*, it was sensitive to context. As predicted by a pragmatic perspective, the context of instruction and the representation of science in discourse were intimately related at each of the three levels: curriculum, conversation, and speech act. Some of these relationships are summarized below.

Curriculum Level

The four beginning teachers were more likely to use lectures and relatively open-ended laboratory activities to teach high-knowledge topics than to teach low-knowledge topics. When teaching low-knowledge topics, they tended to rely on instructional activities like seatwork and non-laboratory group projects.

This knowledge-related preference has two important consequences. First, because different activities represent the subject-matter of science in different ways, a teacher's choice of instructional method (e.g., to lecture rather than assign seatwork) affects public knowledge. Lectures and laboratory activities are, respectively, substantively dense and syntactically dense representations of science. These activities were most common when the teachers taught high-knowledge topics. In contrast, the activities chosen to teach unfamiliar topics focused less on the substantive and syntactic structures of the subject matter and focused more on issues like study skills, cooperative efforts, and student presentations to the class.

Second, choice of instructional activity has important consequences for student participation in classroom discourse. Whole-class instruction, which gives students the opportunity to raise questions publicly about science, was most common when the teachers were topic-knowledgeable. Laboratory activities were also associated with high teacher knowledge topics, and were characterized by high rates of student questioning. Most other classroom activities were characterized by low rates of student questioning and were most common when the teacher was unfamiliar with the subject matter.

In summary, analysis at the curriculum level suggested that when these four teachers were topic-knowledgeable, they were more likely to *create* an instructional context rich in the substance and syntax of science, and in which students were encouraged to participate in discourse. At the most inclusive level of analysis—curriculum—the substantive, syntactic, and pragmatic dimensions of teacher knowledge were closely related.

Conversation Level

Four high-knowledge lessons and four low-knowledge lessons were audiotaped for each of the four teachers. Discourse analysis revealed a number of knowledge-related features of teacher and student discourse; two seen in lectures and recitations are noted here. Like the examples at the curriculum level, these features concern representation of science in teacher talk and opportunities for student participation in discourse.

First, propositional analysis of teacher talk suggested that the teachers in the study: (a) said more per unit of time about high-knowledge science topics than about low-knowledge topics (as measured by the number of substantive propositions in high-knowledge and low-knowledge lessons); (b) tended to devote less time in high-knowledge lessons to anecdotes, stories, and announcements unrelated to the scientific substance of the lesson; (c) were more likely to talk about aspects of high-knowledge topics that were not discussed in the class's textbook; and d) linked discrete propositions into chains of evidence in high-knowledge lessons. In teaching unfamiliar topics to the same students, these same teachers tended to cover less substantive material, spend more time talking about things unrelated to the topic of the lesson, follow the propositional structure of the textbook, and present facts as discrete, unrelated propositions. In summary, there appeared to be a relationship between teachers' substantive understanding of the concepts of science, teachers' understanding of the syntactic or evidentiary links between those concepts, and teachers' portrayal of science as public knowledge.

A second feature of discourse seen at the conversational level concerned teacher encouragement of student talk. When teaching unfamiliar topics, these four teachers tended to discourage student participation. Discourse analysis of lectures by one teacher, Ms. Town, to the same group of students exemplified a number of knowledge-related differences. For example, after asking questions in a low-knowledge lecture, Ms. Town reacted with little affect to correct student responses, simply repeating the response or saying, "Okay." Never during the lecture did she allow a student to change the topic of class discourse.

On two occasions, students asked questions about the subject matter of the lesson, plant biology. Both times, Ms. Town promised to answer the question later in class, but never actually did.

In contrast, in a high-knowledge lecture on the skeletal system, Ms. Town encouraged student talk. She reacted enthusiastically to correct student answers, using words like "good," "great," and "fantastic." Several times, she allowed students to change the topic of discourse. She immediately and directly addressed student questions. For example, in response to a difficult question on the internal structure of compact bone, Ms. Town responded, "Good question," then spent four minutes answering it.

Differences at the conversational level were seen for each of the teachers in the study (some were also documented in an earlier study of six other science teachers; see Carlsen [1987]). They suggest that teacher knowledge affects not only the presentation of science as a set of concepts, but its syntax and its accessibility to students. By closely following the textbook and discouraging student questions, these teachers unintentionally reduced science to a body of known facts. From a sociolinguistic perspective, the teachers actively constructed a communicative context that discouraged student inquiry. Obviously, such a context is inconsistent with a conceptual change model of science education.

Speech Act Level

The relationships portrayed above between teacher subject-matter knowledge and classroom discourse were also seen at the least inclusive level of analysis: individual speech act or utterance.

Analysis of the duration of all teacher speech acts in 32 lessons revealed that when teaching low-knowledge topics, teachers tended to talk more of the time (as measured by the percentage of class time the teacher was talking) and talk for longer periods of time (as measured by the mean length of teacher utterances in seconds). This generalization held for all of the most common instructional activities with the exception of laboratory activities.

During low-knowledge lessons, the four teachers asked questions frequently. Furthermore, although most teacher questions in all lessons were low-level (memory recall) questions, the ratio of low- to high-level questions was highest during low-knowledge lessons. Low-knowledge lessons were characterized by teacher domination of the speaking floor and frequent low-level questions. Students tended to ask questions infrequently; most of their talk consisted of short utterances responding directly to teacher questions.

Context and the Pragmatic Perspective

The substantive and syntactic dimensions of science are by themselves inaccessible to learners. Through their cognitions, learners must actively *make sense* of concepts and scientific arguments, and the process of sense-making is inextricably tied to the context of instruction. Without understanding science, a teacher may be able to communicate the major concepts and principles of the subject matter. In communicating this *content*, however, my research suggests that he or she may build an instructional *context* which is antithetical to the content. In portraying science as a body of discrete propositions, in utilizing general instructional techniques like seatwork rather than science-specific techniques like laboratory experiments, and in discouraging student questions, the syntactical structures of science were sacrificed. Science was communicated to learners, but it was an incomplete view of science.

Although the instruction described above for low-knowledge settings is antithetical to conceptual change teaching, from the teacher's point of view, it may be instructionally sensible. From a pragmatic perspective, teachers are active builders of communicative context, and this built communicative context is the medium through which all instruction proceeds. When a teacher is unfamiliar with the subject matter, the demands of managing a classroom may pressure her into limiting the frequency and range of student questions, adhering closely to written plans, and teaching from the textbook and other conceptually unproblematic materials. Her questions can be used to control the topic of conversation or induce an evaluative atmosphere, rather than serve as cognitive probes. In effect, the teacher compensates for her lack of pragmatic subject-matter knowledge (or "contextual flexibility") by holding the context constant. Unfortunately, when such strategies are used in a science classroom, they run the risk of undermining the syntactical dimension of scientific knowledge, which requires an atmosphere of relatively free inquiry.

The study described above was intentionally restricted to beginning science teachers who had never taught their subject matters before. In the coming years, as these teachers gain experience, they will teach familiar and unfamiliar topics many times, and factors other than their college coursework and research experiences will increasingly affect their subject-matter knowledge and their classroom practices. Thus, the findings documented for these beginning teachers must be carefully qualified. Nevertheless, if we subscribe to the view that effective science teaching is related to the public and private induction of conceptual change, further attention to the pragmatic dimension of teachers' knowledge seems warranted.

IMPLICATIONS FOR FURTHER RESEARCH

This review suggests a number of avenues for further research. Many of these have already been expressed as hypotheses for research from the pragmatic perspective. For example, there is a need for further description of the relationship between instructional setting and teacher and student cognitions. The pragmatic perspective portrays science knowledge as highly contextualized; the aspects of context that make a difference in determining substantive and syntactic knowledge are still unknown. Their elucidation may make it easier to understand why conceptual change is both difficult and often cognitively compartmentalized.

In researching science subject-matter knowledge and classroom discourse, inattention to context may obscure the effects of teacher knowledge. For example, I have found that between-teacher variations in teacher speech are almost always greater than within-teacher variations attributable to subject-matter knowledge. Differences in classroom discourse related to teacher subject-matter knowledge are small compared to differences related to teacher speech habits, average student ability, school, and other factors. If my study had compared high-knowledge teachers with low-knowledge teachers (rather than the same teachers teaching high-knowledge topics and low-knowledge topics), very few knowledge-related effects would have been detected. One implication for future research is that until more is known about the important dimensions of context, it is probably advisable to include within-teacher contrasts in studies of teacher knowledge and classroom discourse.

In a similar way, teacher decisions about instructional activities affect classroom discourse in important ways. Although teachers asked more questions during their low-knowledge lectures than during their high-knowledge lectures, they were less likely to lecture on low-knowledge topics than on high-knowledge topics. Consequently, the research question, "Do teachers ask more questions when they do not understand the subject-matter of the lesson?" is not directly researchable. Instead, it must be broken into two parts: (1) "What curricular (planning) decisions do teachers make about what to teach and how to teach it?" and (2) "While they are teaching, using a specified teaching method, what are the effects of subject-matter knowledge?" Because different teaching methods differ significantly in their communicative characteristics, one cannot directly compare high-knowledge lessons to low-knowledge lessons. Students ask more questions during laboratories than during examinations; comparing high-knowledge laboratories with low-knowledge examinations (or vice versa) is unlikely to reveal anything about the effects of teacher subject-matter knowledge.

The search for the missing subject matter in research on science teaching is complex and problematic. There are many sciences and many different types of science knowledge. The subject matter of science is rapidly changing. Models for describing science as a discipline and as a body of knowledge have been underpowered.

The pragmatic perspective suggests that a new area of research is needed in science education: study of the relationship between instructional context and the substantive and syntactic dimensions of knowledge. While this perspective might appear to further complicate the search for the missing subject matter, it may actually make it simpler. The model of subject-matter knowledge proposed here contains only three categories, and the categories can be used to map between disciplinary knowledge and the knowledge of individuals. The importance of subject-specific pedagogy is acknowledged, but is conceptualized as a relationship between types of knowledge, not an independent category of knowledge. The model predicts the existence of seemingly incompatible (but context-bound) understandings of scientific concepts, and is thus more consistent than other models with the findings of conceptual change research. A pragmatic perspective need not complicate the search for the missing subject matter of science. In fact, if a pragmatic perspective can help us to distinguish science from other subject matters, to describe the subject matter's features, and to understand why the subject matter moves around, it may in the end make the search much easier.

NOTES

1.   Hashweh's sample contained only two teachers whom he considered conceptual change teachers, and because they both taught physics, he was unable to reliably link aspects of their teaching to subject-matter knowledge. Furthermore, he completed his conceptual change interview on only one subject matter for each teacher (the one he or she taught), so contrasts by subject matter could not be made.

2.   Although my remarks here focus on the teaching of science, the historical record of research on the effects of teacher knowledge in other subjects is similar. For an illustrative review in mathematics, see the chapter by Ball in this volume (pp. 1-48).

3.   Lederman does *not* suggest that science teachers do not need to have a working knowledge of their subject matter. Rather, he argues that, for prospective science teachers, the study of teaching methods is much more important than the history and philosophy of science.

4.   In reviewing the videotape of this exchange, I noted a gross error on my part concerning the last of these three skills. Following the student's description of this answer, I began by saying, "Actually, that's an interesting misconception." Undoubtably, this was interpreted as, "Your answer is wrong," even though, as noted above, he possessed a valid mental model. Furthermore, my response stripped away ownership of his idea by labelling it a common misconception (the language of conceptual change research in science), rather than *his* idea. This exchange begs the question, can too much teacher knowledge stifle a conceptual change teaching strategy, if it is inappropriately expressed in classroom discourse?

5.   See, for example, Roger Pool's application of chaos theory to public records of measles outbreaks (Pool, 1989).

6.   The teachers in this study were enrolled in a masters degree teacher certification program, which included a year-long teaching internship. As undergraduates, all had majored in biology or human biology. Distinction between high-knowledge and low-knowledge topics was determined through a combination of card-sort exercises done during the previous summer as part of a curriculum workshop, analysis of undergraduate transcripts, and interviews at the conclusion of fieldwork. During the period of the study, the author served as the subjects' teacher education subject-matter supervisor. Further information concerning the knowledge measures and the author's dual role of researcher and supervisor are detailed elsewhere (Carlsen, 1987, 1988).

REFERENCES

Buchmann, M. (1984). The priority of knowledge and understanding in teaching. In L. G. Katz & J. D. Raths (Eds.), *Advances in teacher education* (Vol. 1, pp. 29-50). Norwood, NJ: Ablex.

California State Department of Education. (1984). *Science framework addendum.* Sacramento, CA: California State Department of Education.

Carlsen, W. S. (1987, April). *Why do you ask? The effects of teacher subject-matter knowledge on teacher questioning and classroom discourse.* Paper presented at the annual meeting of the American Educational Research Association, Washington, DC.

Carlsen, W. S. (1988). *The effects of science teacher subject-matter knowledge on teacher questioning and classroom discourse.* Unpublished doctoral dissertation, Stanford University, Stanford, CA.

Champagne, A. B., Gunstone, R. F., & Klopfer, L. E. (1985). Instructional consequences of students' knowledge about physical phenomena. In L. H. T. Pines & A. L. Pines (Eds.), *Cognitive structure and conceptual change* (pp. 61-90). New York: Academic.

Chi, M. T. H., Feltovich, P. J., & Glaser, R. (1981). Categorization and representation of physics problems by experts and novices. *Cognitive Science, 5,* 121-152.

Confrey, J. (1981). Conceptual change analysis: Implications for mathematics and curriculum. *Curriculum Inquiry, 11,* 243-257.

Dobey, D. C., & Schafer, L. E. (1984). The effects of knowledge on elementary science inquiry teaching. *Science Education, 68,* 39-51.

Druva, C. A., & Anderson, R. D. (1983). Science teacher characteristics by teacher behavior and by student outcome: A meta-analysis of research. *Journal of Research in Science Teaching, 20,* 467-479.

Elbaz, F. (1983). *Teacher thinking: A study of practical knowledge.* New York: Nichols.

Gilbert, J. K., Watts, D. M., & Osborne, R. J. (1985). Eliciting student views using an interview-about-instances technique. In L. H. T. West & A. L. Pines (Eds.), *Cognitive structure and conceptual change* (pp. 11-27). New York: Academic.

Grossman, P. L., Wilson, S. M., & Shulman, L. S. (1989). Teachers of substance: Subject matter knowledge for teaching. In M.C. Reynolds (Ed.), *Knowledge base for the beginning teacher* (pp. 23-36). Oxford, England: Pergamon.

Haney, W., Madaus, G., & Kreitzer, A. (1988). Charms talismanic: Testing teachers for the improvement of American education. In E. Z. Rothkopf (Ed.), *Review of Research in Education, 14,* 169-238.

Hashweh, M. Z. (1985). *An exploratory study of teacher knowledge and teaching: the effects of science teachers' knowledge of subject matter and their conceptions of learning on their teaching.* Unpublished doctoral dissertation: Stanford University, Stanford, CA.

Hashweh, M. Z. (1987). Effects of subject-matter knowledge in the teaching of biology and physics. *Teaching & Teacher Education, 3,* 109-120.

Hewson, M. G., & Hewson, P. W. (1983). Effect of instruction using students' prior knowledge and conceptual change strategies on science learning. *Journal of Research in Science Teaching, 20,* 731-743.

Hofstein, A., & Yager, R. E. (1982). Societal issues as organizers for science education in the 80s. *School Science and Mathematics, 82,* 539-547.

Hurd, P. (1975). Science, technology, and society: New goals for interdisciplinary science teaching. *The Science Teacher, 42*(2), 27-30.

Kuhn, T. S. (1970). *The structure of scientific revolutions.* Chicago: University of Chicago Press.

Lakatos, I. (1970). Falsification and the methodology of scientific research programs. In I. Lakatos & A. Musgrave (Eds.), *Criticism and the growth of knowledge* (pp. 91-196). Cambridge: Cambridge University Press.

Lantz, O., & Kass, H. (1987). Chemistry teachers' functional paradigms. *Science Education, 71,* 117-134.

Lederman, N., & Druger, M. (1985). Classroom factors related to changes in students' conceptions of the nature of science. *Journal of Research in Science Teaching, 22,* 649-662.

Lederman, N. G., & Zeidler, D. L. (1987). Science teachers' conceptions of science: Do they really influence teaching behavior? *Science Education, 71,* 721-734.

Leinhardt, G., & Greeno, J. (1986). The cognitive skill of teaching. *Journal of Educational Psychology, 78,* 75-95.

Lemke, J. L. (1982, April). *Classroom communication of science.* Final report to the National Science Foundation, New York: Brooklyn College, City University of New York. (ERIC Document Reproduction Service No. ED 222 346).

Mayr, E. (1982). *The growth of biological thought.* Cambridge, MA: Belknap.

Morris, C. W. (1938). Foundations of the theory of signs. In O. Neurath, R. Carnap, & C. Morris (Eds.), *International Encyclopedia of Unified Science* (pp. 77-138). Chicago: University of Chicago Press.

National Science Teachers Association. (1984). Recommended standards for the preparation and certification of secondary school teachers of science. *The Science Teacher, 51*(9), 57-62.

Novak, J. D. (Ed.). (1987). *Proceedings of the Second International Seminar on Misconceptions and Educational Strategies in Science and Mathematics.* Ithaca, NY: Cornell University Department of Education.

Ochs, E. (1979). Introduction: What child language can contribute to pragmatics. In E. Ochs & B. B. Schieffelen (Eds.), *Developmental pragmatics* (pp. 1-17). New York: Academic Press.

Phillips, D. C. (1987). *Philosophy, science, and social inquiry.* New York: Pergamon.

Pool, R. (1989). Is it chaos or just noise? *Science, 243,* 25-28.

Posner, G. J., Strike, K. A., Hewson, P. W., & Gertzog, W. A. (1982). Accomodation of a scientific conception: Toward a theory of conceptual change. *Science Education, 66,* 211-227.

Roth, K. J. (1987, April). *Helping science teachers change: The critical role of teachers' knowledge about science and science learning.* Paper presented at the annual meeting of the American Educational Research Association, Washington, D.C.

Schwab, J. J. (1964). Structure of the disciplines: Meanings and significances. In G. W. Ford & L. Pugno (Eds.), *The structure of knowledge and the curriculum* (pp. 6-30). Chicago: Rand McNally.

Shulman, L. S. (1986). Those who understand: Knowledge growth in teaching. *Educational Researcher, 15*(2), 4-14.

Shulman, L. S., & Sykes, G. (1986, March). A national board for teaching? In search of a bold standard. Paper commissioned for the Task Force on Teaching as a Profession, Carnegie Forum on Education and the Economy.

Shulman, L. S., Sykes, G., & Phillips, D. C. (1983). *Knowledge growth in a profession: The development of knowledge in teaching.* Proposal submitted to the Spencer Foundation. Stanford, CA: School of Education, Stanford University.

Smith, D. C., & Neale, D. C. (1987, April). *The construction of expertise in primary science: Beginnings.* Paper presented at the annual meeting of the American Educational Research Association, Washington, D. C.

Toulmin, S. (1972). *Human understanding.* Princeton, NJ: Princeton University Press.

Viennot, L. (1979). Spontaneous reasoning in elementary dynamics. *European Journal of Science Education, 1,* 205-221.

West, L. H. T., Fensham, P. J., & Garrard, J. E. (1985). Describing the cognitive structures of learners following instruction in chemistry. In L. H. T. West & A. L. Pines (Eds.), *Cognitive structure and conceptual change* (pp. 29-49). New York: Academic.

West, L. H. T., & Pines, A. L. (1985). (Eds.) *Cognitive structure and conceptual change.* New York: Academic.

Wittrock, M. C. (1985). Learning science by generating new conceptions from old ideas. In L. H. T. West & A. L. Pines (Eds.), *Cognitive structure and conceptual change* (pp. 259-266). New York: Academic.

*   *   *

CROSS-TALK

The other two chapters on science teaching suggest that the keys to promoting conceptual change teaching are: educating science teachers about the importance of recognizing student misconceptions, developing good curricula for conceptual change teaching, and training teachers to use conceptual change strategies. Your chapter says little about these issues. Do you disagree with the other authors?

Some attention to these issues is clearly warranted, and the research in progress by the other authors should be helpful in determining whether these are indeed the keys to improving science teaching. For argument's sake, however, I would suggest here that the most important determinant of success in science teaching may be a teacher's ability to match instructional context with scientific content, and that the principal determinant of *that* is strong, contextually flexible subject-matter knowledge. Without such knowledge, I am skeptical that most teachers could successfully manage their classrooms and preserve the substance and syntax of science.

Utilization of new curriculum materials (conceptual change oriented or otherwise) by knowledgeable teachers is a topic which merits special scrutiny. Much of the research described in other chapters of this book suggests that the most subject-matter knowledgeable teachers are the least likely to follow textbooks and other curricula closely (see, for example, the chapters in this volume by Wineburg & Wilson [pp. 305-347]; Leinhardt, Putnam, Stein, & Baxter [pp. 87-113]; and Ball [pp. 1-48]). It would be ironic if we found that the most knowledgeable science teachers were the least likely to use high-quality curriculum materials.

How does the "pragmatic dimension" of scientific knowledge that you describe here differ from "subject-matter pedagogical knowledge?"

First, as a term borrowed from semiotics, it is intended to focus attention on the discourse in which knowledge is expressed and the critical role of context in shaping both discourse and knowledge. Second, it serves not as a category of knowledge independent of the substantive and the syntactic, but as that aspect of cognition which allows the substantive and syntactic to be applied in context-meaningful ways. Third, pragmatic knowledge could describe the application of science in settings other than classrooms and for purposes other than pedagogy. Finally, an emphasis on context shaping as well as context sensitivity provides a starting point for understanding the sociolinguistic correlates of scientific knowledge (for example, teacher control of conversational topic) as well as the curricular or cognitive correlates.

Can you elaborate further why teacher knowledge might be sociolinguistically important in the science classroom?

Discourse analysts recognize that there is an imbalance in speaking rights in the classroom, and that, like in the courtroom or the doctor's office, this imbalance is related to authority and knowledge. To date, research on teacher knowledge has been primarily concerned with the cognitive aspects of instruction. So, for example, the content of teacher questions may be scrutinized to identify: (1) whether the teacher understands the instructional topic, (2) what the teacher feels is most important about the topic, (3) whether student misconceptions are anticipated, and (4) whether students understand material that has just been taught. Although each of these issues is worthy of study, we have usually failed to note that teacher questions frequently serve functions related to control and motivation, and that overreliance on such uses may obscure the critical instructional goal of modeling the syntax of science. In her chapter on mathematics teaching, Deborah Ball notes that by using mathematical shortcuts, teachers may unintentionally hide the conceptual base of a mathematical procedure. In a similar fashion, it is possible that a science teacher's reliance on questions to manage discourse may obscure the syntactic significance of questions in science.

Other than for beginning teachers, where might a pragmatic approach to the study of teacher knowledge be undertaken? After all, classroom control is a critical concern of new teachers; one might argue that it is not surprising to see it varying with knowledge. With a few years of teaching experience, knowledge effects may wash out.

As the math-science pipeline for prospective secondary teachers dries up, more and more secondary classes are likely to be taught by teachers whose college majors were in another subject. Although most physics and chemistry classes are currently taught by certified science teachers, increasing numbers of these teachers are displaced biology teachers with a second certification in physics or chemistry (in New York State, this second certification can be obtained with four undergraduate courses). Upon what knowledge base does an experienced biology teacher draw when he finds himself teaching a chemistry class? In what ways does the experienced teacher compensate for his lack of knowledge?

Another interesting focus for pragmatic research might be the knowledgeable but ineffective teacher. There are many well-intentioned teachers with strong backgrounds in science (at least, as measured by courses taken, certification status, standardized test scores, and other "traditional" measures of teacher subject-matter competence) whose students fail to learn much science. A pragmatic approach to studying their teaching might begin by assessing how flexible these individuals are in conceptualizing scientific ideas, and go on to study whether they are able to use context-appropriate representations while teaching. If these teachers are limited by the unavailability of quality instructional materials, then development and dissemination of new curricula may be helpful. If, on the other hand, their problem is inability to match student conceptions about science to teaching strategies, then continuing education in science is probably more likely to be helpful.

SCIENCE TEACHERS' CONCEPTIONS
OF TEACHING AND LEARNING

Robert E. Hollon, Kathleen J. Roth,
and Charles W. Anderson

INTRODUCTION

I kept coming back to those three questions . . . Why a person dies when their heart stops?
. . . Why do we eat? . . . Why do we breathe? . . . especially the first one because they
would say "so what?" And I kept after them until they could tell me "so what." . . . but
if I hadn't asked them that question, I think they would have just memorized . . . they
would have been able to identify the right words in the right places on the test and not
have understood a thing . . . not understood what this has to do with them or living things
or life functions at all (Ms. Copeland, in Hollon & Anderson, 1987, p. 13).

The comment above was made by a seventh grade life science teacher. It reflects
a powerful way of thinking about teaching and learning science, one in which
the teacher is guided by ideas about what students should know, how they
should know it, and why it is important for them to know it. Ms. Copeland
understood the subject matter (cellular respiration) and understood her
students as learners in ways that enabled her to make curricular and

Advances in Research on Teaching, Volume 2, pages 145-185.
Copyright © 1991 by JAI Press Inc.
All rights of reproduction in any form reserved.
ISBN: 1-55938-034-9

145

instructional decisions that fostered the development of understanding. Unfortunately, not all teachers possess this kind of knowledge. For some individuals, many years of teaching experience have not enabled them to develop the sort of knowledge about science and about learners that this teacher had developed.

This chapter presents our current thinking about the kinds of knowledge about subject matter and about learners and learning that is useful to middle school science teachers in planning and in teaching for understanding. The efforts of three middle school science teachers to teach for understanding will provide insights about how such professional knowledge develops in both inservice and preservice settings.

In the first section of the chapter we explain the theoretical perspective on science teaching that informs our studies of teachers' knowledge and thinking. The second section describes some of the patterns of knowledge and of knowledge use that we have seen among science teachers, with particular emphasis on two teachers who participated in a recent study of middle school life science teachers. The analysis focuses on the teachers' knowledge of both subject matter and learners and how that knowledge was used in making curricular and instructional decisions. We also speculate in this section about how those patterns originate and are maintained. Finally, ways in which inservice workshops fail to support these teachers in developing knowledge of learners and of subject matter that was useful in making curricular and instructional decisions are described. In the final sections we consider the potential for change and improvement, discussing ways in which teacher education as well as improvements in teaching materials and the conditions of teachers' work could help teachers use their knowledge more productively. The case of one preservice science teacher's experiences in a program designed to support teaching for conceptual change will be used to frame this discussion.

PERSPECTIVES ON SCIENCE TEACHING

The research discussed in this chapter draws on, and contributes to, two related bodies of research. The first is the recently emerging body of research on teacher thinking, teachers' knowledge, and teacher education. Like the other chapter authors in this volume, we have been strongly influenced by the work of Shulman and his colleagues (cf. Wilson, Shulman, & Richert, 1987; chapters in this volume by Carlsen, Grossman, Wineburg & Wilson), as well as by work in progress at the National Center for Research in Teacher Education at Michigan State University (cf., Ball, this volume, pp. 1-48). This research has generated valuable insights into the nature of the cognitive processes that teachers rely on while planning and carrying out instruction and the knowledge that underlies those processes. The research portrays teaching as a cognitively complex endeavor requiring a substantial body of knowledge and skills, including those that are the focus of this chapter: Teachers' subject-matter knowledge, teachers' knowledge of learners and learning, and the strategies needed to use that knowledge effectively in planning and teaching. The contributions of curriculum materials and teacher training activities in helping teachers develop this knowledge must be reconsidered in light of this research base.

The second body of research on which this chapter is based focuses on curricular and instructional issues in classroom science teaching, with particular emphasis on how classroom teaching helps, or fails to help, students develop conceptual understanding of scientific concepts and theories. Researchers in this tradition have focused on using insights from cognitive psychology (e.g., Larkin & Rainard, 1984; Vygotsky, 1962, 1978) and from the history, philosophy, and sociology of science (e.g., Keller, 1985; Mayr, 1982; Resnick, 1987; Toulmin, 1961, 1972) to inquire into the processes of teaching and learning as they occur in science classrooms and in other settings. Like other researchers in this tradition (cf. Driver, Guesne, & Tiberghien, 1985; Osborne & Freyberg, 1985), we have pursued a dual agenda. We have tried both (a) to understand why so many students have difficulty understanding science in typical science classrooms, and (b) to develop teaching strategies and materials that help students achieve a deeper and richer understanding of science.

It is this research into classroom science teaching (which is discussed in detail in our chapter in Volume 1 of this series: Anderson & Roth, 1989) that provides the conceptual foundation for our inquiries into teachers' knowledge. In particular, this research leads us to make several assertions about the goals of science teaching and the tasks that teachers must accomplish to achieve those goals. These assertions are discussed below.

The Nature of Scientific Understanding

A primary focus of our research has been on the problems of teaching for meaningful understanding of scientific concepts and principles. We have been interested in analyzing students' understanding of the content that they are taught and in describing the qualities of teaching that promote student understanding. In pursuing these questions, we and other researchers in this tradition have often found ourselves engaged in inquiry into the nature of scientific understanding. What emerges from these inquiries is a picture of "understanding" as a multifaceted phenomenon. Among the qualities of thought and action that are commonly associated with understanding, the most important for us are the *usefulness* of the knowledge that a student develops in science class and the *conceptual integration* between that knowledge and the student's personal knowledge of the world.

Scientific knowledge in school classrooms often consists primarily of lists of facts that students use for one purpose: to pass tests. This presents a limited and distorted picture of the nature of scientific knowledge and of its uses. In our research we have treated scientific concepts and theories not primarily as facts, but as intellectual and linguistic tools that scientifically literate people can use for a variety of purposes. These purposes include: *description, explanation, prediction, control,* and *appreciation* of the world around us. Thus we feel that a person can be said to understand a scientific concept or principle only if he or she can use it as a tool (not merely state it as a fact) for one or more of these purposes.

The knowledge that people use for describing and explaining natural phenomena is not solely, or even primarily, scientific. Scientific knowledge is an outgrowth of our common linguistic and cultural heritage, one that enriches that heritage by allowing us to engage in these activities with greater power and precision than would otherwise be possible. As a result, scientific knowledge is not and cannot be divorced from our personal and shared cultural knowledge of the world. To do so is to render scientific knowledge sterile and useless. We witness such sterility in students who can state that photosynthesis is "The process by which green plants make their own food out of carbon dioxide, water, and sunlight," but who do not see that fact as having anything to do with the plants they have in their homes (which get their food "from water and fertilizer that Mom gives them"). In isolating scientific knowledge from their real-world knowledge, students fail to construct understandings of science that are personally meaningful. Thus, students can be said to understand scientific concepts and principles only if they see how those concepts and principles are *connected* with other ideas that they already understand. It is this quality of connectedness that we refer to as conceptual integration.

Learning scientific knowledge in a conceptually integrated and useful form is not an easy process for most students. The "fit" between scientific ideas and students' personal ideas about the world is usually far from perfect. Sometimes students see scientific thought and language as so different from their own that they belong in entirely different spheres; at other times scientific and commonsense ideas are in conflict. Students can come to understand science only if they struggle to overcome these difficulties, and to reconcile the conflicts. Thus learning with understanding is for most students a complex process of *conceptual change,* in which they must reconcile scientific ideas with their own personal knowledge and master the use of these new intellectual tools. In this constructivist view of learning, teachers cannot tell students the answers: Meaningful learning will result only after the learner successfully integrates scientific knowledge into his/her personal knowledge.

Teaching for Conceptual Understanding

A substantial body of research now exists on the question of how teachers can promote conceptual change learning in their students (reviewed in Anderson & Roth, 1989; Anderson & Smith, 1987; Champagne, Klopfer, & Gunstone, 1982; Driver, 1987; Erickson, 1984; Hewson & Hewson, 1984; Nussbaum & Novick, 1982; Posner, Strike, Hewson, & Gertzog, 1982; Resnick, 1987; West & Pines, 1985). Briefly, science teachers must develop knowledge that enables them to make two types of decisions: *curricular decisions* and *instructional decisions.*

Using Knowledge about Science and Learners to Make Curricular Decisions

All teachers must consider what they want their students to learn and decide what kinds of work they will ask their students to do in class. Teaching for conceptual change, though, demands that teachers make such decisions in specific and constrained ways. They must find ways of transforming the knowledge, language, and activities of the adult scientific community into forms that are simultaneously accessible to their students and faithful to the scientific community. Thus, the best goals and academic tasks are those that "bridge the gap" between the scientific community and the student's own knowledge. It is usually impossible to bridge this gap perfectly; teachers must select or invent goals and tasks that improve students' understanding while leaving them somewhat short of complete mastery of scientific thought and language.

Another curricular challenge is selecting which content will *not* be taught. Studies of conceptual change learning have generated a broad consensus among science educators that teaching for understanding requires sacrificing the broad content coverage that characterizes most science textbooks and programs. Thus, in selecting content, teachers need to make difficult decisions about what to omit or deemphasize.

Of course, no teacher ever has a completely adequate understanding of either the subject matter or learners needed to accomplish these curricular tasks. The case studies presented later in this chapter describe how different teachers cope with the curricular functions of their jobs by using the knowledge and resources that are available to them.

Using Knowledge about Science and Learners to Make Instructional Decisions

We have implied that teaching for understanding involves helping students to master complex and difficult tasks. These curricular characteristics are necessary if students are to develop knowledge that is useful and conceptually integrated, but they also pose a major instructional challenge: How can a teacher help 20 to 30 different students achieve these goals when each student must go through his or her own process of conceptual change? In a sense, the task is impossible. We have never studied a teacher who was successful in helping all the students in a class achieve conceptual change learning. But some teachers are more successful than others. Our own research and that of others (cf. Anderson & Smith, 1987; Driver, 1987; Hewson & Hewson, 1984; West & Pines, 1985) has identified characteristics of the classroom environment and of instructional strategies that help a greater proportion of the students in a class to achieve conceptual understanding. Among the instructional strategies that support successful conceptual change teaching are:

1.   *Creating a classroom social environment* where students understand that their thinking is important and are willing to express their ideas, where students listen to each other's ideas seriously without accepting them uncritically, and where they accept that changing one's mind can be a sign of successful learning rather than prior stupidity. The teacher must help create what Collins, Brown, and Newman (1989) refer to as a "culture of expert practice" that the students value and want to become members of.

2.   *Establishing problems* that engage students in scientific thinking. The teacher must help students to become involved in tasks that are both personally meaningful to them and vehicles for the mastery of significant scientific knowledge. To engage students in problems, teachers may find the following strategies to be helpful:

- Eliciting students' ideas about a natural phenomenon
- Challenging students' ideas to create conceptual conflict, dissatisfaction, student debate
- Contrasting students' naive explanations and scientific explanations using a variety of representations

3.   *Understanding and using scientific concepts.* Students need numerous opportunities to use new concepts to explain real world situations. A variety of activities and questions that engage students in using scientific concepts and in refining their understandings of these concepts will help students see the wide usefulness of the concepts. At first, students' misconceptions will persist as they answer these questions. The teacher, therefore, must play the role of "cognitive coach" (Collins, Brown, & Newman, 1989), helping students develop better strategies for comprehending concepts and explaining phenomena by:

a.   *Modeling* solutions to the problems that both demonstrate the application of scientific knowledge and help students to realize the strengths and limitations of their own prior knowledge.

b.   *Coaching* students by creating opportunities for student work in which students can practice using scientific knowledge to describe, explain, make predictions about, and control the world around them. It is often necessary to create situations where students are helped to accomplish difficult tasks by structural feedback from the teacher. Thus, coaching also involves monitoring and responding to student thinking and student performance.

c. *Fading* gradually the amount of teacher direction, scaffolding, and guidance in constructing explanations. Fading suggests both creating tasks that are more open-ended problem-solving tasks and allowing students to take a larger role in defining questions and problems and approaches to solving them.

These characteristics are not unique to science teaching. Collins, Brown, and Newman (1989) describe instructional approaches to reading, writing, and mathematics that have many of these same characteristics.

Conclusion

In this section we have described an approach to science teaching that we will refer to as *conceptual change teaching*. Although this approach to teaching is substantially different from approaches that prevail in schools today, we believe that main elements of conceptual change teaching are necessary for most students to achieve even a basic understanding of the science they study (see Anderson & Smith, 1987; Anderson & Roth, 1989; International Association for the Evaluation of Educational Achievement, 1988).

In order to teach successfully for conceptual change, a teacher must master both a *body of knowledge* and a *pattern of practice*. The body of knowledge includes a useful and conceptually integrated understanding of the nature of science and of the particular science content to be taught. It also includes an understanding of how students think about the natural world and how they can develop conceptually integrated and useful scientific knowledge. Finally, it requires knowledge of curricular goals, academic tasks, and instructional strategies that can successfully link the scientific knowledge to the students' world. The pattern of practice encompasses the use of this knowledge to develop appropriate curricular goals, academic tasks, classroom social environments, and instructional strategies that help students through the process of conceptual change learning.

Accomplishing all of these curricular and instructional functions well puts a large burden on the knowledge, skills, and energy of the most accomplished teacher. Yet, we have worked with teachers who come remarkably close to achieving this ideal. Ms. Copeland, who was quoted at the beginning of this chapter, was such a teacher. Even the short quote illustrates her ability to accomplish the curricular task of recognizing how an apparently dry topic (cellular respiration) in fact has the potential to help her students answer significant questions about their world (e.g., why do we eat and breathe?). She also used her knowledge to engage her students in problems that were significant to them and to help them to master the solutions.

Most teachers, however, rely on different bodies of knowledge and engage in different patterns of practice than those we have described earlier. These prevailing approaches to teaching have so far proven insufficient for the task of helping students to understand science. Thus, most teachers *need* to change. Resolving the conflicts between their own knowledge and practice and the knowledge and practice of conceptual change teachers, though, is a major problem for any teacher. In the next section, we examine some of the forms that such a conflict can take.

CASE STUDIES OF SCIENCE TEACHING

In this section we examine the planning and teaching practices of two different middle school science teachers. The teachers held different personal and professional goals and approached the task of teaching in different ways, but each teacher was engaged in a sincere and intelligent attempt to make use of available knowledge and to respond to new ideas in the profession. In developing these case studies we have attempted both to understand what was reasonable and intelligent about the approach of each teacher and to explain why these approaches fell short of what is necessary to help most students achieve conceptual understanding. We were particularly interested in understanding the ways in which their knowledge of science and of learners supported or constrained them in their efforts to teach for conceptual change.

Research Methods

The case studies presented in the following section are drawn from our recent investigations of middle school science teaching. We were interested in understanding how middle school teachers approached the tasks of science teaching, as well as how specific knowledge about students' learning and about conceptual-change-oriented teaching resources might help them to be more successful (see Smith & Anderson, 1987, for a detailed description of the methodology). The research generated three major data bases: teacher interviews, classroom observations, and written tests measuring students' understanding of photosynthesis, cellular respiration, and matter cycling. Each data base is briefly described below.

Interviews with Teachers

Our investigations involved thirteen experienced teachers. Each teacher was interviewed at the beginning of the project and after teaching each of three seventh-grade science units: Photosynthesis, cellular respiration, and matter cycling. The interviews assessed the teachers' (a) knowledge of science content for these three units, (b) knowledge about students' learning and students' conceptions of these topics, (c) judgments about the important features of planning and about the teaching materials they were using, and (d) instructional judgments about the nature of effective science teaching strategies. The tasks involved card sorting, review of items on the student tests, and discussions of the features of materials and strategies that were actually used to teach each unit. As a result, we were able to develop detailed information about a variety of facets of the teachers' thinking about science content, students, and effective teaching practices.

Observations of Instruction

We observed more than 150 lessons over a period of eight months. Although we were not able to observe all the lessons taught by each teacher, we were able to observe a majority of the lessons for each of the three target units. We collected detailed field notes about instructional activities, teacher-student and student-student interactions, and the use of resource materials. Examples of curriculum materials and any other materials used to plan and teach each unit were also collected and analyzed.

Student Diagnostic Tests

We developed diagnostic tests for each of the target units. The tests used as both pretests and posttests were designed to reveal the extent to which students possessed a conceptually integrated and useful understanding of each unit. Each unit test was administered to more than 300 students in six different school districts.

The case studies presented below include information from all three data bases. They illustrate the knowledge and patterns of practice of two teachers who participated in our research. Ms. Mitchell and Mr. Barnes were thoughtful, experienced teachers who began the study with ideas about teaching and patterns of practice that differed substantially from each other and from our ideas about conceptual change teaching. During the project, each teacher experienced conflicts between his or her own ideas and the ideas and practices we advocated in the workshops and experimental teaching materials. The nature of those conflicts and the resolutions reached by each teacher are the focus of the case studies.

Ms. Mitchell: Struggling with Multiple Resources and Demands

Ms. Mitchell worked at a suburban middle school in a university community. She had been teaching seventh grade life science for 14 years. During our research, Ms. Mitchell participated in two half-day workshops in which she was introduced to the idea of students' misconceptions and the difficulties they could create in students' interpretations of science instruction. We provided general information about the kinds of teaching strategies that would promote conceptual change learning, but not specific examples of teaching strategies to use in teaching the photosynthesis, cellular respiration, and matter cycling units. Ms. Mitchell's reaction to the conceptual change teaching ideas presented in the workshops was positive. She recognized the student learning problems and misconceptions that were discussed as consistent with her own notions about students and their difficulties in understanding the science content.

Knowledge of Students

This positive reaction was due in part to the fact that Ms. Mitchell already knew some of what we were saying. For example, during the initial interview about the photosynthesis unit, she predicted accurately that students would have difficulty in describing how plants get their food:

> Well, kids would say water and minerals, and sun probably, well no, they wouldn't say sun. They'd just say water and minerals, so soil and water. Because they know that you plant a seed in the ground and some of them know you might put fertilizer down because you plant seeds in the ground and put fertilizer and water on it and it grows . . . (Roth, 1987, p. 12).

In the respiration interview, she also predicted accurately that students would talk about respiration as something that humans and animals with lungs would do, and that it involved breathing in oxygen and giving off carbon dioxide. Thus, the idea that students had misconceptions was not surprising to her. She was ready to attempt to integrate the information about students' conceptions, and the teaching suggestions that we made, into her own teaching style.

Ms. Mitchell's responses illustrate a pattern that we saw in many of the stronger teachers in our study. Each held much potentially valuable knowledge about her students' scientific thinking. However, they had few ways of naming or describing what they knew, and thus they had developed and used their knowledge in isolation from other teachers.

Knowledge of Science

Ms. Mitchell always worked to understand the content she was teaching, and she went beyond just memorizing a bunch of facts that the students would learn. She also made sure she understood the relationships among ideas within a unit and how one unit related to another. Thus, she had a good understanding of the connectedness of ideas within science. She had a less solid understanding of the connections between scientific knowledge and real-world phenomena.

Her subject-matter knowledge was often not rich enough to generate different phenomena for students to think about and explain using the concepts they learned in her units. As a result of the workshop, she was committed to improving her knowledge in this area:

> . . . Because I wanted to see . . . like where it (the list of recommended teaching strategies) says explain *why* and those kinds of things, I'm trying very hard to make myself ask those kinds of questions (Roth 1987, p. 14).

In spite of Ms. Mitchell's knowledge of students' misconceptions and her efforts to develop connected, useful understandings of the science content, her students' learning was less than might be expected for a teacher so clearly dedicated to helping students understand science in useful ways. The key reason, as we understand it in retrospect, is that the generic and somewhat superficial introduction to conceptual change teaching in our two half-day workshops was far from sufficient to help Ms. Mitchell successfully restructure her knowledge base and change her pattern to reflect conceptual change teaching. Some of the key problems that she encountered in using her knowledge about learners and about science are described below.

Curricular Decision: Planning to Teach Cellular Respiration

We will illustrate the difficulties that Ms. Mitchell encountered in trying to plan and teach for conceptual change with one of the three target units: cellular respiration. As she always did, Ms. Mitchell began the unit by investing considerable effort to make sure she understood the content she was teaching. In describing her planning for each unit, she always referred to reading college texts and other resources as one of the first things she did in order to "get the content straight." Her descriptions of appropriate answers to our diagnostic test items indicated that she had indeed developed significant knowledge about the important concepts, relationships, and links between units. The interview after the respiration unit illustrated this understanding. Ms. Mitchell stressed the importance of helping students understand "the big picture," which she described as the central relationship between eating and breathing. Thus, she wanted students to understand that both oxygen and food end up in the cells of all living things where they are involved in a chemical reaction that releases both energy and carbon dioxide. This selection of a focus for the topic was in fact quite appropriate for her students.

However, the resources she used in planning did little to help Ms. Mitchell develop this "big picture" as she selected and organized the content. One resource (a college text) focused on distinctions between anaerobic and aerobic respiration at the molecular level, giving step-by-step details of reactions in respiration and glycolysis processes in plants. Another source (the text used in school) described the body systems used for eating and breathing in detail without reference to the ways in which each contributes to cellular respiration. Thus the resources available to Ms. Mitchell provided her with scientific content that was neither conceptually integrated nor useful. To teach successfully for conceptual change, she would have to integrate three isolated bodies of information (about eating, breathing, and cellular respiration) from two different sources. She would have to figure out how her students could use that knowledge to describe, explain, predict, control, or appreciate living systems. Then she would have to figure out how all of this related to her students' own conceptions of how those systems worked. It is not surprising that Ms. Mitchell had difficulty accomplishing this series of tasks.

Instructional Decision: Teaching Cellular Respiration

Ms. Mitchell's teaching of the respiration unit illustrated both the strengths and the weaknesses of the understanding she had developed during her planning. She began and ended the unit using what she called a "brainstorming activity." On the first day, she had the students discuss in small groups the following questions:

Why do we eat?
Why do we need food?
Why do we breathe?
Where do we get energy?
What do oxygen, food, and energy have to do with eating?

The students wrote down their ideas on large posters that were displayed in the room throughout the unit.

It is worth considering where Ms. Mitchell stood at the end of this first day from our perspective and from her own. From our point of view Ms. Mitchell had made an excellent start to the unit. The questions that she had posed focused on important uses of scientific knowledge about cellular respiration, and by having the students write out and discuss their own ideas, she had set the stage for conceptual integration between their personal beliefs and the scientific knowledge to be presented later in the unit. From an instructional standpoint (see earlier section on instructional decisions), Ms. Mitchell had also made a promising beginning. She had established a social environment in her classroom that was conducive to learning. She had successfully established the problem of explaining how our bodies use food and oxygen. Her students were curious about the questions that she had posed and aware of their own uncertainty about the answers. From our perspective, the next step would be for Ms. Mitchell to begin modeling scientific answers to the questions she had posed in the brainstorming activity and to begin coaching her students as they attempted to use the science concepts to make personal sense of real-world phenomena.

From Ms. Mitchell's perspective, however, the situation was more problematic and confusing, for several reasons. In the first place, the description of conceptual change teaching strategies presented in the workshops (conducted three years before this chapter was written) was far less clear and concise than the one given earlier. We had not given Ms. Mitchell explicit guidance as to what she should do next. Even with such guidance, however, the next steps suggested earlier (modeling and coaching) would have been formidably difficult for a teacher in Ms. Mitchell's position. Modeling scientific answers to the questions she had posed was difficult because she did not have any adequate models herself. She had instead materials that gave her bits of information about eating, breathing, and cellular respiration, each part isolated from the other and from the questions that Ms. Mitchell had posed for her brainstorming activity.

Coaching would have presented an even more difficult challenge for Ms. Mitchell. To do a good job of coaching she would have to (a) figure out what sorts of meanings and patterns could be found in the confusing array of student responses to the brainstorming activity and how those patterns related to scientific understanding, (b) develop activities that would give her students opportunities to relate their own beliefs to scientific knowledge and practice using the scientific knowledge, and (c) provide her students with scaffolding and feedback as they struggled with the process of conceptual change. These are confusing and complex tasks. In our curriculum development work (see Anderson & Roth, 1989), they have taken us anywhere from several months to a year to complete for a topic like cellular respiration. Ms. Mitchell, of course, could not spend several months figuring out what to do next. She had to teach the next day! Under these circumstances, it is hardly surprising that she did not begin the modeling and coaching we described it earlier. Instead, her teaching basically followed the pattern established in the materials she was using. The lessons were packed with content and full of vocabulary words for the students to learn. Information about eating, breathing, and cellular respiration was, in the main, presented separately without being linked back to the questions she had posed at the start of the unit.

When Ms. Mitchell had her students come back to the brainstorming activity at the end of the unit, the results were disappointing but not surprising. Although they added some technical details, the students' answers were essentially similar to the ones they had given at the beginning of the unit. The unit posttest results were similar: A few students had developed a useful and conceptually coherent understanding of cellular respiration, but most had not.

Conclusion for Ms. Mitchell

Ms. Mitchell's teaching of the other target units followed a pattern similar to the one described for the respiration unit above. Occasional conceptual-change-oriented questions and activities were variations on a pattern that was basically congruent with the teaching materials available to her and with her own established practice. Her students listened to lectures, read and answered questions in textbooks, and worked on laboratory activities that Ms. Mitchell described as opportunities to practice science "process skills" and as interesting breaks from the book-bound routine.

Without the extensive instructional support that they needed, most students were not able to develop the knowledge they needed to answer the difficult conceptual-change-oriented questions that Ms. Mitchell added to her existing patterns of teaching. These questions, thus, were essentially peripheral to the primary instructional process; they were interesting but frustrating sidelights for both Ms. Mitchell and her students.

Ms. Mitchell herself was sometimes quite critical of her teaching, often along lines similar to those suggested earlier. While her self-criticism correctly identified important limitations in her teaching, the criticism was perhaps pointed in the wrong direction. The task of teaching for conceptual change was formidable, and neither the materials she had to work with nor the minimal guidance we had given her in the workshops was adequate for the job.

Mr. Barnes: Describing An Expanding Universe of Scientific Knowledge

Mr. Barnes had taught for 13 years in the same rural school district in a farming community near a midwestern university. He was trained as a high school science teacher, and had spent ten years teaching biology and ecology to high school students. In addition to his Bachelor of Science degree in biology, he had completed several graduate courses in education. Mr. Barnes was in the "materials only" group in our research project. He was provided with experimental student texts and teachers' guides for the photosynthesis and cellular respiration units (Anderson, Roth, Hollon, & Blakeslee, 1986; Roth & Anderson, 1987), and with unit goals for the matter cycling unit. He did not participate in any workshops before teaching the three target units.

Understanding of Science

Unlike Ms. Mitchell, who sometimes lacked confidence in her own biological knowledge, Mr. Barnes had a deep and well developed understanding of the scientific content to be taught and of the relationships among the three units in our research. He was adept at relating scientific phenomena to everyday events familiar to the students. In one lesson in the photosynthesis unit, for example, he linked plants' food making to the tapping of sugar maple trees in Michigan, to the ways that corn on the cob acted as food, and to the reasons why plants placed on a window sill in the winter don't grow as well as they would in the summer.

In addition, he displayed excellent understanding of how scientific concepts had developed within the scientific community. He used this knowledge during classes to describe to students how scientists had come to understand various phenomena. For example, in discussing Von Helmont's experiments, he began with a short discussion of scientists' notions about plants getting food from soil, then related Von Helmont's observations and conclusions to the scientific ideas existing at that time, and followed with a description of scientists "scratching their heads" about the apparent contradiction.

Beyond that, Mr. Barnes *liked* science and worked hard to stay current in any subject that he taught. When his teaching assignment was changed to include earth science, for example, he took a physical science course during the summer, then took his family on a camping trip through the western United States. He explained the reason for this particular trip was that he needed to see the geological formations that he was talking about in class.

Knowledge of Learners

Our interviews revealed that, like Ms. Mitchell, Mr. Barnes was aware of many of his students' misconceptions about photosynthesis, respiration, and matter cycling. He was consistently able to predict students' responses to the diagnostic test questions and describe the patterns of thinking that led to those responses. Mr. Barnes was also like Ms. Mitchell in that he attributed less importance to his students' conceptions than we did. For example, his explanations of why students failed to learn focused on factors such as students' information processing limitations and the abstractness of scientific concepts rather than on factors related to student conceptions. The excerpt below is from the interview at the end of the respiration unit:

M.B.: Some of the kids have difficulty relating to abstract things here, and I think that this unit caused some problems in that they couldn't see it, that respiration was always breathing to them and they couldn't see the stuff being produced.

I: Did it end up with some of them still believing that respiration was breathing?

M.B.: I had some of them saying that down to the bitter end! They still didn't get it. I think it's the number of steps along the way, too. You get beyond two or three in sequential thinking, kids, they lose it and go back to the use that they feel is real (respiration interview, Hollon & Anderson, 1987, p. 24).

While these comments are sensible and probably correct, they also tended to distract Mr. Barnes from problems involving the relationship between students' prior knowledge and the scientific knowledge presented in class. Neither did this view of learning lead Mr. Barnes to think extensively about the relationship between knowledge acquisition and knowledge use. In focusing on the difficulties that students encountered in absorbing or acquiring knowledge, he often described students as relatively passive. As we shall see below, most students also had relatively passive roles in his classroom.

Mr. Barnes was aware that not all of his students understood the content that he was teaching. He had come to accept that, especially for the weaker students, this would probably be the case. For these students, he described his primary goal as helping them to become more proficient learners. In each interview, he indicated that he felt it was more important to help his students become better learners or "processors of information" than to help them learn science content:

> I would not feel bad as a science teacher if many of the students didn't remember the science concepts but at least learned to organize themselves and learned to organize and process information better . . . I think there is a majority whose minds are going through such change that I sometimes question whether they are learning a great deal (photosynthesis interview, Roth, 1987, p. 35).

> My goal is to teach them to work . . . science concepts are less important than learning to be organized (respiration interview, Hollon & Anderson, 1987, p. 23).

At the same time, he felt it important to challenge the upper group of students, and provide them with instruction and information that would enable them to understand the details of important scientific principles and processes.

In summary, Mr. Barnes's knowledge of the content he was teaching, his understanding of how scientific knowledge develops, and his love of science were apparent in all aspects of his planning and teaching. In many respects, his scientific knowledge exemplified the conceptual integration and usefulness that we would like to see in all teachers. However, in spite of this background, which was very unusual among the teachers that we observed, Mr. Barnes was not always successful in helping his students understand photosynthesis, cellular respiration, and matter cycling. To understand why his teaching did not have the intended impact, it is necessary to examine how his goals for student learning and his understanding of students' learning processes shaped the way he approached both curricular and instructional tasks. These issues are explored below.

Curricular Decisions: Planning for the Respiration Unit

As a member of the "Materials Only" group in our study, Mr. Barnes received copies of the teachers' guides and instructional materials for the photosynthesis and respiration units (Anderson, Roth, Hollon, & Blakeslee, 1986; Roth & Anderson, 1987) with instructions to use them in whatever way he thought appropriate. His understanding of their purpose and rationale came from what he read in the teacher's guides themselves. When he looked at the materials, he was troubled by what he saw. In particular, he judged our experimental materials to be too "watered down" for his top students:

> [The photosynthesis materials] were at a lower level maybe than what I would present. But then I think maybe that . . . we'll see. Maybe it will hit the middle kids a lot better . . . but I do think that for some of the kids, the brighter kids, they don't need as much repetition . . . so I think the materials hit the kids in the middle a lot better.

> [The respiration materials] were very watered down . . . it wasn't anywhere near the detail that I . . . I mean this material wasn't anywhere near the detail, it didn't have as many terms and things for them to understand. It seemed like a general theme emphasized and reemphasized. Maybe I like to identify parts and things. Maybe that confuses them. I think the brighter kids can handle a lot of that without getting confused. But I am sure that there are those on the other end who are going to be confused by it. It depends on where you put the focus. I would like to focus on the kids who are above the middle somewhere . . . but I know I'm going to lose some kids.

For Mr. Barnes, our materials raised a set of troubling questions. As described above, his goals focused on helping students learn how to deal with large amounts of scientific content. He knew that the weaker students did not fully understand the content that he exposed them to, but he was not convinced that they could understand, and he reasoned that in any case they were learning "to organize and process information better." Our materials clearly were not very well suited to helping him achieve these goals. They focused on a different goal: Conceptual understanding for all students. Associated with the different goals were different teaching patterns, one comfortable and familiar, the other new and unfamiliar. In the end, he resolved the conflict between these alternative goals and strategies neither by abandoning the pattern of his practice nor by rejecting our materials. Instead, he pursued a course of action that had aspects of both.

Instructional Decision: Teaching about Cellular Respiration

Our analysis of Mr. Barnes' teaching focuses on the second lesson in the cellular respiration unit. During the introductory lesson, the students had written individually and discussed their answers to a set of questions posed in the text that were similar to those posed by Ms. Mitchell during her brainstorming activity:

Where do our bodies get the energy we need?
What happens to the food we eat?
What happens to the air we breathe in?
What is respiration?

The class had also read the portion of the experimental text that discussed the answer to the first question: Food is the only source of energy for human beings, and substances such as water and minerals are not food in this sense.

Mr. Barnes began the second lesson with a reminder about the day's assignment, which was to answer a series of questions in the experimental text about whether various substances serve as sources of food for humans. After checking to see who had trouble answering the questions, he spent 20 minutes reviewing students' responses to questions posed in the text. He began the discussion by relating the content of the chapter (sources of energy) to the theme of the unit in general (cellular respiration).

> T: (Opening the text to the page with the questions) Respiration has something to do with breathing and also getting energy from food and oxygen in cells. In chapter two it talks about people and respiration. Can you get energy from water?
> S1: No.
> T: Why can't you?
> S1: Because it only has hydrogen and oxygen.
> T: Did you all have that? (Most students raise a hand in response.) Can you get energy from vitamins? (A few say yes, most say no.) Why not?
> S2: It doesn't contain energy . . .
> T: What do they give us?
> S3: Extra nutrients?

At this point, Mr. Barnes described the properties of vitamins, referring to them as catalysts or co-factors which help chemical reactions release energy, pointing out that "we need them, but they don't give us energy."

The remaining questions were reviewed in similar fashion. Mr. Barnes asked a student to answer the question, then checked to see how many other students agreed with that answer. He usually asked at least one follow-up question, encouraging several different students to respond, after which he summarized the point of the question. At several points, he compared students' responses to "ways that scientists used to think" and told them that "a lot of people besides you think that, too."

After the last question was discussed, Mr. Barnes read the definition of food in the text:

> FOOD refers only to materials that contain energy for living things. All living things must have food, and the energy it provides, to live and grow.

He asked "Does 'all living things' include plants?" Most students nodded their heads in agreement. "So plants not only make their food, they also use it. Remember from here on that all living things use food."

At that point, Mr. Barnes began a detailed 20-minute lecture describing the processes by which humans deliver food and oxygen to their cells. He used a transparency to illustrate important steps in the digestion process. In addition to descriptions of food being digested and transported to cells (with brief interruptions to define diffusion and fat storage), the lecture included descriptions of the passage of waste products through the blood to the kidneys, skin, and lungs, the production of urea (and its use as a fertilizer but not as an energy source for plants). He used a second transparency to illustrate the movement of oxygen to the brain and described in detail how oxygen entered the blood stream and eventually diffused into each cell. He concluded the lesson by answering a question and linking the important points of the lecture to the next day's activity (an investigation in the text focusing on the effects of physical activity on respiration).

The lesson described above was typical of the way that Mr. Barnes conducted his class. In later lessons, he presented the functions of the circulatory system and respiratory system in similar detail. Lessons not involving some sort of lab activity were usually divided into two parts: short question-answer sessions during which the students responded to Mr. Barnes' questions or asked questions themselves, and "mini-lectures" in which the students sat quietly and listened to Mr. Barnes. In many classes, the lectures were supplemented by movies or filmstrips which served as the basis for question-answer sessions. In some instances, there were several rounds of question-answer and mini-lecture sessions in a single class.

Question-answer sessions usually took place at the start of class, but sometimes occurred after Mr. Barnes presented some new material. These sessions were often "virtuoso performances" in which Mr. Barnes supplied cogent and well informed answers to just about any question that the students cared to ask. He valued student questions and understood their importance:

> . . . and I do try to stimulate them to ask questions if they don't understand a particular thing. And if they don't understand something, or are not sure about something I would really focus in on that and try to give them—that's what I call the teachable moment . . . and to me the teachable moment is more valuable than anything else because that's what they're interested in at the time and they are ready to focus in on that particular item . . . if I can stimulate them to ask questions, I know they are focused on what's going on (respiration interview, Hollon & Anderson, 1987, p. 25).

Both his lectures and his answers to student questions were models of the connectedness of scientific knowledge and its usefulness for making sense of the real world.

Classes involving laboratories or other activities were always carefully introduced and linked to the topic being studied. After the activities were completed, Mr. Barnes carefully reviewed the activity and discussed the students' data. Their results were related to the topic and ambiguous results explored. Mr. Barnes purposefully left some questions unresolved if he felt that further study of the topic would provide students with the additional information they needed to resolve the issue.

At the end of the respiration unit, Mr. Barnes constructed a test that contained 55 multiple choice, true-false, and fill-in-the-blank items. In contrast with the questions contained in the respiration materials and on our pre- and posttests, the test questions did not require the students to use cellular respiration concepts to explain the functions of living things. Many of the questions addressed details of the digestive, circulatory, and respiratory systems that were not included in the teaching materials that we had supplied. Similar questioning patterns were evident in the photosynthesis and matter cycling unit tests.

Conclusion for Mr. Barnes

In the end, Mr. Barnes's teaching reflected an uneasy compromise between his own habits and beliefs and the patterns of practice built into our teaching materials. He used our materials, but he modified them in significant ways. The most obvious of these was that through his lectures and the question-answer sessions he added back much of the scientific content that we had omitted. He also maintained a pattern of interaction in his classroom in which he was the primary source of information and his students were primarily questioners and listeners. In our terms, Mr. Barnes provided his students with an admirable model of scientific reasoning, but he did not give them enough coaching—enough opportunities for structured practice and feedback—to enable them to emulate the model that he provided. Again, it is hardly surprising in retrospect that this was the case. We supplied Mr. Barnes with materials that were based on assumptions about curriculum and instruction different from his own, then left it up to him to resolve the differences. We were impressed by his insight and the serious manner in which he considered the alternative that we offered, and his ability to articulate differences between our approach and his own. We will let Mr. Barnes himself have the last words:

> What's really hard is for a person who has been in the classroom to change something that they've ingrained themselves into a method of presenting something . . . Anyway, I like to try different things but some things get me real excited and some things don't, so, yeah, I think I can change, but it's hard. I'm not stuck in a rut, but I know what things will work for me. I have an inner sense of what I can pull off, and maintaining control of my personality and when I read . . . like some goals and objectives, sometimes just reading them doesn't

make sense to me. I was always a doing person, so maybe just observing it in
a different way . . . maybe if I had been in that (the training) group . . . maybe
that'd turn me on more (respiration interview, Hollon & Anderson, 1987, p. 26).

Conclusions from the Study: Changing Conceptions of Science and Science Teaching and Learning

In observing and talking with the teachers who participated in the study,
we saw a wide range of teaching practices. At one extreme was Ms. Copeland,
the teacher quoted at the beginning of this chapter, whose practice coincided
to a remarkable degree with our own recommendations for science teaching
(cf., Anderson & Roth, 1989; Hollon & Anderson, 1987). At the other extreme
there was one teacher (whom we considered to be a case of "teacher burnout")
who rarely exerted the effort necessary to maintain order in his classroom,
let alone think about deep issues concerning science curriculum and instruction.
Those teachers who lacked strong science backgrounds had developed
patterns of practice quite different from those of Ms. Mitchell and Mr. Barnes.
Mr. Armstrong (cf., Hollon & Anderson, 1987) was typical of most of these
teachers. Rather than providing science instruction directly, Mr. Armstrong
acted primarily as a manager who put students in contact with instructional
materials such as books, films, and commercially prepared worksheets. In
contrast with Ms. Mitchell and Mr. Barnes, Mr. Armstrong treated the science
content as a relatively unstructured list of facts or objectives to be covered one
at a time. His understanding of students was also substantially different; neither
he nor the other teachers like him could predict how their students would
answer the questions on the diagnostic tests. Their lack of knowledge about
students was associated with a tendency to define their practice in terms of
managing student work rather than monitoring student understanding. Of the
five teachers in the study who had not been science majors in college, four
followed patterns of practice similar to Mr. Armstrong's. The fifth was Ms.
Copeland!
We have chosen in this chapter to focus on Ms. Mitchell and Mr. Barnes
not because they are "typical" but because in many ways they exemplify the
best of current practice in science teaching. Both are intelligent, experienced,
dedicated professionals who take seriously their obligation to help their
students learn and understand science. Both volunteered to participate in the
study because they were concerned about their students' understanding and
were searching for ways to help their students learn with more understanding.
Yet, each experienced profound difficulty in enacting teaching practices like
those described at the beginning of this chapter.
In this respect Ms. Mitchell and Mr. Barnes were typical of the teachers
who participated in our study. None of the teachers underwent a profound
transformation in his or her teaching practice, and all retained patterns of

thought and behavior that differed significantly from those we consider necessary for helping most students through the process of conceptual change.

It is a commonplace to suggest that learning to teach for conceptual change is itself a conceptual change process. While this is true, it understates the difficulty of the change process. The students in Ms. Mitchell's and Mr. Barnes's classes were being asked to change their thinking about science, not the patterns of their lives. For the teachers, however, engaging in conceptual change teaching involves more than changing their *thinking* about science, about students, and about curriculum and instruction. They would also have to change patterns of *practice* that are deeply embedded in the materials that they use, in the social organization of their classrooms and their schools, and in the institutional context of their work.

Although learning to teach for conceptual change is difficult, the help that we gave the teachers in the learning process was minimal. In our instructional terms (cf., section on instructional decisions in this chapter), we left the teachers in social environments that were not particularly conducive to conceptual change teaching. The teaching materials that we provided were reasonably useful for establishing a problem and modeling solutions to it, but we provided no coaching to support the teachers who had to use their own materials to teach for conceptual change. Our workshops were adequate for establishing the problem of students' difficulties in understanding science, and we provided a general model for addressing the problems. However, we included no coaching for the teachers as they worked to incorporate our ideas into their teaching. Thus, it is not surprising that the teachers chose courses of action that allowed them to maintain their own knowledge bases and patterns of practice while incorporating some ideas from our workshops and teaching materials. While this pattern of change is understandable and sensible, it did not lead to the more fundamental changes that are necessary if science teachers are to help most of their students achieve conceptual understanding.

In summary, our study of middle school science teaching was a failure in helping teachers develop new conceptions of science teaching and learning, but not as a learning experience for us. In particular, the study helped us to see how conceptual change teaching requires a long and difficult change process involving both teachers' knowledge bases and their patterns of practice. This change process is made more difficult by the fact that current patterns of practice are deeply embedded in the materials that teachers use and in the social and organizational context of their work.

Such changes are not impossible. For example, during the last century, doctors' work has undergone changes in its knowledge base and its patterns of practice far more extensive than those suggested above for teaching. The difficulty of the change process does suggest, however, that we must learn to be satisfied with—even proud of—partial successes achieved through great effort. One of those partial successes is described in the next section.

EDUCATION FOR CONCEPTUAL CHANGE TEACHING

The middle school study described in the previous section leaves us with an obvious question: If the approaches to teacher education that we used in the middle school study were inadequate, then what should we do? This section describes an alternative that we feel points in the right direction: The Academic Learning teacher education program at Michigan State University. Our primary vehicle for describing the program will be a case study of a recent graduate, "Dave," and the development of his knowledge about science, about science learning, and about science teaching during his two years in the program.

Description of the Academic Learning Program

The Academic Learning program is one of five alternative teacher education programs at Michigan State University. Each program is intentionally kept relatively small to facilitate experimentation with alternative forms of organization and instructional strategies. The Academic Learning program is limited each year to about 65 students (typically 25 prospective elementary teachers and 40 secondary) who intend to focus on the teaching of academic subjects: mathematics, science, social studies, and English/language arts. The first cadre of students entered the program in the fall of 1981. One of us (Anderson) has been associated with the program since its inception. Roth has been associated with the program for five years. Most faculty associated with the program assume a variety of roles, including administration, teaching, advising, and supervision of student teachers.

We have made a conscious effort to incorporate the principles of conceptual change teaching into the organization and activities of the Academic Learning program. The following description of the program therefore uses the categories that we used to describe conceptual change teaching at the beginning of this chapter.

Curriculum of the Academic Learning Program

We would like to have a program whose goals are to produce conceptual change teachers: Teachers whose knowledge and practice had the qualities described earlier in this chapter. Unfortunately, this is an impossible goal, for two reasons. First, the knowledge base for conceptual change teaching is large, complex, and often topic-specific. No student can master it during the two year duration of the program. Second, such a goal ignores the degree to which teachers' knowledge is embedded in the tools that they use and in the social and institutional context of their work. Nineteenth-century doctors, for example, would not be well served by a program that trained them to use twentieth-century surgical tools and techniques, then sent them back to work in nineteenth-century hospitals.

Thus we have, of necessity, settled for more modest goals. We hope to graduate students who function well in present school contexts, yet at the same time hold higher aspirations for themselves and for their profession. We would like our graduates to share our commitment to helping students achieve conceptually integrated and useful scientific knowledge, and to possess some important parts of the knowledge base and patterns of practice that foster meaningful student learning. In addition, we hope to produce graduates who are prepared and motivated to learn from their own experiences as teachers, graduates who can analyze the degree to which they are helping their students understand and who can modify their practice accordingly. The case study of Dave, below, suggests the kinds of support needed to help preservice teachers develop the knowledge of subject matter, of learners, and of teaching that will enable them to reach these goals.

Instruction in the Academic Learning Program

Students enter the Academic Learning program thinking about teaching and learning in much less sophisticated ways than Ms. Mitchell and Mr. Barnes and devoid of many of those teachers' practical skills. The students therefore must go through a series of difficult conceptual changes to achieve the goals outlined above. The instructional problems confronting the program, therefore, are similar to the problems that science teachers encounter with their K-12 students. The program must provide a social environment that encourages conceptual change learning, establish the problem of teaching for understanding as a major goal, provide the students with appropriate and understandable models, coach them as they develop their own knowledge bases and patterns of practice, and eventually fade out of the picture. A few of the ways that we have tried to accomplish these instructional functions are illustrated in the case of Dave, below.

When Dave entered the Academic Learning program he became part of a social environment—a community—that has developed over the life of the program. This community includes the *students*, who enter the program each fall and stay together as a cadre (sometimes splitting into smaller groups) throughout their two years in the program. The community also includes *university faculty* members, many of whom, like Roth and Anderson, have worked with the program for several years and in a variety of roles. Finally, the community includes *mentor teachers*, each of whom works with a single Academic Learning student from the time the student enters the program through the completion of his or her student teaching. Like Ms. Mitchell and Mr. Barnes, both of whom have served as mentor teachers, the mentors are experienced teachers who share our commitment to teaching for understanding.

The Academic Learning community is not as coherent as we would like. Meeting time between university faculty and mentor teachers, for instance, is limited to seven after-school meetings each year plus more extensive contact during student teaching. Nevertheless, this community has several characteristics that make it a social environment that can help Dave and other students work toward becoming conceptual change teachers. The community encompasses both the university and the schools as locations, and university faculty, mentor teachers, and students as members. The university faculty and mentor teachers share an appreciation of the importance and difficulty of the craft of teaching, a commitment to helping children understand science, and a desire to improve teaching as a profession. Over time, the Academic Learning students gradually come to share many of these beliefs and commitments.

Dave: Learning to Become a Conceptual Change Teacher

"Dave" is our pseudonym for a student who graduated from Michigan State University in June, 1988. He was one of 12 students who were observed and interviewed regularly as part of the evolution of the Mentor Teacher component of the Academic Learning program. Those interviews and observations are the basis for this case study. Roth, Rosaen, and Lanier (1988) provide a more complete report.

Dave's Knowledge of Science, Learners, and Teaching

Like most Academic Learning students, Dave entered the program in the fall of his junior year. Dave was a bright, handsome, and articulate biology major. He was one of 10 students in his cadre preparing to be secondary science teachers. He had the potential to be an excellent teacher. At that time, however, he was still a long way from realizing that potential.

Because he had consistently done well in biology courses, Dave expressed confidence in his conceptual understanding of the subject matter:

> . . . I feel really strong in my conceptual knowledge and I guess that's about it. I would be able to explain most concepts, you know, after reviewing them and going over the items that I have to know. Because that's what hangs me up in class. I go to class and they're doing something, and I can't answer something simply because I haven't reviewed it. I don't know the word or you know the term for that. I've just forgotten it . . . (Roth, Rosaen, & Lanier, 1988).

Further, he viewed biology as "the ideal thing to teach because it's so related to their (students') everyday world and things they might wonder about." Thus, Dave began his teacher education with a reasonably coherent understanding of the subject matter he was to teach, and he viewed that knowledge as serving important functions in explaining everyday events and empowering individuals to better appreciate their natural world. He felt confident that he knew the subject well enough to teach it to middle school students. Dave would later come to understand that his confidence was not completely justified.

Dave's confidence was based in part on ignorance of what is involved in being a teacher. He knew little about students, about curriculum, or about instruction that supports the development of understanding. Because he knew so little, he did not know how much there was to learn. Similarly, he did not appreciate how much knowledge and how much hard work it would to take to establish even a rudimentary pattern of practice, let alone one that could help his students engage in conceptual change learning. Thus instruction in the program would have to help Dave discover and define the central problems of teaching, then help him to construct plausible solutions to them.

The First Courses: Discovering the Problems

During his first two terms in the Academic Learning program Dave took courses in learning and in curriculum. Each course involved lectures, readings, discussions, and, most importantly to Dave, assignments to be done in his mentor teacher's classroom. Dave's mentor, "Mr. Williams," was, like Ms. Mitchell and Mr. Barnes, a middle school life science teacher who had formerly participated in the middle school study. He had a good knowledge of his students, but like Ms. Mitchell and Mr. Barnes, his teaching strategies sometimes lacked enough coaching to help students develop meaningful understanding.

The readings, discussions, and assignments in the first course in the program focused on student learning, with a particular emphasis on cognitive science/ constructivist theories of learning. These learning theories, however, had little immediate effect on Dave, who was still trying to decide whether he wanted to be a teacher or a doctor. The most important experiences for Dave during this course were readings and discussions with his mentor and his fellow students about alternate approaches to teaching. These discussions convinced him that he really did want to become a teacher, and that teaching was a more complex activity than he had believed. Dave wrote extensively about these issues in the journal that he kept as a course requirement. He wrote very little, however, about constructivist or any other theories of the learner. At the end of the term, Dave's final paper for the learning course reflected his emphasis on *teaching* approaches rather than *learning* issues:

> How can I summarize the ways in which my views on teaching have changed when my head seems to be whirling with questions that, as of yet, have been unanswered. Perhaps the most important function of my first teacher education course was not only to present me with several differing approaches to teaching,

but to get me to raise questions, by seeing flaws in my beliefs, concerning all aspects of teaching and the learning environment, and on this point it has succeeded tremendously (Roth, Rosaen, & Lanier, 1988).

Dave began his second teacher education course, the curriculum course, confident that explaining scientific concepts to his students would not be a major problem for him, and that he could do so without a lot of advance preparation.

I: Suppose you're going to teach a unit like this (about food chains), before you consider yourself actually ready to teach them, what kinds of things would you have to know . . .

D: First of all, I'd go through and make sure that I knew the concepts very well, and I'd study all the parts of that, and I'd probably make out a list of exactly all I wanted them to get out of it, and the different representations that I could use. I could think about that a lot, but I think I'm a lot better on the spot. That's the way I've always been, in creating analogies right on the spot depending on the misconceptions of the children (Roth, Rosaen, & Lanier, 1988).

However, by the end of his curriculum course, Dave had gained a quite different appreciation for the notion of "thinking on the spot." This change was brought about by course assignments that required him to examine the ways that subject-matter was represented in his mentor's science text and the ways that students in his mentor's classroom constructed subject matter understanding as the result of instruction. Dave was particularly surprised by the results of a series of clinical interviews with middle school students to assess how they had understood content presented during class:

My interviews were very surprising to me. I had assumed that the material would easily be grasped . . . the problems they had . . . I was certainly shocked by them. What I begin to see now is that children may be able to do very well on a test, but when asked to begin telling what they learned it becomes apparent that they really might not know the interconnections among the facts. It also seems obvious that the children can do well on a test even though they have holes in their schema of the subject matter. It's a very difficult dilemma (Roth, Rosaen, & Lanier, 1988).

As a result of these experiences, Dave developed a much deeper appreciation of the importance of integrating his knowledge of the subject matter with knowledge about students' development. Dave also began to recognize that even his mentor teacher, whom he admired greatly, was not as effective as he had thought, because the representations developed by the teacher did not match well with the knowledge constructed by the students:

The entire situation is so frustrating. [My mentor] is such a great teacher and is very capable of getting his children on task. But the children still aren't learning what they should be (Roth, Rosaen, & Lanier, 1988).

At the same time as he was becoming aware of his mentor teacher's limitations, Dave was developing a deeper appreciation of the difficulty of representing subject matter to students and of the depth of his mentor's science knowledge:

> What we're talking about this term really shook me up because I am confident in my knowledge, but how to put it across so that the students will understand it? Not just that they'll memorize it. . . . With the many different representations, what's the best way to do it? Because it's so hard when I can sit there and think forever and it just comes to (my mentor teacher) (Roth, Rosaen, & Lanier, 1988).

By the end of the curriculum course, Dave's understanding of teaching was changing and becoming more complex. He now saw student understanding as a critical issue, and he realized how much he would have to learn before he could help all his students to understand the science that he taught. Constructivist views of the learner now began to intrigue him in ways they had not during the "learning" course. Now that he understood the central problems, he needed help in figuring out some solutions to them. He left the curriculum course wondering if he could ever develop the content and pedagogical knowledge needed to teach for conceptual change.

Developing Knowledge and Practice

Dave began trying to put his knowledge into practice during his methods courses (Science methods, Reading and Learning Strategies in the Content Areas) for which he had to plan and teach a week-long unit using a conceptual change framework for planning, teaching, evaluation, and reflection. After teaching the unit, Dave was required to evaluate students' learning and critique his own teaching. He realized that what he needed was not *more* knowledge about energy flow in ecosystems (the topic of the unit), but a different *kind* of knowledge about it. He commented that "examples are hard to come by and its hard to have a storehouse of representations." At the end of his methods course, Dave's vision of the ideal teacher had changed again:

> . . . Where before I thought it all dealt primarily with the teacher and how he presented the material, I see now that the students have to play such an active role in their learning or they won't learn at all. Especially during my week of teaching—that was my major drawback. I was discussion-based, but I didn't have them participate to the extent that I wanted them to. So, I think that looking at the content, it would have to involve the children interpreting the information, drawing inferences on their own, I guess, and guided by the teacher (Roth, Rosaen, & Lanier, 1988).

At this point, Dave's understanding of his subject matter and how to transform it in ways that fostered effective communication were of primary importance. His goals for planning now included using *students' conceptions* of the subject as an important cornerstone in planning and teaching.

By the end of his methods courses, "conceptual change teaching" was much more than a set of academic ideas for Dave. It was becoming a personally meaningful construct. When asked in the interview how he would explain conceptual change ideas to someone who had never heard about them, he responded:

> Okay. I've done this before (with friends). First of all we have to, when I first start talking about this to someone I like to tell them, ask them what they think goes on in learning, how you learn something and they usually say modeling, coaching and fading, not in those words but that's what they mean—well the teacher shows me how to do it and I work at it and he helps me a lot and then gradually I do it on my own. And then I ask them, well what do you have to know to be a good teacher? What does it take to really teach someone something? And I talk a little bit about knowing what they know already, some preconceptions and then maybe to show them the flaws in their thinking. You have to understand what a student doesn't understand correctly and create discontent in their thinking. And then I don't want to make it sound like I'm just telling them the definition of things but basically you have to know what a student learned, what a student knows, what he doesn't know correctly and what he has misunderstood, show them, show him a way, in such a way that he sees that and then present him with the correct way of thinking and help him work along to seeing that correct way and seeing how it's more useful (Roth, Rosaen, & Lanier, 1988).

Thus Dave completed his first year of teacher preparation and entered student teaching holding a well articulated conception of conceptual change teaching. Building this framework for thinking about learning, teaching, and subject matter was a gradual process that required Dave to make significant changes in his conceptions of teaching and learning.

Dave's early field experiences played a critical role in this conceptual change process. Along with readings and other course assignments, they helped Dave to appreciate the difficulty of conceptual change teaching, to see and criticize his mentor as a model, and to benefit from coaching by his mentor and course instructors. Although Dave was becoming increasingly articulate in *talking* about conceptual change teaching, he recognized that his actual *practice* as a teacher often fell far short of the ideas that he articulated.

During student teaching the next fall, Dave extended and deepened his knowledge base while working to establish a pattern of conceptual change practice. Like other student teachers, he was often consumed with issues of management, maintaining students' interest, and adjusting to the demands of full-time teaching. However, he never became solely preoccupied with day-today survival. By the end of his experience he was able to focus his energies again on the issues of subject-matter knowledge and student understanding:

> . . . It won't bug me to spend six or seven minutes on one certain thing to tie it all back in to everything that we've done so far . . . Because I'll ask a question, maybe an application question, and I can see where all the loopholes were where I missed. I had an incomplete concept map if you want to describe it that way. You have to be really specific. I learned that you can't assume that the kids know something or that the kids are going to make the connections (Roth, Rosaen, & Lanier, 1988).

Because of his mentor's earlier participation in the middle school study, Dave used the same experimental teaching materials as Mr. Barnes to teach photosynthesis and cellular respiration. Dave's response to those materials, however, was different from Mr. Barnes's:

> The conceptual change model. Modeling, coaching, and fading, too. I think that a strength I have comes directly from that, because now I'm looking at my students the way I was taught to do it. It's not something that I've lost. I can see weaknesses in my teaching that don't conform to that now. I wish we had used *The Power Plant* (the experimental photosynthesis materials) earlier because it has helped me, especially at the beginning where they go through and at least they can see what they think and have it down on paper and have it clear in their minds (Roth, Rosaen, & Lanier, 1988).

The impact of the materials on Dave was strikingly different from their impact on Mr. Barnes. These curriculum materials supported Dave's development. Dave had already come to value the conceptual-change goals embedded in the materials during his first year of professional study. He began student teaching trying to achieve these goals using materials that were not supportive of these goals. Dave recognized the philosophical incongruities between his text and his goals. Thus, the conceptual change materials provided at least a partial solution to dilemmas he had been struggling to solve. Thus, in a conceptual change learning model, he had engaged the problem of teaching for understanding, and the materials provided one source of coaching. In contrast, when Mr. Barnes received the curriculum materials, he was not dissatisfied with his own teaching and he held teaching goals that conflicted with those embedded in the materials. The materials did not provide meaningful support for his learning. They did stimulate some dissonance for him, but were insufficient to help him rethink his understanding of science teaching and learning.

Dave ended his student teaching experience confident that he was developing a pattern of conceptual change practice:

D: I look at teaching totally different now after I've been doing it. What I can see, what's happening, just like the model I've been using.

I: I wasn't sure what you meant when you said that you look at teaching totally different now that you've done it. Is that what you said?

D: Yeah, because it all seemed like words, maybe, yeah. Well, I understood, but it was on a superficial level, and now I think it's a part of me where I'm using that as a basis for everything. I see that when I wrote (in a journal) about my mentor teacher, I could see the teacher's point of view but not the students'. Now, I can see what's happening with my students. [My understanding of] subject matter knowledge, too. I think that's changed a lot. No matter what, you don't know enough about something to answer every question the way it should be answered. It's hard sometimes . . . there have been times where I feel that even though I tried to simplify it for them, that the explanation wasn't good enough. I didn't know enough about something to put it into terms that they would understand. I could explain it to someone else, another college student, but not to the kids because I didn't know it enough. Does that make sense? (Roth, Rosaen, & Lanier, 1988).

Conclusion for Dave: A Well-Started Beginner

After completing the Academic Learning program, Dave still is not a "complete" conceptual change teacher. In many respects his performance is still that of a beginning teacher—sometimes disorganized, clumsy, and ineffective. Nevertheless, we feel that the confidence Dave expressed at the end of the program was far more justified than his confidence at the beginning. We would argue that he has developed a set of beliefs and conceptual tools that prepare him to reflect on and learn from his experience as a teacher. At the time of this writing, a few months after Dave's graduation, we cannot say to what extent this potential will be realized. We doubt that Dave (or anyone else) can fully realize his potential without a work environment that encourages and nurtures conceptual change teaching.

We offer Dave's case as an existence proof, an example of the kind of "partial success achieved through great effort" to which we referred above. Not all Academic Learning students have been as successful as Dave, but enough have been successful to convince us that we are learning what it takes to help beginning teachers construct a knowledge base and a pattern of practice consistent with the principles of conceptual change teaching.

DISCUSSION

Even teachers like Mr. Barnes and Ms. Mitchell, who are among the best teachers we have worked with, are failing to teach science well in the sense that they help most of their students develop conceptually integrated and useful knowledge. Can we afford to settle for their best efforts? What are the consequences of settling for less?

If science education will continue as it has in the past, a few students, the elite 10 percent, will continue to develop significant understanding of important scientific concepts and relationships. The other 90 percent will continue to find science confusing, intimidating, uninteresting, and unrelated to their daily lives. They will continue to get through the school science courses using memorization strategies and opt out of science as soon as it is no longer required. The separation of those individuals who understand science from those who cannot and do not value scientific knowledge will further the development of a "scientific elite." The majority of citizens will continue to emerge from schooling unprepared to make reasonable decisions about scientific issues.

We believe, as do most other educators, that this state of affairs is an unacceptable scenario. Thus, we are faced with a dilemma: One the one hand, our best and most dedicated teachers experience limited success in teaching science for understanding, yet we as a society cannot afford any less. It is critical that we search for ways to resolve the dilemma. We must find ways to provide both beginning and experienced teachers with the knowledge, skills, and support systems that they need to foster meaningful understanding in their students. What conclusions can we draw from our work with experienced teachers like Ms. Mitchell and Mr. Barnes and the modest, yet encouraging success with beginning teachers like Dave?

Facilitating Change in Professional Knowledge and Patterns of Practice

For experienced teachers such as Mr. Barnes and Ms. Mitchell, long-term changes in professional subject-matter knowledge and patterns of teaching practice involve restructuring deeply held patterns of thought and action that have developed over many years. The teachers must, in many ways, initiate those changes themselves. Thus, an important issue is that of finding ways to support teachers who are seeking productive changes in their practice.

The broad range of subject-matter knowledge and teaching practices that we observed suggests that not all teachers need, or will even benefit from, one type of experience. In addition, it is clear that the typical short-term, sporadic inservice workshops cannot provide the sustained attention to teaching, learning, and subject matter that is needed to promote meaningful teacher change. Our experience suggests that efforts to help individuals teach science well in the sense that we have defined in this chapter must focus on several specific goals. These goals are described below.

Developing Knowledge of Science and of Students

Professional development experiences must foster the development of a conceptually integrated base of knowledge about the content to be taught and the ways in which students understand and learn that content. Such knowledge is not easily developed. Only one of the five teachers in our research who were not trained in science (Ms. Copeland) was able to accomplish the curricular and instructional tasks as we have defined them in this chapter. A primary reason for her success was that she had invested considerable time and effort to develop both the conceptual knowledge for each unit, and the deeper understandings of the interrelationships among units and the importance of the content in everyday settings. Further, she had developed patterns of practice that generated information about her students' thinking that she was able to use in productive ways. However, Ms. Copeland was atypical. Even Ms. Mitchell, who possessed significant knowledge about the content she was teaching and the ways that her students thought about the content, was limited in her ability to use her knowledge because it was not integrated in functional ways.

Our research suggests that knowledge of subject matter and students' thinking, while necessary, is not sufficient to enable teachers to engage successfully in conceptual change teaching. Like Ms. Mitchell and Mr. Barnes, many of the teachers held well-developed functional theories and practical knowledge about their teaching, and understood much about their students' learning problems. However, they lacked the collegial support that would have validated their insights, and often lacked a language and communication channels for articulating their ideas.

As a result, they were often unaware of the power of the knowledge they possessed and could not share it to improve the effectiveness of their teaching. For these teachers, the social environment of teaching presented critical barriers to professional development.

Establishing New Professional Relationships

A critical element in improving science teaching is to provide opportunities and support for teachers to engage in collaborative investigation of important problems of practice, and channels for sharing expertise. Traditional relationships between schools and universities must be re-examined and restructured to remove some of the traditional distinctions between roles, and establish a better language for talking about important problems of practice.

Efforts to accomplish these goals are encouraging. There are projects where teachers and university researchers have learned to collaborate in ways that enable each group to contribute to the formulation of important problems and to their investigation. The partnerships foster exchanges of expertise, sharing of services and resources, and provide a richer understanding of important problems (cf., Erickson, 1984, 1986). The settings for these collaborations vary from individual classrooms or buildings, to preservice teacher education programs such as the Academic Learning program, to professional development schools devoted to teacher training and research. In these environments, experienced teachers, university faculty, and beginning teachers come together to develop teaching skills, examine new curricular resources and instructional strategies, and participate in discussions of enduring problems of practice. Individuals can experiment with new approaches to teaching without fear of collegial or administrative disapproval and with support from other teachers and university faculty.

Providing Professional Development Experiences That Include Modeling and Guided Practice

It is clear from our research that providing teachers with general information about conceptual change teaching is not sufficient to enable them to accomplish the difficult transitions in their own conceptions of teaching, even in teachers like Ms. Mitchell and Mr. Barnes. Like their students, who undergo conceptual change in learning different ways of thinking about scientific theories, teachers need to have experiences that help them really understand both the importance of the curricular and instructional tasks and guided practice in successfully accomplishing them in their classrooms. One would not expect a doctor to read about a new surgical technique, attend a seminar describing general issues about the procedure, then sally forth and begin using the technique without further practice under supervised conditions. It is equally unreasonable to expect teachers to make fundamental changes in their practices without appropriate instruction and practice in applying new instructional strategies.

Reducing the Cognitive Complexity of Teaching Tasks

Teaching for conceptual change involves a series of cognitively complex tasks demanding that teachers possess a rich and diversified knowledge of the subject they are to teach, knowledge about the ways that learners think about that subject, and knowledge about teaching strategies that will help students bridge important gaps between their knowledge and the more scientifically mature understanding that is the goal of instruction. In order to help teachers better accomplish such complex tasks, we must seek ways to reduce their cognitive and technical complexity. We need to identify tasks that lend themselves to simplification, and to develop tools that help teachers to routinize these tasks, thus freeing cognitive capacity and real time to better address those tasks that do not lend themselves to simplification.

Our experimental materials represent one attempt to address this issue (cf., Anderson & Roth, 1989). The materials were structured to provide students with problems that engaged them in thinking about the topics. They provided teachers with questions and information useful for diagnosing students' difficulties in understanding the content and supplied corrective feedback, and included multiple opportunities for students to apply new ideas to real-world events. Thus, they differed significantly from typical texts and teacher resource materials. A critical feature of the materials was the *organization* of information. Rather than combining all the information for the teacher into a section at the beginning of the text, commentary was supplied at appropriate points in the text using a teacher page-student page format. Important information about the topic was available at the point in the text where it was most directly applicable. Although our experience with materials organized in this matter is still limited, it is worth noting that the largest gains in student understanding were obtained for those cases where the teachers used the materials.

We believe that such changes in teaching materials can only enhance our efforts to develop teaching into a true profession. Providing teachers with more powerful technical and conceptual tools can only work in favor of their developing patterns of practice that are rewarding to themselves and their students. One characteristic of professions such as medicine, law, and engineering is the development and use of a broad variety of specialized tools. Practitioners are expected to be able to use the tools made available to them in order to solve complex problems. A similar argument can be made for the development and use of more sophisticated conceptual and technical tools in teaching: They provide teachers with the means to engage in more complex problem-solving tasks than would otherwise be possible because they can access and analyze information in complex ways that would not be possible without the tools.

Provision for Collegial and Institutional Support

Improving teachers' professional knowledge alone is not the answer. We must also find ways to restructure the institutional demands of teaching in ways that make the curricular and instructional tasks possible to accomplish in typical classroom and school environments. This suggests that the larger institutional structure must evolve in ways that provide support (and accountability) for teaching in ways that lead to meaningful understanding. Teachers cannot be expected to engage in professional growth and development in an environment that fails to provide both the support for innovation and the tolerance of some ambiguity that are needed to foster change.

In his book *A Place Called School: Prospects for the Future*, John Goodlad (1984) described "teachers' personal attention" as the interest in the subject matter and the learner, the "pedagogical traits" as those techniques designed to keep the student covertly or overtly engaged in learning. He noted that

> The development and improvement of both sets of qualities and abilities become realistic goals for both preservice and inservice teacher education. We do not need to wait for profound changes in the social fabric of society or the organization of schooling to begin work on what appears to be a cornerstone in improving the quality of education in elementary and secondary schools (Goodlad, 1984, p. 125).

REFERENCES

Anderson, C.W., & Roth, K.J. (1989). Teaching for meaningful and self-regulated learning of science. In J. Brophy (Ed.), *Advances in research on teaching*, Vol. 1 (pp. 265-309). Greenwich, CT: JAI Press.

Anderson, C.W., Roth, K.J., Hollon, R.E., & Blakeslee. T. (1986). *The power cell* (Occasional Paper No. 113). East Lansing, MI: Michigan State University, Institute for Research on Teaching.

Anderson, C.W., Sheldon, T.H., & Dubay, J. (1986). *The effects of instruction on college non-major's conceptions of respiration and photosynthesis* (Research Series No. 164). East Lansing, MI: Michigan State University, Institute for Research on Teaching.

Anderson, C.W., & Smith, E.L. (1987). Teaching science. In V. Koehler (Ed.), *The educator's handbook: A research perspective* (pp. 84-111). New York: Longman.

Champagne, A.B., Klopfer, L.E., & Gunstone, R.F. (1982). Cognitive research and the design of science instruction. *Educational Psychologist, 17*(1), 31-53.

Clark, C., & Peterson, P. (1986). Teachers' thought processes. In M.C. Wittrock (Ed.), *Handbook of research on teaching (3rd ed.)* (pp. 255-296). New York, NY: Macmillan.

Collins, A., Brown, J.S., & Newman, S.E. (1989). Cognitive apprenticeship: Teaching the craft of reading, writing, and mathematics. In L.B. Resnick (Ed.), *Knowing, learning and instruction: Essays in honor of Robert Glaser*. Hillsdale, NJ: Erlbaum.

Driver, R. (1987, July). Promoting conceptual change in classroom settings: The experience of the children's learning in science project. In J. Novak (Ed.), *Proceedings of the Second International Seminar: Misconceptions and Educational Strategies in Science and Mathematics, Volume II*. Ithaca, NY: Cornell University.

Driver, R., & Easley, J. (1978). Pupils and paradigms: A review of the literature related to concept development in adolescent science students. *Studies in Science Education, 5*, 61-84.

Driver, R., & Erickson, G. (1983). Theories in action: Some theoretical and empirical issues in the study of students' conceptual frameworks in science. *Studies in Science Education, 10*, 37-60.

Driver, R., Guesne, E., & Tiberghien, A. (1985). *Children's ideas in science*. Philadelphia, PA: Open University Press.

Erickson, F.E. (1984). School literacy, reasoning, and civility: An anthropologist's perspective. *Review of Educational Research, 54*(4), 525-546.

Erickson, F.E. (1986). Tasks in times: Objects of study in a natural history of teaching. In K.K. Zumwalt (Ed.), *1986 Yearbook of the Association for Supervision and Curriculum Development*. Washington, DC.

Gilbert, J.K., & Watts, D.M. (1983). Concepts, misconceptions, and alternative conceptions: Changing perspectives in education. *Studies in Science Education, 10*, 61-98.

Hewson, P.W., & Hewson, M.G.A. (1984). The role of conceptual conflict in conceptual change and the design of science instruction. *Instructional Science, 13*, 1-13.

Hollon, R.E., & Anderson, C.W. (1986, March). *Teachers' understanding of students' thinking: Its influence on planning and teaching.* Paper presented at the annual meeting of the National Association for Research in Science Teaching, San Francisco, CA.

Hollon, R.E., & Anderson, C.W. (1987). *Teachers' beliefs about students' learning processes in science: Self-reinforcing belief systems.* Paper presented at the annual meeting of the American Educational Research Association, Washington, DC.

International Association for the Evaluation of Educational Achievement. (1988). *Science achievement in seventeen countries: A preliminary report.* Elmsford, NY: Pergamon.

Keller, E.F. (1985). *Reflections on gender and science.* New Haven, CT: Yale University Press.

Larkin, J.H., & Rainard, B. (1984). A research methodology for studying how people think. *Journal of Research in Science Teaching, 21*(3), 235-254.

Mayr, E. (1982). *The growth of biological thought.* Cambridge, MA: Belknap.

National Commission on Excellence in Education. (1983). *A Nation at Risk.* Washington, DC: U.S. Department of Education.

National Science Foundation—Department of Education. (1980). *Science and engineering education for the 1980s and beyond.* Washington, DC: National Science Foundation.

Nussbaum, J., & Novick, S. (1982). Alternative frameworks, conceptual conflict, and accommodation: Toward a principled teaching strategy. *Instructional Science, 11*(3), 183-200.

Osborne, R.J., & Freyberg, P. (1985). *Learning in science: The implications of children's science.* Portsmouth, NH: Heinemann.

Posner, J., Strike, K., Hewson, P., & Gertzog, W. (1982). Accommodation of a scientific conception: Toward a theory of conceptual change. *Science Education, 66*, 211-227.

Resnick, L.B. (1987). Learning in school and out. *Educational Researcher, 16*(9), 13-20.

Roth, K.J. (1987). *Helping science teachers change: The critical role of teachers' knowledge about science and science learning.* Paper presented at the Annual Meeting of the American Educational Research Association, Washington, DC.

Roth, K.J., & Anderson, C.W. (1987). *The power plant: Teacher's guide to photosynthesis* (Occasional Paper No. 112). East Lansing, MI: Michigan State University, Institute for Research on Teaching.

Roth, K.J., Rosaen, C.L., & Lanier, P.E. (1988, August). *Mentor teacher project: Program assessment report.* East Lansing, MI: Michigan State University.

Shulman, L.S. (1986, February). Those who understand: Knowledge growth in teaching. *Educational Researcher, 15*(2), 4-14.

Shulman, L.S., & Carey, N.B. (1984). Psychology and the limitations of individual rationality: Implications for the study of reasoning and civility. *Review of Educational Research, 54*(4), 501-524.

Smith, E.L., & Anderson, C.W. (1987, April). *The effects of training and use of specially designed curriculum materials on conceptual change teaching and learning.* Paper presented at the Annual Meeting of the National Association for Research in Science Teaching, Washington, DC.

Toulmin, S. (1961). *Foresight and understanding.* Great Britain: Anchor Press.

Toulmin, S. (1972). *Human understanding.* Princeton, NJ: Princeton University Press.

Vygotsky, L.S. (1962). *Thought and language.* Cambridge, MA: MIT Press.

Vygotsky, L.S. (1978). *Mind in society.* Cambridge, MA: Harvard University Press.

Wertsch, J. (1985). *Vygotsky and the social formation of mind.* Cambridge, MA: MIT Press.

West, L.H.T., & Pines, A.L. (Eds.). (1985). *Cognitive structure and conceptual change.* Orlando, FL: Academic.

Wilson, S., Shulman, L., & Richert, A. (1987). 150 different ways of knowing: Representations of knowledge in teaching. In J. Calderhead (Ed.), *Exploring teacher thinking*. Sussex: Holt, Rinehart, & Winston.

*   *   *

CROSS-TALK

You talk strictly in terms of teacher *knowledge*. However, to use some of the terms used in other chapters in this book, isn't it true that you are concerned not only about teachers' knowledge, but also about their *beliefs* and teaching *orientations*?

In other papers (e.g., Anderson & Smith, 1987; Hollon & Anderson, 1987) we have contrasted teachers in terms of beliefs or orientations. Teachers like Mr. Armstrong were described as exhibiting a *fact-acquisition* orientation. Teachers like Mr. Barnes and Ms. Mitchell were described as exhibiting a *content-mastery* orientation. Teachers like Dave and Ms. Copeland were described as exhibiting a *conceptual-development* orientation.

We chose not to discuss these orientations in this chapter partly because of limitations of space, and partly because they are peripheral to the central point of this chapter, which is that the *amount* of learning necessary to teach for conceptual change is very large. Thus, changing a pattern of practice from one orientation to another is not primarily a matter of re-orientation or conversion to a different point of view; it is primarily a matter of learning and using a great deal of new knowledge.

You have proceeded by developing your own model of ideal teaching and then attempting to train teachers in the use of the model. What are the pros and cons of this approach compared to the other approach used by many of the other authors in the book—studying expert teachers to see what they think and do?

We began our research about 10 years ago with the intention of studying expert teachers. We soon discovered a fundamental problem with this approach: Most students were not learning with understanding, even in the classes of the best teachers that we observed. We therefore concluded that it was necessary to develop interventions that supported alternative—and more effective—patterns of practice that are virtually impossible to find in naturalistic studies of existing classrooms. We reached this conclusion because, in contrast to many studies of teacher knowledge, assessment of student learning was an important part of all of our research.

Could you comment on the tradeoffs inherent in more or less emphasis on fidelity versus teachers' ownership of the curriculum in implementation of new programs? We have struggled with how much to scaffold teachers'

implementation through provision of detailed curriculum materials, in contrast to having teachers construct their own versions of activities and lessons, with some resulting loss on the conceptual change features which we seek to have implemented.

If "teachers' ownership of the curriculum" is taken to mean that teachers should become committed to teaching units or materials that they have developed personally, then we regard it as ultimately harmful rather than helpful. We take the fact that teachers often find it necessary to develop their own materials as a symptom of the general lack of professionalism in our field; we certainly do not have similar expectations for doctors, or farmers, or engineers. We would like teachers to "own" a commitment to finding and using the best possible materials and techniques and to developing their own materials only as a last resort when nothing adequate is available.

Unfortunately, most teachers, most of the time, find themselves teaching in situations where no adequate materials are available. In these situations teachers must learn to modify existing materials or to develop their own; so preparing teachers for these situations must be considered an important goal of teacher education. In keeping with the instructional principles outlined in our chapter, we can expect that extensive coaching, with scaffolding and feedback, will be necessary, and that some loss of conceptual change features will be apparent in teachers' first attempts to plan and teach in fundamentally different ways. We also believe that exposure to models, including carefully developed conceptual change materials, will make the coaching process less difficult and traumatic.

Neither of the experienced teachers you describe used his or her subject-matter knowledge in ways that facilitated children's conceptual change. Have you concluded that experienced teachers have such imbedded patterns of practice that change is exceedingly difficult for them? Is it more effective in the long run to concentrate on preservice teachers such as Dave, making sure that he has the foundational knowledge and orientation to enable him to construct his own continuing education? Could you comment on your current assessment of where we should be placing our limited resources and energy?

We feel that Dave's success relative to Ms. Mitchell and Mr. Barnes was due not to his greater flexibility, but to the extent and nature of the program. Dave's experience in the Academic Learning program included (in addition to practice teaching) about 150 hours of contact with university instructors, more than 1500 pages of reading, more than 400 pages of writing, and dozens of individual meetings with university staff or his mentor in which he received individual feedback on his writing, his planning, or his teaching; all in the context of a program where a commitment to conceptual change teaching was a conscious norm. In contrast, Ms. Mitchell had about 7 contact hours for instructional purposes, about 50 pages of materials to read, no opportunity to write and receive feedback, and no feedback on her teaching.

Ms. Mitchell and Mr. Barnes started out as better teachers than Dave; it is likely that at the end of comparable treatments they would still be better teachers than Dave.

Again we would emphasize that our fundamental concern is not with teachers' difficulties in being flexible with regard to orientation; it is with the amount of time and energy necessary to develop and maintain a pattern of conceptual change practice. Although we present Dave's case as a success story, it is also important to keep in mind the limited nature of his success. Dave was just starting to develop a true pattern of conceptual change practice, and we are not confident that even someone as intelligent and committed as Dave can develop to his full potential without additional support over the next several years.

So where would we place our limited resources and energy? Our first priority would probably be on support systems for teachers, including teaching materials, allocation of time for planning and professional development, and reward systems that encourage teaching for understanding. Without such support systems, we see little chance that most teachers will have the time, energy, or commitment to develop and maintain a pattern of conceptual change practice.

The development of better support systems will not change the need for extensive programs of professional development. We feel that there are many teachers, both inservice and preservice, who could benefit from such programs, and we see little reason to favor one group over the other. At the moment, our main concern is that we have not yet found reasonable "halfway measures," programs less extensive than Dave's that are clearly beneficial to the teachers and their students.

Ms. Copeland's case raises issues that I touch on in my discussion in the concluding chapter for the volume. In particular, what do you think of the following hypotheses? (1) Beyond a few basic courses, continued coursework in the academic disciplines might be unhelpful or even counterproductive for elementary school teachers. (2) What elementary school teachers might need, in addition to or even instead of disciplinary courses is courses that would provide them with pedagogical-content knowledge concerning how to teach the content that they will be teaching at the grade levels they will be working in.

The suggestion that additional content knowledge might be unhelpful or even counterproductive is not supported by our research. In general, teachers who had more content knowledge were far better at identifying key points or issues, at developing instructional representations, and at analyzing students' thinking than those who had less. We interpret Ms. Copeland's case as supporting two points: (1) No amount of scientific knowledge can substitute for a lack of knowledge or skill in other important areas, and (2) number of science courses taken may not be a very good measure of critical scientific knowledge, especially knowledge having to do with the nature of science as opposed to particular science content.

As we pointed out earlier, the question of what to do when time and resources are insufficient to help teachers develop adequate knowledge is one that we find troubling because none of the current suggested answers seem likely to work. We would not support approaches that would substitute narrowly defined "pedagogical-content knowledge" for scientific understanding. On the other hand, it may be that prospective teachers are better off developing a thorough understanding of the content and pedagogy of a limited number of topics than acquiring a smattering of knowledge about a wider range of topics. It may also be that teachers who are alienated from science can approach understanding of scientific content more effectively if it is learned in a pedagogical context.

REFERENCES

Anderson, C.W., & Smith, E.L. (1987). Teaching Science. In V. Koehler (Ed.), *The educator's handbook: A research perspective* (pp.84-111). New York: Longman.

Hollon, R.E., & Anderson, C.W. (1987). *Teacher's beliefs about students' learning processes in science: Self-reinforcing belief systems.* Paper presented at the annual meeting of the American Educational Research Association, Washington, DC.

THE CONSTRUCTION OF SUBJECT-MATTER KNOWLEDGE IN PRIMARY SCIENCE TEACHING

Deborah C. Smith and Daniel C. Neale

Science teaching in the primary grades has been a persistent problem (e.g., Craig, 1927; Henry, 1947; Stake & Easley, 1978). Teachers in those grades are under pressure to focus on reading and mathematics (e.g., McCutcheon, 1980); in addition, they feel untrained and uncomfortable with science (Schmidt & Buchmann, 1983; Welch, 1981; Wier, 1987). Science is not allocated much time in the school day (Rosenshine, 1980; Weiss, 1987), and when taught, is usually in a recitation format that relies mainly on a textbook (Pratt, 1981; Stake & Easley, 1978; Weiss, 1987).

Some efforts have been made to change this situation, most notably the National Science Foundation's funding of new elementary science curricula in the 1960s and 1970s. It is not clear, for reasons to be discussed later in the chapter, that these programs would have resulted in students' improved conceptual understanding of science had they been fully implemented in elementary classrooms. However, few of these programs became a permanent part of the elementary curriculum (Welch, 1981).

Advances in Research on Teaching, Volume 2, pages 187-243.
Copyright © 1991 by JAI Press Inc.
All rights of reproduction in any form reserved.
ISBN: 1-55938-034-9

Research on school improvement has identified a number of reasons why this may be so. Successful implementation of new programs and practices is now understood as a complex process that depends upon such factors as: (a) the extent to which local needs are met, (b) staff involvement in decisions about new practices, (c) the provision of continuous staff development activities, (d) feedback and support to teachers, (e) flexibility in coping with problems arising from the changes, and (f) adaptation of the innovations to local conditions. (See, for example, Berman & McLaughlin, 1975; Fullan & Pomfret, 1977; Fullan, Bennett, & Rolheiser-Bennett, 1989; Griffin, 1983; Hall & Hord, 1987; Purkey & Smith, 1985; Stallings & Krasavage, 1987). It appears that earlier attempts to implement science and mathematics curricula were too often delivered top-down to schools, with too little follow-up support for teachers.

Although knowledge about the process of school improvement is helpful in designing new efforts to strengthen science instruction, at the same time this knowledge calls attention to a difficult problem for science educators. If successful implementation involves a process of adaptation to local conditions and staff involvement in decisions about new practices, then many opportunities are present for the content and practice of the new curriculum to be distorted (Brophy, 1982). Indeed, as Shulman and Tamir (1973) suggested, and as one might expect, there appear to be no "teacher-proof" curricula. And recent work in science education (e.g., Anderson & Smith, 1983a; Hashweh, 1985; Munby, 1984; Olson, 1981) provides further evidence that teachers whose own competencies, and/or views of what science should be, differ from those embodied in the curriculum, often dramatically adapt curricula by rearranging the sequence of activities, changing the focus of discussions, or omitting intended activities.

A particular problem with science teaching as currently practiced in schools is indicated by another growing body of research on students' understanding of science lessons. It appears that students of all grade levels and across content domains are failing to understand basic scientific concepts (Champagne, Klopfer, & Anderson, 1980; Driver & Erickson, 1983; Strike & Posner, 1982). Researchers have identified powerful preconceptions about phenomena that students bring with them to lessons (see Helm & Novak, 1983; Novak, 1987). Although students may learn factual content and terminology in order to pass tests, their own preconceptions interfere with an understanding of scientific explanations for phenomena (Eaton, Anderson, & Smith, 1984). Even teaching that is "good" by standards applied to reading and mathematics lessons (e.g., Brophy & Good, 1986) often fails to bring about change in students' preconceptions (Anderson & Smith, 1983a).

A number of science educators have been at work investigating the kinds of teaching that are effective in facilitating students' conceptual change (Anderson & Smith, 1983a; Driver, 1987; Nussbaum & Novick, 1982; Posner, Strike, Hewson, & Gertzog, 1982; Strauss & Stavy, 1983). Drawing on current views in the history and philosophy of science, this kind of teaching for conceptual change puts the teacher's focus on students' ideas and their predictions and explanations for phenomena. Lessons often include "discrepant events" that contradict students' preconceptions, make them dissatisfied with their own explanations, and lead them to search for better ones. The emphasis is upon encouraging the children to see themselves as a community of scholars who debate ideas and their explanatory adequacy as an important part of lessons. There is evidence that these teaching strategies do promote students' conceptual change (Anderson & Smith, 1983a; Driver, 1987; Hewson & Hewson, 1983; Neale, Smith, & Wier, 1987; Smith & Anderson, 1984).

Unfortunately, because conceptual change teaching places difficult demands on teachers, it is particularly vulnerable to the kinds of distortions that teachers may introduce into intended teaching strategies (Brophy, 1982; Hollon & Anderson, 1987; Munby, 1984; Olson, 1981; Smith & Sendelbach, 1982). Thus, teachers may weaken or delete exactly those features that are critical for students' conceptual change (Anderson & Smith, 1983a; Smith & Lott, 1983).

At the Curriculum Development Laboratory at the University of Delaware, we have been working on the design of conceptual change teaching strategies for the primary grades (K-3). Having developed an effective set of unit activities on light and shadows (Neale et al., 1987) and demonstrated the model in a lab classroom (Smith & Johns, 1985), we were interested in investigating its use in public school classrooms. While recognizing the need for teachers to adapt the conceptual change model to their local circumstances, at the same time we were concerned that the science content and critical features of the model not be distorted. In search of solutions, we turned to another research base—that concerned with teachers' knowledge and its use in classroom lessons (e.g., Anderson & Smith, 1985; Berliner, 1986; Leinhardt & Greeno, 1986; Shulman, 1986)—as a source of possibilities.

We believed that earlier curriculum innovations had failed to recognize the complexity of the knowledge required for good science teaching. If we could identify the kinds of knowledge that are required for successful conceptual change teaching, we could plan for, encourage, and support teachers' construction of that knowledge. Teachers could then adapt conceptual change science teaching to their own classrooms, with a principled and knowledgeable appreciation for the critical features of the instruction. In this way we hoped, as Cohen (1985, p. 279) has suggested, to support teachers' change of "not only what people do, but how they think about their behavior and the meaning they and others give to it." We next consider recent research on teachers' knowledge and its relevance to science teaching.

TEACHERS' KNOWLEDGE

Much research on teaching has now broadened its focus from the identification of effective teaching behaviors to the related study of the knowledge and beliefs that underlie effective teaching. In the next section, we briefly review some relevant research on teachers' knowledge for teaching content, especially as it relates to teaching for conceptual change in science.

Substantive Content Knowledge

Some researchers have concentrated on teachers' knowledge of the content they teach (Buchmann, 1983; Leinhardt & Smith, 1985; Shulman, 1986). Shulman's (1986) discussion of knowledge for teaching content suggests that expertise in teaching requires substantive content knowledge (Schwab, 1978) which is not only factually correct, but also rich in relationships and organized by a conceptual model of the domain. Leinhardt and Smith's (1985) studies of expert elementary math teachers provide insight into the ways in which expert teachers' knowledge is organized and how it differs from that of novices. For example, semantic nets of experts' knowledge revealed rich conceptual links, ordered in hierarchical relationships. Novices, on the other hand, could sometimes state the algorithm but not apply it.

In secondary science, Hashweh (1985) found that more knowledgeable teachers reorganized the sequence of topics in the text and added activities where they felt the text was weak. Less knowledgeable teachers followed the text sequence closely, deleted sections that they themselves did not understand, and maintained their own errors about the content, even when the text directly contradicted them. Similarly, Carlsen (this volume, pp. 115-143) describes how differences in the same teacher's knowledge of various science topics led to differences in the opportunities for students to ask questions in those lessons.

Primary grade teachers are well aware of their weak background in the sciences (e.g., Schmidt & Buchmann, 1983). They may even hold some of the same misconceptions that their students do (e.g., Apelman, 1984; Smith, 1987). In fact, it may be useful to consider them as adult novices in some, if not all, of the science domains they teach (e.g., diSessa, 1982).

In science teaching, and especially in conceptual change teaching, it is critical that the teacher be able to present and explain the current scientific model clearly and to contrast it with student models (Anderson & Smith, 1985). Yet, Roth, Anderson, and Smith (1986) observed teachers whose own content knowledge was insufficient to clear up children's confusions during science lessons. Anderson and Smith (1983a) found that even teachers who could state scientific principles correctly in lessons sometimes made mistakes when trying to explain phenomena. Thus, not only is correct content knowledge needed for conceptual change teaching, but teachers must be confident enough and fluent enough with the scientific model to lead discussions, provide examples and explanations, and generate problem solving applications. This translation of content into teaching is the next area of teaching knowledge we discuss.

Pedagogical Content Knowledge: Knowledge of Students' Concepts

The translation and interpretation of content during teaching is what Shulman (1986) has called pedagogical content knowledge. Hawkins (1980) has discussed this as the teacher's ability to make content "penetrable" for students. One aspect of this pedagogical content knowledge is the teacher's knowledge of typical student errors and the usual developmental path along which students progress (e.g., Carpenter, Peterson, Fennema, & Carey, 1987). Leinhardt's (1987) expert math teachers provide examples of how this knowledge is important to effective teaching. These teachers were aware of usual student errors and in which lessons they would typically appear. Further, because of their importance for students' progress in understanding mathematical concepts, experts planned for ways to elicit these errors and then to use them in lessons to teach the correct concepts. Hashweh (1985) found that less knowledgeable high school science teachers failed to recognize student errors and actually corrected a (simulated) student who was especially insightful about underlying principles in the lesson. In primary science, teachers are rarely aware of students' preconceptions, or of their power to interfere with science learning (Hollon & Anderson, 1986; Neale, 1987). Even when informed of these student ideas, teachers often assume that they can be ignored or easily changed (Hollon & Anderson, 1987).

Pedagogical Content Knowledge: Strategies for Teaching Content

Yet another important aspect of pedagogical content knowledge is knowledge of particular teaching strategies that enable students to make progress in conceptual understanding of the content (Carpenter et al., 1987; Leinhardt, 1985). Anderson and Smith and their colleagues (Blakeslee, Anderson, & Chadwick, 1986; Roth, et al., 1986; Smith & Anderson, 1984; Smith & Lott, 1983) have carefully described strategies that work in facilitating students' conceptual change in science. These include (a) eliciting students' preconceptions and predictions about phenomena, (b) asking for clarification and explanation, (c) providing discrepant events, (d) encouraging debate and discussion about evidence, and (e) clearly presenting alternative scientific explanations. What is remarkable about these strategies is that elementary teachers so rarely use them in science lessons (Anderson & Smith, 1983a; Neale, 1987; Smith & Lott, 1983). Yet, knowledge of these teaching strategies appears to be crucial to success in bringing about significant change in students' conceptions (Anderson & Smith, 1983a, 1985; Hewson & Hewson, 1983; Minstrell, 1984; Nussbaum & Novick, 1982).

Pedagogical Content Knowledge: Shaping and Elaborating the Content

A third kind of pedagogical content knowledge is the teacher's use of examples, good explanations, metaphors, analogies and representations. For example, Collins and Stevens (1982) describe the varied array of examples and counterexamples with which an expert teacher challenged a student's thinking about rainfall cycles. In math, Putnam and Leinhardt (1986) report the repertoire of examples, alternative representations, good explanations, and categories of activities which expert teachers revealed in their interviews and teaching. Similarly, Wilson, Shulman, and Richert (1987) describe the "150 ways of knowing" that secondary teachers construct for helping their students to learn the subject.

In science lessons, teachers with limited content knowledge may generate metaphors that are conceptually misleading for students (e.g., Smith & Sendelbach, 1982), or may severely limit activities and discussions because of their own inability to apply concepts to new situations (Dobey & Schafer, 1984). In Hashweh's (1985) dissertation study of secondary science teachers, those with better content knowledge in the domain generated more representations of the physics content, and these were qualitatively different from those generated by less knowledgeable teachers.

Knowledge of particular curriculum materials and activities to use with students (Clark & Elmore, 1981; Leinhardt, 1987; Shulman, 1986) is yet another important aspect of teachers' knowledge for teaching content. Teachers with better content knowledge in Hashweh's (1985) study also reorganized the text's sequence of topics and inserted some of their own activities, in order to emphasize important conceptual themes.

Teachers' Orientations Toward Science Teaching and Learning

Other researchers have focused on the dispositions—theories, beliefs, and roles—that frame teachers' work (e.g., Clark & Peterson, 1986; Peterson, Carpenter, Fennema, & Loef, 1987). Clandinin (1986), in his detailed case study of one teacher, found that the teacher's images of teaching and learning served to "mind" her practice, that is, to shape the decisions and actions; this is similar to Schon's (1983) characterization of the "role frame" with which professionals frame their work. McCutcheon's work (1980), among others (Anderson & Smith, 1985; Harlen, 1975), has suggested that these beliefs and roles may often conflict with the belief systems and roles implicit in curriculum and may result in modifications of the curriculum. For this reason, programs of research on teachers' content knowledge have also considered how teachers' beliefs about particular content, how it is established and accepted as knowledge in the discipline (Schwab's [1978] syntactical knowledge), and how it should be taught and learned (Anderson & Smith, 1985; Hashweh, 1985; McCutcheon, 1980; Peterson et al., 1987), play a part in effective teaching.

As Shulman (1986) points out, subject-matter disciplines have accepted methods for establishing knowledge and deciding claims of truth. Although authority is rarely a sufficient warrant for truth in the scientific community, teachers may act as if their own authority or that of the text is sufficient in science lessons (Russell, 1983). While it is unlikely that elementary teachers will have knowledge of the history and philosophy of science (or of mathematics, see Peterson et al., [1987]), they often do have strong beliefs about what science is, how scientific knowledge becomes established, and how it ought to be taught and learned. Anderson, Smith, and their colleagues (Blakeslee et al., 1986; Hollon & Anderson, 1986; Smith & Anderson, 1984) have described several kinds of *orientations* to science teaching and learning which are held by elementary and junior high science teachers.

The familiar and persistent recitation format in science lessons (Helgeson, Blosser, & Howe, 1977; Kilbourn, 1983) often rests on a teacher's assumptions that science consists of "just facts" and that these facts are effectively transmitted to students through memorization and practice. These *didactic* teachers turn discussions into lectures, delete investigative activities, and transform problem-solving exercises into objective tests (Hollon & Anderson, 1987; Munby, 1984; Smith & Anderson, 1984).

Activities-oriented teachers share many of the same assumptions about science teaching and learning; however, in addition to the text and lectures, they rely on activities such as demonstrations, experiments, films, and worksheets to provide students additional sources of content mastery (Anderson & Smith, 1985). Unfortunately, such teachers often seem unsure as to how these activities contribute to students' learning. As a result, their students rarely develop understanding.

In contrast to didactic teachers, those who hold a *discovery* orientation appear to assume that scientific claims rest on the empirical discovery of the truth that lies in the sensory world. For these teachers, children learn by "hands-on" experience with phenomena in open-ended experiments; if enough experiences are provided, teachers assume that children will assimilate the intended science content directly (Smith & Anderson, 1984). In lessons, children are encouraged to come to their own conclusions, and their ideas are accepted without challenge. Discussions are often deleted because teachers assume that children have correctly induced the "truth" as revealed in the empirical phenomena.

Teachers sometimes follow a somewhat different variation, focusing more on the *processes* or methods of science. In their lessons, content and understanding matter less than does students' correct performance of the "scientific method." So students observe, hypothesize, manipulate variables and materials, and draw (possibly incorrect) conclusions. In the teacher's eyes, however, they have "done" the correct scientific procedures, and are therefore successful learners.

In contrast, a *conceptual change* orientation to the teaching of science lessons assumes a student who comes to lessons with already structured ideas about the content of the lesson. As we have discussed, teachers focus on children's explanations for phenomena, the predictive adequacy of alternative explanations, the use of evidence in supporting and justifying claims, and the role of discussion and debate in establishing knowledge and making progress in understanding (Anderson & Smith, 1983a). They plan for students' misconceptions and provide discrepant events (Nussbaum & Novick, 1982) which contradict them. Clearly, conceptual change teaching requires an orientation (or principles of practice, Elbaz [1983]; or image of teaching, Clandinin [1986]; or role frame, Schon [1983]) to appropriate ways to establish knowledge claims in science, and the teaching strategies (which are different from those in the primary teacher's usual repertoire) through which to implement that orientation. Lack of such understanding and strategies may be a major source of adaptations that distort and weaken conceptual change lessons, just as McCutcheon (1980) has suggested.

Pedagogical Knowledge of Organization and Management

Leinhardt and her colleagues (Leinhardt, 1983; Leinhardt & Greeno, 1986; Leinhardt, Weidman, & Hammond, 1984) have examined a particular kind of pedagogical knowledge in mathematics lessons, the teacher's knowledge of lesson structures and accompanying rules and routines that help lessons flow easily. One might expect that teachers' knowledge of strategies for management and organization would be important in elementary science lessons, too. Although strategies for management have been well studied (Evertson et al., 1981) for reading and mathematics classes, little work has been done in science lessons, especially in the primary grades. This is unfortunate, for while reading and math lessons involve familiar activity structures and familiar rules and routines (e.g., recitation, two-way presentation, seatwork), science lessons often involve new and complicated activity structures. For example, students may move around the room gathering materials, work in small groups to test out ideas, talk with other children as they work, and meet as a whole class to discuss and debate results and explanations. In science lessons, teachers must be prepared for and have clear rules and routines for such activities (Sanford, 1984; Tobin & Fraser, 1987); if not, their attention may be occupied by monitoring children's movement, talk, and activities (as observed by Anderson & Barufaldi [1980], and Smith & Sendelbach [1982]), to the detriment of the conceptual content of the lessons.

Summary

We have discussed several kinds of teachers' content knowledge and beliefs that we believe to be critical in successful conceptual change science teaching. If teachers lack knowledge in any or all of these areas, science lessons could be intentionally or unintentionally modified in ways which reduce students' opportunities for conceptual understanding. From another perspective, these aspects of teaching knowledge constitute important targets for teacher development. If teachers had such knowledge, learning to use conceptual change strategies should be facilitated.

While we have discussed them separately, it is clear from considerations of teacher thinking (Berliner, 1989; Clark & Peterson, 1986; Doyle et al., 1983; Leinhardt & Greeno, 1986) that many of these kinds of teaching knowledge would be in simultaneous use during science teaching and that their selection and integration would contribute to the complexity of that teaching (e.g., Shulman's [1986] "strategic" knowledge, and Brophy's [1988]"conditional" knowledge). In the most recent phase of our research, we have followed teachers back into their own classrooms to document teachers' uses of content knowledge and cognitive processes while teaching science lessons. In this paper, we discuss the first phase of the longitudinal program in some detail and briefly report recent results from the classroom studies.

METHOD

Ten primary teachers in grades kindergarten through three were recruited (by recommendation, application, and observation) from three local school districts, for a four-week summer program (funded by EESA Title II) on teaching primary science. Two of these teachers joined the program after much of the preliminary data collection was completed; they are not included in most of the analyses. Teachers had from 5 to 27 years of experience and ranged in age from mid-twenties to mid-fifties. For purposes of confidentiality, all were given feminine pseudonyms.

Program and Data Collection

One of the main purposes of the program was to understand, facilitate and document conceptual change in the teachers' content knowledge. With this in mind, we used the conceptual change framework (Anderson and Smith, 1985; Posner et al., 1982), and Case's (1978) recommendations for instructional design for the four-week program. Case suggests that diagnosis of the learner's spontaneous strategies and of particular areas of difficulty is crucial for designing instruction aimed at changing that thinking. Much of our initial data collection was devoted to diagnosing teachers' thinking and understanding their current science teaching, so that we could provide opportunities for and support teachers' construction of knowledge in the areas we believed to be important for expertise in conceptual change teaching.

During the Spring of 1986, prior to the summer program, teachers were videotaped in their own classrooms while teaching a science lesson of their choice. All teachers also completed a questionnaire/application concerning their views of teaching school science. Each then was individually interviewed in depth about her: (a) educational background, teaching experience, school environment, and science curriculum knowledge; (b) knowledge of the physics of light and shadows, and (c) knowledge of children's ideas in that domain. The physics content interview was a clinical interview about instances (Osborne, 1980; Posner & Gertzog, 1982), in which paper and pencil tasks were presented (see, for example, Figure 1); teachers were asked to draw, then discuss their answers, and the interviewer then probed their answers. Similarly, for each task they were asked to predict what they thought children in their own classes would say. All interviews were audiotaped, then transcribed. After the interview, each received the syllabus and readings for the course.

For four weeks in June and July, 1986, teachers participated in the Summer Institute, held at the College of Education's Curriculum Development Lab classroom. They were paid by their districts (from EESA Title II funds) and received four graduate credits for the course. In the first week, teachers read and discussed research on children's misconceptions (e.g., excerpts from Piaget [1930]; Eaton et al. [1984]; DeVries [1986]) and on teaching strategies that facilitate conceptual change (e.g., Anderson & Smith, 1983a). Readings were chosen to provide contradictory and alternative evidence to teachers' own views. In addition, they explored their own knowledge of light and shadows in activities aimed at revealing their own misconceptions and facilitating their own progress in understanding the content. Activities were designed to meet Case's (1978) suggestions for instructional design and incorporated the conceptual change teaching strategies which we hoped they would learn (Anderson & Smith, 1983a).

We viewed the program's main goals to be conceptual change not only in teachers' substantive content knowledge, but also in their ideas about teaching science and their knowledge of children's ideas. We had already videotaped their spontaneous teaching of what they believed to be good science lessons and diagnosed their knowledge and beliefs in a number of areas. In this first week, our aim was to provide discrepant events in several of these areas, in order to have teachers begin the search for alternatives. For example, in addition to reading about children's misconceptions, teachers learned how to conduct clinical interviews with materials and interviewed the children coming to the summer camp. In this way, they were able to check the research findings against their own findings with young children.

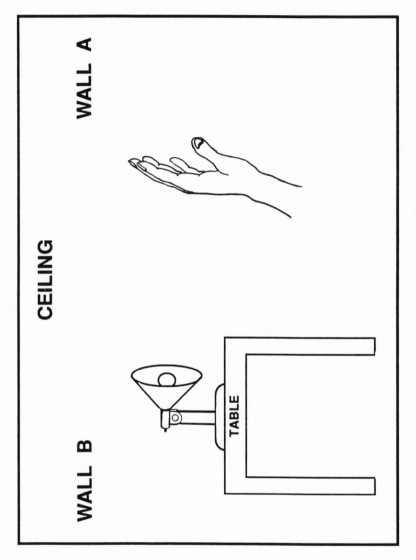

Figure 1. Illustration Used in Teachers' Interview about Subject Matter

In activities about light and shadows, lessons with teachers were organized around the central problems they had revealed in their own clinical interviews. Lessons opened with a problem or puzzle to explain; proceeded to predictions, reasons, explanations and debate from the entire group; led to activities in which they sought solutions with a peer and represented their results in some way (writing, graphs, tracings, etc.); and ended with discussion of their ideas, previous predictions and explanations, unresolved problems, and so forth. Having other adults express misconceptions and difficulties in understanding (e.g., one teacher who, for days, could not understand why moving the screen closer to the object made the shadow smaller) was an especially striking reminder that conceptual change takes time and involves giving up strong intuitive beliefs.

For the second and third weeks, teachers taught small groups of children, ages five to eight, in a morning summer camp. Two teachers were responsible for each small group; one taught the group and the other coached, with roles reversing for the second week. Although the small groups were unrealistic in terms of their usual teaching loads, we wanted to follow Case's (1978) instructional design and reduce the cognitive load on teachers while they were learning new content and new strategies. During each teacher's week of teaching, one lesson was videotaped; in the afternoons, that teacher and her coach met with us to discuss the tape (other teachers were welcome, but not required to attend). Afternoons were also spent exploring new light and shadows activities, discussing issues of children's understanding in lessons, and constructing materials and activities for the next lessons. Each teacher kept a log in which she reflected on teaching, learning, feelings about lessons, etcetera.

In the last week of the summer program, teachers interviewed children again to assess their progress, then met in grade-level teams to discuss activities and plan a two-week unit for their own classes in 1986-87. This week turned out to be a considerable frustration, because many were inexperienced at constructing and writing curriculum and had difficulty transforming their new knowledge of content, children, and activities into a workable unit.

In October of 1986, each teacher was interviewed about her substantive content knowledge and orientation again in a clinical interview with questions parallel to, but not identical to, the June interview.

Before each teacher began teaching her unit in the winter and spring of 1987, the first author interviewed her about her plans. This planning interview included probes of the teacher's knowledge of children's thinking about light and shadows, of conceptual change science teaching strategies, of criteria for curriculum design, of the substantive content, and of management.

Children's conceptual understanding of light and shadows was assessed before and after instruction in a clinical interview with familiar materials. A stratified random sample of half of each class, representing both sexes and three ability levels (as determined by total score on the California Test of Basic Skills), was interviewed by a trained interviewer in a quiet setting at the child's school.

During the unit, at least four lessons were videotaped. These four lesson tapes began with a brief pre-lesson interview with the teacher about her plans and goals. During the lesson, the first author took notes. After the lesson, the teacher and researcher discussed the lesson—first, without the videotape; then, while watching the tape. Either teacher or researcher could stop the tape to comment at any point. For these four lessons, the researcher offered "coaching" comments on three aspects of the lesson that went well and one suggestion for improvement. Teachers kept written logs throughout the unit teaching.

After the unit, teachers completed a written self-evaluation of their teaching and of children's progress in understanding light and shadows. One year later, each was interviewed again about her substantive content knowledge, pedagogical content knowledge, pedagogical knowledge of management, and orientation. Teachers were also asked to rate and discuss their evaluation of various components of the program, and to describe its implications for their teaching, both in science and in other subjects.

DATA ANALYSIS

Videotapes of teachers' Spring (1986), Summer (1986), and Spring (1987) summer lessons were transcribed. Each lesson was then independently described and rated by a trained rater according to a configurations checklist (Hall & Hord, 1987) of features associated with conceptual change teaching (drawn from Anderson & Smith, 1983a; Blakeslee et al., 1986; Hollon, Anderson, & Smith, 1980; and Posner et al., 1982) and with young children's thinking in science (Kamii & DeVries, 1978). These configurations represented the ideal and several possible alternatives for each feature.

Each feature was represented by an item in the following form, in which a rating of three represented a high level of implementation.

3	2	1
Activities are clearly tied to concept in lesson.	Activities not clearly tied to concept.	Activities are not included.

Features were grouped into the following categories:

Lesson Segments. These included the eight lesson structures identified in the analysis of expert performance during the demonstration unit: (1) introduction, (2) review, (3) development (focus), (4) development (elicit), (5) investigation, (6) representation, (7) discussion, and (8) summary.

Content Features. Included were five items indicating: (1) an emphasis upon conceptual understanding, (2) accuracy of subject-matter content, (3) focus on scientific conceptions, (4) appropriateness of subject-matter representations, and (5) conceptual ties across lesson(s).

Teacher Role. Three teacher actions were specified: (1) eliciting and diagnosing misconceptions, (2) presenting discrepant events to challenge student thinking, and (3) encouraging discussion and construction of scientific conceptions.

Student Role. These were six student actions associated with constructing subject-matter knowledge, including: (1) making predictions and explanations, (2) conducting investigations, (3) representing findings, (4) describing results, (5) applying new conceptions, and (6) discussing results and explanations with others.

Activities and Materials. Three features were included: (1) materials permit students to produce immediate, salient, and varied effects; (2) activities are clearly related to concepts in the lesson; and (3) activities include discrepant events.

Classroom Management. Six features were rated, including: (1) appropriate spatial arrangements, (2) discussion of rules and routines, (3) monitoring and feedback on rules and routines, (4) application of appropriate consequences, (5) degree of student responsibility, and (6) student cooperation in following rules and routines.

Disagreements about ratings were resolved by returning to the tapes and transcripts. Inter-rater agreement on these ratings ranged from 94 to 100 percent for pairs of raters. Considerable time was spent viewing lesson tapes and reading transcripts to refine the definitions of features being rated and to clarify interpretations of items on the checklist (see Neale, 1987; Neale, Smith, & Johnson, 1989, for details).

Audiotapes of teachers' interviews were transcribed. Questionnaires and the background section of the interview were read independently by two researchers, and evidence of the teacher's primary orientation to teaching and learning science (drawn from Anderson & Smith, 1985) was noted. Preliminary categorization was made independently, and discrepancies (which were few and involved the extent to which traces of other orientations were present) were resolved by a return to the interview transcripts and discussion between the raters. Raters agreed about orientation categories on 90 percent of the items.

The physics content section of the June and October interviews was scored and summarized for all teachers. Content sections for two teachers were lost due to recording difficulties. Four teachers' knowledge of the targeted conceptions for light and shadows were coded (again by two independent raters) for their June and October interviews. Raters agreed 87 percent of the time, and discrepancies usually involved the degree of confidence in the teacher's knowledge of the targeted concept.

Teachers' knowledge of children's ideas in the Spring, 1986, and Spring, 1987, interviews was summarized independently in a similar way by two researchers. There were no disagreements in coding these predictions.

Logs were transcribed and inspected for further evidence of teachers' changes in beliefs and content knowledge, and their feelings about these changes. Audiotapes of stimulated recall sessions for lessons were transcribed and teachers' comments coded for issues which related to the kinds of knowledge under study and which were raised by the teacher.

Children's interview responses were scored for accuracy of predictions and quality of explanation, and a total score computed for all items. t-tests of the differences between pre-and post-instruction class means were conducted.

RESULTS

In this section, we present summaries of teachers' knowledge of the substantive content; their orientations to science teaching and learning; and their pedagogical content knowledge of children's misconceptions, of teaching strategies in science, and of the uses of content in lessons. We focus on five teachers in particular because they are especially interesting cases, but use data from other teachers to provide contrasts or additional examples. In each of the kinds of teaching knowledge under study, we discuss ways in which teachers made progress or encountered barriers.

Next, we discuss a recent follow-up study (Neale, Smith & Johnson, 1989) of the extent to which teachers were able to implement the conceptual change teaching strategies in their own classrooms. Finally, we briefly summarize findings from an in-depth case study of one teacher (Smith, 1989).

Substantive Content Knowledge

Spring Substantive Content Knowledge

With one exception, teachers' content knowledge was limited, both in science in general (as revealed in their Spring, 1986, lessons) and in the physics of light and shadows (in their June interviews). For example, in the different spring lessons, teachers made such mistakes such as implying that birds migrated because they were cold-blooded, or switching the terms *rotation* and *revolution* when referring to the motion of the earth.

In their June interviews, all but two teachers discussed at some length their lack of science background and feelings of inadequacy in science content. Ms. Clark summed up the feelings of many others:

> You know, kids enjoy it [science] but I think they [teachers] shy away from
> teaching it, and I think my own lack of, not knowing what to do is the reason
> I am not doing it . . . .
> Science always has sort of a special feel when you hear the word—"Oh, that's
> for smart people," and you are an elementary major and you will stick with
> reading and math and that kind of thing.

Teachers admitted that they avoided teaching science, and physics in particular, because of their own lack of knowledge. In fact, Ms. Duke revealed that she had wanted to quit upon hearing that we were to do physics in the summer program.

> I was thinking I would love to do something about the beach and seashore. I
> had no idea. And [another teacher] said, "I heard it's physical science." Well,
> you have ruined my day. I hate you; why did you say that? I don't know, I guess
> . . . well, I guess magnets would be physical science. I never had physics.

It is worth remembering, especially as we discuss teachers' content knowledge, that for most of the teachers with whom we worked, the summer program demanded courage as well as cognitive growth (Gruber, 1974).

In the content interview about light and shadows (see Table 1 for targeted conceptions), teachers' knowledge was fragmented and often provided evidence of conceptual flaws similar to children's misconceptions. Teachers groped for memories of terms like *reflection* and *refraction*. They could sometimes remember the words *waves, rays, or particles*, but these appeared to be isolated fragments in memory. One would ask "Isn't it rays?" but then fail to use the idea in later explanations. Answers often seemed to be based on personal experience (e.g., "I know I've done that, so the shadow gets bigger"). At best, their knowledge was procedural in nature; they could tell *what* to do but when pressed for an explanation, admitted they did not know. The exception was an experienced upper-grades teacher (Ms. Rochester) who correctly answered all except one of the interview questions and referred to a conceptual model (rays travelling, bouncing, refracting) throughout her explanations.

Most teachers referred to light as something that "lights up" an area or gave examples (e.g., the sun or electricity), much as children do (Anderson and Smith, 1983b; DeVries, 1986). Although nearly all knew that a shadow resulted when light was blocked in some way, one called it a *reflection* and another a *projection*. However, their general lack of a conceptual model of light travelling in all directions from a source led to faulty predictions about the size of shadows. Most were procedurally correct in describing how to make a hand shadow bigger or smaller; however, half then predicted that, in order for the shadow to be the same size as the hand, the hand should be halfway between the light and surface (see Figure 1).

Table 1.   Targeted Conceptions For Teachers

1. Light is a form of energy.
2. Light exhibits properties of particles.
3. Light travels in straight lines.
4. Light is emitted by a source in all directions.
5. Light sometimes exhibits properties of wave behavior.
6. Light is composed of different wavelengths.
7. Light is absorbed by many objects.
8. When light is reflected, the angles of incidence and reflection are equal.
9. When light passes into a medium of a different density, it is bent or refracted.
10. When light is absorbed or reflected by an object, a shadow is formed where the light doesn't get through (is blocked).
11. We see most objects because of light reflected from them to our eyes.
12. We see colors because some wavelengths have been absorbed by the object and others are reflected to our eyes.
13. Shadows can be made bigger: by blocking more of the light (decreasing the object/light distance) or by projecting the shadow over a larger area (increasing the object/surface distance).
14. Shadows cannot be smaller than the object surface making them unless we distinguish between the umbra & penumbra as in the case of solar eclipses.
15. The length and shape of a shadow is affected by the orientation of the light and object, and the angle between the light and surface.
16. Objects can only have a shadow if light is hitting them; if one is in the other's shadow, the shaded object will not create a new shadow (merges).

The lack of a model of light actively travelling in a direction also led to predictions that a dog sitting within the shadow of a house would have a shadow (or maybe a faint one), because light was available around the dog. The active role of light in vision was similarly not well understood; only one referred to the reflection of light from the dog to the boy's eyes as the reason why the dog could be seen, when the house was blocking the light. Others fell back on assertions ("I know you can see him") or mentioned the available light as necessary to "look through" in order to see the dog. This latter notion of light as static substance which brightens, and of the eyes playing the active role in reaching out and "grabbing" images, is common among children as well (Anderson & Smith, 1983b).

When asked for explanations of phenomena that required conceptual knowledge of the wave properties of light, (e.g., what would happen to light falling on a prism), teachers answered that light would reflect off, go through unchanged, be bent but emerge as white light, and so forth. Even those who knew that the spectrum would appear could not explain why or how that happened. Explanations for the red color of an apple also sometimes resembled those which children give; one suggested that the color was part of the apple and "light had nothing to do with it." While others could mention words like spectrum, or tried to recall some knowledge about light and color, (e.g., "Isn't

Table 2. Teachers' Knowledge of Targeted Conceptions

Targeted Conceptions		Rochester Spring	Rochester Fall	Clark Spring	Clark Fall	Stein Spring	Stein Fall	Lake Spring	Lake Fall
energy	1	+	+	∅	+	∅	∅	+	∅
rays, particles	2	√	+	√	+	∅	+	√	+
straight lines	3	√	+	∅	√	∅	+	√	√
diverges	4	√	+	∅	√	∅	+	√	+
waves	5	+	+	∅	∅	∅	∅	∅	∅
refraction	6	+	+	∅	∅	∅	∅	−	∅
absorption	7	+	+	∅	∅	∅	∅	√	∅
reflection	8	+	+	−	∅	∅	∅	√	+
refraction	9	√	+	∅	∅	√	∅	√	+
shadow	10	+	+	+	+	∅	+	+	+
reflected to eye	11	+	+	−	√	∅	+	∅	+
color	12	+	+	−	∅	∅	√	√	√
size	13	√	+	√	+	√	+	√	+
smaller	14	−	+	−	+	√	+	√	−
angles of light	15	√	+	√	√	−	+	+	+
merges	16	√	+	−	−	+	−	−	√

Notes: + = strong evidence, explicitly stated
√ = some evidence, answers appear to use
∅ = no evidence, not mentioned or used
− = said opposite or used incorrect model

204

white the absence of all colors?"), only three correctly explained the absorption and reflection of wavelengths to the eye.

For four of the five teachers who collaborated closely with us and agreed to have their results individually presented, their June answers were examined for evidence of conceptual knowledge about light and shadows (see Table 2). (Ms. Duke's June content interview was lost due to recording difficulties.) There was a wide range of knowledge among these teachers. One showed evidence of a clear, scientific conceptual model that was consistently applied throughout the interview (Ms. Rochester); another was missing some of the finer details, but correctly applied the general model to most questions (Ms. Lake). Others were clearly missing a coherent, scientific model, although they could predict some solutions accurately (e.g., Ms. Clark and Stein).

Summer Substantive Content Knowledge

Over the four-week summer institute, teachers struggled with their fears about content as well as the content itself. While they enjoyed the physics activities (e.g., covering an entire wall of the classroom with paper in order to make the biggest thumb shadow), their comments and logs revealed many difficulties. Ms. Stein wrote about making the huge hand shadows:

> Seemed very complex to grasp and takes time to sort out each situation. It is necessary to become actively involved in order to understand concept of light and shadow.

In another activity, Ms. Rochester and Ms. Evans were trying to make double shadows, using just one light and one object, with the aid of a mirror. The first author and Ms. Rochester were trying to figure out why the "reflected" shadow appeared where it did; when Ms. Rochester used the terms "angles of incidence and reflection," Ms. Evans exclaimed in dismay and panic, "Oh, I knew it was going to get like this!" For her, still struggling with constructing an initial model of light as travelling, such terminology was a reminder of too many science courses in which content was covered too fast, understanding fell by the wayside, and memorization sufficed (see Anderson, 1986, for examples).

Teachers did come to realize some of the power of a conceptual model and the excitement of coming to understand physical phenomena. Ms. Lake commented in her log, after an afternoon making mirror mazes:

> Reflected light is collected and reflected by each successive mirror. I loved the afternoon of discovery.

And later wrote:

One big help is knowing that the light travels in straight lines—the principle is the same with cameras and the reflection in the mirror. The logical approach to solving the problems that we have encountered makes it seem easier. The talking through the "why" of things is helpful, too.

While working as a group on a lesson about mirrors and reflection, Ms. Duke (whose aversion to physics was quoted earlier) exclaimed

This is so fascinating! I can see why people become physicists.

and in her log wrote

Later after lunch, we came back to play with mirrors; it was fun, yet mind boggling. I'm still pondering how we see, let alone this new information! I guess I could be here all summer.

For teachers who began with naive conceptions of the nature of light, one week's activities were obviously not enough. By the end of the first week, teachers were interviewing children and planning for the summer camp. Ms. Evans later commented about the interviewing in this way

Yeah, that was confusing to me even when we tested the kids . . . we had the one doll in front of the other and I was asking those questions like crazy and I was going, "Oh (expletive deleted), I really don't know this."
You know, really, especially when we do the pre-interviews, we had done that stuff but it just really hadn't, you see it still hasn't all, it takes a while.

Fall Substantive Content Knowledge

Teachers' substantive content knowledge did change, often dramatically, over the summer. Table 2 shows the progress made by four of the teachers we studied. Ms. Evans' comments in her fall interview provide the clearest example of changes and her feelings about her growth in content knowledge. In answer to the question, "What is light?", she responded:

S: It's the absence of darkness, I know that much, and it's energy, and it travels, and moves, and bends, and is all around except when it's dark, and you break it up into different colors of the spectrum, and it could be a force, like a laser. If you concentrate it, it spreads.
D: You know a lot.
S: More than I knew when I came in the summer time.

And later in the interview, she commented:

S: I just love it because I know so much.
D: I know. Doesn't it feel great?
S: Must be how kids feel. . . .

Subject-matter content knowledge represented both barriers and triumphs for the teachers with whom we worked. Throughout the monthly seminars (1986-87), it remained a primary focus, as they continued to struggle with difficult ideas and to help each other understand. (See Smith [1987], for further discussion of changes in teachers' substantive content knowledge.)

Orientations to Teaching and Learning Science

Table 3 gives the definitions of the four orientations to science teaching and learning that were used in the study. Table 4 describes the major orientations of the five teachers whom we have studied most closely. Except for Ms. Rochester, the predominant view was that of a "hands-on" discovery approach, although Ms. Clark and Ms. Stein also revealed minor commitments to the Processes and Content Mastery orientations. Teachers' beliefs appeared to center most clearly around an empiricist view of learning. Young children learned science best by direct experience with events, materials, and natural phenomena; their own natural curiosity would lead them to discover scientific truth directly. Ms. Lake articulated this view of "good science" in this way:

> I think it's more hands on. It's more manipulating materials and watching things change and touching things and tasting them and feeling them and smelling them. It's a completely different thing. It's using all your senses and it's, your whole body is involved . . . It's something that you are going to experience rather than just talk about.

As part of this discovery orientation, many teachers viewed their role as that of "opening a door," "providing a key," or "exposing" the children to experiences; they were there to motivate children's curiosity about the "magic of science."

This teacher role as motivator is also part of the didactic/content mastery orientation, as Ms. Rochester's description revealed:

> I think a lot of teaching, at least for me, is performing, being on stage, captive audience. That is my, you know, Mr. Wizard type of aspect; seems like, that is what I would fit with, . . . if I had all the time in the world, all the money in the world, just the kids get so into it and you have so much fun doing it. That would be ideal.

Table 3. Orientations to Science Teaching and Learning

	Science is	School science is	Learning science is	Teaching science is
Discovery	inquiry, discovery of natural laws, curiosity, creativity	inquiry science, exciting, interested, trying out ideas, drawing own conclusions, exciting, fascinating	discovering with five senses, being curious, interested, trying out ideas, drawing own conclusions, exciting, fascinating	providing materials and interesting activities, encouraging children to try things, motivating children's interest and curiosity, posing questions, managing activities
Processess	scientific method, processes of science	learning scientific method, process approaches	learning steps in scientific method and practicing them: observing, drawing conclusions, collecting data, testing hypotheses, inferring, observing that model correct steps.	demonstrating and teaching steps in scientific method, providing opportunities to practice, maintaining children's correct use of method, managing activities
Didactic/Content Mastery	body of facts, laws, formulas; established by scientists	exposure to content, memorizing known facts, laws and formulas, assimilation of known content.	reading text, adding on new information, practicing, answering factual questions, watching films, listening to teacher talk, being tested, watching demonstrations.	presenting content clearly, showing and demonstrating, getting films, asking factual questions, correcting students' errors, giving clues and hints, providing practice, giving tests
Conceptual Change	construction and evolution of theories within conceptual ecology; criteria of predictive and explanatory adequacy.	focus on fundamental concepts and theories in science, provide opportunities for children to construct and reorganize knowledge.	articulating own ideas, predicting, explaining, contrasting alternative explanations, debating and arguing, making sense of discrepent events, solving problems, contrasting evidence and predictions.	eliciting children's ideas, providing discrepant events, challenging children to predict and explain, contrasting alternatives, presenting scientific conceptions, providing ways to apply new concepts, encouraging debate.

Table 4.   Teachers' Initial Orientations to Science Teaching and Learning

	Data Source (*Spring, 1986*)		
Teachers	*Program Application*	*Interview*	*Teaching*
Experienced (15-25 years)			
Lake	D	D	D,A
Mid-Career (5-15 years)			
Clark	D	D,CM	CM
Rochester	P	CM,P	CM/A
Beginning Career (0-5 years)			
Duke	D	D	D/A
Stein	D	D	D/A

Note: Discovery = D
Processes = P
Content Mastery/Didactic = CM
Activities = A

Ms. Clark, a first grade teacher, commented in a similar vein:

> It's just maybe just in my mind, that I feel that science should almost be like a magic act . . . .I feel that it should be done with such big fanfare that if I am not going to do it with a big fanfare, then I am not doing a good job.

Although most of the teachers shared this discovery orientation, Table 4 shows that other concerns, especially content mastery, were also evident in their interviews. Their Spring, 1986, lessons were the most striking evidence that orientations often collided with the reality of content coverage in the classroom. Except for the kindergarten teachers, whose teaching practice and interview beliefs were most "consonant" (i.e., consistent, see Thornton, 1985), other teachers had solved the problem of covering content while maintaining the commitment to discovery learning by simply doing both in their lessons. For example, five of the eight whom we videotaped devoted part of the lesson to straightforward didactic teaching of this sort:

> Clark: Can anybody tell me something they can remember about the sun? Is the sun a planet, too?
> Child: No.
> Clark: What is the sun?
> Child: A star.
> Clark: The sun is a star. What special things do the planets get from the sun?
> Child: Light.
> Clark: Light. What else?
> Child: Heat.

Clark: Heat. If we didn't have sun, what would happen?
Child: Die.
Clark: Right. Okay, it would be so cold that we would freeze. Ann said there are also planets in the solar system. How many planets? Lenny?
Lenny: Nine.

In the second part of the lesson, children sometimes went off to activities such as investigating rotten logs, making terrariums, pouring water through different kinds of soil, making butter from cream, and so forth. In this way, teachers covered content, yet provided children with the exciting "hands-on" activities which they believed were important.

What is interesting about this compromise is that neither the classroom observation data nor the interview data on its own would have revealed the depth of these discrepancies. In fact, Ms. Clark, who was strongly committed to "hands-on" discovery science, taught science lessons which were the epitome of straight didactic lessons: short answer, factual, with reading of text and brief explanations by the teacher.

Only one teacher was clearly aligned with the didactic/content mastery orientation in both her interview and classroom teaching. Ms. Rochester, a third-grade teacher, relied heavily on the text, although she supplemented with "experiment type things." However, these experiments were usually practice or applications of material covered in the text, as her interview indicates:

> Generally, I would tell them what, I would go through the whole thing that they were going to do, step by step. And then give them some time to work on it. Then we usually close with maybe ten minutes of what did you see happening, or what did this group get, that kind of thing.

In spite of their different orientations to content mastery or discovery learning, almost all teachers shared a common, deeper view about children's learning in science, as we have seen: the content was outside the child—in the sensory world, in the text, or in the activities—and their job was to facilitate children's assimilation of the content through discovery, activities, or didactic lessons. Throughout the interviews and the classroom lessons, what is striking is the lack of attention to children's ideas, predictions or explanations. Only two teachers mentioned the role of prediction, prior ideas, or explanations in science. Two commented on the need for children to make their own meaning out of experiences, but only one explicitly raised the issue of children's sometimes mistaken ideas. Ms. Duke, a kindergarten teacher, remarked that she sometimes had to provide contradictory examples, so that children didn't "go off with the wrong idea." No other teacher seemed aware that children's wrong ideas could be a problem in science lessons.

Pedagogical Content Knowledge

In this section, we present results of three kinds of teachers' pedagogical content knowledge, or the translation of substantive content into classroom teaching. First, we discuss their knowledge of children's ideas in science and how this was used in their spring and summer lessons. Next, we examine their teaching strategies and how they changed from spring to summer lessons. Finally, we present teachers' uses of metaphors, analogies, and examples in lessons.

Pedagogical Content Knowledge: Knowledge of Students' Concepts

In Table 5, we can see that few teachers focused on children's ideas, predictions, and explanations in their Spring, 1986, lessons (see Teacher Role). Children rarely were involved in predicting, explaining, generating ways to test ideas, and so on (see Student Role in Table 5). In most of Ms. Rochester's, Clark's and Stein's Spring, 1986, lessons, the focus was on the familiar didactic, question-response-evaluation format (e.g., Cazden, 1986) and content coverage or review.

When problems arose in children's answers, teachers sometimes resorted to giving hints in order to shape children's answers, rather than probing or diagnosing children's ideas in order to understand why they were incorrect. In the lesson described earlier, Ms. Clark runs up against this problem:

Clark:	When it spins, there is a special word we use for that in science. Paul, can you remember what that is, when it spins?
Other child:	Rotates.
Clark:	Well, that is right, but let Paul answer. It rotates when it is going around like this (demonstrates with globe). It is rotating. When it goes around the sun, there is another name. Paul, we will give you a chance again. (Paul is silent.) What do we call it when it takes its path all the way around the sun? Do you see it in that list of words? Want to help him, Mary?
Mary:	Rotates.
Clark:	It rotates and spins around like this (demonstrates again). It is just staying in one spot. We want it to go around in its orbit around the sun. What do we say when it goes all the way around the sun? Paul?
Paul:	Rotates.
Clark:	It re . . .
Paul:	Revolves.
Clark:	Revolving. When it goes this way, it is revolving.

Table 5.   Mean Ratings on Configurations Checklist for Six Teachers

Feature	Before Institute (Spring, 1986)	During Institute (Summer, 1986)	After[a] Institute (Spring, 1987)
Lesson Segments			
1. Introduction	1.5	1.5	1.8
2. Review	1.3	2.5	2.7
3. Development (Focus)	1.0	2.5	2.4
4. Development (Elicit)	1.8	2.7	2.7
5. Investigations	2.2	2.7	2.7
6. Representation	1.2	2.2	2.4
7. Discussion	1.3	2.5	2.3
8. Summary	1.5	1.3	1.7
Content			
1. Conceptual emphasis	1.0	2.0	2.3
2. Accurate	2.5	2.7	2.9
3. Scientific emphasis	1.3	2.7	2.7
4. Appropriate developmentally	1.2	2.3	1.8
5. Ties concept across lessons	1.2	2.3	2.6
Teacher Role			
1. Elicits S conceptions	1.7	2.7	2.9
2. Provides discrepant events	1.5	2.3	2.6
3. Facilitates S constructions	1.7	2.3	2.3
Student Role			
1. Predict, explain	1.5	2.5	2.8
2. Test predictions	2.0	2.3	2.5
3. Represent results	1.2	2.3	2.7
4. Describe, discuss results	1.5	1.8	2.2
5. Apply everyday experience	1.0	1.3	1.3
6. Cooperate in small groups	1.8	2.5	2.4
Activities/Materials			
1. Permit salient effects	2.0	3.0	2.8
2. Tied to lesson concept	2.0	2.7	2.9
3. Include discrepant event	1.2	2.0	2.3
Management			
1. Workspace, materials ready	2.2	3.0	2.8
2. Rules, routines discussed	2.3	2.8	2.8
3. Rules, routines in place	1.8	2.3	2.6
4. Monitoring, consequences	2.0	2.7	2.7
5. Ss take responsibility	1.8	2.3	2.0
6. Ss on task	1.8	2.8	2.5
Average Rating	1.61	2.37	2.45

Note: 1 = Low implementation
         3 = High implementation
         [a] Mean of ratings for lessons 4 and 9

When teachers did try to respond to children's mistaken ideas, they usually corrected the child and tried to explain in more detail. For example, in the discussion of revolution and rotation, a child raised her hand to comment that the earth "goes around once a month." Ms. Clark corrected her ("The earth goes around and it is not once a month"), and launched into a long explanation using a globe to demonstrate the difference between day/night changes and seasonal changes. However, the reasons behind the child's answer were not explored, and her understanding was not further probed during either the explanation or the end of the lesson.

Even in the discovery lessons (Ms. Duke and Ms. Lake), while there was a lot of talk about activities, the focus was still rarely on children's ideas. In Ms. Lake's lesson on coconuts, the focus was on children's five senses and their descriptions of tasting, smelling, feeling, seeing and hearing the coconut. Although children were asked to predict what was inside, they were not asked for explanations; answers were merely repeated or written down on a chart, not discussed and probed. Ms. Duke's magnification lesson appeared to be focused on children's discovery of what happened when various items were placed under the lens. Children's predictions about what might happen and ideas about why were not sought, nor were their explanations for the results.

In their June interviews, summarized in Table 6, teachers in the program were asked to predict children's answers to the same questions about light and shadows which they had answered. Because many of the teachers shared views of light and shadows which were similar to those children hold, their predictions were sometimes accurate by accident; they incorrectly predicted that children would give the "adult" answer, but because their own answer was mistaken, ended up giving the answer children actually would say. For example, two teachers whose own answers about how we see the red of an apple had revealed their lack of knowledge about the role of absorbed and reflected light, predicted that children would say the same thing—"red is part of the apple" and "we define red that way."

In general, teachers were accurate about what children would not know or would have trouble understanding. They predicted difficulties in children's understanding of reflected and refracted light and of merged shadows, and suggested that most would think of light as something which "lights up" like the sun or electricity (another example of accidentally correct predictions). They were also accurate in predicting that children would be able to find procedural solutions (e.g., for making a shadow bigger), but would be unable to explain why.

However, only two mentioned that children believed that shadows were "tangible things." None of the others knew that children sometimes think of shadows as projections or emanations, or that they often think shadows remain, unseen, in the darkness. Several incorrectly predicted that even young children would already know that shadows were the result of light's absence.

Table 6.   Teachers' Knowledge of Children's Preconceptions (Spring, 1986)

Children's Preconceptions	Rochester	Clark	Stein	Lake
1. Shadow is concrete or tangible.	−	∅	∅	+
2. Shadow is projection from body.	−	∅	∅	∅
3. Shadow is pushed out or made by light.	−	/	/	/
4. Shadow is reflection from object.	−	∅	∅	∅
5. Light is static "stuff" all around.	/	∅	∅	∅
6. Light travels in a straight tunnel from source.	∅	∅	∅	∅
7. In general, knew that children had alternative preconceptions.	∅	∅	∅	/
8. Children's ideas interfere with instruction.	∅	∅	∅	∅

Note: + = explicitly stated
        / = some evidence
        ∅ = not mentioned
        − = asserted child would know scientific conception

In spite of this lack of knowledge about children's ideas, teachers were concerned about what children could understand in science lessons. As Ms. Clark commented about her college background:

> They gave you courses so that you could have an educational background in science that you could apply . . . . Which I think is a lot different than actually showing you lessons that are applicable for first or second grade.

As one way of solving this dilemma, teachers relied heavily on the text for guidance in teaching concepts appropriate for young children, or on library books which they assumed had "gotten it down to a level that the children can understand."

Most important for conceptual change teaching, only Ms. Duke was aware that children's own ideas could interfere with their understanding of scientific concepts.

> . . . because you want the child to see a certain result. You can take a lot from the children, and almost like brainstorming, they can come up with some ideas. Then you accept what they say for face value. But I think a lot of times in science, you can't leave it up to that. You can't brainstorm over, like, say when I did the unit on buoyancy, because you don't want them to go away with a false concept, so you might direct their thinking or what they are doing. (She then went on to describe her giving children counter examples in order to contradict their ideas.) . . . so they weren't going away with a mistaken idea about something.

In the summer program, teachers were intrigued and interested to find out, in their readings, that children's ideas changed from a notion of shadows as *projections* to one seeing them as *reflections*, as they understood more about light travelling and having direction. Most powerfully of all, when they interviewed children themselves, they were clearly amazed yet challenged by the explanations which children gave. As they compared the results of the interviews across age groups, they could see how children's ideas changed and why they needed to plan to address different issues with the five-year-olds than with the eight-year-olds.

In their summer lessons, teachers' use of their knowledge of children's misconceptions varied. Misconceptions seemed to provide the background for many lessons, rather than the focus. For example, because children's ideas of a shadow as a projection led to incorrect predictions about locations of shadows, lessons focused on "how to" move the shadow by moving the light. Then, when children were procedurally successful at moving the shadow, this was taken as evidence of deeper underlying conceptual understanding of the active nature of light. Although teachers paid more attention to children's ideas, and asked them to predict more often (see Table 5), procedures and activities often took priority in the summer lessons as they often do in activity-based science lessons (see Smith & Sendelbach, 1982).

When children did come up with misconceptions or evidence of confusion in lessons, teachers sometimes passed over them or struggled for ways to respond and failed. For example, children in the older group had been asked to predict the shape of a doll's shadow with the light angled overhead. One confidently predicted a long shadow directly on the screen, and gave an audible gasp when the light was turned on to reveal a small shadow at the doll's feet. Ms. Evans noticed the gasp, paused and looked at the child for a long time with her face showing uncertainty and tension, made a brief comment, then went on to the next part of the lesson. In her interview about the lesson, the teacher later recalled:

> I don't know . . . I let that go, too. I should have pursued that more . . . should probably have capitalized more, if I could redo it.

In instances like these, teachers seemed able to recognize that a child was expressing a misconception, but unable to decide what to do; most often, they simply continued with the lesson as planned. It appeared that teachers knew about children's misconceptions, elicited them by asking for predictions, recognized them when they occurred in lessons, but then were unsure how to use them to contrast alternatives or to move the lesson and children's understanding along.

There were also successes in recognizing and using misconceptions. Ms. Clark reported, in her stimulated recall, that she had noticed when Dennis made an incorrect prediction for changing the size of the shadow:

> He made a prediction. He was the only one whose prediction wasn't right about moving the light. He was going to make it smaller, and he put the light right up to it. I was surprised. Of course, we didn't put the light on . . . so I asked him to do it and see what he had to do to make it bigger, and of course, maybe since he had a chance to see it, did predict and then with trying it, maybe it will make a big enough impact that it will just . . . you know, when he turned that light on, and there it was, I'm sure he nearly died. So it might make the difference.

Although she did not probe his prediction or follow up his reaction to the result, this teacher knew enough to arrange for the discrepant event, in order to provide feedback which was contradictory.

Pedagogical Content Knowledge: Teaching Strategies

As we have discussed earlier, none of the Spring, 1986, lessons was aimed at children's misconceptions, and in none of them were children actively predicting, explaining, and contrasting alternative ideas. In the summer lessons, three teachers made important changes in their uses of the conceptual change teaching strategies which they had read about and discussed; the two teachers whose primary orientation was to discovery science did not.

Ms. Rochester, Clark and Stein were successful in focusing lessons on the scientific concepts, eliciting students' preconceptions by asking for predictions, increasing requests for explanations, probing and requesting clarification of ideas, asking children how to test out ideas, contrasting alternatives, asking children to apply their newly constructed ideas to events, and providing ways for them to represent and discuss results. Children were more cognitively active in these lessons, compared to the same teachers' spring lessons.

For example, in contrast to Ms. Clark's didactic Spring, 1986, lesson, her summer lesson opened with a playful review in which she "played dumb" (see Leinhardt, 1985) so that children would correct her and articulate their own ideas about the light and object relationship. She then reviewed the previous day's findings (how to move a shadow without moving the light), and presented a variation on that problem (now move it without moving the object). Next, she cycled through each child's predictions (although she usually forgot to probe for explanations), demonstrated how to represent the predictions and actual results, and sent them off to work in pairs on a problem (move the fish's shadow into the house on the screen). This lesson represented considerable skill in diagnosis, discussion, demonstration, and flexibility in responding to children's ideas (remember her posing of the discrepant event to Dennis).

In contrast, the two discovery teachers (Lake and Duke) made few changes in their teaching strategies. They rarely took the time to ask children to predict or give explanations, and spent most of the lesson allowing children to try things and find out "what happened." For example, Ms. Lake had planned a lesson on what was needed to make a shadow, but after a short review, she turned the light on. A child immediately put his hand in front of the light to make a shadow (preventing her from asking for predictions and explanations, or setting up any discrepant events). She responded in this way:

> Oh look at Larry! Larry has got something. Okay, Larry would you like to do that again? What did you do, Larry? You discovered what you needed. What did you need?

As the lesson progressed, children chose items from a basket and held them in front of the light, trying various actions. Children's choices of positions for the object, their predictions about where the shadow would be or what it would look like were not probed; instead children "discovered" effects. Ms. Lake's comments were generally of this nature:

> We've discovered something, didn't we? Oh look, what happened to it? What happens to it? As you bring it closer and farther away, what happens? That's very good.

In Ms. Lake and Ms. Duke's lessons, the teachers rarely probed or challenged children's ideas or provided discrepant events, so that their ideas would be elicited or contradicted. Although the children were excited and interested, the focus of the lesson was on having fun, not changing ideas. When Danny brought in a tracing of his body shadow from home, Ms. Lake tried to elicit his explanation for the difference between his morning and noontime shadows:

> Lake: What do you think made that difference?
> Danny: I don't know. This morning it was lighter than . . . and the other time, it wasn't that light.
> Lake: All right. Yesterday morning when we went outside, where was the sun? Do you remember where we were looking? Where was the sun?
> Cam: In the middle.
> Lake: Okay, and so the shadow wasn't quite as long was it? But in the morning it was very long, wasn't it?

In this little exchange, Danny raises the idea that the shadow was longer because the sun was brighter. Ms. Lake accepts the idea, does not probe or clarify what he means, and tries to call on Cam to give her the "right" answer; when that fails, she simply summarizes what happened and goes on to the next activity. Danny's ideas are probably still intact, Cam's contribution is not clarified, and the opportunity for a substantive discussion of shadow length and reasons why it changes are lost. (Although we were not able to probe this incident in Ms. Lake's stimulated recall for the lesson, it appears that her decision to move on was a principled one. Elsewhere, she had commented about the children's activities, "I felt that my questions were almost an interfering extra in the experimentation.") The difference between this exchange and Ms. Clark's discrepant event for Dennis points out how teaching strategies play a critical role in children's progress in understanding the content in lessons.

Pedagogical Content Knowledge: Examples and Representations

Despite some teachers' struggles with the physics content, in their summer lessons they were accurate and made few errors (see Table 5). For the most part, this was because many stuck closely to the kinds of activities they themselves had done in the first week, or modified them slightly. These activities were familiar; teachers knew what to expect, and had a sufficient level of procedural success to insure safety. However, what was missing in most of these lessons was exactly the kind of examples, analogies, and metaphors which are evidence of content knowledge in use to serve pedagogical purposes.

The one exception, again, was Ms. Rochester. Her excellent conceptual knowledge appeared to allow her to generate new activities, new representations to assist children's understanding, and more use of examples and applications to everyday events. For example, she constructed a "spaghetti model" of light (strands of spaghetti stuck into a styrofoam ball), and used it in most of her lessons for children to predict what would happen in activities. She assisted their cognitive movement back and forth between the model and concrete materials and events. In her videotaped lesson, she asked children to consider the limitations of the model by pointing out that some materials (e.g., a hair) would pass in between the spaghetti, and then asking children whether that meant some items would be too thin to make a shadow.

There were some problems inherent in the spaghetti model; these will be discussed in a later section on Nan's unit in her own classroom (see Smith [1989], for further discussion of these problems). However, this kind of familiarity and flexibility with the content, in order to construct activities, examples and explanations to facilitate children's understanding, is what teachers whose own content knowledge was under construction seemed to lack.

We have presented a description of teachers' substantive, syntactic (in this study, their orientations to teaching and learning science), and pedagogical content knowledge, and how changes in that knowledge were related to their teaching in the summer lessons. Next, we briefly summarize two recent studies of the teachers' implementation in their own classrooms.

IMPLEMENTATION IN TEACHERS' CLASSROOMS

Results from the configurations checklist ratings of videotaped classroom lessons are summarized in Table 7 for the six teachers for whom both pre- and post-Summer Institute data were complete. (Two teachers joined late and did not submit tapes of prior teaching; two others did not implement the unit because of personal or professional difficulties in their lives that year. Our initial study of five teachers was limited to those who had given their permission; eventually, six teachers gave permission to be included in this study.)

Each of the six teachers made substantial progress in implementing conceptual change teaching, as measured by the mean of the total ratings on the 31 features. As shown in Table 7 and Figure 2, increased levels of implementation occurred in every category of lesson features.

A more detailed picture of the ratings is given in Table 5, which reports mean ratings of the six teachers on each of the 31 features both before, during and after the Summer Institute. Despite the small sample size, differences between the means of all the ratings before and after training proved to be statistically significant for the group, as indicated by the Wilcoxon Signed-Ranks Test ($Z = -2.20; p = .028$).

The results of ratings must be interpreted carefully, remembering the context in which each set of lessons was taught. Before the Institute, each teacher selected a lesson to be videotaped in her own public school classroom. During the Institute, the teaching was scaffolded in several ways: (1) the "class" was a small group of summer campers, (2) the content and activities were suggested by Institute materials, and (3) coaching was provided. After the Institute, lessons were taught with some of the scaffolding removed. Although lessons still included some content and materials suggested during the Institute and coaching was provided, now teachers were teaching in their regular public school classrooms as part of a two-week unit.

Thus, changes from "Before" to "During" are best interpreted as evidence of significantly greater implementation of principles of conceptual change teaching in a highly supportive environment. These levels of implementation appeared to be maintained "After" as teachers taught lessons in a much less supportive environment, that is, their regular classrooms many months after the Summer Institute had concluded.

While all of the rated features showed a change toward implementation, teachers appeared to be more successful with some features than with others. For example, in the Spring, 1987, lessons, teachers were rated as more successful in eliciting students' conceptions than they were in facilitating students' construction of new knowledge during the lessons (see Teacher Role in Table 5). Teachers were not as successful in asking students to apply conceptions to their everyday experiences. Students in 1987 lessons were rated as more likely to be predicting and explaining than in the previous Spring, 1986, lessons (see Student Role in Table 5).

Table 7.   Ratings on Features of Conceptual
Change Teaching for Six Teachers

Feature	Before Institute (Spring, 1986) Mean (s.d.)	p^a	During Institute (Summer, 1986) Mean (s.d.)	p^a	After[b] Institute (Spring, 1987) Mean (s.d.)
Lesson Segments	1.4 (0.18)	<.05	2.2 (0.50)	n.s.	2.3 (0.41)
Content	1.4 (0.23)	<.05	2.4 (0.33)	n.s.	2.5 (0.27)
Teacher Role	1.4 (0.39)	<.05	2.4 (0.62)	n.s.	2.5 (0.38)
Student Role	1.5 (0.24)	<.05	2.1 (0.65)	n.s.	2.3 (0.46)
Activities/Materials	1.7 (0.14)	<.05	2.6 (0.46)	n.s.	2.7 (0.38)
Management	2.0 (0.62)	n.s.	2.7 (0.41)	n.s.	2.6 (0.38)
All Features	1.61 (0.21)	<.05	2.37 (0.44)	n.s.	2.45 (0.37)

Note: 1 = Low Implementation
3 = High Implementation
[a] Wilcoxon signed-ranks test (for differences in pairs of ratings)
[b] Mean of rating for lessons 4 and 9

In terms of content accuracy and emphasizing scientific conceptions, teachers were rated as more successful in their Spring, 1987, lessons. However, there still appeared to be some problems in choosing developmentally appropriate content in lessons, although progress was made on that feature.

Lesson materials and activities were rated as more successful in producing salient effects when children acted on materials, but less successful in including discrepant events (although more so than in the teachers' Spring, 1986, lessons).

For organization and management of the classroom, videotaped lessons in Spring, 1987, were rated as more successful in having the workspace and materials ready, having rules and routines discussed and monitored, and consequences applied. Students in those lessons were rated as on task more often than students in Spring, 1986, lessons, although, as might be expected, ratings were slightly lower for the full class lessons in Spring, 1987, than for the small group lessons in the Summer Institute.

As discussed in the more complete report of this study (Neale, Smith, & Johnson, 1989), these group averages fail to depict the range of successful implementation across the six teachers. Some teachers showed dramatic

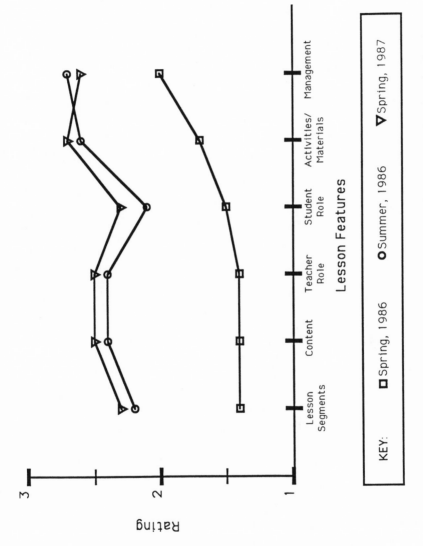

Figure 2. Mean Ratings on Features of Conceptual Change Teaching for Six Teachers

changes in their use of conceptual change teaching strategies, while others experienced more difficulty. It appears that classroom management was one important factor in the teachers' success in implementation. For example, Carol wrote in her final report:

> I thought (to myself) that I was a pretty good teacher as far as my management went—until you opened my eyes. Now I see my flaws and since last summer, have tried to be more conscious of the skills necessary to develop a good unit. . . . My problem with discipline was because I'm just too easy.

We are currently exploring this and other factors in implementation in a series of case studies focusing on teachers' knowledge and its uses while teaching, their written comments in their final reports, and their reflections in their interviews one year later.

Beyond the specific changes as seen in the ratings, a general theme emerged. In their final interviews, all eight teachers said, in one way or another, that the biggest changes occurred in the new attention that they gave to students' thinking. Denise put it this way:

> I learned how to listen more carefully to children, think about what they're saying, let them go on their predictions, to be patient, to plan my lessons according to what the class knows and not what I think should be taught, and not take for granted that they already know something.

Betsy noticed in her math teaching that:

> I used to just get up and do it; it never occurred to me to find out what they already knew. I now realize the amount of misconceptions that children come to school with and it was something that I never thought about before. . . . It's amazing to me the depth of children's thinking; it is not always "correct," but they just feel so strongly or think so strongly about their ideas and maybe I just never gave it credibility.

This underlying shift in teachers's perspectives on children's learning in science may represent a change even more important than those captured by the observable behaviors on the configurations checklist. In the next section, we discuss one longitudinal case study which examined the teacher knowledge, beliefs and cognitions underlying changes in teaching.

CHANGE IN TEACHER KNOWLEDGE, THINKING, AND PRACTICE

In this section of the chapter, we briefly summarize a longitudinal case study (Smith, 1989) of one of the Summer Institute's teachers, Nan Rochester. We describe her prior knowledge and teaching practice before the Summer Institute, her participation and change in knowledge during the summer, her plans and planning for her own classroom unit, and her thinking, teaching, and uses of her knowledge during that unit, in the winter of 1987.

Spring 1986 Knowledge

Some of Nan's prior knowledge has been described earlier in the chapter. Her subject-matter knowledge of the physics of light and shadows was the strongest and most accurate of any of the teachers in the program. Her model of light included its straight line travel, its divergence in all directions from the source, its ability to be bent or reflected, and the fact that, upon reflection, the angle of incidence would be equal to the angle of reflection. Nan had taken a physical science course as an undergraduate, and had taught a unit on light and color to her previous fourth-grade class. Because she reported usually "boning up" on the content before teaching, it is likely that these experiences played a role in her good content knowledge.

Like most of the other teachers, Nan had no knowledge that children came with their own alternative ideas about light and shadows. However, her intuitive hunches about what would be hard for them, and why, were on target.

> It [light] is a tough one for kids . . . . It has some of the things you can do to something that has substance, but it doesn't have any substance itself. Which is hard to deal with, for a kid, I think.

Nan's orientation to teaching and learning science was predominantly the content/didactic orientation found in most elementary science lessons. Her questionnaire responses, interview responses and teaching practice all reflected this orientation before the Summer Institute, although there were also some traces of the processes orientation.

Spring 1986 Science Teaching

In her spring lesson, children read the text about forest habitats and answered Nan's questions about the text. When children were wrong, Nan asked another child for the correct answer or corrected the child and explained what was wrong. Children then went on to small group work in which they examined rotting logs through plastic bags, to see what kind of animals lived there. While children acted on the materials and were sometimes surprised by the results, the activity was not set up to contradict previous predictions or explanations.

In terms of management strategies during science lessons, Nan relied primarily on a point system, in which both individual children and the whole class had point cards. Children received points for complete work and good behavior, and lost points for incomplete work and misbehavior. In her spring lesson, the whole group segment of the lesson went smoothly, with the common question-response-evaluation (QRE) format.

However, when children went to their small groups, Nan did not discuss needed rules and routines. The noise level rose steadily, children wandered from group to group, and when they needed help either called to Nan or followed her around the room. In her interview, she had commented,

> That [management] is something I often have, not trouble with, but it is always in the back of my mind when I am doing an experimental type lesson . . . . What is the effect going to be on the kid? Do you have them do this thing first? Is it going to make them so excited and talkative . . . that the rest of the lesson is going to be shot? Or, if you put it at the end, the lesson will be over then, and it doesn't matter . . . . There are times when I shy away from doing something that would be really good to do, but I know if I do that, the kids are going to be just totally crazy and not get much out of it, because they are getting so wound up . . . . So you have to consider as a big thing, to think about when you are planning experimental type things.

The small group activities segment of her spring lesson demonstrated why Nan (and other teachers) felt uncomfortable about science activities in her classroom.

Summer Institute, 1986

In the Summer Institute program, Nan appeared to enjoy playing with the content in the activities teachers did themselves, and in designing curriculum for the children in the summer camp. Her activities for her small group were designed with the results of her previous interviews with children in mind, and aimed at misconceptions children might have.

In her videotaped lesson, she sometimes fell back into her QRE routine in questioning children. She often asked children for their predictions, but sometimes forgot to follow up with probes for their explanations. A new teaching routine, the prediction/try, appeared to be a combination of her old QRE routine and the prediction/explanation routine from the conceptual change teaching strategies: Nan would ask for a prediction, then she or the child would try it out, to find out. In this case, she no longer provided the correct answer; the child's action on the materials did.

There were two sections of her summer lesson in which she and the children discussed unusual results—with a bent paper tube which let no light through, and with sunprints that worked less well than others. In these sections, children were interested, curious, and eager to propose explanations for what had happened, and Nan did a careful job of probing their thinking.

As discussed earlier, Nan's ease with the content appeared to enable her to play with ideas and representations, for example, the spaghetti model of light. But this same representation also posed some problems in her lesson. With the paper tube around the light bulb, she explained that the tube was "forcing" the light down the tube and gestured as if the light bent or curved at the tube's edge (instead of being absorbed or reflected). Nan also broke the spaghetti pieces off to demonstrate the light rays being blocked by a surface; this worked well to represent the light rays not reaching an area behind the surface, but may have misled children into thinking that light could break off (instead of being absorbed or reflected).

In terms of management of the summer class, with only six children there were few problems, although Nan reported worrying about possible problems as she was teaching. She did make some changes, compared to her spring lesson. She reviewed rules and consequences before children went to work, reminded children of rules and routines when transitions occurred, and monitored them as she circulated among the small groups.

Perhaps most importantly, in her log for the summer camp, Nan thought ahead to teaching in her own classroom, and commented on the discrepancy between her usual science teaching and the conceptual change strategies that she was practicing in the summer camp.

> Then there will be the problem of either trying to do this with other areas of science throughout the year, and going crazy trying to keep up with the work, or teaching science the way we used to and having more time, but knowing that we are doing many of the wrong things as cited in the research. Aargh!

Dissatisfaction with the current perspective is the first step in the process of conceptual change (Posner et al., 1982). Nan was all too aware of the difference between the way she had been teaching and the way she now wanted to teach.

Fall Interview and Planning for Unit

In the Fall interview about subject matter and orientations to science teaching and learning, Nan's content knowledge appeared to have taken on a new dimension: in solving the physics problems, she used logical necessity (Piaget, 1983) to reason from what she knew about light to solutions about events and their causes. For example, in reasoning about how light would be reflected from the hatchback of a car, she said,

> Well, let's see, if it's [light] in your eye, and it's gotta be coming in off of the glass . . . so it's coming off the glass like that [draws ray from glass to driver's eye], . . . is going to be like that [draws ray from car hatchback to the sun, with equal angles of incidence and reflection]. So it's gotta be morning time, 'cause the sun's coming up.

She sometimes went beyond what the problem asked, and posed an even harder problem for herself to solve—for fun.

Her orientation to teaching and learning science appeared to be a patchwork of many sources. While there were definitely conceptual change ideas present, there were also ideas from the content/didactic, processes, and discovery orientations. As Nan commented later, in reading the case study,

> At this point, I think they [her ideas] were [under reconstruction]. I was trying to put the conceptual change ideas together with the way I had taught science for the previous ten years.

In Nan's plans for her unit, she mentioned by name or described all the misconceptions which children might have about light and shadows. Lesson activities nearly all met the curriculum criteria we had discussed. Her lessons were aimed at diagnosing and addressing children's ideas, and nearly all of the conceptual change teaching strategies were explicitly included in her plans. One exception was the teaching strategy of encouraging children to discuss among themselves the evidence for their alternative explanations.

What was also noticeable in the plans was the omission of some of her previously used teaching strategies, for example, reading from the text and telling children when they were wrong. Some traces of the content orientation were still present. For example, the prediction/try and ask a vote routines were included; both provide the teacher with information about who is right, but not about the child's reasoning behind an answer.

In her plans for organization and management of the unit lessons, Nan had thought through the storage and workspace requirements, and clearly had a lesson structure in mind.

> Basically what I've broken this down to is the intro and review, development and activities; so intro and review is kind of like we were just starting to talk about or reviewing from the day before. Development and activities is talking about the problem for today and giving them directions, laying the bulk of the work on that. Representation, what they're going to bring back to the group follow-up discussion and how we're going to talk about what things they found, and then just a materials list and suggestions for early finishers.

She planned to discuss and/or review rules and routines in many of her plans for lessons, while continuing to use her point system. In our planning interview, she discussed her recognition of that system's limitations.

> . . . it doesn't give them as much of a chance of molding their behavior or developing inner ways of controlling themselves . . . . But it's hard to let go of,

because I've been on the other end where it's been . . . they've been in control, and I haven't, as a student teacher . . . . And it's so reinforcing to be able to have that control and say, " This is the way it's going to be." . . . I think the main reason I use it is 'cause it works and it makes my day easier . . . because you are always on top of things, and you're pretty much always feeling in control.

As we went through her plans, she occasionally made decisions to limit some activities, because of management concerns.

On the whole, Nan's plans and her discussion of them revealed that she had consciously incorporated the various kinds of knowledge that we had targeted for the summer program. While there were also traces of her prior orientation, and some concerns about management of the small groups, she appeared to be adequately prepared for teaching the unit.

Classroom Unit, Spring, 1987

In this section, we discuss what Nan's teaching and children's learning looked like in her unit lessons, and the various kinds of knowledge which she reported using while teaching. We also discuss ways in which her knowledge was insufficient, or her prior orientation interfered with her efforts to teach for conceptual change.

Nan's lessons were clearly different from her previous science lessons. In these lessons, she had set up events as ways to elicit and diagnose children's thinking. For example, in the first lesson, she read part of *Peter Pan* and brought out a tracing of her own shadow, to provoke children's thinking about whether it could really be her shadow. Throughout her lessons, she used a variety of teaching strategies to find out what children were thinking: asking for several children's predictions for the same event, asking children to explain their predictions, probing and clarifying children's answers, asking for predictions and then trying them out, contrasting alternative ideas, asking children to represent their predictions in some way, emphasizing results which contradicted predictions, asking children to demonstrate what would happen, and asking the class to vote on outcomes. Throughout her discussions with the class, she rarely gave away the "right" answer, either by her facial expression or by her verbal responses; instead, she highlighted children's reasons, evidence and arguments, and asked children to evaluate their effectiveness.

When a common misconception surfaced in these lessons, she sometimes left her planned lesson, probed the child's thinking, and invented a discrepant event on the spot. In her stimulated recall interviews (conducted after four of the lessons), she reported thinking about children's ideas, recognizing misconceptions, and making decisions about whether to address them right away or leave them for later lessons. For example, when Jerry says his shadow is always in front of him, in the first lesson, she reported,

> Jerry said, as soon as Jerry hit me with that, I said, this is a classic, you know, my shadow's always in front of me, so I said okay, I'll have to deal with this now, . . . so I jumped on that to try and see if we could present graphically for him that that wasn't the way it was, that's why I had him come up and start standing there, and put the light in different places and everything, to see if, to let him see that it wasn't always going to be in front of him. . . .

Her knowledge of children's thinking also appeared to enable her to remember individual children's thinking from lesson to lesson, and to use that knowledge to make decisions while teaching.

As mentioned earlier, the activities in Nan's lessons were planned to meet the curriculum criteria we had discussed. She reported monitoring the success of these activities in terms of those criteria, as the lesson progressed. For example, she was disappointed when children were not as surprised as she had hoped they would be by the large area of light from a small hole.

> Like I said, I thought the demonstrations would be more striking, so I thought I'd get more of a reaction out of the little hole with the big light on the screen.

In addition, she reported constructing practical knowledge of how well different activities worked, whether children had difficulty with the physical demands of the activities, and what changes she might make the next time she taught the unit.

Throughout her lessons, Nan's content knowledge of the physics of light and shadows benefitted her teaching and children's learning. She often reviewed content themes at the beginning of a lesson, and related the current lesson to previous lesson themes. Within lessons, she recognized unexpected opportunities to work on important scientific conceptions. For example, in one lesson, the children had noticed that the window shades on the classroom's three windows had shadows of different widths. Nan reported recognizing this situation as a variation on a problem children had encountered the day before. She used this puzzling event to diagnose which children were able to apply what they had learned about how light travelled in straight lines, and to help the children think through where the sun must be outside the window, and what must be making the uneven shadows.

Her subject matter knowledge also enabled her to predict the results of events, to recognize children's answers which were right or wrong before trying them out, to generate demonstrations and explanations on the fly, and to solve unexpected problems when they arose during lessons. For example, in one lesson, light from a slide projector made an unexpected rectangular shape on the screen. Nan noticed that the hole through which the light was going was a pinhole, and reasoned her way through the paths of light in a pinhole camera to figure out what had happened.

In one lesson, however, content knowledge which we had only briefly addressed in the summer program was required to explain why a hair shadow disappeared when the hair was held close to the light bulb. While Nan had some good intuitive ideas about what was happening, she lacked knowledge of extended light sources and the resulting umbra and penumbra, and was not able to explain the results for children.

In another lesson, on the afternoon of the Valentine's Day party and before a four-day weekend, the small group activities were hectic and several small groups argued over turns and results. In her summary of the lesson, Nan described the relationship between the size of the shadow and the distance of the object from the light as exactly opposite to the correct relationship. Thus, her good content knowledge was not always adequate for unexpected results in the lessons, and sometimes appeared to be affected by increased demands on her in the lesson.

In the management of her unit lessons, Nan made some clear progress. Even though the whole group segments of her lessons relied on familiar lesson structures (e.g., shared presentation, seatwork), and familiar rules and routines (e.g., hand up for a turn, one person talks), there were some initial problems. Children were excited by events and ideas, and called out; Nan sometimes allowed this and sometimes did not. In addition, the new teaching strategies— asking for predictions and explanations, and providing wait time—slowed down the pace of her lessons and made the timing feel awkward and uneven at times.

> I was about to say, "Now this light's different because it doesn't have a shade on it, so the light's going up," and I just said, 'Wait a second, the kids are supposed to be telling me this,' so I stopped and said, "How's this light different from . . . ." and actually that bogged me down a little bit because they started giving me all these things about how the light was different, other than what I was aiming at, which was how the light given off was different . . . . They were giving me about a metal thing instead of this, and you can't bend it and—which is interesting observations, but that's the kind of things that come up that— you know— slow you down a little, but you really can't ignore that because you asked, how is it different, so . . .

Gradually, over the ten unit lessons, the whole group discussions smoothed out, children consistently used rules and routines, and the conceptual focus of lessons improved along with the quality of children's discussions.

However, in the small group activities, a lesson segment not well practiced for Nan or the children, it was not until the second week that things began to go smoothly. In the first week's lessons, Nan rarely remembered to review rules and routines before children went off to work in their small groups; as a result, noise levels were high, children argued over turns and sometimes wandered to other groups, and Nan found herself followed around the room by children needing help. When she did enforce rules and routines, she did so inconsistently, sometimes reviewing the rule and sometimes ignoring the infraction. In her stimulated recall interviews, Nan reported not wanting to spend time to review rules and routines, so that children had more time to work on their activities.

Gradually, over the second week, she began introducing, reviewing, and consistently monitoring more rules and routines related to the small group work. In addition, her focus in both her discussions and her interactions with children changed. Instead of emphasizing consequences in terms of the point system, she began emphasizing the consequences for children in terms of their learning.

> Because what did we say about group work? Why is it important for everybody to get a chance? Ronnie?
> So they'll know how to do it.
> Okay, they get a chance to know how to do it. Okay, anything else? Ollie?
> To learn.
> To learn, yeah. If everybody doesn't get a chance to try it for themselves, they won't get a chance to learn it as well. Okay, so everybody will take a turn with these things.

As she and the children became more practiced in the rules and routines needed for small group work, that work began to flow more smoothly, also. Nan reported being able to focus on listening to children as she circulated among the small groups, instead of solving disagreements and preventing fights.

Nan's lessons clearly showed the influence of the conceptual change orientation to teaching science, but also included aspects of other orientations, especially her prior commitment to content. Although the kind of talk had changed for both herself and the children, she was still doing most of the talking in lessons. She reported wanting to lead or tell children the right answer, and wanting to bring each lesson to closure, even though not all children might understand the lesson's objectives. She sometimes fell back on the question-response-evaluation format, or emphasized whether children were right or not. Her stimulated recall interviews revealed the extent to which she was actively monitoring her teaching, in order not to fall back on these teaching strategies related to her old orientation.

> Yeah, I felt like I was putting words in their mouths when they said you can see it [light] on the ceiling and I said, "Yeah, these metal beams are shining," you know, which is like jumping ahead to the light reflecting off that, and I was kind of throwing that in there but usually I try to correct myself afterwards, like I remember after I said that, I said, "Of course, it could've been shining before we turned it on." You know like—you know, I still jump into the old teacher

mode of—telling them what it is, but then if I think about it, I try and—you know, say, "No, wait, I shouldn't be doing that," so I try to find some way out of it, which is why I said that.

And as discussed previously, her stimulated recall comments also revealed the extent to which she was now actively seeking out and diagnosing children's thinking, and deciding what to do on the basis of that thinking. Rather than replacing her old orientation, Nan appeared to have broadened it, changed her criteria for what understanding the content meant, and changed her role and methods for helping children to reach her goals of understanding the science content.

Other Knowledge and Orientations

It was clear from Nan's lessons, interviews, and log that the six kinds of knowledge we studied were insufficient for understanding her thinking and teaching. Nan reported using many other kinds of knowledge while teaching, including her knowledge of individual children, their personalities, their family backgrounds and friendships, their academic abilities in other subjects, and tricks or strategies that worked with particular children to solve problems. She also had extensive knowledge of other teachers and their classrooms, expectations in the school milieu, and the principal's expectations, as well.

Furthermore, it was clear that knowledge about Nan's orientation to teaching and learning science was insufficient for understanding her science teaching. Her image of herself as a science teacher appeared to be embedded in other, broader images of herself as a teacher of young children; these included things like providing fair turns, making sure children with low self-esteem participated in lessons, providing challenges for her academically gifted children, and being sensitive to children's feelings.

Finally, Nan's willingness to share her point of view with us revealed the depth of feeling involved in making changes in her teaching. The challenges she faced were not solely those of knowledge construction or of complex information processing while teaching. Her log and stimulated recall comments over the year's time ranged from apprehension to frustration, from discouragement to joy. The rewards of having mastered something difficult and seen it work with children in her classroom are clearly expressed in her final report on her unit.

> In general, I felt fantastic about the unit, the kids' work in it, what they learned, and what I learned. This was a totally new topic for me to teach to my kids and I think that really contributed to my pleasure. There was so much going on, so much to be pleased with, and so much to notice because it was all so new. I felt like the kids were really learning some science concepts and without the encumbrance of a text and the reading and vocabulary problems that

accompany it. The best feelings were when kids made verbal statements of excitement about discoveries they made, when they verbalized many of the misconceptions I was told I would hear, and when normally shy, quiet students, or low-achieving ones, gave explanations, predictions and ideas. The worst feelings were the lack of cooperation that some groups experienced (and the attempts at reducing this), and the frustration of not having the necessary time or expertise to develop all my science lessons after this model.

Summary

This extensive case study of one third-grade teacher revealed the ways in which her new knowledge was used in planning and in teaching, and described how that knowledge was related to changes in her science teaching. It has helped us to understand the complexity involved in such changes, and the demands, both cognitive and affective, placed on the teacher.

DISCUSSION

We began the chapter with a question about whether a focus on teachers' content knowledge offered a promising way of investigating and understanding the difficulties they experience in implementing science curricula and teaching effective science lessons. Our work thus far with these primary teachers has convinced us of the usefulness of this approach and its importance for both staff development and curriculum change projects. Our findings in this study with primary teachers reveal many similarities to Anderson and Smith's work (1985; see also Hollon, Roth, & Anderson, this volume, pp. 145-185), to Leinhardt's (1986; see also Leinhardt et al., this volume, pp. 87-113) studies of novice math teachers, and to Carpenter et al.'s (1987; see also Peterson et al., this volume, pp. 49-86) study of primary-grade math teachers.

Teachers' declarative knowledge of the physics content, of children's likely preconceptions to be encountered in lessons, and of effective teaching strategies for addressing them, all proved to be critical components in the changes they were able to make in their teaching.

The translation of this declarative knowledge into plans for appropriate and workable curriculum activities, and from plans into the many kinds of procedural knowledge needed for teaching the lessons, represented yet another level of mastery. Changes in customary lesson structures and the construction of new, cooperative interactive routines, both between teacher and children and among children, presented a considerable challenge even for a teacher like Nan Rochester, who appeared to be established and competent in her teaching before the Summer Institute. Finally, our study of Nan's thinking and teaching revealed the depth and complexity of the information processing and decision making that occurred underneath her observable teaching behaviors.

It appears to us that, rather than staff development programs that focus on content-free skills and strategies, or even on particular curriculum packages, it is especially beneficial for teachers to focus on a particular content and the ways in which that content is translated in teaching. In this way, teaching principles are embedded in teaching practice and case knowledge of teaching (Shulman, 1986) can be constructed. For experienced teachers who are novices at teaching science, this case knowledge of a prototypical unit may be an important beginning. When combined with a program of support in which teaching is modelled, and then their own teaching is coached, such a focus provides a chance for teachers to comprehend what the whole performance looks like (Collins, Brown, & Newman, 1986). For many primary teachers, comprehending what is possible may be the scaffolding within which the different kinds of knowledge and their coordination can be more easily constructed.

As Hord and Huling-Austin (1986) have reported, implementation of science programs often takes up to three full years of support before teachers begin to feel comfortable. If teachers have different configurations of knowledge in each of the areas we studied and different rates of progress (as we have found), then programs of support will require opportunities to individualize their development (Hord & Huling-Austin, 1986) just as the teachers with whom we work have done.

If teachers are trying to master a more challenging and more complex kind of teaching, they and their supervisors may need to allow time for mucking about and failing, just as children sometimes go through U-shaped curves in development (Strauss, 1982). In fact, these curves may more appropriately be thought of and planned for as J-shaped curves (R. Smith, 1989), in which even the most dedicated and competent teachers may need extra support at the bottom of the curve, so as to reach eventual mastery and expertise at a new level of competence. We believe that the teachers with whom we have worked provide evidence that this kind of progress can be made in many of the areas of knowledge that appear critical for conceptual change teaching.

Beyond the complexity of the cognitive aspects of the changes teachers made, their stimulated recall interviews, final reports, and final interviews highlighted the very real affective aspects involved. In many ways, we were asking teachers to put their comfort and certainty at risk, by disassembling parts of their teaching that were already working, and constructing ways of teaching that increased the risk and ambiguity for the teacher, as well as for the students (see Doyle, 1983). As with any new curriculum, teachers were unsure of the timing and pace of lessons. In addition, conceptual change teaching by its very nature involves looking for and taking into account children's own ideas, some of which are predictable, some of which are not; trying out activities and materials which may work as planned or may provide some unexpected discrepant results that challenge the teacher's own content knowledge; and setting up and monitoring cooperative small group activities which may provoke social/emotional altercations, thus adding to the complexity and risk of the teaching. Teachers reported satisfaction, pleasure, and joy as they changed their science teaching, as well as disappointment, embarrassment, and confusion.

It is clear that, even after this intensive experience, the teachers with whom we worked do not yet possess the characteristics associated with expertise generally (e.g., Chi, Glaser, & Rees, 1982) or in teaching (e.g., Berliner, 1989; Leinhardt, 1986). The speed and automaticity of processing are not yet present. While some can recognize patterns of student thinking, they sometimes have difficulty knowing the conditions under which to use particular teaching strategies or forget important parts of those strategies. Certainly, the deeply principled conceptual knowledge of the content is still under construction for some, as is principled understanding of the nature of science teaching. And the ability to combine strategies so as to reach goals in lessons still may be awkward and uncertain (e.g., Hall's [1986], mechanical stage of usage; Shulman's [1986], strategic knowledge; and Brophy's [1988], conditional knowledge). However, they do represent interesting mileposts along the road to expertise (see Berliner, 1989), and as such, may help us to understand what the transformation may look like.

Many questions remain—about grade level effects, influences of orientations to science, the relative influence of teaching experience—and especially about the development of strategic knowledge (Shulman, 1986), as teachers coordinate different kinds of knowledge and make decisions during teaching. If we can understand, for these teachers of varying experience, grade levels, and knowledge, what their individual paths to increased expertise look like, we may be in a better position to design more effective staff development programs in science education.

ACKNOWLEDGMENTS

An earlier version of this paper was presented at the Annual Meeting of the American Educational Research Association, April, 1987. The authors wish to thank our research associates, Dr. Katherine Manger, Julia Schmidt, Matthew Onstott and Dr. Elizabeth Wier, and the secretarial staff, Ginny Ferguson, Claire Blessing and Patricia Howell. The research was funded by an EESA Title II grant; the opinions expressed do not necessarily reflect those of the funding agency.

REFERENCES

Anderson, C. (1986). *Improving college science teaching: Problems of conceptual change and instructors' knowledge*. Paper presented at the annual meeting of the National Association for Research in Science Teaching, San Francisco, CA.

Anderson, C., & Barufaldi, J. (1980). *Research on elementary school science teaching: A study using short-term outcome measures* (Occasional Paper No. 37). East Lansing, MI: Michigan State University, Institute for Research on Teaching.

Anderson, C., & Smith, E. (1983a). *Teacher behavior associated with conceptual learning.* Paper presented at the annual meeting of the American Educational Research Association, Montreal, Canada.

Anderson, C., & Smith, E. (1983b). *Children's conceptions of light and color: Developing the concept of unseen rays.* Paper presented at the annual meeting of the American Educational Research Association, Montreal, Canada.

Anderson, C., & Smith, E. (1985). Teaching science. In V. Koehler (Ed.), *The educator's handbook: A research perspective* (pp. 80-111). New York: Longman.

Apelman, M. (1984). Critical barriers to the understanding of elementary science: Learning about light and color. In C. Anderson (Ed.), *Observing science classrooms: Observing science perspectives from research and practice* (pp. 3-36). AETS Yearbook. Columbus, Ohio: Clearinghouse for Science, Mathematics, and Environmental Education.

Berliner, D. (1986). In pursuit of the expert pedagogue. *Educational Researcher, 15*(7), 5-13.

Berliner, D. (1989). Implications of studies of expertise in pedagogy for teacher education and evaluation. In *New directions for teacher assessment, Proceedings of the 1988 Educational Testing Service Invitational Conference* (pp. 39-68). Princeton, NJ: Educational Testing Service.

Berman, P., & McLaughlin, M. (1975). *Federal programs supporting educational change: Vol. IV. The findings in review.* Santa Monica, CA: Rand Corporation.

Blakeslee, T., Anderson, C., & Chadwick, J. (1986). *Defining and observing instructional strategies for conceptual change teaching.* Paper presented at the annual meeting of the National Association for Research in Science Teaching, San Francisco, CA.

Brophy, J. (1982). How teachers influence what is taught and learned in classrooms. *The Elementary School Journal, 83*(1), 1-14.

Brophy, J. (1988). Educating teachers about managing classrooms and students. *Teaching and Teacher Education, 4*(1), 1-18.

Brophy, J., & Good, T. (1986). Teacher behavior and student achievement. In M.C. Wittrock (Ed.), *Handbook of research on teaching* (3rd ed., pp. 328-375). Chicago: Rand McNally.

Buchmann, M. (1983). *The priority of knowledge and understanding in teaching* (Occasional paper No. 61). East Lansing, Michigan: Michigan State University, Institute for Research on Teaching.

Carpenter, T., Peterson, P., Fennema, E., & Carey, D. (1987). *Teachers' pedagogical content knowledge in mathematics.* Paper presented at the annual meeting of the American Educational Research Association, Washington, DC.

Case, R. (1978). A developmentally based theory and technology of instruction. *Review of Educational Research, 48*(3), 439-463.

Cazden, C. (1986). Classroom discourse. In M. C. Wittrock (Ed.), *Handbook of research on teaching* (3rd ed., pp. 432-463). Chicago: Rand McNally.

Champagne, A., Klopfer, L., & Anderson, J. (1980). Factors influencing the learning of classical mechanics. *American Journal of Physics, 48*(12), 1074-1079.

Chi, M., Glaser, R., & Rees, E. (1982). Expertise in problem solving. In R.Steinberg, (Ed.), *Advances in the psychology of human intelligence* (vol. 1, pp. 7-76). Hillsdale, NJ: Erlbaum.

Clandinin, J. (1986). *Classroom practice.* Philadelphia: Falmer.

Clark, C., & Elmore, J. (1981). *Transforming curriculum in mathematics, science and writing: A case study of teacher yearly planning* (Research Series No. 99). East Lansing: Michigan State University, Institute for Research on Teaching.

Clark, C., & Peterson, P. (1986). Teachers' thought processes. In M. C. Wittrock (Ed.), *Handbook of research on teaching* (3rd ed., pp. 255-296). Chicago: Rand McNally.

Cohen, M. (1985). Introduction. *Elementary School Journal, 85*(3): 277-279.

Collins, A., Brown, J., & Newman, J. (1986). Cognitive apprenticeship: Teaching the craft of reading, writing and mathematics. In L.B. Resnick (Ed.), *Cognition and instruction: Issues and agendas.* Hillsdale, NJ: Erlbaum.

Collins, A., & Stevens, A. (1982). Goals and strategies of inquiry teachers. In R. Glaser (Ed.), *Advances in instructional psychology II.* Hillsdale, NJ: Erlbaum.

Craig, G. (1927). *Certain techniques used in developing a course of study in science for the Horace Mann Elementary School.* New York: Columbia University.

DeVries, R. (1986). Children's conceptions of shadow phenomena. *Genetic, Social, and General Psychology Monographs, 112*(4), 479-530.

diSessa, A. (1982). Unlearning Aristotelian physics: A study of knowledge based learning. *Cognitive Science, 6*(1), 37-75.

Dobey, D., & Schafer, L. (1984). The effects of knowledge on elementary science inquiry teaching. *Science Education, 68*(1), 39-51.

Doyle, W. (1983). Academic work. *Review of Educational Research, 53*(2), 159-199.

Doyle, W., Sanford, J., Clements, B., Schmidt-French, B., & Emmer, E. (1983). *Managing academic tasks: An interim report of the junior high school study.* Austin: University of Texas at Austin, Research and Development Center for Teacher Education.

Driver, R. (1987, July). *Promoting conceptual change in classroom settings: The experience of the Children's Learning in Science Project.* Paper presented at the Second International Seminar, Misconceptions and Educational Strategies in Science and Mathematics, Cornell University, Ithaca, NY.

Driver, R., & Erickson, G. (1983). *The study of students' conceptual frameworks in science.* Paper presented at the annual meeting of the American Educational Research Association, Montreal, Canada.

Eaton, J., Anderson, C., & Smith, E., (1984). Students' misconceptions interfere with science learning: Case studies of fifth grade students. *The Elementary School Journal, 84*(4), 365-379.

Elbaz, F. (1983). *Teacher thinking: A study of practical knowledge.* New York: Nichols.

Evertson, C., Emmer, E., Clements, B., Sanford, J., Worsham, M., & Williams, E. (1981). *Organizing and managing the elementary school classroom.* Austin: University of Texas at Austin.

Fullan, M., Bennett, B., & Rolheiser-Bennett, C. (1989). *Linking classroom and school improvement.* Paper presented at the annual meeting of the American Educational Research Association, San Francisco, CA.

Fullan, M., & Pomfret, A. (1977). Research on curriculum and instruction implementation. *Review of Educational Research, 47*(1), 335-397.

Griffin, G. (1983). Implications of research for staff development programs. *Elementary School Journal, 83*(4), 414-426.

Gruber, H. (1974). Courage and cognitive growth in children and scientists. In M. Schwebel & J. Ralph (Eds.), *Piaget in the classroom.* New York: Basic Books.

Hall, G. (1986). *Deriving teaching skill from studies of the implementation of innovations in education.* Paper presented at the annual meeting of the American Educational Research Association, San Francisco, CA.

Hall, G., & Hord, S. (1987). *Change in schools: Facilitating the process.* Albany: State University of New York.

Harlen, W. (1975). *Science 5/13: A formative evaluation.* London: Macmillan Education.

Hashweh, M. (1985). *An exploratory study of teacher knowledge and teaching: The effects of science teachers' knowledge of subject matter and their conceptions of learning on their teaching.* Unpublished doctoral dissertation, Stanford University, CA.

Hawkins, D. (1980). Conceptual barriers encountered in teaching science to adults: An outline of theory and a summary of some supporting evidence. In M. Apelman, R. Colton, A. Flexer, and D. Hawkins (Eds.), *A report of research on critical barriers to the learning and understanding of elementary science* (SED 80-08581). Boulder: University of Colorado.

Helgeson, S., Blosser, P., & Howe, R. (1977). *The status of pre-college science, math, and social science education, 1955-1977: Vol. 1. Science education.* Washington, DC: U.S. Government Printing Office.

Helm, H., & Novak, J. (Eds.). (1983, June). *Misconceptions in science and mathematics. Proceedings of the International Seminar, June 20-22, 1983.* Ithaca, NY: Cornell University.

Henry, N.B. (Ed.) (1947). *Science education in American schools. The Forty-sixth Yearbook of the National Society for the Study of Education.* Chicago: The University of Chicago Press.

Hewson, M., & Hewson, P. (1983). Effect of instruction using students' prior knowledge and conceptual change strategies on science learning. *Journal of Research in Science Teaching, 20*(8), 731-743.

Hollon, R., & Anderson, C. (1986). *Teachers' understanding of students' scientific thinking: Its influence on planning and teaching.* Paper presented at the annual meeting of the National Association for Research in Science Teaching, San Francisco, CA.

Hollon, R., & Anderson, C. (1987). *Teachers' beliefs about students' learning processes in science: Self-reinforcing belief systems.* Paper presented at the annual meeting of the American Educational Research Association, Washington, DC.

Hollon, R., Anderson, C., & Smith, E. (1980). *A system for observing and analyzing elementary school science teaching: A user's manual.* East Lansing: Michigan State University, The Institute for Research on Teaching.

Hord, S., & Huling-Austin, L. (1986). Effective curriculum implementation: Some promising new insights. *Elementary School Journal, 87*(1), 97-115.

Kamii, C., & DeVries, R. (1978). *Physical knowledge in the preschool.* Englewood Cliffs, NJ: Prentice-Hall.

Kilbourn, B. (1983). *Socialization and science teaching in the junior high school.* Paper presented at the annual meeting of the American Educational Research Association, Montreal, Canada.

Leinhardt, G. (1983). *Routines in expert math teachers' thoughts and actions.* Paper presented at the annual meeting of the American Education Research Association, Montreal, Canada.

Leinhardt, G. (1986). *Math lessons: A contrast of novice and expert competence.* Paper presented at the annual meeting of the American Educational Research Association, San Francisco, CA.

Leinhardt, G. (1987). Development of an expert explanation: An analysis of a sequence of subtraction lessons. *Cognition and Instruction, 4*(4), 203-223.

Leinhardt, G. (1987, July). *Situated knowledge: An example from teaching.* Paper presented at The Teachers' Professional Learning Conference, University of Lancaster, England.

Leinhardt, L., & Greeno, J. (1986). The cognitive skill of teaching. *Journal of Educational Psychology, 78*(2), 75-95.

Leinhardt, G., & Smith, D.A. (1985). Expertise in mathematics instruction: Subject matter knowledge. *Journal of Educational Psychology, 77*, 241-271.

Leinhardt, G., Weidman, C., & Hammond, K. (1984). *Introduction and integration of classroom routines by expert teachers.* Paper presented at the annual meeting of the American Educational Research Association, New Orleans, LA.

McCutcheon, G. (1980). How do elementary school teachers plan? The nature of planning and influences on it. *The Elementary School Journal, 81*(1), 4-23.

Minstrell, J. (1984). Teaching for the development of understanding of ideas: Forces on moving objects. In C. Anderson (Ed.), *Observing science classrooms: Observing science perspectives from research and practice* (pp. 56-74). Columbus, OH: Clearinghouse for Science, Mathematics and Environmental Education.

Munby, H. (1984). *A qualitative study of teachers' beliefs and principles.* Paper presented at the annual meeting of the American Educational Research Association, Montreal, Canada.

Neale, D. (1987). *Primary teachers' current practices and needed expertise in science lessons.* Paper presented at the annual meeting of the National Association for Research in Science Teaching. Washington, DC.

Neale, D., Smith, D., & Johnson, V. (1989). *Implementing conceptual change teaching in primary science.* Adapted from a paper presented at the annual meeting of the American Educational Research Association, San Francisco, CA.

Neale, D., Smith, D., & Wier, E. (1987). *Teacher thinking in elementary science instruction.* Paper presented at the annual meeting of the American Educational Research Association, Washington, DC.

Novak, J. (1987). (Ed.). *Misconceptions and educational strategies in science and mathematics. Proceedings of the second international seminar.* Ithaca, NY: Cornell University.

Nussbaum, J., & Novick, S. (1982). Alternative frameworks, conceptual conflict and accommodation: Toward a principled teaching strategy. *Instructional Science, 11*(3), 183-200.

Olson, J. (1981). Teacher influence in the classroom: A context for understanding curriculum translation. *Instructional Science, 10,* 259-275.

Osborne, R. (1980). Some aspects of students' views of the world. *Research in Science Education. 10,* 11-18.

Peterson, P., Carpenter, T., Fennema, E., & Loef, M. (1987). *Teachers' pedagogical content beliefs in mathematics.* Paper presented at the annual meeting of the American Educational Research Association, Washington, DC.

Piaget, J. (1930). *The child's conception of physical causality.* Totowa, NJ: Littlefield, Adams.

Piaget, J. (1983). *Le possible et le necessaire* [The possible and the necessary]. Paris, France: Presses Universitaires de France.

Posner, G., & Gertzog, W. (1982). The clinical interview and the measurement of conceptual change. *Science Education, 66*(2), 195-209.

Posner, G., Strike, K., Hewson, P., & Gertzog, W. (1982). Accommodation of a scientific conception: Toward a theory of conceptual change. *Science Education, 66*(2), 211-227.

Pratt, H. (1981). Science education in the elementary school. In N. Harms & R. Yager (Eds.), *What research says to the science teacher* (Vol. 3, pp. 73-93). Washington, DC: National Science Teachers Association.

Purkey, S., & Smith, M. (1985). School reform: The district policy implications of the effective schools literature. *Elementary School Journal, 85*(3), 353-389.

Putnam, R., & Leinhardt, G. (1986). *Curriculum scripts and the adjustment of content in mathematics lessons.* Paper presented at the annual meeting of the American Educational Research Association, San Francisco, CA.

Rosenshine, B. (1980). How time is spent in elementary classrooms. In C. Denham & A. Lieberman, (Eds.), *Time to learn* (pp. 107-126). Washington, DC: National Institute of Education.

Roth, K., Anderson, C., & Smith, E. (1986). *Curriculum materials, teacher talk and student learning: Case studies in fifth grade science teaching* (Research Series #171). East Lansing: Michigan State University, The Institute for Research in Teaching.

Russell, T. (1983). Analyzing arguments in science classroom discourse: Can teachers' questions distort scientific authority? *Journal of Research in Science Teaching, 20*(1), 27-45.

Sanford, J. (1984). Management and organization in science classrooms. *Journal of Research in Science Teaching, 21*(6), 575-587.

Schmidt, W., & Buchmann, M. (1983). Six teachers' beliefs and attitudes and their curriculum time allocations. *Elementary School Journal, 84*(2), 162-171.

Schon, D. (1983). *The reflective practitioner.* London: Temple Smith.

Schwab, J. (1978). *Science, curriculum, and liberal education* (selected essays). Chicago: University of Chicago Press.

Shulman, L. (1986). Those who understand: Knowledge growth in teaching. *Educational Researcher, 15*(2), 4-14.

Shulman, L., & Tamir, P. (1973). Research on teaching in the natural sciences. In R. Travers (Ed.), *Handbook of research on teaching* (2nd ed., pp. 1098-1148). Chicago: Rand McNally.

Smith, D. (1987, April). Primary teachers' substantive, syntactic and pedagogical content knowledge. Paper presented at the annual meeting of the National Association for Research in Science Teaching, Washington, DC.

Smith, D. (1989). *The role of teacher knowledge in teaching conceptual change science lessons.* Unpublished doctoral dissertation, University of Delaware, DE.

Smith, D., & Johns, D. (1985). *Teaching for conceptual change: Rationale and description of activities in a first grade science unit.* Paper presented at the annual meeting of the Northeastern Educational Research Association, Kerhonkson, NY.

Smith, E., & Anderson, C. (1984). *The planning and teaching intermediate science study: Final report.* East Lansing: Michigan State University, Institute for Research on Teaching.

Smith, E., & Lott, G. (1983). *Ways of going wrong in teaching for conceptual change* (Research Series #139). East Lansing: Michigan State University, Institute for Research in Teaching.

Smith, E., & Sendelbach, N. (1982). The program, the plans and the activities of the classroom: The demands of activity-based science. In J.K. Olson (Ed.), *Innovation in the science curriculum: Classroom knowledge and curriculum change.* London: Croom-Helm.

Stake, R., & Easley, J. (1978). *Case studies in science education.* Urbana, IL: University of Illinois, Center for Instructional Research and Curriculum Evaluation.

Stallings, J., & Krasavage, E. (1987). Program implementation and student achievement in a four-year Madeline Hunter follow-through project. *Elementary School Journal, 87*(2), 117-138.

Strauss, S. (Ed.) (1982). *U-shaped behavioral growth.* New York: Academic Press.

Strauss, S., & Stavy, R. (1983). Educational developmental psychology and curriculum development: The case of heat and temperature. In H. Helm & J. Novak (Eds.), *Proceedings of the International Seminar, Misconceptions in Science and Mathematics* (pp. 292-303). Ithaca: Cornell University.

Strike, K., & Posner, G. (1982). *Epistemological assumptions of college students.* Paper presented at the annual meeting of the Northeastern Educational Research Association, Ellenville, NY.

Thornton, S. (1985). *Curriculum consonance in United States History classrooms.* Unpublished doctoral dissertation, Stanford University, CA.

Tobin, K., & Fraser, B. (1987). *Exemplary practice in science and mathematics education.* Perth, Western Australia: Curtin University of Technology, Science and Mathematics Education Centre.

Weiss, I. (1987). *How well prepared are science and mathematics teachers? Results of the 1985 National Survey of Science and Mathematics Education.* Paper presented at the annual meeting of the American Educational Research Association, Washington, DC.

Welch, W. (1981). Inquiry in school science. In N. Harms & R. Yager (Eds.), *What research says to the science teacher* (Vol. 3, pp. 53-72). Washington, DC: National Science Teachers Association.

Wier, E. (1987, April). *Primary teachers' perceptions of barriers to teaching science.* Paper presented at the annual meeting of the National Association for Research in Science Teaching, Washington, DC.

Wilson, S., Shulman, L., & Richert, A. (1987). 150 different ways of knowing: Representations of knowledge in teaching. In J. Calderhead (Ed.), *Exploring teachers' thinking.* London: Cassell Educational Limited.

*   *   *

CROSS-TALK

What is the difference between Schwab's syntactic knowledge and the orientations to science teaching and learning that you used in your studies?

The two are not equivalent, as Grossman, Wilson, and Shulman (n.d.) have pointed out. While the line between the two is not clean, syntactic knowledge involves knowledge of the acceptable methods, tools of inquiry, and criteria for evidence in a discipline; this is knowledge that is justified in some sense (e.g., as in Scheffler's [1965] justified true belief) or related to evidence about the history of science. Orientations to, or beliefs about, teaching and learning science rest more on a personal values system about that subject in schools, although they may include beliefs about what science is or ought to be.

We suspect that these two aspects are related for teachers and that, had we probed more deeply into their knowledge about scientific methods and about how progress is made in constructing scientific knowledge, their answers would have been related. While some teachers used terms like *hypotheses* and *experiments* in their initial interviews about teaching science, the only direct data we have about their syntactic knowledge comes from two items on the Fall questionnaire. Their answers to "What do scientists do?" and "How do scientists decide what is true?" revealed a wide range of beliefs, and little evidence of knowledge of the history and philosophy of science. This is an area which deserves more attention because of its implications for teachers' orientations to teaching and learning science.

It is also of interest because teachers' orientations to science teaching appeared to be nested within larger images or networks of beliefs about their roles as teachers of young children—in Nan Rochester's teaching, for example. What teachers may know or believe about the history of science and scientists' work may not be compatible with other systems of belief about teaching and learning which affect their thinking and teaching. For example, this may be one possible explanation for the smaller changes made by the teachers with discovery orientations, who were mostly the teachers of the youngest children. Since our study was not causal in nature, and only descriptive, there are several alternative explanations to be explored.

Elementary teachers' lives center around teaching several different subjects, and thus differ from the more limited focus of secondary teachers. It would be interesting to see whether elementary teachers' orientations to the different subjects that they teach are compatible with each other or whether they may be quite different. For example, an orientation to child-centered interpretations of literature may contrast with a more fact-oriented orientation to science. Another fruitful area for future investigation is the relationship of elementary teachers' general theories about teaching and learning to their orientations to particular subjects. The teachers with whom we worked appeared to find the new conceptual change teaching orientation applicable, at least in some cases, to other subjects they taught. In their final interviews, some expressed the view that coming to use conceptual change teaching strategies in science had revolutionized their conceptions of teaching generally (and even their views of their own value as teachers).

Finally, we have been asked about our decision to model and teach actively one particular orientation to science teaching, conceptual change. Other authors have noted that, especially in the humanities at the secondary level, multiple interpretations are the norm, both in the field itself, for example, history, and in the teaching of that discipline. Unfortunately, we do not yet know much about the effects of these different models on secondary students' understanding in that discipline. As we discussed earlier in the chapter, we are persuaded by growing evidence that other orientations to teaching and learning science often do not result in children's conceptual understanding of the substantive content; since this understanding is something we value, our current choice is a conceptual change orientation. In addition, other orientations may misrepresent the nature of the discipline, given current thinking about the history and philosophy of science; a conceptual change orientation is most compatible with our current understanding of the nature of progress in science. Should evidence arise that either of these can be replaced by a more effective and more representative model, then our decision might be to choose a different orientation as our current "best bet."

What would be necessary for elementary teachers to teach conceptual change science well?

Our experience so far suggests that there are no straightforward or simple answers. It is unlikely that even a well-written, conceptual change oriented, student text or a scripted teacher's guide that provided some of the needed knowledge (e.g., about students' misconceptions) would be sufficient. Roth's dissertation study (1985) found that some children did make conceptual changes with such a text, but only when they themselves noticed the discrepencies and tried to resolve them. In a classroom situation, teachers might use the text in the service of other orientations and not highlight such discrepancies or ask children to resolve them. Hollon and Anderson (1987; Hollon, Roth, & Anderson, this volume, pp. 145-184) have reported the many ways in which their conceptual change materials and activities have been modified and weakened in classrooms.

A shift in the teacher's image of, or orientation to, science teaching appears to be one necessary component, although it is not clear that this has to take place first. Some teachers with whom we worked appeared to shift their orientations only *after* trying the strategies in their own classrooms, and noticing how children responded and worked. This was not a sudden, all or nothing shift, but one which appeared to be a major reorganization of their frameworks to teaching science. Previous orientations, especially in the form of usual teaching routines, intruded on attempts to teach in a new way, for example, in our case study of Nan Rochester.

Once a shift was at least under consideration, it was clear that this was not simply a matter of slotting in a new set of teaching techniques. So far there appears to be no substitute for, or more economical solution to, the problem of the many different kinds of teacher knowledge that are used in conceptual change teaching (and probably in any kind of expert teaching). Teachers need a repertoire of the kinds of knowledge we have discussed and this knowledge needs to be flexible and quickly accessible for use in decision making while teaching.

There is no script or simple algorithm for the teaching, especially, as Leinhardt and her colleagues point out in their chapter, when the teacher's decisions depend in a substantial way on what children's responses indicate about their understanding. This kind of conditional, contextual knowledge for decisions while teaching may account for some of the differences in teachers' abilities to implement conceptual change teaching consistently, as Carlsen discusses in his chapter. Teachers may, in some sense, be able to "understand" more than they are successful in doing; that is, they may have an image of conceptual change teaching but have difficulty negotiating the fast-flowing, complex, interactive waters of particular classroom contexts. There may also be times when they can "succeed" procedurally in conducting a conceptual change lesson, but only later "understand" why that occurred.

Pedagogical knowledge of agendas, activity structures, and rules and routines also appear to be particularly important. As Leinhardt and her colleagues discuss in their chapter, and as our case study of Nan Rochester revealed, the organization and management of materials and activities for science lessons proved to be an aspect of conceptual change lessons which often rocked the classroom boat.

Fortunately, once the conceptual change framework/orientation and some basic knowledge of the teaching and management strategies are in place, teachers may be able to take their case knowledge from one unit and move more easily into other science units. In the final interviews for our project, teachers were asked what they thought they would need in order to teach a conceptual change unit in another science topic. First, they said they would need to master the conceptual content themselves, preferably by working through the activities and materials. Ironically, their improved conceptual understanding of light and shadows seemed to highlight for them their meager scientific understanding of other topics, and they were reluctant to take on new topics without improved understanding. Second, they said they would need to know the common children's misconceptions to look out for in the new topic. In addition, they said they would want coaching and a regular time to meet with other teachers who were also trying to teach in this way—just as Hollon, Anderson, and Roth suggest in their chapter.

When we consider what we have learned about the complexity of teaching for conceptual change, it appear to us that our program was modest in its support for teachers' change. Teachers had one week of work on all the kinds of knowledge under construction, four or five days practice in the summer camp, with only one day of coaching and one stimulated recall interview, and then experience with one unit in which they were coached and offered one suggested improvement four times. Our studies point out how much we still do not know about the processes by which teachers move from one level of expertise to another, for example, in Berliner's (1989) scheme. Here is our current best bet: an ongoing staff development program in science teaching, with materials which supported teachers with important information about children's thinking and possible curricular pathways and activities, in which teachers modelled for each other various levels of expertise, and which enabled teachers to construct the different kinds of knowledge over time, to apply them in their own classrooms more gradually, to ask for coaching and feedback on a regular basis, and to collaborate with others in assessing effects on children's learning, might provide the environment in which elementary teachers could construct expertise and extend it to the different science units they teach.

References to Cross-talk

Berliner, D. (1989). Implications of studies of expertise in pedagogy for teacher education and evaluation. In *New directions for teacher assessment, Proceedings of the 1988 Educational Testing Service Conference* (pp. 39-68). Princeton, NJ: Educational Testing Service.

Grossman, P., Wilson, S., & Shulman, L. (n.d.) *Teachers of substance: Subject matter knowledge for teaching*. Unpublished manuscript.

Hollon, R., & Anderson, C. (1987). *Teachers' beliefs about students' learning processes in science: Self-reinforcing belief systems.* Paper presented at the annual meeting of the American Educational Research Association, Washington, DC.

Roth, K. (1985). *Conceptual change learning and student processing of science texts.* Unpublished doctoral dissertation, Michigan State University, East Lansing, MI.

Scheffler, I. (1965). *Conditions of knowledge: An introduction to epistemology and education.* Chicago: Scott, Foresman.

WHAT ARE WE TALKING ABOUT ANYWAY?

SUBJECT-MATTER KNOWLEDGE OF SECONDARY ENGLISH TEACHERS

Pamela L. Grossman

See, that's something that I'm struggling with right now! I don't even know what it means to learn English. What are we talking about anyway?
—Martha, pre-service teacher (in Grossman, 1987b)

Certainly, something special is called for to see a concept of overall structure in English as a discipline in schools and colleges today. To begin with: the structure of what? There is language . . . literature . . . and composition . . . Our discipline is diverse.
—Wilson (1964)

SUBJECT MATTER OF ENGLISH

In discussing the implications of teachers' subject-matter knowledge in English, we are faced with a dilemma similar to Martha's and Wilson's—knowledge

Advances in Research on Teaching, Volume 2, pages 245-264.
Copyright © 1991 by JAI Press Inc.
All rights of reproduction in any form reserved.
ISBN: 1-55938-034-9

of what? A diffuse discipline, English has been catgorized according to the tripartite division of content mentioned above—literature, language, and composition—as well as according to a more functional approach, which specifies the four basic skills acquired in the study of English—reading, writing, listening, and speaking. In a history of the teaching of English, Applebee reiterates the difficulties in defining the nature of the subject matter in English.

> Beyond the cliche that each of these studies deals with language, they have no real unity as *subject matter*; attempts to interrelate them have been artificial, and for the most part, short-lived. Whether the model for the educational process has been growth in language, the four basic skills (reading, writing, listening, speaking) or the three basic disciplines (language, literature, and composition) some aspects of what teachers considered to be important has been lost . . . Inevitably, the edges of the subject have blurred and wavered, creating for the teacher of English a perpetual crisis of identity (Applebee, 1974, pp. 245-246).

In order to sharpen our perspective on subject-matter knowledge in English, it seems necessary first to simplify the task by focusing on one aspect of English. Because I am discussing the subject-matter knowledge of secondary school English teachers, for whom literature plays a central part in the curriculum, and because literature generally receives primary emphasis during subject matter preparation in college, I have chosen to focus on the role teachers' knowledge of literature plays in teaching.

KNOWLEDGE OF LITERATURE

While limiting the focus of this chapter to teachers' knowledge of literature simplifies the task significantly, we must still ask ourselves what we mean by "knowledge of literature." As is true of the humanities in general, knowledge of literature results not from scientific proofs but from interpretations. Literary interpretation, in turn, rests on how one reads a text, using a set of conventions that determines what elements of a text to pay attention to and the relative order of importance of the different elements.

Knowledge of literature, then, emerges from a process of interpretation that necessarily focuses on particular aspects involved in reading a literary text. What one knows about literature will in large part depend upon one's interpretative stance. To help clarify the possible approaches towards reading a single text, I will refer to a model of the act of communication developed by Roman Jakobson, which was revised by Scholes (1982) to describe the reading of a literary text. The six elements which comprise the act of reading include the author, the text itself, the context in which the author wrote, the medium in which the author wrote, the codes which govern the production of a literary text, and finally, the reader of the text.

Different schools of critical theory argue for the relative importance of various elements of this model (Eagleton, 1983; Scholes, 1982; Tompkins, 1980). For example, in the school of New Criticism, interpretation is rooted in the text itself; biographical information about the author, in this framework, is irrelevant to the meaning of a text (Wimsatt & Brooks, 1957). In other schools of criticism, the author is the key to the meaning of a text; only by understanding the author's intention can the reader hope to understand a text (Hirsch, 1967). Inherent in both of these approaches is the belief that there are correct and incorrect readings of texts; the reader must deal with the text objectively in order to interpret a work correctly. Theories of reader response, however, argue that the reader makes meaning of the text, and that interpretation in large part rests on the subjective interaction between a text and an individual reader (Tompkins, 1980). Other schools of critical theory emphasize the personal or historical context in which the writer wrote, using theoretical models from outside English, such as Marxist or psychoanalytical theories, in the interpretation of literary texts. While differences among these various schools of literary criticism may be important for graduate students in English, and may even make the pages of the *New York Times* (Campbell, 1986), why are they important for high school teachers? Is knowledge of semiotics and deconstruction essential for teaching in the secondary classroom? While battles concerning the appropriate way to read literature occur mostly in the upper echelons of higher education, how high school teachers learn to read literature influences how they themselves will teach literature to their own students. English teachers' interpretative stances, which I term orientations towards literature, become important in understanding their goals for instruction, curricular choices, instructional assignments, and classroom questions. In this chapter, I will outline three of the most common orientations towards literature, a reader-orientation, a text-orientation, and a context-orientation, and illustrate the role of orientation towards literature in classroom planning and teaching through the case studies of two beginning English teachers.

Clearly, these orientations do not comprise the whole of teachers' knowledge of literature. Teachers also possess content knowledge of literature, including knowledge of key terms for literary analysis (e.g., plot, theme, figurative language, metonymy), knowledge of genres and of major authors, and knowledge of significant historical periods of literature (e.g., American Renaissance, Romanticism). While this content knowledge remains constant across orientations, the relative importance of such knowledge is determined within a particular orientation to literature. Because of the importance of these interpretive frameworks in the conceptualization of subject-matter knowledge in English, I have chosen to focus on orientations to literature rather than on content knowleldge per se, while recognizing that this focus represents a necessarily simplified perspective.

ORIENTATIONS TOWARDS LITERATURE

More than a casual attitude towards the subject matter, an orientation towards literature represents a basic organizing framework for knowledge about literature (Grossman, 1987c). An orientation draws from both the substantive and syntactic structures of a discipline (Schwab, 1964), including the critical theories which frame how one reads literature, representing the substantive structures, and the sources of evidence one uses to ground an interpretation, the syntactic structures. While there are a number of possible orientations towards literature, as suggested by the discussion above, three of the most prevalent orientations are the reader-orientation, the text-orientation, and the context-orientation.

The text-orientation has its roots in the New Criticism, advocated by Robert Penn Warren and Cleanth Brooks, among others. In this orientation, an isolated text, or literary work, becomes the locus of interpretation. The reader looks within the text, at literary devices, at the use of language and structure, for clues to its meaning. Literary analysis follows formal patterns, such as analyzing for tone, theme, and structure. While there is some latitude in interpretation, the text itself must serve as the source of evidence to "prove" an interpretation.

The reader-orientation, which has its roots in reader-response theory (see Tompkins, 1980, for overview) focuses not on an isolated text, but the reader's responses to a particular text. Within this orientation, the meaning of a text is personal and subjective, rather than universal and objective. Idiosyncratic personal response assumes priority over formal literary analysis. Reading a text involves an interaction between the reader and text, as readers connect the text to their own experience and personalize it.

An orientation towards the context suggests that the reader's interpretation of a literary work is mediated by theoretical frameworks and analytical tools from another discipline, such as psychology or history. Readers of this orientation may use analytical frameworks from Freudian psychology or Marxist thought, for example, in their literary interpretations. The meaning of a text becomes psychological or political, rather than purely literary as in the text-orientation, or personal, as in the reader-orientation.

These orientations represent a continuum of possible interpretive stances towards a literary text. While readers may approach a literary work from a dominant orientation, their interpretation may include elements of other orientations as well. For example, while a text-oriented reader may interpret a poem from the perspective of its structure, imagery, meter, and theme, using the words of the poem as evidence for the interpretation, the reader may also identify personally with the theme of the poem. A specific orientation may predominate, but it is rarely exclusive. To illustrate the influence of these orientations towards literature on the teaching of literature in the secondary classroom, I will use the case studies of two prospective English teachers, Colleen and Martha, two participants in the Knowledge Growth in a Profession research project that took place at Stanford University. Colleen illustrates an orientation towards the text in both her knowledge and beliefs about literature and in her teaching, while Martha represents an orientation to the reader.

METHODOLOGY

The Knowledge Growth in a Profession research focused on the subject-matter knowledge of beginning secondary school teachers and the role subject-matter knowledge played in their teaching (Wilson, Shulman, & Richert, 1986; Grossman, Wilson, & Shulman, 1989). During the first year of the research, which focused on the year of teacher education, we interviewed twenty prospective teachers in four fields—English, social studies, math, and science. In the second year of the research, we followed a subset of these teachers into their first year of full-time teaching. I interviewed and observed both Colleen and Martha during their year of professional preparation and followed Martha into her first year of teaching.

During the first year of data collection, I interviewed Colleen and Martha at least ten times about their knowledge and beliefs about English, their conceptions about teaching English, their academic backgrounds, and their specific knowledge about literature and writing. One set of interviews focused on a particular piece of text, a short story entitled "The Stone Boy" (Berriault, 1966). The first interview asked the prospective teachers about their own understanding of the story, probing for the interpretive process in which they engaged. The second interview, which took place several weeks later, asked the teachers to think about teaching the short story—their goals for teaching the story, how they might use the story in a unit, what activities or writing assignments they might use in conjunction with the story, and how they would evaluate student understanding.

In addition to the interviews, I observed Martha and Colleen teach in their classrooms, interviewing them beforehand about their plans and objectives and afterwards about the observed lesson. During the course of the study, I observed both Martha and Colleen teach poetry. The interviews concerning "The Stone Boy" and the observations of poetry lessons serve as the primary sources of data for this analysis, although in my sketches of the two teachers, I draw upon the larger set of data. Prior to my analysis of the role of orientations in planning and teaching about literature, I will provide a brief description of the two teachers and their knowledge and beliefs about English.

COLLEEN

Always an avid reader, Colleen entered college with the intention of majoring in English. Both her mother, a former English teacher herself, and one of Colleen's high school English teachers encouraged Colleen's love of words and books. During her four years of college, Colleen earned both a bachelor's degree and a master's degree in English, having completed twenty four English classes. Colleen feels that her greatest area of expertise in literature lies in twentieth-century American fiction; her undergraduate major emphasized creative writing.

Colleen brings to her study of English a passion for language and a sensitivity to its nuances and possibilities.

> Something about people and their words I find really invigorating, really exhilarating to me, and my students make fun of me because I'm so into the words, the words themselves I think are really neat [Colleen, PS1, 2:5] (Grossman, 1987a, p. 5).

Colleen's orientation towards literature centers around the text itself. In interpreting a story, she refers constantly to the text, reading passages aloud to support her conclusions. Colleen pays close attention to the specific language of a story and notes the use of imagery. Colleen's evaluations of literature revolve around the author's ability to depict ambiguity. For this reason, she prefers writers such as Chekhov, Virginia Woolf, and William Faulkner to writers such as Hemingway or D.H. Lawrence.

Although Colleen had always considered the possibility of becoming an English teacher, she initially planned to teach at the college level. She decided to get a credential for teaching secondary school English because "it was closest to college, which is where I wanted to end up" [Colleen, PS1, 1:4] (Grossman, 1987a, p. 4). Colleen entered teaching because of her deep love of the subject matter.

MARTHA

Unlike Colleen, Martha did not enter college with the intention of majoring in English; she planned to major in engineering. When her first calculus class convinced her to abandon engineering, she decided to major in political science with the goal of becoming a lawyer. Only when she realized that she had taken primarily English classes did she declare her major in English. Martha describes her English major as a self-designed one, with an interdisciplinary and comparative emphasis. As part of her junior year abroad in Vienna, Martha took a number of German literature courses. Martha feels her strengths lie in ninteenth- and twentieth-century American, British, and German literature.

Martha's preference is less for the critical and analytical aspects of English and more for what she terms the human aspect of literature.

> One of the reasons why I really like the study of literature is because it draws on different aspects of the human condition . . . I like to approach literature from this perspective: what can I learn about people, about myself, about society through literature [Martha, IB, 2:2] (Grossman, 1987b, p. 2).

Martha's orientation to literature focuses on the reader. In discussing a short story, Martha concentrates on the experiences of the characters, comparing their experiences to her own. She does not focus on the language of the story and rarely refers to individual passages. Instead, she discusses the overall theme of the story as a statement on the human condition. She contrasts her approach to literature with that of a scholar, suggesting that she needs to personalize a literary work, while a scholar analyzes the story more objectively.

> I don't think I would make a good scholar because I just can't take something isolated and bring a bunch of techniques for critical analysis or whatever and impose that on it. I have to be able to relate it to what I see and what I've experienced and that is the basis, the way I will attack a piece of literature. I'll find some angle that is real to me and work from that [Martha, IB, 3:4] (Grossman, 1987b, p. 3).

Martha's evaluation of literature centers around thematic concerns. She responds particularly to literature connected to the theme of the outsider; "There's always something that appeals to me about the one that no one seems to understand . . . I always feel, for some reason, sympathetic to that" [Martha, SS2, 5:2] (Grossman, 1987b, p. 3). Her favorite books include *An American Tragedy* and *Native Son*, both novels about outsiders to society.

Martha decided upon a teaching career almost as a quirk of fate. Still planning to go to law school, Martha discovered in her senior year that she needed to earn some extra units. She found that she could earn the necessary units by engaging in a teaching internship in a local public school. Her experience in the schools led her to discover her own passion for working with students who needed extra help.

> And then I worked with a special help junior class. And it was the special help junior class, those kids in there, who were losers by everybody's standards, that I absolutely fell in love with . . . I felt so good about working with them that it made me apply to the teacher education program [Martha, PS1, 1:1] (Grossman, 1987b, p. 4).

Martha entered teaching because of her love not for the subject matter but for the students.

ORIENTATIONS IN PRACTICE: GOALS FOR INSTRUCTION

Martha and Colleen entered teacher education with differing conceptions about what it means to interpret literature. Colleen saw the text as central to the process of interpretation, while Martha emphasized the personal response of the reader.[1] These differing orientations play themselves out in the context of curricular planning, as the teachers' goals for their classes reflect their own orientations towards literature, as was apparent both in their stated goals for teaching poetry and their simulated planning to teach "The Stone Boy."

Colleen's first concerns about teaching "The Stone Boy" focused on how the text fit within the larger curriculum. She asked whether she would be teaching it in a short story unit, an American literature unit, or a unit on creative writing. In considering how to teach the text, Colleen discussed the elements of the short story that could fit into the various units and also talked about how the story might be taught in relation to other texts she might be teaching. A secondary concern focused on the students and their ability levels. Colleen's goals for teaching the story focused on her desire for her students to become close, critical readers.

> I mostly would like them to have this very nebulous skill of paying attention to details in reading. And I think any of those activities . . . would have them looking at the story enough to let them be in the story to see the words and what's being said, not just fly through it and not remember any of it [Colleen, SS3, 11:1].

Colleen's goals for teaching "The Stone Boy" reflect her own concerns with close textual interpretation. Her evaluation of student understanding of the story would emphasize "how much detail they used from the story, explaining to you their opinions or their answers or whatever" [Colleen, SS3, p. 12:1]. Her ultimate goal, consistent with her own text-orientation, is to encourage students to pay close attention to the details of a text in their interpretations of literature. This emphasis on the text appears in her goals for teaching poetry as well.

In talking about her goals for teaching poetry, Colleen again focused on the importance of close attention to a literary text.

> One of the things you have to teach them is that you have to take the time, look at every word. And I want them to look at words . . . I guess all you could do to get them to look at poetry in the future is to have them look at the words and know how important it is to look at the words and not just look it through and say "I don't understand it." [Colleen, Obs. #1] (Grossman, 1987a, p. 6).

While Colleen acknowledges the importance of supporting students' interpretations of poetry, she asserts that the basis for their interpretations must lie within the poem itself.

> So that's my major goal, to get them to understand that what they interpret is just as valid
> as what the next person interprets and also to look at the words. That what the poem
> means is right there in front of you, you don't need someone to stand there and say this
> is what it means [Colleen, Obs. #1] (Grossman 1987a, p. 6).

While she encourages students to express their opinions about literature, Colleen's emphasis on the importance of looking to the text in literary interpretation reflects her dominant orientation towards the text. Student responses to literature, while interesting to Colleen, were not acceptable as interpretations unless they could be supported with proof from the text, as she suggests in her goals for teaching her students to write about literature.

> You make a point and prove it with the text, and you prove it with the poem in front
> of you, with the text. I've even said, you can have the option of saying, 'I believe this,
> it's a gut reaction, but I can't back it up.' That's an option, you can't use it in an essay,
> you still have to make three major points that you can back up, but you can use it as
> a fourth point [Colleen, Obs. #1] (Grossman, 1987a, p. 7).

In this comment, student response becomes extra credit—the fourth point—not the focus of the writing assignment.

Colleen's overall goal for teaching literature—that students learn to look toward the text in their literary interpretations—mirrors her own orientation toward literature. Believing in the primacy of the written text, she translates this belief into her goals for student readers.

Martha's goals for teaching literature center around the encouragement of student responses to literary works. In contrast to Colleen's consideration of the text, Martha began her consideration of how to teach "The Stone Boy" by focusing on the responses of her students.

> I probably would deal more . . . with the reaction that people have after reading it, what
> their response to it is [Martha, SS3, 1:2].

Rather than wanting students to focus on the language of the story, Martha wants them to focus on their own reactions to the story, suggesting that she approaches the teaching of literature from an experiential perspective.

> [I] focus on literature as experience. What has happened to you as a result of reading this
> story? How do you feel? What goes on in your mind now that you reflect back over what
> you've read? [Martha, SS3, 1:3].

Martha's goals for teaching the story would be to encourage students to talk about their own responses to the story and how it affected their ideas about human nature. She stresses that she finds this goal more compelling than making sure students are able to identify literary elements within a text.

> What's wrong with just reading something and talking about it? To me, it was enough to read it and to think about it . . . This is a story that kind of lodges itself there in your consciousness because it's disturbing, because you wonder, these are people, how can they do these things to one another? . . . I see that as infinitely more important than whether they can tell me where the rising action is or whatever [Martha, SS3, 6:3].

Martha's emphasis on student response, which is consistent with her own approach towards reading literature, appears again in her goals for teaching poetry. She sees the study of poetry as a chance to examine and broaden one's personal experience.

> I like poetry a lot and I enjoy teaching it. I think it allows us to look at various human experiences in a very concise, condensed form . . . And these are ideas that either the students have had and can relate to or have not had and we can have our own selves broadened a bit because we've experienced something our own lives don't provide. So I have no problem with teaching poetry, if you're looking at literature from a Rosenblatt[2] point of view [Martha, Pre-obs. 13:3] (Grossman, 1987b, pp. 10-11).

Although Martha borrowed a poetry curriculum which emphasized the formal analysis of poetry using technical terms, she later rejected the unit, claiming it was inconsistent with her goals of encouraging student response.

> I've been thinking philosophically through what's being accomplished in my approach to this unit, and everything I value, such as reading the poem to find some common element that they can relate to, that this is a part of the human experience as we've talked about for a year or more. All that stuff is getting brushed off because I don't have time. No, I can't talk about what these poems mean in our lives because I have to tell you the difference between an iamb and a trochee [Martha, Pre-obs., 2:2] (Grossman, 1987b, pp. 11-12).

Martha's goals for teaching literature all revolve around the importance of encouraging student response to the works. Her focus is less on the text than on the reader, reflecting her reader-orientation towards literature in general.

ORIENTATIONS IN PRACTICE: PLANNING FOR INSTRUCTION

Orientations towards literature inform not only these teachers' goals for instruction, but also their actual plans for teaching literature and their choices of activities for students. In planning how to teach "The Stone Boy," Colleen thought of various activities that would require students to focus on the text. Her first choice of an activity involved textual interpretation.

> [I would] think of a question that would get them looking at that passage . . . This passage on page 243 related to this one on page 244. In what way can they be compared? [Colleen, SS3, 4-5].

Other ideas for activities included having students rewrite the ending of the story and asking students what they might have done in the protagonist's place. Colleen's predominant strategy for planning the lesson, however, involved picking out particular lines and passages from the short story which she would ask students to explain. Colleen gave the following example for what she might assign college bound students.

> Explain the ending to me. What does he mean when he says, "He was trembling from the fright his answer gave him?" What does that mean? And don't just give me an answer from the top of your head. Go back to the story and from the story tell me what it means. Give me an example [Colleen, SS3, 13:2].

Again, Colleen's ideas for teaching "The Stone Boy" reflect her own concern for close textual interpretation. Her planning began with the text itself, as she chose passages, images, and language for students to interpret. While Colleen said she would vary the type of activity assigned to students on the basis of student ability, all of the activities share a common focus on the text. Colleen stated that she would have lower-level students summarize the story for the class, slightly more advanced students explain "self-explanatory passages," and the advanced students interpret more difficult passages, putting "together things that aren't put together for them; also the language would be kind of fun for the advanced students to look at" [Colleen, SS3, 7:1]. As mentioned above, Colleen would evaluate students' understanding of the story by seeing how much detail they used from the text in supporting their interpretations. Colleen's plans are consistent with her desire that students become readers who pay attention to details of the text, readers, in fact, very much like herself.

Colleen's choice of activities in teaching poetry echoed her hypothetical plans for teaching "The Stone Boy." As a pre-activity for a unit on poetry, Colleen had her students paraphrase the lyrics of their favorite song. Her objective was to have students think about the actual words of the song and why particular words had been chosen. Again, Colleen's choice of activity parallels her orientation towards the text.

> And I want them to look at words. I had them Monday, as a pre-activity to start the unit, I had them bring in their lyrics to their favorite song, and I told them, 'I want you to look at every word and paraphrase it' . . . I had them paraphrase each line, so some words they could leave, but try to look at every single word . . . Just to look at the words. I wanted them to see other words meaning the same thing [Colleen, Obs. #1, 7-8], (Grossman, 1987a, pp. 5-6).

In contrast to Colleen's plans for teaching the short story and her choice of activities that focus on the text, Martha chose activities that encourage students to respond affectively to the story. In talking about how she might teach "The Stone Boy," Martha suggested that she would ask students to write a page or so on how the story left them feeling and then use their responses to start a classroom discussion. Martha did not refer to the text in her planning, but talked about the story as a whole and how it might affect students. Martha would not feel compelled to evaluate students' understanding of the story beyond their written responses and classroom discussion, believing that it is enough to read and respond to a story, without having to analyze it.

In her first year of full-time teaching, Martha inherited a unit on poetry which she planned to teach to her class. The unit embodied an orientation to the text, as the lessons stressed the technical terminology for close textual analysis of poetry. In preparing to teach the unit, Martha altered the curriculum she had been bequeathed, tailoring it to fit her own goals. Martha began the unit with a project she designed on experimental poetry, in which the class first discussed "found" and "concrete" poems and then worked on their own poems which were then used to decorate the classroom walls. Martha also added the requirement that students keep a poetry journal throughout the unit, in which they were to write their personal responses to the poetry they were reading. Uncomfortable with the orientation of the curriculum she was using, Martha struggled to find ways to emphasize students' responses over technical analysis. Martha's immediate adaptation of the curriculum materials suggest the importance of a teacher's dominant orientation in curriculum implementation. In implementing the curriculum, Martha began to shift the emphasis of the unit away from the textual analysis of poetry and toward student response.

These beginning teachers' orientations toward literature influenced not only their goals for teaching literature but the types of activites they chose for their students. While Colleen's activities share a common focus on the text, Martha's activities are designed to encourage student response.

ORIENTATIONS IN PRACTICE: CLASSROOM QUESTIONS

These orientations toward literature find their way into the classroom, as the teachers' questions and interactive teaching reflect their predominant concerns about the teaching of literature.

In teaching the poem "Complaint" by William Carlos Williams, Colleen led a discussion that emphasized the language of the poem. She opened the class by reading the poem aloud twice and then asked students for a definition of "jalousie," pointing out the play on words between "jealousy" and "jalousie." Colleen then focused the students' attention on the words of the poem, asking "What does 'great' mean?" "Why does he say 'Joy' twice?" "Why 'pick' a hair?" [Colleen, Obs. #1] (Grossman, 1987a, p. 6). During the discussion of the poem, Colleen reminded her students, "In a poem, every word counts," and asked them to think about how the sentences of the poem were organized to make a poem, telling them, "I want you to see how they take ordinary language and make it a poem" [Colleen, Obs. #1] (Grossman, 1987a, p. 6).

This emphasis on the words and language of literary texts was apparent in all of the observations of Colleen's teaching. In teaching a short story by Edgar Allan Poe, "The Cask of Amontillado," Colleen began the class by putting a list of unfamiliar words from the story on the board and asking students for their definitions. During the discussion, she pointed out the meaning of the names of the two protagonists Montresor, my treasure, and Fortunato, lucky, and also pointed out the play on the words cask and casket in the story.

The content of Colleen's interactive teaching was filled with references to the language of the literary texts. While she believed that multiple interpretations of a single text were possible and desirable, she felt strongly that these interpretations had to be grounded in the details of the text.

The text played a much less central role in Martha's classroom. During her student teaching, Martha emphasized the teaching of writing in her classroom and taught relatively few literary works. In her first year of full-time teaching, Martha taught more literature, although she still preferred to teach writing. Martha was less concerned with students' understanding of particular texts than with their general responses to literature. Her frustration with the poetry unit she inherited centered around its lack of attention to students' personal responses to the poems and its emphasis on technical analysis. Martha's desire for the students to respond personally to poetry overshadowed her desire that they understand the poems, as is evident in class discussions such as this.

Martha: What do we learn from "the house was like a ship?"
Student: It moves.
Martha: It's floating and what is the water in this poem?
Student: I don't know.
Martha: Night is like water.
Student: I don't understand.
Martha: Oh, I don't want you to not like poetry. Don't worry about right answers. We're not looking for right answers [Martha, Obs. 11-85].

In this dialogue, Martha shows her discomfort with emphasizing textual analysis over student response.

The orientations toward literature that these two teachers bring to the classroom influence their goals for instruction, their choice of activities, and their emphasis in classroom discussions. In learning to teach English, both Colleen and Martha rely on their own conceptions of what it means to read literature, as their dominant orientation towards literature becomes a leitmotif of their teaching. Their frameworks for reading literature become frameworks for the teaching of literature as well. Colleen continues the tradition of the New Criticism in her emphasis on the text as the locus of literary meaning, while Martha represents the tradition of reader-response theory, in which meaning emerges from an interaction between a text and a particular reader.

The influence of orientations towards literature does not seem limited to beginning English teachers. In an analysis of the contrasts between two expert and two novice English teachers (Grossman & Gudmundsdottir, 1987), we found evidence that the more experienced teachers' orientations towards literature were also reflected in their curricular decisions and classroom teaching. The more experienced teachers, Nancy and Naomi, had developed more explicit models of the teaching of literature than had the novice teachers, but their models of teaching literature each embodied a dominant orientation. Nancy's model, which illustrated a dominant orientation towards the text, articulated four levels of reading a work that moved from literal understanding to interpretation to application and evaluation. While her fourth level encompassed students' response to literature, Nancy emphasized the third level of interpretation, in which students grapple with the text itself to find its meaning. Naomi provides a vivid contrast to Nancy, as she had developed a model for teaching literature that centered on the student-reader. Like Martha, Naomi wants her students to respond personally to literary texts and to make connections between literature and their own lives. (See Gudmundsdottir [1989] for a full discussion of Nancy and Naomi.) While Nancy and Naomi were equally experienced teachers with similar subject-matter backgrounds, their teaching of literature embodied their differing orientations toward literature itself.

The contrasts between Colleen and Martha, as well as between Nancy and Naomi, suggest implications for both research on teaching and teacher preparation. While an orientation towards literature is only one facet of teachers' subject-matter knowledge in English, this analysis argues against research on subject-matter knowledge that ignores the underlying structures of disciplinary knowledge.

IMPLICATIONS FOR RESEARCH ON TEACHING

Past research on teachers' subject-matter knowledge of English (Hook, 1965; Veal, Butler, Hulme, & Hudson, 1983) used teachers' scores on standardized tests of English and numbers of college English courses taken as measures of subject-matter knowledge. The research found little or no relationship between teachers' subject-matter knowledge and either pupil achievement (Hook, 1965) or general teaching performance (Veal et al., 1983). Yet the lack of findings and paucity of studies in this area perhaps tell us as much about our difficulties in conceptualizing the role of subject-matter knowledge in teaching as about the relationship between knowledge and teaching itself.

According to the measures previously used in research on teachers' subject-matter knowledge, such as undergraduate major, knowledge of literary terms, or number of courses taken in a subject, Colleen and Martha might look very much alike. Although Colleen took more English courses, they both graduated from the same undergraduate institution, from the same department, and even took some of the same English classes. A multiple choice test on the content of American literature in which teachers were asked to identify major authors and important texts might similarly fail to distinguish between the two teachers. In order to reveal the influence of subject-matter knowledge on classroom teaching, in this case, researchers would need to attend to the substantive and syntactic structures underlying the teachers' knowledge of literature, as well as paying close attention to the actual content of classroom instruction.

As suggested by the discussion of orientations, subject-matter knowledge is multidimensional, encompassing not only the content of a discipline but the theories which frame investigations by posing questions for study, and the analytic tools and rules of evidence used in the production of new knowledge. In considering how best to represent teachers' subject-matter knowledge, researchers must look beyond teachers' knowledge of the facts of a discipline, which in literature might include knowledge of authors, texts, and literary terms, and investigate what theoretical knowledge, either tacit or explicit, informs teachers' approach to the subject-matter content and the teachers' understanding of how new knowledge enters the field.

The schools of literary theory referred to early in this chapter represent some of the major substantive structures of literature. These literary theories guide interpretation, by suggesting what is most salient to the process of reading literature through their focus on either the text, the author's intention, or the reader's response, to name just a few alternative approaches. As the array of literary theories from the New Criticism to structuralism to semiotics and deconstruction (Eagleton, 1983) indicates, there is more than one way to read a book. *How* one reads reflects the choice, either conscious or unconscious, of a substantive structure.

Colleen and Martha rarely discuss literary theory. They show little interest in the battles being waged over critical theories of literature. Yet through a probable combination of personal values and disciplinary training, each teacher has adopted a way of reading literature which reflects differing literary traditions. Colleen and Martha bring these "ways of reading," their knowledge and beliefs about literary interpretation, into their classrooms as their ideas about what is important in the interpretation of literature in turn help determine how they teach their own students to read and make sense of literary texts. (See Wilson and Wineburg [1988] for a discussion of a related pattern in history teaching.)

While the substantive structures of a discipline guide the type of questions asked in a field, the syntactic structures provide the tools of inquiry and canons of evidence through which new knowledge is admitted to a field (Schwab, 1964). Knowledge of the syntactic structures may be particularly important for teachers, as they rely on their knowledge of literary analysis, in the case of English teachers, to increase their own knowledge within the field (Grossman, Wilson, & Shulman, 1989).

An orientation towards literature, as I have defined it, encompasses aspects of both the substantive and syntactic structures of English as a discipline. These orientations become visible in classrooms, however, only by paying close attention to the content of classroom instruction, by looking not only at the number of questions asked, but at the literary implications of those questions, by looking not only at the number of papers assigned, but at the topics of the papers. Research which involves teacher planning must also take into account the nature of the subject matter to be taught. Without a focus on the content of instruction, the influence of subject-matter knowledge may well be rendered invisible (Shulman, 1986).

In doing research on teachers' subject-matter knowledge, we need to be aware of the multiple dimensions of subject-matter knowledge and belief and to pay attention to the expression of knowledge in the actual content of teachers' plans and classroom instruction. Researchers also need to work with subject-matter experts in developing research methods that are sensitive to the unique nature of a discipline.

Research on teachers' subject-matter knowledge also holds implications for the preparation of teachers. As we begin to understand more about the role prior subject-matter knowledge plays in teaching, teacher educators, in both departments of education and in liberal arts departments, must grapple with how prospective teachers can best acquire the knowledge of their subjects they will need for teaching.

As the story of Colleen and Martha reminds us, prospective teachers do not enter teacher education as blank slates; they arrive with an extensive "apprenticeship of observation" in teaching methods (Lortie, 1975) and with prior knowledge and beliefs about their subject areas. In the case of English, the orientations teachers have formed towards literature affect their ideas about the teaching of literature. Teacher educators can help prospective students examine their knowledge and beliefs about a subject and reflect on how this knowledge influences both their beliefs about teaching their subject and their classroom practice.

While this discussion of orientations towards literature reveals only one facet of research on teachers' subject-matter knowledge, it illustrates the dangers of oversimplifying the construct of subject-matter knowledge. To ask whether Colleen or Martha possesses more knowledge of English would be to miss the point—the crucial difference in the interpretive stance each teacher assumes towards literature. By paying attention only to differences in amount of subject-matter knowledge, researchers may miss the underlying differences in structure and character of knowledge that result from further study. Knowledge and belief are not easily quantified, nor are quantitative differences always of most consequence.

ACKNOWLEDGMENT

The research on which this chapter is based was made possible through a grant from the Spencer Foundation for the Knowledge Growth in a Profession research project at Stanford University. The Spencer Foundation also supported the writing of this chapter through a pre-doctoral fellowship to the author.

NOTES

1. Interestingly enough, their motivations for entering teaching in the first place mirror their orientations to literature. Colleen is more text-centered, citing her love of the subject matter, while Martha is more student-centered, attributing her desire to teach to her enjoyment of students.

2. Martha refers here to Louise Rosenblatt, an early advocate of reader-response theory and author of the book *Literature as Exploration* (1938).

REFERENCES

Applebee, A. N. (1974). *Tradition and reform in the teaching of English: A history*. Urbana, IL: National Council of Teachers of English.

Baxter, J., Richert, A., & Saylor, C. (1985). *Content and process of biology* (Tech. Rep. of the Knowledge Growth in a Profession research project). Stanford, CA: Stanford University, School of Education.

Berriault, G. (1966). The stone boy. In J.M. Moffett and K.R. McElheny (Eds.), *Points of view: An anthology of short stories* (pp. 342-353). New York: New American Library.

Campbell, C. (1986, February 9). The tyranny of the Yale critics. *New York Times Magazine*, pp. 20-28, 43-48.

Carlsen, W. S. (in preparation). *The effects of science teacher subject-matter knowledge on teacher questioning and classroom discourse*. Unpublished doctoral dissertation, Stanford University.

Eagleton, T. (1983). *Literary theory: An introduction*. Minneapolis: University of Minnesota Press.

Grossman, P.L. (1987a). *A passion for language: The case study of Colleen, a beginning English teacher*. (Tech. Rep. of the Knowledge Growth in a Profession Research Project). Stanford, CA: Stanford University, School of Education.

Grossman, P.L. (1987b). *Conviction-that granitic base: The case study of Martha, a beginning English teacher*. (Tech. Rep. of the Knowledge Growth in a Profession Research Project). Stanford, CA: Stanford University, School of Education.

Grossman, P.L. (1987c, April). *The tale of two teachers: The role of subject matter orientation in teaching*. Paper presented at the annual meeting of the American Educational Research Association, Washington DC.

Grossman, P.L., & Gudmundsdottir, S. (1987, April). *Teachers and texts: An expert/novice comparison in English*. Paper presented at the annual meeting of the American Educational Research Association, Washington DC.

Grossman, P.L., Wilson, S.M., & Shulman, L.S. (1989). Teachers of substance: Subject matter knowledge for teaching. In M. Reynolds (Ed.), *Knowledge base for the beginning teacher.* Washington DC: American Association of Colleges for Teacher Education.

Gudmundsdottir, S. (1989). *Knowledge use among experienced teachers: Four case studies of high school teaching.* Unpublished doctoral dissertation. Stanford University, Stanford, CA.

Hashweh, M. Z. (1987). Effects of subject matter knowledge in the teaching of biology and physics. *Teaching and Teacher Education, 3,* 109-120.

Hirsch, E.D. (1967). *Validity in interpretation.* New Haven, CT: Yale University Press.

Hook, E. N. (1965). *Teacher factors influencing pupil achievement in elementary school English.* Unpublished doctoral dissertation, Colorado State College.

Lanier, J. E., & Little, J. W. (1986). Research on teacher education. In M. C. Wittrock (Ed.), *Handbook of research on teaching,* (3rd ed.). New York: Macmillan.

Leinhardt, G., & Smith, D. (1985). Expertise in mathematics instruction: Subject matter knowledge. *Journal of Educational Psychology, 77,* 247-271.

Lortie, D. C. (1975). *Schoolteacher: A sociological study.* Chicago: University of Chicago Press.

Rosenblatt, L. (1938). *Literature as exploration.* New York: Modern Language Association of America.

Scholes, R. (1982). *Semiotics and interpretation.* New Haven: Yale University Press.

Schwab, J.J. (1964). The structure of disciplines: Meanings and significance. In G. W. Ford & L. Pugno (Eds.), *The structure of knowledge and the curriculum* (pp. 6-30). Chicago: Rand McNally.

Shulman, L. S. (1986). Those who understand: Knowledge growth in teaching. *Educational Researcher, 15*(2), 4-14.

Steinberg, R., Marks, R., & Haymore, J. (1985). *Teachers' knowledge and structuring in mathematics* (Tech. Rep. of the Knowledge Growth in a Profession research project). Stanford, CA: Stanford University, School of Education.

Tompkins, J. P. (Ed.). (1980). *Reader-response criticism.* Baltimore: The Johns Hopkins University Press.

Veal, R., Butler, R., Hulme, G., & Hudson, S. (1983). Relationships between knowledge and performance assessment measures of prospective English teachers. *English Education, 15*(3), 131-135.

Wilson, G. C. (1964). The structure of English. In G.W. Ford & L. Pugno (Eds.), *The structure of knowledge and the curriculum* (pp. 71-86). Chicago: Rand McNalley.

Wilson, S.M., Shulman, L.S., & Richert, A.E. (1987). "150 different ways" of knowing: Representations of knowledge in teaching. In J. Calderhead (Ed.), *Exploring teachers' thinking* (pp. 104-124). London: Cassell.

Wilson, S. M., & Wineburg, S. S. (1988). Peering at history through different lenses. *Teachers College Record, 89,* 525-539.

Wimsatt, W. K. & Brooks, C. (1957). *Literary criticism: A short history.* Chicago: University of Chicago Press.

*   *   *

CROSS-TALK

What is the best orientation for teaching literature?

A number of other authors in this volume raised the question of the relative value of the orientations I describe for the teaching of English. I deliberately shy away from making a normative judgment on these orientations, partly because little evidence exists to support such a judgment, and partly because I am not sure that there is only one right way for teaching literature. Just as there are many ways of reading a text, there are many ways of teaching a text. All three orientations discussed in this chapter have their proponents. All are valid interpretive frameworks for the study of literature. I would also argue that one could find examples of both excellent and mediocre teaching within each of these orientations. Each orientation, however, is prey to overgeneralizations which may distort disciplinary understanding. Overgeneralizing the text orientation might lead students to believe that a single truth resides in a text, a true interpretation that can be perceived only by a discerning reader. Overgeneralizations of the reader orientation might lead students to believe in absolute relativity; any interpretation is acceptable, regardless of evidence.

Given the range of possible orientations towards literature, there remains a concern over the content of instruction and its relationship to student learning. While a text-oriented English teacher and a reader-oriented teacher might be equally good teachers in a general sense, I would argue that they could be teaching quite different things about literature. One of the agendas for further research, then, will involve studying student learning in classrooms of teachers with differing orientations. We will also need to struggle with the relative value ascribed to each of these orientations within the cultures of the community, school, and university.

While differing orientations represent differing schools of literary theory, these orientations are not mutually exclusive categories in practice. A teacher who is predominantly text-oriented may ask students for their personal responses to literature, just as a teacher who is primarily concerned with the context may still ask students to explicate a poem. The diversity of approaches towards literature accurately reflects the nature of the discipline. We need to be concerned, however, about the sense students make of teachers' diverse orientations. Do students see these differences as idiosyncratic preferences of individual teachers to which they must accommodate their literary responses? In order for students to construct an accurate representation of the discipline of English, students and teachers alike will need to talk more openly about different orientations towards reading and teaching literature and begin to see these differences as disciplinary, rather than purely personal, in nature.

What is the relationship between orientations to literature and orientations to other subject matters?

While the concept of subject-matter orientation may be particularly useful in understanding subject-matter knowledge in interpretive disciplines such as literature or history, which typically have multiple and competing substantive structures, other authors in this volume also refer to orientations to subject matter. Wineburg and Wilson indicate that Price and Jensen share a similar orientation to history. What would an alternative orientation to history look like and what are its pedagogical implications? The three teachers in Ball's chapter seem to represent three differing orientations towards math that might be seen as procedural, instrumental, and conceptual. Smith and Neale also discuss teachers' diverse orientations towards science, which include a didatic orientation, an activities orientation, a discovery orientation, and a conceptual change orientation.

Our common use of the construct of subject-matter orientation raises the question of whether the nature of subject-matter orientations is subject-specific or whether orientations reflect more general epistemological orientations towards the nature of knowing. How would Martha and Colleen teach history, for example? Would Colleen focus on an analysis of historical documents while Martha encouraged students to respond personally to historical events? How might the three teachers in Ball's chapter teach social studies? This issue seems particularly germane to discussions of subject-matter knowledge for elementary teachers. Could a fourth grade teacher hold a conceptual orientation towards math and a factual orientation towards social studies or do elementary teachers hold general orientations towards knowledge that cut across particular subject matters? While the specific differences among particular subject-matter orientations might necessarily be subject specific (e.g. a conceptual change orientation to science), there may be general similarities across subject matters which turn on questions on the nature of truth, evidence, and justification. As particular orientations also embody conceptions of teaching and learning, we might look across subject matters to find commonalities in general conceptions of what it means to learn or teach. If I hold a general orientation towards knowledge that holds knowledge to be disputable, I might teach students that knowing "facts" is less important than knowing how to enter the argument. If I believe that knowledge consists of a well-organized body of factual material, the truth of which is indisputable, I might be more interested in students acquiring these facts than in discussing how they know what they know. These questions suggest both avenues for further research on teachers' subject-matter knowledge as well as implications for the role of liberal education for prospective teachers.

PEDAGOGICAL MODELS
OF SUBJECT MATTER

Sigrun Gudmundsdottir

INTRODUCTION

The transmission of knowledge is one of the goals of public education. Teachers are central to this process since it is through them that the goals are realized. Yet, it is not enough for teachers to know their subject matter, they also need to know how to teach it. While content knowledge and pedagogy are considered important components in the knowledge base of teaching, the nature of the relationship between the two has evaded researchers on teaching.

Research on teaching, however, has been concerned with the knowledge base of teaching. This topic has been approached from different perspectives, providing important insights about a complex process (Shulman, 1986). Researchers examining teaching have traditionally been interested in relationships between classroom management and other general features of pedagogy and the academic achievement of students. These are certainly important issues in the process of education but not the whole story. The relative absence of attention to curriculum content in research on teaching has been noted by several scholars in the field (Brophy, 1979; Fenstermacher, 1978;

Advances in Research on Teaching, Volume 2, pages 265-304.
Copyright © 1991 by JAI Press Inc.
All rights of reproduction in any form reserved.
ISBN: 1-55938-034-9

Green, 1971; Smith, 1980). Teacher educators have been warned that teacher preparation is more than a mastery of procedures (Scheffler, 1973). There are obligations that teachers should take seriously regarding the knowledge they teach (Buchmann, 1986). While content knowledge alone is not enough for teaching, management skills are no substitutes (Buchmann, 1984; Shulman, 1974). In the area of research on teacher education, the absence of content in teacher preparation has been noted by Feiman-Nemser and Buchmann (1986).

Dewey, writing in 1904, not only empathizes the role of subject-matter knowledge in teaching, he also suggests that scholarly knowledge of the discipline is different from the knowledge needed for teaching. The teachers' context is different from that of the scholar. Unlike scholars, teachers cannot focus only on content. They have to take into account many factors. They have to think about students' preconceptions and misconceptions. They have to generate appropriate analogies, explanations and examples to explain the subject matter, and they have to engage a group of students in an activity that facilitates learning. This means that teachers must restructure their content knowledge to make it pedagogical. Some veteran teachers have created new knowledge, called pedagogical content knowledge, that is unique to teachers and teaching (Shulman, 1987).

Pedagogical content knowledge draws on a range of ideas that relate to students, curricular materials, educational contexts, and in particular content and pedagogy, and includes both general and topic specific strategies. In this chapter, through four case studies of high school teachers, I focus on the relationship between content and pedagogy, both general and topic specific, and describe how the teachers use their pedagogical content knowledge in teaching.

Nancy, Naomi, David, and Harry are veteran teachers, having taught between 20 and 37 years.[1] They are considered excellent teachers by their students and colleagues. They have reorganized their content knowledge by constructing pedagogical models of the subject they teach. The models bring together content and pedagogy in a unique and personal way. Moreover, the models are the centerpieces of their pedagogical content knowledge and the main source for their professional excellence.[2]

THEORETICAL FRAMEWORK

This study is part of the "Knowledge Growth in Teaching" research program. A logical model of the knowledge base of teaching has grown out of this project (Shulman, 1987). The model includes seven types of knowledge. *Content knowledge* is the teachers' content background in the subject they teach. *General pedagogical knowledge* includes "broad principles and strategies of classroom management and organization that appear to transcend subject matter" (Shulman, 1987, p. 8). *Curriculum knowledge* is knowledge of curriculum materials that can be used to teach a particular topic. *Knowledge of learners* informs teachers about how students learn, their developmental levels, motivation, preconceptions, and misconceptions, information that is vital in representing new knowledge to students. *Knowledge of educational contexts* extends from understanding group dynamics in the classroom to educational financing and character of communities. *Knowledge of educational aims* and their historical and philosophical origins helps teachers put their own goals into a larger perspective. Finally, there is pedagogical content knowledge which is "that special amalgam of content and pedagogy" (Shulman, 1987, p. 8). It is the most important part of the knowledge base of teaching and distinguishes the veteran teacher from the novice, and the teacher from the scholar.

The content in pedagogical content knowledge is especially important for high school teachers. They often teach a subject in which they have a bachelor's degree, and they tend to see themselves as subject-matter specialists. Moreover, many teachers have a specialization within their discipline. There is no way that a teacher, or anyone else, can know everything there is to know within a discipline. Teachers and scholars alike have to specialize. For example, historians tend to know a small part of the discipline of history, like American history, Medieval history, European history, and so on. The diversity within history (and other disciplines as well) means that there are many structures by which knowledge and ideas can be organized. Disciplines differ even more in the ways they investigate the world. The psychologist sets up experimental studies or does clinical interviews. The historian studies artifacts, oral history transcripts, and documents. Each discipline has its own distinctive ways of determining what are valid data and how they should be interpreted.

Schwab (1961/1978) calls these two aspects of knowledge the "structures of the disciplines" and argues that there are several structures within each. He identifies basically two kinds of structures within disciplines, syntactic and substantive structures. Substantive structures include the key concepts that characterize the discipline. Examples in literature are tragedy, comedy, romanticism, plot, character, and the novel. In history, chronology, revolution, monarchy, and democracy are examples of conceptual devices making up substantive structures. This kind of structure determines how scholars view their discipline and the kinds of research questions they pursue. The substantive structures often precede and determine the syntactical structures by influencing what scholars consider important ideas. The syntactic structure determines the ways in which researchers move from raw data through interpretation to conclusion. Everyone who studies a discipline will encounter these structures. The historian takes courses on Marxist history, political history, or social history; the English scholar takes courses on poetry, drama, the short story,

British literature, Romanticism, literary analysis, and so on. Moreover, most people end up specializing within their discipline. That means they study in greater depth a few substantive and syntactic structures. Historians who specialize in Marxist history will tend to know more about the areas that contribute to this school of history and be ignorant of others. The biologist specializing in microbiology will know more about concepts critical to microbiology. This kind of specialization within a discipline gives rise to different orientations to the subject matter (Herron, 1971).

The disciplines are value laden organizations of knowledge and give rise to a range of orientations. English (or literature) focuses on texts and interpretation and facilitates a range of values, or orientations. The orientations influence what one thinks important to know, how to interpret texts, and seek evidence for interpretation. Similarly, the discipline of history has an inherent set of values. Historians decide what to investigate before they seek the relevant data, and their preferences and interpretations are guided by substantive structures. This means that historians start out with a value that influences what they will see. In this way, values act as filters for what is considered important to know in a discipline.

Three orientations to literature have been identified: text, context, and reader (Grossman, Ringstaff, Reynolds, & Sykes, 1985). Two of those, text and reader, are relevant for this study. In the textual orientation:

> one may know periods of literature, major authors within periods, and individual texts. The sources of evidence exist within the text itself, and the reader may use the traditional tools of literary analysis to understand texts (Grossman, et al., 1985, p. 7).

A reader orientation is also described:

> the meaning of a text depends upon the individual reader. Knowledge of a text is idiosyncratic, tied to the personal experiences of the reader. In this orientation, the evidence for the interpretation of texts resides in personal experience. Personal responses assume priority over literary analysis (Grossman, et al., 1985, p. 8).

Even though Grossman et al. (1985) are referring to literature, there is reason to believe that their classification also refers to other interpretative disciplines, such as history.

Making content knowledge pedagogical means a reorganization that focuses on a disciplinary orientation. Case studies of student teachers show that they try to figure out ways to communicate their disciplinary orientation to their students (Grossman, 1987a, 1987b; Grossman & Gudmundsdottir, 1987; Gudmundsdottir, 1987; McGraw, 1987; Reynolds, 1987; Wilson & Gudmundsdottir, 1987). In some cases it involves a major intellectual shift (Feiman-Nemser & Buchmann, 1986; Gudmundsdottir, Carey & Wilson, 1985;

Wineburg, 1987). An important part of the restructuring process is to find new relationships between content (Arzi, 1987). It is a process that has matured in seasoned veterans, who often have elaborate models to guide their practice (Clandinin, 1986; Elbaz, 1983; Grant, 1988; Gudmundsdottir, 1990).

The pedagogy in pedagogical content knowledge is also related to teachers' orientation to the subject matter. A particular orientation legitimates a range of pedagogical strategies that enable teachers to communicate it. For example, a teacher who feels literature should relate to peoples' personal meaning will figure out ways for students to make connection between literary ideas and emotions. Similarly, a history teacher who feels the historical method is most important will figure out ways to make students interpret documents and historical events.

The pedagogical models combine content and pedagogy in a meaningful and efficient way. The models include a process that segments and structures content to make it accessible to students. At the same time, each model facilitates a range of pedagogical strategies that communicate content to students (Byrne, 1983). Researchers have described different types of pedagogical structures. There are agendas, curriculum scripts, explanations and representations (see Leinhardt, Putnam, Stein, & Baxter, this volume, pp. 87-113). General pedagogical models can have three levels, reflecting varying degrees of generality: rules of practice, practical principles, and images (Elbaz, 1983). Pedagogical models have been conceptualized as two types of curricula (Bussis, Chittenden, & Amarel, 1976); a deep curriculum that organizes content and establishes priorities for students and a surface curriculum that includes the activities observed in the classroom.

There is a topic-specific element in pedagogical models, generated by the more general pedagogical models. The topic-specific element includes knowledge identifying the appropriate teaching methods and segmenting a topic to make it accessible to a group of students. It also includes knowledge of the representational possibilities of a topic that can be used with different kinds of students in different kinds of courses (Byrne, 1983). The teachers' representations have to relate to and build upon the ideas students already hold about that topic.

Nancy's, Naomi's, David's, and Harry's pedagogical models build on their orientation to the discipline and their ideas about learning. The models combine pedagogy and content, are both general and topic specific, and generate pedagogical strategies that relate to the teachers' disciplinary orientation.

METHODOLOGY

The data for this study consist of transcribed interviews, transcribed classroom tape recordings, observer's notes, and documents collected in the field. Data collection covered a period of four months during the 1984-1985 academic year. Nancy, Naomi, David, and Harry are subjects in a dissertation study (Gudmundsdottir, 1988). They teach in a San Francisco Bay Area high school. They were recommended as experienced teachers by their principal.

The teachers were interviewed four to seven times, each interview lasting from 1 to 1 1/2 hour. The interviews focused on the teachers' conception of subject matter, the course they were teaching, students in the class, and their approaches to transforming their content knowledge. The teachers were observed between 18 and 22 times. All classroom tape recordings and interviews were transcribed verbatim. In addition, various documents related to the school and classes were collected.

Initial data analysis consisted of coding the data using categories from the theoretical framework. Several of the theoretical categories were particularly relevant for the data: content knowledge, general pedagogical knowledge, pedagogical content knowledge, and knowledge of learners. Using the coded data, case studies of Nancy, Naomi, David, and Harry were compiled. In the case studies, the description of the teachers' knowledge base centered around these four theoretical constructs.

The idea of a pedagogical model emerged early during fieldwork—Nancy announced in her first interview that she had a "model of English." She vividly described her model and gave examples of how she used it. The following day and for months, I watched her use it implicitly and explicitly in the classroom. This gave me the idea that the other teachers might also have such structures. None of the other teachers described their models unsolicited. However, extensive observations in their classrooms revealed that they had a method that appeared to grow out of a pedagogical model. Interviews with Naomi, David, and Harry, focusing on a number of selected classroom events, revealed that they had a model.[3]

The teachers' models turned out to be similar in some ways. This is not surprising, since they are all dedicated teachers who are sensitive and responsive to their students. They also work in a similar environment where they have to manage ideas and students. One set of cross-case comparisons, which is the subject of the present chapter, involved analysis of the questions the teachers asked their students during lessons. Nancy's model was used as a comparison for the other models because it seemed best suited for such analysis. The teachers' questions were selected for such analysis because they appeared to relate to the ways in which the teachers communicated their ideas to students. The teachers asked many questions during class. Some of them were intended as "thought stimulations" and the teachers did not expect students to answer. The teachers also asked questions that they expected students to answer, or non-rhetorical questions. These questions were coded using Nancy's model, a kind of emic coding (see Tables 1-4).

Nancy's model includes three categories. Category one relates to understanding the literal meaning of the text. For example: What is the name of the innkeeper (in *Moby Dick*)? Once students understand the words and the plot, they can either move to category two, which is interpretation, or category three, which relates the ideas in the text to students' lives.[4] An example of a category two question is: Queequeg goes under the bed to put on his boots. What does it mean? An example of a category three question is: What kind of job would Bartleby have today if he lived here in the Bay Area?

Coding strictly non-rhetorical questions provided some problems, however, because on four occasions the teachers used group work where students worked on one question for a whole period. For these classes the number of group assignments was multiplied so that it represented one question every five minutes, excluding the five minutes at the beginning of the class that the teachers used to get students to settle down to work. This makes nine five-minute blocks during each session. This method, however, was only used for those sessions where the teachers did not ask any questions beyond the assignment. It is a very conservative estimate because the teachers asked more than nine questions in most classes.

NANCY

Nancy is in her early forties, attractive, of medium build with shoulder length blond hair. She is quick and direct in her movements. She has been teaching for twenty years. Literature is her passion and "turning students on to the book" is her mission. Her passion and mission provide an important driving force in her personal and professional life. This study focuses on her teaching American literature to college preparatory juniors. The course begins with a unit on Hawthorne, followed by a unit on Melville. First, students read a short story "Bartleby the Scrivener" and then a novel, *Moby Dick*. Next, they read *The Adventures of Huckleberry Finn* by Mark Twain, followed by works by Fitzgerald, Miller, Hemingway, and Salinger.

Nancy has invented a pedagogical model of literature (see Figure 1). It is a hierarchical model, according to her, where interpretation begins with category one questions and then moves on to categories two and three. Nancy uses her model to enhance her own literary experience when reading all kinds of literature, from Hemingway to Agatha Christie. She also uses the model in all her teaching of literature, no matter the type of class or kind of text. She explicitly teaches students to use it when they try to make sense of texts. Nancy claims that her purpose, both in course design and teaching in general, is to move the students through all categories. The literary works students read are different in nature, according to Nancy. Some are difficult for students to read and understand, like the Melville works. Others are easy to understand,

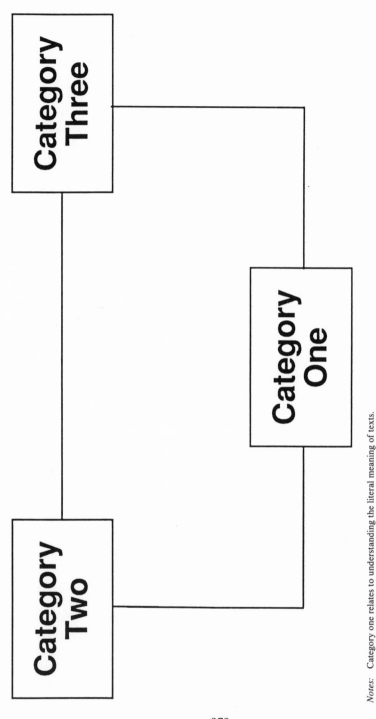

Notes: Category one relates to understanding the literal meaning of texts.
Category two is interpretation.
Category three involves connecting ideas in the text to students' lives.

Figure 1. Nancy's Model of English

272

Table 1. Analysis of Questions Nancy Asks in the Units on Melville and
Huck Finn Using her Reading Categories

| Observations | Categories | | | Explanations |
	One	Two	Three	
1	16	1	4	"Bartleby the Scrivener"
2	8	5	5	"Bartleby the Scrivener"
3	6	0	0	Introducing *Moby Dick*
4	17	7	0	Discussion of Queequeg
5	0	48	0	Discussion of characters
6	5	5	0	Discussion of whaling
7	13	9	0	Discussion of Ahab
8	0	48	0	Discussion of Ahab
9	8	1	1	Literary style
10	1	13	0	Discussion of Ahab
11	0	0	0	Study questions
12	0	0	0	Test
13	0	0	0	Movie
14	3	23	0	Introducing *Huck Finn*
15	0	0	0	Test review/ *Moby Dick*
16	0	0	0	Essay review/ *Moby Dick*
17	3	4	7	*Huck Finn* group work
18	7	13	0	*Huck Finn* group work
19	3	6	4	*Huck Finn* group work
20	3	2	0	*Huck Finn* group work
Total	93	200	20	(303)
Percent	30	66	7	(100)

like *The Adventures of Huckleberry Finn* (from here on, to be referred to as
Huck Finn). Consequently, she adapts her questioning pattern to take into
account students' difficulties with understanding texts.

Table 1 shows how Nancy uses her model. In 20 observations Nancy asks
the students a total of 303 questions. Most of the questions are category one
(30%) and two (66%). This emphasis on questions relating to the text reveals
a textual orientation to literature. The first two observations show many
category one and three questions. Nancy is teaching a Melville short story to
familiarize the students with his language, which she feels they have difficulty
understanding. She asks category one questions to make sure students
understand the words. Then, she moves to categories two and three. The high
number of category three questions at the beginning of the unit can be
explained. Nancy thinks the text is difficult for students, so they need extra
motivation. That motivation comes from asking students to link the text to
their own lives.

Moby Dick starts in observation 3, and a growing number of category two questions begins to appear. Here, Nancy seems mostly interested in getting students to interpret the text. Even though Nancy claims that her aim is to move students from category one to category three, it appears that her real goal is getting students to category two. That is in accordance with her textual orientation because the movement between category one and two emphasizes questions that are textually oriented, while category three tends to be reader oriented. *Moby Dick* is, in Nancy's view, difficult to read and understand. The high number of questions in the Melville unit shows that Nancy feels students need to be led carefully through the process of interpretation.

Huck Finn begins in observation 17. According to Nancy, the novel is both easy to read and to understand. Consequently, she changes her strategy because the students do not need her help in moving between the categories. Nancy organizes students into groups that trace themes through the novel. With Twain's text, they are able to understand the meaning of the words on the page, interpret the novel on their own, and relate it to their lives. The help they may need can come from fellow students who are working with them in the group.[7]

During the unit on *Huck Finn* there are two rounds of reporting; one in the middle and one at the end of the unit. While the category two questions are still frequent, the number of category three questions begins to rise. When teaching "easy" novels, Nancy feels that students are able to understand the words and the plot (category one) and to interpret (category two) on their own. For these novels, she concentrates on relating the students' understanding and interpretation to their lives (category three).

While Nancy's approaches to the teaching of *Moby Dick* and *Huck Finn* are different, her pedagogical model is central to both. Melville's works, according to Nancy, are difficult texts to teach. When she teaches "difficult" texts she relates them to the students' lives (as in "Bartleby the Scrivener"). Once the students are used to the language of Melville, she moves to category two questions (in Moby Dick). When teaching difficult texts, Nancy remains center stage asking many questions. With an easy novel like *Huck Finn*, she does not feel she has to lead the students as carefully as with the more difficult works. She asks many category two questions in observation 14 when introducing the novel. But, once the students are working in their groups, she takes a back seat and listens to their presentations. The 20 observations in Table 1 show that Nancy's pedagogical model is general enough to enable her to organize the course of study and, at the same time, topic-specific, providing her with pedagogical strategies to teach different kinds of text.

Observation 7 shows how Nancy's general model can be topic-specific (see Figure 2). In this observation she is teaching a difficult text, both in terms of

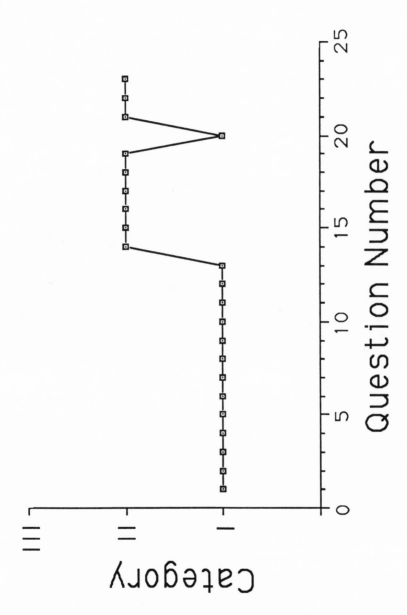

Figure 2. Questions Nancy Asks in Observation 7 Analyzed Using her Reading Categories

language and ideas. Although the students are well into Moby Dick, it is the first discussion on Ahab. Nancy begins the lesson by asking a series of category one questions (1-13) to make sure students understand the plot. The details she asks about are all relevant to the interpretation that follows. She brings students' attention to the word "coffin." It is the name of the innkeeper and a coffin plays a role in the plot. She then asks questions that address the details of Ahab's appearances on the bridge. The questions make sure students notice that Ahab does not emerge from his cabin until the ship is far out to sea. The category one questions also bring students' attention to the details of the event where Ahab presents his mission to the ship's crew, particularly the reactions of the officers. The category two questions (14-23) begin where Nancy asks: "What does this tell you about Ahab?" Nancy asks interpretive questions about Ahab throughout the lesson. She pauses at Ahab's comments about "striking the sun" and asks: "Who strikes the sun?" The students answer and she asks: "Ahab is seeing himself as?" Nancy then looks at Ahab's interaction with Starbuck, one of the officers. She asks a series of category two questions that make sure students understand how and why Starbuck relents. She asks, for example: "What choice does [Starbuck] have? What will happen if he doesn't go along?" This series of category two questions is interrupted once by one category one question (20) where students missed an important detail. By generating questions about the text, Nancy goes from category one to two and stays there most of the time. It seems as if her goal is interpretation, that is, category two.

Nancy's general approach to literature both as a literary scholar and teacher show that she has a textual orientation to literature which appears in her course organization and her model. This orientation brings together a range of substantive structures that form a tradition within literature which is often called "traditional literary criticism." This also appears in her course design. There, she is concerned with major periods in literature and key authors and literary works in American literature. Her pedagogical model also reflects the syntactic structures related to traditional literary criticism in that she seeks support for her interpretation within the texts.

It is clear from Nancy's descriptions of her pedagogical model, and from observations of her using it, that she has taken her own private "literary learning theory" or "literature study method" and turned it into a "pedagogical model." She claims she uses the model to enhance her own literary experience. When she reads detective novels, she reads at category one, or "plot level," because "there is nowhere else to go." Then, there are authors like Hemingway, Steinbeck, and Dostoevsky, who provide her with the opportunity to explore interpretations at categories two and three.

NAOMI

Naomi is a tall handsome woman in her early fifties, with short curly brown hair and gentle brown eyes. Her manner is quiet and unhurried, a stark contrast to the busyness of high school life. Naomi is deeply religious and active in her church and various other charitable associations. She has been teaching English for 25 years. This study focuses on her teaching efforts with a general track class. Naomi's American literature course starts with a unit which includes a selection of short stories and essays. Next, students read *Huck Finn* followed by novels, plays, and poems by nineteenth- and twentieth-century authors. Naomi's general students take twice as long to read *Huck Finn* as the college preparatory students.[8]

Naomi has a model of English (see Figure 3). It shows how she appreciates English and how she approaches the teaching of literature. The model is like an onion with layers that she peels away. In the middle there is a core, which she designates as "English." Surrounding the core are the layers: the first is called "Understanding the language," and includes words and sentence structure; the second "Deeper significance," asks, "what is it saying?" The third "Multiple interpretations," probes "what else does it say?" She has developed a teaching technique, which I have called circling, to communicate her model to students. The circling technique is based on questions and flows directly from her model of English. It has three phases that are parallel to the model. The first questioning phase falls directly in the first layer of the model: understanding the language. Naomi focuses on clarifying the text, making sure students understand the words and the plot. The second questioning phase of circling flows from the second layer in her model of English—interpretation—whereas the third phase of the circling process is parallel to the third layer in the model—multiple representations and what they mean for students. Naomi prompts students to use their understanding of the text to examine their own lives. In the circling process, the focus is on this phase. Most of the time Naomi circles several times. Each time she circles, she picks out a different aspect of the content and interprets it through categories two and three, giving students the opportunity to add layer upon layer of meaning in a unique mixture of the personal and textual.

If Nancy's model can be characterized as "steps to follow" in the process of literary analysis, then Naomi's model can be characterized as "an onion." Although these analogies represent different conceptions of literature and literary analysis, they have some similarities that appear when Naomi peels away the layers of her "onion" in the circling process. Naomi's circling can be related to Nancy's reading categories. The first phase of the circling process is like Nancy's category one; both focus on the literal meaning of text. Naomi's second phase is like Nancy's category two, because she focuses on interpretation. Her third phase resembles Nancy's category three, asking students to relate literature to their lives. Because Nancy's model is particularly relevant for analyzing questions and because it describes the approach to

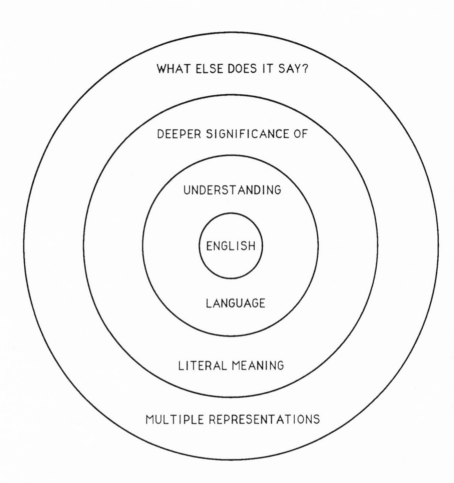

Figure 3.   Naomi's Model of English

teaching for both herself and for Naomi, it was used to analyze the questions that Naomi posed for her class. All the non-rhetorical questions Naomi asked students about literature and for which she expected answers were analyzed using Nancy's three categories, a total of 356 questions (see Table 2). 35 percent are category one, 28 percent are category two, and 37 percent are category three.

Table 2. Analysis of Questions Naomi Asks in the Units on
Huck Finn Using Nancy's Reading Categories

| Observations | | Categories | | | Explanations |
		One	Two	Three	
1		0	0	0	Vocabulary
2		0	0	15	Themselves
3		2	11	9	Character
4	(total 31)	6	4	21	Prejudice
5		9	0	9	Character
6		0	0	0	Vocabulary
7	(total 45)	21	10	14	Character
8		7	3	4	Huck with father
9		0	0	0	Vocabulary
10		12	1	1	Character
11	(total 24)	17	5	2	Running away
12		0	8	10	Character
13		7	3	0	Character
14		0	9	0	Character
15		9	12	0	Character
16		8	1	0	The Bible
17		0	1	0	Character
18	(total 61)	13	6	32	Jim and Huck
19	(total 45)	3	25	17	Character
20		13	0	7	Bounty hunters
Total		127	99	132	(356)
Percent		35	28	37	(100)

Table 2 shows Naomi's questions in the unit on *Huck Finn*. Relatively few observations have the largest number of questions (observations 4, 7, 11, 18, and 19). The topics discussed during these classes were: prejudice, character, running away from home, the friendship between Huck and Jim, and Huck's moral dilemma when he meets the Bounty Hunters. According to Naomi, these topics are critical to students' understanding of the novel, and important pedagogically because they enable her to make connections between the novel and students' realities.

The high number of category three questions shows her emphasis on encouraging students to examine their lives in light of the literature. This emphasis reveals a reader orientation to literature. Naomi makes sure they get the meanings of words (35% category one questions), and then interpret these meanings (28% category two questions). Then they are able to spend more time and energy examining their own lives in light of an understanding gained from the text (37% category three questions). In this way Naomi's general pedagogical model provides a framework for the whole course of study.

Naomi's model is also topic specific. With some variations, Naomi's model and the circling technique can be used in teaching a range of topics in the course. A typical circling pattern takes place as follows: the first phase usually begins with category one questions, the second phase with category two questions, and the last phase with category three questions, completing the process. Observation 7 is an example of how Naomi's model and her circling technique are topic-specific as well.

In observation 7, one which came soon after *Huck Finn* was introduced, Naomi discusses the character of Huck—a central consideration as she teaches this novel. Naomi attempts to make the students identify with Huck and how he handles his life. To achieve this end she circles approximately five times. Figure 4 is a graphic representation of how Naomi uses the categories in circling. She begins phase one by asking a category two question (question 1): "What are the things we know about Huck that tell us who he is and what he is like and why?" The students are unable to answer so she moves to category one to get the facts straight (questions 2-7). For example, she asks: "What kind of boy is he?" Naomi wants students to support their views and asks: "What tells you that?" Once she is confident that the students understand the facts about Huck's life she initiates phase two by asking category two questions (8-9) where the subject of interpretation is the family: "What do you sense in him? . . . What is missing in Huck's life?" Students' responses reveal that they feel that no one loves or cares for Huck. The first circling is completed in phase three where she moves to category three. This class session occurs near Thanksgiving, so the subject becomes the family being together (questions 10-11): "What are all of you going to do on Thursday? . . . When I say family, what do you think of?" The questioning pattern in the second circling (questions 12-24) is not as clear. It is a mixture of all categories but seems to develop the idea of family. Naomi asks about Huck's feelings toward his father, his attitudes toward the rules set by the widows and Huck's feelings toward Jim at the beginning of the novel. The first phase in the third circling begins in question 25. Here, Naomi returns to the text, asking the students: "What kind of boy is Huck?" She moves quickly through phase two (question 27) where she asks about Tom's and Huck's wild imaginations. The third phase begins in question 28 as Naomi focuses the students on their own lives. Here, the topic is still the family (as in the first circle) but this time she focuses on relationships among siblings: "Many of you have younger brothers and sisters. What are they like?" Here, Naomi is referring to the wild imaginations of younger siblings, something students had mentioned in the discussion. She pursues the topic of sibling relationships in a series of questions. For example, "You have older brothers and sisters. What do you expect them to feel about you?" The first phase in the fourth circling begins when Naomi brings the students back to the text (question 35). She refers students to a text they read earlier and the character of "Walter Mitty" and his vivid imagination, and asks: "Why

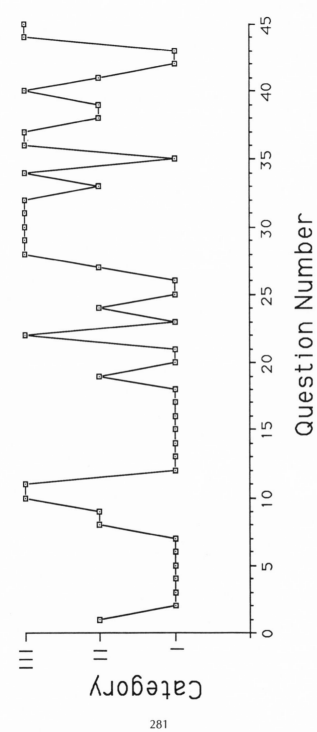

Figure 4. Questions Naomi Asks in Observation 7 Analyzed Using Nancy's Reading Categories

did Walter live in such an imaginary world?" In this question, Naomi is developing further the idea of imagination and pretense play. The second and third phases are mixed together (questions 36-41). The subject is still the family, in particular the students' own childish play. For example, "You played soldiers. What did that make you feel? . . . What about Walter? . . . Why do kids want to be grownups?" The fifth and last circling is short. It begins in question 42 and the subject is parental love: "What does Huck's father want? How would you feel about your father if you were Huck?"

Naomi varies the way she uses the circling technique. In Figure 4 there are five smaller circling events gradually building up an image of family, younger siblings' wild imaginations, and parental love. On another occasion (observation 18) she brings the students around in one grand circle. The subject of that discussion is friendship. This variation in the circling process shows how she adjusts her model to the text and the ideas she wants to pursue with students. In one (observation 7, Figure 4) she moves rather carefully, picking up events and gradually building up an image of family relationships. In the other (observation 18) she executes one grand sweep of circling. The first topic, family relationships, is emotionally loaded, and according to Naomi's knowledge of students, a common cause of distress for students. The second topic is friendship, which is also important, but not as emotionally loaded, in Naomi's view. It seems that Naomi does not believe she needs to be as careful in building up the image as she did in the first topic.

As Naomi circles from the text to students' lives and back to the text, she is working within established traditions in her discipline. One of the orientations to literature Grossman (1985) describes is a reader orientation. This orientation draws upon a range of substantive and syntactic structures that justify the priority of personal responses which Naomi encourages. It seems that Naomi mainly draws on the syntactic structures that relate to this orientation because as students interpret literature, they mostly seek evidence for their interpretation outside the text in their personal experiences. In other words, Naomi seems to support her pedagogic strategy on the syntactic structures relating to a reader orientation.

Naomi's course design reflects a different orientation to literature (as described by Grossman et al. [1985]). She attends to major periods in American literature and includes the important works and authors. It seems that in this respect she supports her course design on important elements in the substantive structures that contribute to a textual orientation. In doing so, she clearly respects an important tradition in the teaching of American literature in American high schools. This tradition shows considerable agreement across the country with regard to defining major literary periods, key authors, and literary works in American literature.

DAVID

David is tall and lean, and his youngish looks make it hard to believe he has passed the half-century mark in age. He is a man with a mission as symbolized by a little lapel needle in his jacket: it carries a picture of the earth as seen from space. It is the symbol for the Beyond War Movement. David has a B.A. degree in the social sciences which has given him an interdisciplinary background. He has been teaching for twenty-seven years. This study focuses on his teaching of juniors enrolled in an advanced placement U.S. history course. The course of study covers the major periods in the history of the United States starting with the Age of Jackson. The periods David covers are traditional and reflect a chronological organization in the textbook.

David has a model of history that is the centerpiece of his pedagogical content knowledge (see Figure 5). It consists of pieces of information, or historical facts, that he has learned through thinking, life experience, and reading newspapers, history journals and books, and cartoons like *Doonesbury*. The different pieces of information are connected through interpretation. These connected pieces are funnelled together and meet in current events: nuclear arms race, poverty, prejudice, wars, pollution, technology, and equal opportunity.

The aim of this model is to connect historical events and ideas over time, interpret and make students identify with them. This process makes continuity in history very important. David achieves continuity and personal identification through a range of techniques that enable students to get personally involved and to realize how ideas behind events in the past are influencing current events. He plays his guitar and sings songs from the period they are studying and compares them with present-day pop songs. The poor during the Age of Jackson did not have their biographies written or their pictures taken. However, some of them wrote songs about their dreams and the stark realities of their lives in factories and ghettoes. David spends time examining the texts because they are primary source materials and illustrate important historical themes. Students also work in groups creating their own utopian community and role playing the conflict between the robber barons and the union leaders.

Like Nancy's, David's model seems to be his private learning model which he has made into a pedagogical model. His model reflects the interdisciplinary nature of his education and the integration of his professional interests and his private mission. David's model begins with facts, knowing about the events, which corresponds to Nancy's category one. He connects facts through interpretation, which is like Nancy's category two, and he links interpretations with current events, which is similar to Nancy's category three. Table 3 shows that he asks a total of 252 questions in 18 observations. The percentages show the emphasis in his teaching: 24% of the questions are category one, 51 percent are category two, and 25 percent are category three. David claims his model

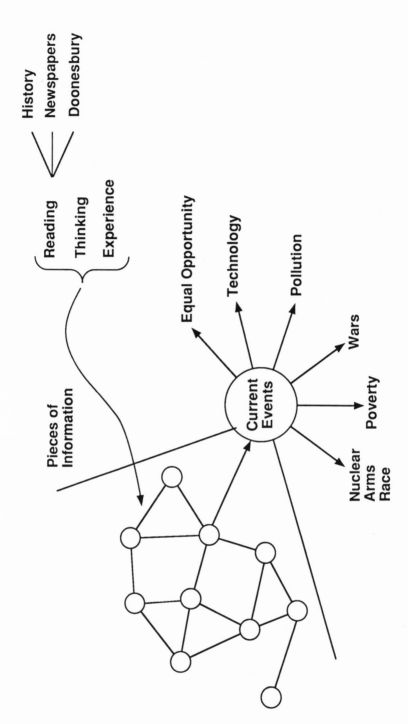

Figure 5. David's Model of American History

Table 3.   Analysis of Questions David Asks in Class Using
Using Nancy's Reading Categories

Observations	Categories			Explanations
	One	*Two*	*Three*	
1	7	10	0	Test preparation
2	9	19	4	Utopia group work
3	2	2	0	T plays guitar
4	2	25	1	8 interpretations of Civil War
5	0	0	9	Utopia group work
6	0	0	9	Utopia group work
7	12	6	0	Oneida
8	2	12	3	8 interpretations of Civil War
9	7	25	6	Civil War and foreign powers
10	0	0	0	Test review
11	0	0	0	DBQ practice
12	0	0	9	Robber barons
13	14	7	5	Big business
14	5	3	16	Group work review
15	0	3	0	Test preparation
16	8	0	0	Test
17	0	9	0	Student presentations
18	0	9	0	Student presentations
Total	60	129	62	(252)
Percent	24	51	25	(100)

emphasizes all the categories, but in practice he spends more time with category two questions. This mismatch can be explained. David teaches an advanced placement (AP) class and the questions on the test are almost exclusively category two. Asking many category three questions, however, does not fit into his advanced placement course. David asks this kind of question because he feels they are an important part of historical knowledge, whether they appear on the AP test or not. In three of the observations (4, 8, and 9) David is discussing the Civil War. These observations are also characterized by a high number of category two questions, or questions asking students to interpret. War, according to David, is the most important topic in the study of history, and the Civil War is the most devastating experience in U.S. history. Therefore, it is not surprising that he should ask many interpretative questions when he is dealing with this topic.

David's model is also topic-specific. Observation 9 shows him using all the categories, moving from facts to interpretation and linking to current events (see Figure 6). At the beginning of class, a student asks a question about presidential power and the Constitution during wartime, with reference to the Civil War, the period they are studying. David answers by asking a series of questions (1-8). In question 9 David addresses the topic of the day: the battle at Antietam. He makes reference to prior knowledge: "In the Revolutionary War, what were some of the key battles?" Students answer, and he turns their attention to the Civil War battle that he thinks was a turning point in the war, the battle of Antietam. He asks (question 10): "High casualties, but was it a decisive victory?" He moves them through several interpretative questions (11-15) that establish the role of foreign intervention in the Civil War. For example, "How important do you think foreign policy was [in previous wars]? . . . What about this war [Civil War]? . . . Why was it logical that [foreign powers] should lean to the South?" In question 16 he has to ask a category one question to establish the fact that the North, as a powerful industrial area, was a competitor with European countries, and therefore, made the Europeans favor the South. The next questions (17-19) clarify the role of tariffs established by the North in foreign intervention. Now that David has explored industrial competitiveness and foreign intervention in wars, he is ready to link students' understanding with current events. In question 20 he asks: "How would we feel if we could split up the power of the Soviet block and the communist world?" In questions 21-33, students use their understanding of Civil War foreign policy to analyze present-day U.S. foreign policy. For example, "Do you think [splitting up the communist block] is part of our [present day] foreign policy? . . . Are all the countries we support democratic? . . . What does that tell you about our choice of allies?" The class ends with a series of category two questions (33-37) that bring the students back to interpreting Civil War events: "Why didn't the Blacks in the South revolt? . . . Were there not some easy things [Blacks] could have done that would have disrupted the war?"

In observation 9 David moves through all phases of his model. He begins by referring to students' prior knowledge, connects it with the events they are studying, interprets, brings the students' understanding to the present, and finally returns to the text they are studying. After all, students will not be asked about current foreign policy toward the Communist world on the AP exam.

Although David's model, as described by him, does not seem to reflect specific syntactic or substantive structures of history, these ideas are present in his teaching. His emphasis on the substantive structures of history appear in many activities. For example, on one occasion students were asked to respond to the election of 1860 from the Republican party platform, from the point of view of an abolitionist, immigrant, Western farmer, industrialist, or member of Southern slave power. On another occasion, students were asked to try to interpret events during the Age of Jackson as if there was no Civil War coming. The reason is, according to David, that the Civil War is such an important and emotional event in American history that it tends to force itself upon most historical interpretations in the periods leading up to it and, therefore, blind students to alternative interpretations. Students also learn about the different substantive structures of history by interpreting important

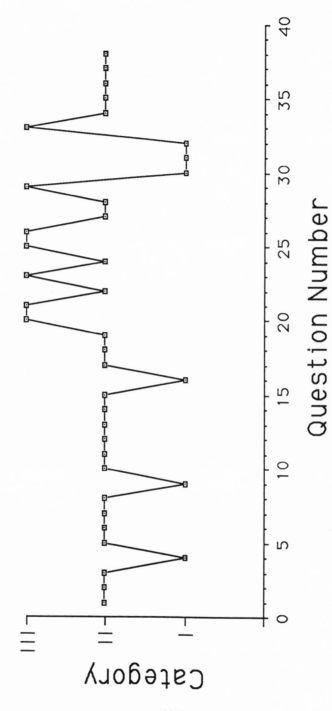

Figure 6. Questions David Asks in Observation 9 Analyzed Using Nancy's Reading Categories

events, like the coming of the Civil War, through eight different theoretical interpretations. The syntactic structures of history also appear in David's class, although not as frequently. David's use of the substantive and syntactic structures of history show that he is concerned with how we know what we know, and that we can be made aware of the biases that are an essential part of historical interpretation.

HARRY

Harry is in his early sixties, heavy set, quick and alert. He has been teaching for thirty-seven years and is considering an early retirement. This study focuses on his teaching a general track U.S. history class. The course of study covers the period from Columbus's discovery of the Americas to the present day. It features a chronological progression that tends to emphasize political history.

Harry's content knowledge is particularly impressive. He majored in history, specializing in the American Revolution. As an undergraduate, he encountered the ideas that were to shape his approach to history. One of his professors converted him to a neo-progressive view of American history and turned him into a "conflict historian." These historians see conflict in American history as the key unit of analysis. Content knowledge is particularly influential in Harry's pedagogical content knowledge. This influence appears in his model of American history (see Figure 7). Harry sees American history as the growth of opportunities for participation in the democratic process. It is like a slice of the American pie, a slice that becomes more and more inclusive the closer we are to the present day. The pie begins with the American Revolution and the Constitution. At the time, a very small part of the population was eligible to vote. The boundaries of the pie, that is the right to vote and become an American citizen, are a constant source of conflict. Harry's model of history begins in time with his specialization, American Revolution. This framework represents a restructuring of American history for pedagogical purposes. In this restructuring, Harry's specialization is the primary influence, it is a structuring that draws primarily on the substantive structures of history that conflict historians find inspiring.

Harry asks many questions in class. He needs them to drive class discussions and to get students to think and interpret historical events. Nancy's reading categories can be used to analyze Harry's questions. Table 4 shows the non-rhetorical questions Harry asks in class, analyzed using Nancy's reading categories. The table shows that the majority of the questions Harry asks are category one (41%) and two (49%). It appears that Harry is pursuing facts and their interpretation and occasionally relating students' understanding of history to their realities.

A Slice of the American Pie

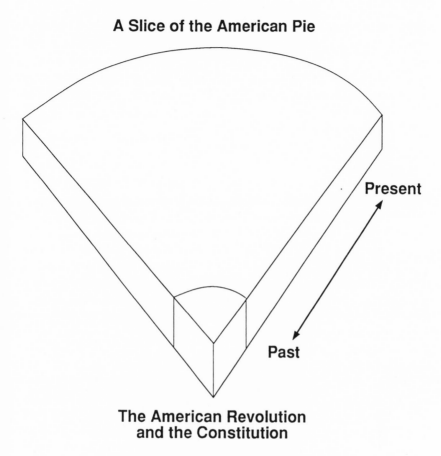

**The American Revolution
and the Constitution**

Figure 7. Harry's Model of American History

Table 4 shows that, like David, Harry focuses on war. The choice of this topic is not surprising for a conflict historian because war is the ultimate conflict. The largest part of category two questions comes from four observations (5, 18, 20, and 21). The topics for those classes are the Crane Brinton theory of why revolutions occur, and the causes of the Civil War. When the topic becomes important, it seems as if Harry asks more interpretative questions—questions that are harder for students to answer. The table also shows that Harry uses tests frequently (in 6 out of 22 classes observed). His students are reluctant for most of the time, according to Harry, and need to be threatened by a test to read the textbook.

Observation 5 shows that the Student Model is also a subject-specific strategy. In this class he asks 11 category one questions and 15 category two. A detailed breakdown of the questions he asks shows more clearly how he

Table 4.   Analysis of Questions Harry Asks in Class
Using Nancy's Reading Categories

	Categories			
Observations	*One*	*Two*	*Three*	*Explanations*
1	12	1	2	Test and discussion
2	0	0	11	Group work and discussion
3	0	1	0	Housekeeping
4	1	6	0	Test
5	11	15	9	Crane Brinton
6	1	4	1	Group work and discussion
7	0	0	1	Class assignment
8	14	1	0	Test
9	5	0	0	Test
10	0	4	0	Lecture and discussion
11	11	3	0	Chronology
12	0	8	0	Newspaper
13	0	8	0	Newspaper
14	1	2	0	Lecture and discussion
15	0	5	0	Test and discussion
16	0	3	0	Lecture and discussion
17	5	6	1	Test and discussion
18	2	12	0	Causes of the Civil War
19	13	8	1	Causes of the Civil War
20	8	12	1	Causes of the Civil War
21	12	23	1	Statistics discussions
22	7	3	0	Causes of the Civil War
Total	103	125	26	(254)
Percent	41	49	10	(100)

moves between categories (see Figure 8). The subject of the discussion is the
Crane Brinton theory. Harry begins with a category two question: "What is
a speculation?" He is referring to the Crane Brinton theory as a speculation.
The students cannot answer so he asks category one questions (questions 2
and 4-7): "What is the name of the man [who is speculating]? . . . What is
he trying to do? . . . Brinton thinks this is a pattern, with how many stages?
. . . What is important in the first stage of revolutions?" Harry is trying to
find out if students have read the material and understand the role of the British
War debt in bringing on the American Revolution. He feels confident that they
know and asks category two (question 8) and three questions (9-15). In these
questions Harry refers students' understanding of the role of the British War
debt in the American Revolution to current events. Once Harry feels confident
students understand this important issue, he asks question 10: "Have you ever
heard of another nation saying that the national debt is getting so high that
it could really hurt the society?" This topic is developed in a series of questions.

For example, "Do you know how big the debt is?" Harry writes the sum on the board: $1,500,000,000. He continues his questions: "To whom do we owe the money? . . . Does this spell trouble? . . . If the British war debt spelt trouble, does this spell trouble? . . . How? . . . Why?" To develop this point further Harry asks for details, or facts (category one questions 16-17): "Do the presidential candidates agree that we are going to have to raise taxes to pay the debt? [This discussion took place in October 1984, the day after the Reagan/ Mondale debate on TV.] . . . Which one says we are going to raise taxes?" This is interpreted in category two questions (18-25). For example, "What does the debt mean in terms of your pocketbook and mine if the taxes go up? . . . Many people say we are passing on the price of prosperity to whom?" In question 25, Harry brings the class back to the text and has students consider other factors contributing to revolutions: "What happens when you have a disastrous crop?" In the next series of questions he moves between all three categories. For example, "What begins to cost more money? . . . If bread is most important, or sometimes the only diet, what is going to happen to those people? . . . But before they starve, what are they likely to do?" In this way, Harry not only deals with complex historical ideas such as the Crane Brinton theory of why revolutions occur, but he also relates those ideas to important present-day issues in a way that is meaningful for students. He establishes connections between the past and present and demonstrates how "real" history was on TV last night.

Nearly four decades of teaching have made Harry a commanding figure in the classroom. He is particularly skilful as a storyteller and discussion leader in catching and holding students' attention. Harry chooses to tell stories of events that are examples of major historical ideas. He often retells important events from the textbook because he knows that many of his general track students do not read it. As a skilled storyteller he is able to transmit the important ideas into a medium that penetrates the passivity of a large group of students. In spinning his story, Harry the storyteller is animated, spicing the story with his personal views and constantly drawing the students into the story. As a discussion leader, Harry is precise and probes for meaning. As an efficient organizer of group work, Harry frequently uses this mode so students can discuss ideas and work on collaborative projects.

The range of substantive structures in history that conflict historians find inspiring appear in Harry's model and in his teaching. In observation 5 Harry takes on revolution, an important substantive structure in history and his model makes him focus on events and ideas that represent conflict. The syntactic structures of history that conflict historians draw upon, however, do not appear as vividly in his teaching or in his model. Harry is primarily concerned with interpretation, primary sources, and the events of American history where people and ideas are in conflict.

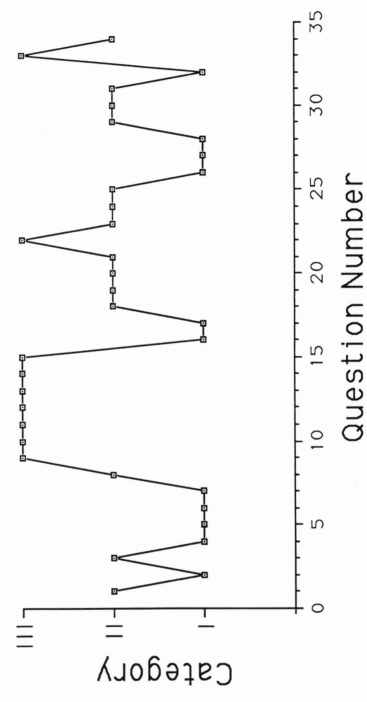

Figure 8. Questions Harry Asks in Observation 5 Analyzed Using Nancy's Reading Categories

DISCUSSION

Naomi's, Nancy's, Harry's, and David's pedagogical models are different in nature. This is not surprising since the models are "homemade" and represent the teachers' disciplinary perspective, their private learning theory, and their values. Each teacher's disciplinary perspective draws together a range of substantive structures. This gives them an orientation that is reflected in their pedagogical models. The models, however, reflect to a different degree the substantive structures of history and literature. Harry's model most clearly represents a distinct set of substantive structures in history, and in the classroom he works with some of the key concepts conflict historians consider important. Nancy's model represents a sequence of steps to follow that lead her students to a particular view of literature, a view that represents an orientation which draws on a range of substantive and syntactic structures that all relate to traditional literature criticism. Naomi's model also reflects an orientation to literature, but it draws on different concepts and represents different syntactical structures. Her model focuses on layers of meaning, where personal meaning has priority. Because Nancy and Naomi draw on different substantive and syntactic structures in literature, they identify and validate evidence for their interpretation differently: Most of the time Nancy goes to the text and Naomi to students' personal lives and feelings.

David's model does not, it seems, represent distinct substantive or syntactic structures of history (or any other discipline). Instead, its primary objective seems to be to integrate, through interpretation, information from a range of sources. When David uses this "un-disciplinary" model in the classroom, however, he highlights the substantive and syntactic structures of history. By critically examining these structures, his students have the opportunity to see how they shape interpretation. No matter how much or how little the four models mirror a few of the structures of the disciplines the teachers teach, the models always end up representing an orientation to literature or history the teachers feel is important and worthwhile for students to understand and appreciate.

The models are different, yet they have one important element in common: they are the teachers' homemade maps of the discipline they teach and they show how the teachers feel the discipline should be sequenced for pedagogical purposes. These disciplinary maps function in many ways like regular maps. They show routes through a given terrain, routes that will expose the traveller to different views of the landscape while at the same time excluding other views. The map-making process for all the teachers seems to start with their own ways of making sense in their discipline. In that respect the models, to some extent, represent the teachers' private learning models of their discipline. This is especially true for Naomi, Nancy, and David, less so for Harry.

Nancy's model has important similarities with Gagne's (1970) theories of learning. Gagne's idea of task skill hierarchy and different types of learning appear in a general way in Nancy's model. Nancy seems to have analyzed broad skills needed for reading and interpreting literature. Students need to understand the words on the page. They need to be able to interpret the ideas using textual evidence and to link this understanding to their reality. This analysis has lead her to define a distinctive type of learning that is relevant for her discipline. The type of learning Nancy pursues in her model is problem solving where no one solution is correct. Instead, a range of solutions is acceptable. In the problem-solving activities Nancy organizes in her classroom, students interpret texts and seek and validate textual evidence to support their interpretation.

Nancy never made any reference to learning theories to support her model. She claims she invented this model herself, drawing mostly on her experience in the classroom. She had been teaching for about 20 years when I sat in her classroom (winter of 1984-85). This means that she may have been exposed to some of Gagne's early work in teacher education. Initially, she may have found this work useful, but now two decades later she no longer remembers Gagne's influence.[9] Her model, however, remains a powerful and useful pedagogical tool regardless of where she may or may not have initially gotten the ideas. Similarly, David's model can also be related to Gagne's theories of learning in a general way. David identifies a general skill his students need to master, knowledge of historical facts and their theoretical interpretation, and he organizes a range of classroom activities around problem solving, where students interpret historical events through historical theories.

The clear disciplinary orienation that appears in the teachers' models shows that values are central to their pedagogical content knowledge. Naomi, Nancy, David, and Harry hold strong personal and disciplinary values. These values relate to one of two issues: the discipline they teach, or people and their social contexts. Nancy and Harry are united in their focus on their respective disciplines, but each does so in a unique and personal way. They look to their discipline for central questions about life and their purpose for teaching. Nancy's focus is on working with the text, as reflected in high percentages of category one and two questions. She sees literature, and the ability to make sense of literature, as the central purpose of her teaching. Harry's focus on the discipline of history has a parallel function, also reflected in a high percentage of category one and two questions.

David and Naomi are united in their focus on people and their social contexts. David's model that funnels historical ideas to current events enables him to connect these ideas with the present, as reflected in a relatively high percentage of category three questions for an advanced placement class (25%). He is also the peace activist who points out the futility of wars. His choice of the bloodiest Civil War battle to explain fighting communicates his values to students through the study of American history. Naomi's mission is to help students understand themselves and the problems they face through the study of literature. At times, her teaching has almost a therapeutic purpose, especially when they spend almost as much time discussing students' problems as they do the text (37% category three questions).

Tables 1 and 2 show how Naomi's and Nancy's different values are reflected in the questions they ask in class. Both teachers ask a similar percentage of category one questions because they feel that they have to make students read and understand the text. The difference between them is evident when examining what they make students do with the words they now understand. Nancy stays with the text at category two (66%). Naomi divides her time and energy between category two (28%) and three (37%), emphasizing the latter. This means that Naomi and Nancy use models similar in nature to get to different destinations. Their destinations are different because they have different values.

While the English teachers use a similar model to get to different destinations, the social studies teachers use different models to get to similar destinations. The different content background of the social studies teachers is reflected in different models. David has an interdisciplinary background and his model organizes knowledge from several disciplines. Harry has a Master's degree in the subfield of history he is teaching. With this background, the social studies teachers have constructed different models of teaching American history. Harry's model is entirely the organization of content, and illustrates his command over American history. This kind of model is unique to Harry, because none of the other teachers in this study talk about content in the same way as he does.

Tables 3 and 4 show that Harry and David use their different models to get to similar destinations. Category two is their destination because 46 percent of the questions Harry asks are category two as are 53 percent of David's questions. This is not surprising since history is an interpretative discipline. Harry asks more category one questions (41%) than David (24%). David does not need as many category one questions to proceed to interpretation. His are advanced placement students who read the textbook. Harry, who teaches a general track, cannot rely on his students to do their homework. The high percentage of category one questions shows that he feels he has to make sure students know the facts. This is the only difference found in this study that can be accounted for by students' academic standing.

There are differences between Harry and David in terms of the percentage of category three questions. Table 4 shows that 10 percent of Harry's questions are category three, and Table 3 shows 25 percent of David's are category three. It seems that both teachers have the tendency to tie historical understanding to students' lives, but David more than Harry. The high percentage of category two questions in David's class can be accounted for by the nature of the class he is teaching (advanced placement) and the relatively high percentage of category three questions by his values.

The models are versatile tools that help teachers cope with long-term planning as well as teaching a difficult topic to reluctant students. As a general strategy in organizing a course, the models are closer to content than pedagogy. When the teachers plan their courses they think about the development of ideas. Naomi identifies the ideas she can link to students' realities, while David is torn between his values that encourage the same, and the nature of his course that calls for an emphasis on interpretation. Nancy progressively introduces students to the difficult language of Melville, and Harry highlights conflict in his course design. The models are an efficient way to structure content in a course of study so that it becomes a meaningful whole. As a topic specific strategy, the models are closer to pedagogy. This is vividly exemplified in Nancy's and Naomi's teaching. When Nancy teaches difficult texts, like the Melville works, she remains center stage asking questions. When she teaches easy texts, like *Huck Finn*, she abandons the stage and lets students work on their own, tracing themes through the chapters. Similarly, Naomi changes her circling depending on how emotionally loaded the topic is.

The teachers imply that their models are entirely their own inventions that have developed over time as they have had to teach different kinds of courses to different types of students. This raises questions about why they felt the need to construct models of the subject they teach, and about the kinds of functions the models serve other than to restructure content for pedagogical purposes and communicate their values. In the classroom, teachers deal with two problems: subject matter and students. Content and students constitute a complex and fluid world that needs to be comprehended if teaching and learning are going to take place. The models are the teachers' representations of what they think is important to comprehend. The process of constructing models is facilitated and shaped by prior knowledge (Simon, 1957; Shulman & Carey, 1984). As high school teachers they teach a discipline: English or U.S. history. A discipline includes a wide range of topics, ideas, theories, and research approaches. It is not easy to reduce a slice of a discipline into a high school course, and at the same time retain what the teachers think is important to that discipline. The models help them organize this wide range of ideas into what teenagers can learn, understand, and find meaningful, and at the same time communicate the teachers' values.

Naomi, Nancy, David, and Harry are considered excellent teachers by their colleagues. They are not excellent because they have pedagogical models of the subject they teach. Excellence in teaching requires more. Bad teachers can have efficient models that make them uninspiring teachers (Hardgreaves, 1989). Nevertheless, the models are a critical element in their excellence. Novices, who often have excellent content knowledge but have not structured it for pedagogical purposes, have problems with managing their classrooms and communicating their conceptions of the subject matter (Grossman et al., 1987; Gudmundsdottir, 1987). They also seem to find it difficult to organize ideas into a course of study. They are more often able to develop individual units without seeing how they connect into a course of study (Gudmundsdottir and Shulman, 1987). Pedagogical models, therefore, seem to provide for efficiency in dealing with texts, good or bad.

CONCLUSIONS

The four veteran teachers in this study have pedagogical models of their discipline that are the centerpiece of their pedagogical content knowledge. Their disciplinary orientation and their values shape the goals they set for themselves, and consequently influence the way in which they use their models. The pedagogical models are both general and topic-specific. The general element influences content organization into a unit and course of study. The topic-specific element is closer to pedagogy and influences the methods teachers use in communicating their ideas to students.

The results of this study have implications for research on teaching. Nancy, Naomi, David, and Harry are all recognized as excellent teachers, but what is the nature of the models that less competent teachers use? There are also implications for teacher education. Student teachers need to be given the opportunity to begin the process of restructuring their content knowledge for pedagogical purposes. They can, among other things, study examples of models invented and used by experienced teachers. It should not be necessary for novices to begin to invent the wheel in their first years of teaching.

ACKNOWLEDGMENTS

The research reported in this chapter was sponsored by a grant from the Spencer Foundation to Stanford University for the "Knowledge Growth in a Profession" research program, Lee S. Shulman, principal investigator. The author would like to thank Jere Brophy and Michael Huberman for their helpful criticism, and Debbie Smith and Dan Neale for their cross-talk questions.

NOTES

1. All names are pseudonyms.

2. The four teachers in this study are veteran teachers who have the reputation among their colleagues and students to be excellent teachers. I am using the work "excellent" for "expert" since the latter word has taken on far too many connotations from a series of psychological studies of experts and novices in teaching (Carter & Berliner, 1987). The word "expert" no longer supports

the modest but important claims that I want to make about teaching. I did not do systematic studies of the students' learning, but I lived in the four teachers' classsrooms for many months. As an experienced teacher and researcher on teaching I came to the conclusion that they were excellent teachers.

3. Only Naomi and David sketched their models. Nancy's and Harry's models (shown in Figures 1 and 7) are my reconstructions of their descriptions. These reconstructions were approved by them as accurate.

4. Nancy made the comment on this analysis that moving from category one to categories two or three is "moving up in interpretation." I have tried to capture this in my reconstruction of her model.

5. Observations covered the period when students read the works of Melville and Twain.

6. The observation covered only part of the course of study. It is possible that the number of questions in all categories evens out throughout the school year.

7. Nancy made the comment that this teaching method works for juniors only when they are working with "easier" novels like *Huck Finn*. According to her, this teaching method does not work when teaching *Moby Dick* to this age group.

8. Observations covered the period when students read *Huck Finn*.

9. My colleagues at Pedagogisk Institutt at the University of Trondheim in Norway have put forward an alternative explanation of the apparent influence of Gagné's theories in Nancy's pedagogical model. They suggest that the positivistic influence has been so pervasive in education in America that it makes many researchers and practitioners "think that way." While I am not prepared to endorse this explanation, I must admit that I feel American and European educators think somewhat differently.

10. This does not exclude the possibility that the other teachers have such models. They probably have them, but I did not know how to ask.

REFERENCES

Arzi, H.J. (1987). *Teachers' knowledge of science: An account of a longitudinal study in progress.* Paper presented at the annual meeting of the American Educational Research Association, Washington, DC.

Brophy, J.E. (1979). Teacher behavior and its effects. *Journal of Educational Psychology, 71*(6), 733-750.

Buchmann, M. (1984). The use of research knowledge in teacher education and teaching. *American Journal of Education, 92*(4), 421-439.

Buchmann, M. (1986). Role over person: Morality and authenticity in teaching. *Teachers College Record, 87*(4), 529-543.

Bussis, A.M., Chittenden E.A., & Amarel, M. (1976). *Beyond surface curriculum.* Boulder, Colo.: Westview Press.

Byrne, C. (1983). *Teacher knowledge and teacher effectiveness: A literature review, theoretical analysis and discussion of research strategy.* Paper presented at the 14th Annual Convention of the Northeastern Educational Research Association, Ellenville, NY.

Carter, K., & Berliner, D. (1987). *Expert and novice interpretation of classroom data.* Paper presented at the annual meeting of the American Educational Research Association, Washington, DC.

Clandinin, J. (1986). *Classroom practice.* Sussex: Falmer Press.

Dewey, J. (1904/1964). The relation of theory to practice in education. In R. Archambault (Ed.), *Dewey on education* (pp. 313-339). Chicago: University of Chicago Press.

Elbaz, F. (1983). *Teacher thinking: A study of practical knowledge.* London: Croom Helm.

Feiman-Nemser, S., & Buchmann, M. (1986). The first year of teacher preparation: Transition to pedagogical thinking? *Journal of Curriculum Studies, 18*(3), 239-256.

Fenstermacher, G. (1978). A philosophical consideration of recent research on teacher effectiveness. In L.S. Shulman (Ed.), *Review of research in education* (Vol. 6, pp. 157-185).

Grant, G.E. (1988). *Teaching critical thinking.* New York: Praeger Press.

Green, T.F. (1971). *The activities of teaching.* New York: McGraw Hill.

Grossman, P. (1987a). *Conviction–that granitic base: A case study of Martha, a beginning English teacher.* Unpublished research report. Stanford, CA: Stanford University, School of Education, Knowledge Growth in Teaching research project.

Grossman, P. (1987b). *A passion for language: From text to teaching.* Unpublished research report. Stanford, CA: Stanford University, School of Education, Knowledge Growth in Teaching research project.

Grossman, P., & Gudmundsdottir, S. (1987). *Teachers and texts: An expert/novice comparison in English.* Paper presented at the Annual Meeting of the American Educational Research Association, Washington, DC.

Grossman, P., Ringstaff, C., Reynolds, A., & Sykes, G. (1985). *English major to English teacher: New approaches to an old problem.* Paper presented at the annual meeting of the American Educational Research Association, Chicago.

Gudmundsdottir, S. (1990). Curriculum stories: Case studies of social studies teaching. In C. Day, P. Denicolo & M. Pope (Eds.), *Insights into Teacher Thinking and practice* (pp. 107-118). England: Falmer Press.

Gudmundsdottir, S. (1987). *Learning to teach social studies: Case studies of Cathy and Chris.* Paper presented at the annual meeting of the American Educational Research Association, Washington, DC.

Gudmundsdottir, S. (1988). *Knowledge use among experienced teachers: Four case studies of high school teaching.* Unpublished doctoral dissertation, Stanford University.

Gudmundsdottir, S., Carey, N., & Wilson, S. (1985). *Role of prior subject matter knowledge in learning to teach social studies.* (Tech. Rep. of the Knowledge Growth in a Profession research project). Stanford, CA: Stanford University, School of Education.

Gudmundsdottir, S., & Shulman, L.S. (1987). Pedagogical content knowledge in social studies. *Scandinavian Journal of Educational Research, 31*(2), 59-70.

Hardgreaves, A. (1989). *Curriculum and assesment reform.* Milton Keynes, England: Open University Press.

Herron, M.D. (1971). The nature of scientific enquiry. *School Review, 79*(2), 171-211.

Leinhardt, G., & Smith, D. (1985). Expertise in mathematics instruction: Subject matter knowledge. *Journal of Educational Psychology, 77*(3), 247-271.

McGraw, L. (1987). *The anthropologist in the classroom: A case study of Chris, a beginning social studies teacher* (Tech. Rep. No. CS-07).

Reynolds, A. (1987). *Everyone's invited to the party: A case study of Catherine* (Tech. Rep. No. CS-09).

Scheffler, I. (1965). *The conditions of knowledge.* Chicago: The University of Chicago Press.

Schwab, J.J. (1961/1978). Education and the structure of the disciplines. In I. Westbury & N. Wilkof (Eds.), *Science, curriculum, and liberal education.* Chicago: University of Chicago Press.

Shulman, L.S. (1974). The psychology of school subjects: a premature obituary? *Journal of Research in Science Teaching, 11*(4), 319-339.

Shulman, L.S. (1986). Paradigms and research programs for the study of teaching. In M.C. Wittrock (Ed.), *Handbook of research on teaching* (3rd ed., pp. 3-36). New York: Macmillian.

Shulman, L.S. (1987). Knowledge and teaching: Foundations of the new reforms. *Harvard Educational Review, 57*(1), 1-22.

Shulman, L.S., & Carey, N.B., (1984). Psychology and the limitations of individual rationality: Implications for the study of reasoning and civility. *Review of Educational Research, 54*(4), 501-524.

Simon, H.A. (1957). *Models of man: Social and rational: Mathematical essays.* New York: Wiley.

Smith, B. O. (1980). *A design for a school of pedagogy.* Washington, DC: U.S. Department of Education.

Wilson, S., & Gudmundsdottir, S. (1987). What is this a case of? *Education and Urban Society, 11*(1), 42-54.

Wineburg, S. (1987). *From fieldwork to classwork: A case study of a beginning social studies teacher.* Unpublished research report. Stanford, CA: Stanford University, School of Education, Knowledge Growth in Teaching research project.

*   *   *

CROSS-TALK

Many critics are suggesting that the structures of disciplines idea was overblown, that disciplines do not actually have inherent structures or even structures that endure for very long. Do you accept the ideas about the structures of the disciplines?

I accept, to some degree, the idea of the structures of discipline as put forward by Schwab (1961/1978), Hirst (1965/1974), and Kuhn (1970), and I use them because I find them useful for the kind of work I do. I find it useful to think of the disciplines to include different kinds of scholarly traditions, research programs, paradigms or structures, because of the variety of scholarship that exists within each (see, for example, Hilgard & Bower, 1975; Tyack, 1976). The teachers encounter a range of these structures in their college education and a few of them shape their view of the discipline for years to come. The fact that disciplines change and structures fade away is less important for this work because I am dealing with teachers who are the product of their years in college. Harry makes reference to this when he says that one of his professors turned him into a "conflict historian." "Conflict history" may not have been an enduring structure in historical scholarship as practiced at the university level, but it has endured in Harry's high school classroom. There, it has had an active life for 37 years, inspiring generations of young Americans.

You indicate that Nancy sometimes used category 3 questions as motivational gimmicks when introducing new content that was difficult for students. Is the nature of the category three questions asked at this point for this purpose different from that of the questions asked following the understanding and interpretation of the material?

Yes, there is a range of difference in the type of category three questions, but not just in those asked by Nancy. Each of the teachers, in their own way, tries to help students find a connection between the content they are studying and their lives. It is a process that is shaped by the teachers' pedagogical models of subject matter. A fine-tuned analysis of all the category three questions that the four teachers asked will show how the teachers' pedagogical models and their goals give rise to variations in this type of question. The presence of category three questions shows that the teachers try to touch base with different aspects of students' lives. The timing of this type of question is critical, and so is their aim. It is clear, for example, that Harry's questions focus on critical incidents in U.S. domestic policy, that David's category three questions usually come at the end of a longer interpretative discussion as kind of "peak insight," and that Naomi's category three questions penetrate deep into the students' emotions. As different as these types of category three questions are, they still have one important element in common, and that is finding a connection between content and reality. This process is accounted for in Shulman's (1987) Model of Pedagogical Reasoning and Action, as "adaptation." It is important and deserves the attention of researchers investigating pedagogical content knowledge. I left it out because there simply was not enough space to deal with this complex issue.

Why were you focused on questioning to the exclusion of other things that the teacher might do, and is there any evidence in support of your implicit assumption that the number of questions asked during a lesson translates directly into the time spent on a topic and the degree of importance placed on it by the teacher?

I am not aware that I make implicit claims about questions translating into time on a topic, but I accept that I consider that the questions teachers ask in class tell something about what they want students to learn. It was obvious from my observations in the four teachers' classrooms that the questions they ask are very important. The teachers seem to formulate and develop important content ideas into questions that they asked verbally in class or on tests. I am not sure "time on a topic" would, on its own, capture the important qualities of Nancy's, Naomi's, David's, and Harry's teaching. In this case study, I have chosen to give an overview of the teachers' questions in the tables, and at the same time go beyond the numbers and show, in other diagrams and excerpts from data, what they stand for. Category three questions are especially difficult, no matter how one "quantifies" them. I see few of these questions stay longer with the students than a number of category one or two questions. Furthermore, I am convinced that some students work on a few of these questions in their minds for days, even weeks, as they ponder the meaning of their existence, and I do not know of a way to quantify that.

Do you think different analyses or conclusions might have resulted if you had used one of the history teachers' models rather than Nancy's as the prototype?

The teachers' pedagogical models are different in nature and focus on different aspects of their pedagogical content knowledge. Moreover, the models do not equally concern themselves with the questions teachers ask in class. Harry's model, for example, is different from the other teachers' models in that it shapes a disciplinary orientation in history. While this model does not generate questions in the way that Nancy's model does, his model probably creates an important content target for the questions Harry asks in class, because they frequently address conflict rather than consensus. Harry's conception of the role of history in the lives of youngsters, however, makes him ask the different types of questions. He wants them to know the important facts of history. He wants his students to interpret those facts historically, and to use their historical understanding to examine conflict in society today. David's model, on the other hand, is more concerned with process. It identifies areas that are the source for questions about fact, interpretation, and connection with current events. Had this model been used initially as a source of comparison, it would probably have yielded similar results.

How do you think the quality of David's course was affected when he deviated from what otherwise would have been his ordinary behavior in order to make sure that his students were prepared for the AP test?

The deviation concerned is a larger percentage of category two questions, that is, interpretation. To do well on the AP test, students need to be able to interpret events, figures, tables, diagrams, and pictures using historical concepts, ideas, or theories. These are the document-based questions, something David identified as very important on the test. He spends more class time on this activity than he would have liked to. Given the freedom, he would probably explore category three type of questions more thoroughly. These are the questions that link students' lives with history. It is a very important element in historical understanding, and in my mind, a sign of excellence in teaching. This connection between students' lives and history has to build on a strong knowledge of facts and solid historical interpretation, otherwise it is "empty." History teaching at the high school level would be ineffective without a sense of history in our lives.

You state that your teachers are experienced and highly regarded by their colleagues and students, but you do not present any evidence in terms of achievement data suggesting that they are particularly effective with their students. Could you comment on your criteria for identifying expert, experienced, successful, and excellent teachers?

I did not set out to study excellent teachers, so I did not collect student achievement data. When I approached the school to ask for permission to do the study, I said I needed experienced teachers who taught college preparatory and general classes. Once I started observing Nancy, Naomi, David, and Harry, I realized they were excellent teachers. I base this judgment on my experience as a teacher in Scotland and Iceland, as a student in six countries, and as a researcher in California. I was impressed with the teachers' understanding of the subject they teach, the ways in which they are able to communicate it, students' responses and participation in class, the kind of respect I sensed there existed between the teachers and students, and the teachers' dedication to the education enterprise. At first, I thought I was just making it up, so I cross-checked my observation. A discussion with the principal and other teachers revealed that they also felt my four teachers were outstanding. Visits to the counselor's office revealed that Castile High has a higher percentage of graduates going on to a four-year colleges than any other school in the district. There is more information that I came across later which confirms my observation of the four teachers' excellence. A study by one of the leading universities in the United States recently identified the school I call "Castile High" as having one of the ten best social studies departments in the country. Here, I am reminded of all the years David and Harry have spent in that school teaching social studies and building up the curriculum. Finally, it is worth mentioning that another researcher, Grace Grant, (1988) was in Nancy's classroom and also independently characterized her as excellent. Grant calls Nancy "Linda" and, interestingly enough, also independently calls the high school concerned "Castile High." I do not want to deny that students' grades are important in judging teacher quality, but I feel very strongly that this cannot be the only criterion. This is especially true for the Nancy, Naomi, David, and Harry because many of the important qualities of their excellence may not show up on a test. Perhaps it is my European background that makes me focus on this aspect of teaching because I feel there is more to education than grades.

Are your statements about what Nancy feels and knows about the therapeutic quality of Naomi's teaching, and about Harry's story teller role, based on what the teachers told you or on your own interpretations of their teaching? In general, to what extent do you feel we ought to have teachers corroborate the conclusions we make about their teaching?

The data on the teachers' feelings, knowledge, and actions come mainly from observations and interviews, but also other sources such as curriculum materials. I encountered methodological problems when working with these fine teachers which relate to this question. They were so impressive as teachers and so articulate and thoughtful as informants, that it was tempting for me as a relatively inexperienced researcher to accept everything they said as "the truth." It is not that they were trying to mislead me. On the contrary, they were just presenting their view of the world because I asked them. And, initially, their view of the world became my view as well. Gradually, I began triangulating elements of this world, and it appeared that things were not exactly as the teachers described them. For example, in the first interview with Nancy she claimed she had a "model of English" which she described. For weeks afterwards I observed her use this model and I interviewed her about it. However, it was not until I began coding the questions she asked in class and counting instances that I realized she indeed had a model, but not the one she described. I confronted her with this "new model" and she basically agreed with my reconstruction, but emphasized that I had lost the hierarchical nature of her questioning. She explained that in English teaching, the interpretation moves on up to higher levels of understanding. I subsequently added this element to the reconstructed model, which is described in the chapter. It was the same case with the other teachers. Their account of their classroom was initially my lens to view it. I collected enough data to understand this view as they saw it, but then I tried moving beyond it and triangulating in different ways. I always shared my interpretation with them and invited them to respond. Their responses to my interpretation of their ideas and actions often produced some of the most important data in this study. In those interviews, I could explore gaps in my understanding and also figure out ways to collect contradictory evidence. For example, early on I identified the influence of the Beyond War Movement in David's teaching. I shared this with him, but he said this was not true and I was "overdoing it." I rechecked my data looking for contradiction and I also focused subsequent observation in the classroom on this issue. I did find some insignificant contradictions, but nothing that made me change my view. David eventually agreed that perhaps his philosophy was coming through. I would like to add that, when you are a dedicated teacher like David who gives so much of himself in his work, your view of the world is bound to come through.

References to Cross-talk

Grant, G. (1988). *Teaching critical thinking*. New York: Praeger.

Hilgard, E., & Bower, G. (1975). *Theories of learning*. (4th ed.). New York: Harcourt Brace Jovanovich.

Hirst, P. (1965/1974). *Knowledge and the curriculum*. London: Routledge and Kegan Paul.

Kuhn, T. (1970). *The structure of scientific revolutions* (2nd ed. enlarged). Chicago: University of Chicago Press.

Schwab, J. (1961/1978). *Science, curriculum, and liberal education* (selected essays). Chicago: University of Chicago Press.

Tyack, D. (1976). Ways of seeing: An essay on the history of compulsory schooling. *Harvard Educational Review, 46*(3), 355-389.

SUBJECT-MATTER KNOWLEDGE IN THE TEACHING OF HISTORY

Samuel S. Wineburg and Suzanne M. Wilson

INTRODUCTION

We begin our discussion of subject-matter knowledge in the teaching of history[1] with the following sketch:

> The topic for the day in Mr. Bellack's American history class is the background to the American Revolution. When the bell rings, Bellack tells his 32 eleventh-graders to take out the review questions assigned over the weekend. The first question on the list asks students to identify these terms or persons: inalienable rights, John Hancock, Henry Lee, and John Locke. A boy in the front row, quoting from his textbook, volunteers the first answer: "Inalienable rights are the rights that can't be taken away from the people—not by the government, not by the people themselves"[2] (Todd & Curti, 1982, p. 119). Nodding, Bellack says "good job" and moves on. A girl in the next row identifies Henry Lee: "Richard Henry Lee of Virginia introduced a resolution in the Second Continental Congress declaring, 'These United Colonies are, and of right ought to be, free and independent states'" (pp. 119-120). "Nice job, Jennie" says Bellack who then passes out a worksheet to help students determine what they need to

Advances in Research on Teaching, Volume 2, pages 305-347.
Copyright © 1991 by JAI Press Inc.
All rights of reproduction in any form reserved.
ISBN: 1-55938-034-9

know for the chapter test. Bellack explains that this test will be composed of 30 multiple-choice questions and 20 true-false questions. There will also be two short-answer questions: "What were three main purposes of the Declaration of Independence?" and "Why can the Declaration be called a 'practical document'?" Students work independently on the worksheet for the next 20 minutes. As the hour comes to an end, two students, somewhat distressed, raise their hands. "Mr. Bellack, we *still* can't find the answers to the short-answer questions." "Read your books carefully," Bellack assures them, "and you'll find everything you need." Bellack is right, for on page 119 the textbook states: "The Declaration . . . was a practical document with three major purposes"—"Preamble and Reasons for Separation," "A Theory of Government," and "A Formal Declaration of War." When the bell rings, Bellack reminds students that if they didn't do well on the worksheet, they should study hard for tomorrow's test.

Although this sketch is fictional, it is based on what many researchers, ourselves included, have observed in history classrooms. In *A Place Called School*, based on observations in over 1000 classrooms, John Goodlad (1985, p. 212) noted that topics in history and social studies classrooms "become removed from their intrinsically human character, reduced to the dates and places readers will recall memorizing for tests." And while most teachers in Goodlad's study listed the "development of reasoning" as their main objective, their tests revealed a different story. Composed largely of multiple-choice, matching, or true-false questions, the typical social studies test often requires nothing more than the regurgitation of memorized information.

Goodlad's findings are not the exception; sadly, they are the rule. Shaver, Davis, and Helburn (1979), in their review of the National Science Foundation study of social studies instruction (Wiley & Race, 1977), noted that in most classrooms, textbooks—not teachers—determine the subject matter to be taught, serving as a script for recitations and the basis for student assessment. Similar findings emerged from a study of social studies instruction in Indiana nearly 25 years ago (Baxter, Ferrell, & Wiltz, 1964), and recent surveys report few deviations (cf. Christopoulos, Rohwer, & Thomas, 1987; Howard & Mendenhall, 1982). Ravitch and Finn (1987), in their analysis of data from the National Assessment of Educational Progress, summarized the current state of affairs:

> In the eyes of the students, the typical history classroom is one in which they listen to the teacher explain the day's lesson, use the textbook, and take tests. Occasionally they watch a movie. Sometimes they memorize information or read stories about events and people. They seldom work with other students, use original documents, write term papers, or discuss the significance of what they are studying (p. 194).

In light of the consistency of these findings, it may well be that we have reached the point of diminishing returns in studying the "typical" or the "representative" history classroom. We have a fairly good sense of what occurs in such classes; it is unlikely that another study of randomly selected history teachers will yield dramatically new knowledge about social studies instruction. This is not to suggest that the study of representative social studies teachers is fruitless; there are many questions raised by educational researchers left to be answered in social studies classrooms. However, the consistency of the results concerning the nature of typical social studies instruction suggests that this particular area has been sufficiently documented.

But the study of the representative is not the only way to advance our knowledge of teaching. In fact, in our work we have conscientiously avoided the ordinary to focus on the extraordinary, moving from the study of the probable to a close examination of the possible. Shulman (1983, p. 495) explains the advantages of such a strategy: "It is often the goal . . . to pursue the possible, not only to support the probable or frequent. The well-crafted case instantiates the possible, not only documenting that it can be done but also laying out at least one detailed example of how it was organized, developed, and pursued." In a similar vein, Robert K. Merton (1947, p. 197) quipped many years ago, "Whatever is, is possible."

What follows is an account of two nonrepresentative teachers. In examining these teachers, we first characterize their instruction and then reflect on the ways in which their teaching is informed by a particular kind of professional knowledge. But first, we briefly review the conceptual foundations of our work.

THE WISDOM OF PRACTICE

Questions concerning the professional knowledge base of teaching alternately intrigue and plague the world of educational scholarship, practice, and policy. State and national mandates calling for new standards for teacher certification presume the existence of a knowledge base that can guide the assessment of prospective and practicing teachers. Similarly, teacher education programs presume that a professional knowledge base can be communicated through such programs. While researchers and policymakers alike believe in the existence of a knowledge base, they have been frustrated in their attempts to delineate its contents and boundaries.

Shulman (1987b) enumerates the sources from which we can draw inferences regarding the knowledge base of teaching, including scholarship in the content disciplines, educational materials and structures, and formal educational scholarship. Shulman also suggests an additional source, one that remains largely untapped and uncodified. This source is what he calls the "wisdom of practice"—the knowledge, skills, beliefs, and values that wise practitioners have acquired through years of experience and reflection.

Although several researchers have documented the practical knowledge of teachers (e.g., Clandinin, 1985; Connelly & Clandinin, 1985; Elbaz, 1983), few have examined the practical knowledge of teachers as it relates to the subject matters they teach. The wisdom of practice studies conducted under the auspices of the Teacher Assessment Project were designed expressly for this purpose. The Teacher Assessment Project was a research and development initiative designed to generate a set of prototypes for alternative ways to assess teaching. These prototypes were then used to inform the development of a certification process for the newly formed National Board of Professional Teaching Standards. Beginning in the areas of high school social studies and elementary school mathematics, we have drawn on many sources to guide our decisions about the knowledge and skill that should be assessed by the Board. Experienced teachers have contributed to all phases of this work—as consultants on advisory boards, as collaborators in the wisdom of practice research, and as examiners in exercise administration. See Shulman (1987a) and Shulman, Haertel, and Bird (1988) for overviews of this work.

Eleven experienced history and social studies teachers in the San Francisco Bay area, nominated as "expert"[3] by university professors, school administrators, and teachers, were recruited for a series of in-depth interviews and classroom observations. These teachers ranged in years of experience, subject-matter preparation, and cultural and ethnic backgrounds. They also differed in the types of schools they worked in and the kinds of students they taught.[4] Data collection focused on one part of the U.S. history curriculum: the American Revolution and the formation of government.[5] Two considerations guided this selection. First, after polling our wisdom of practice teachers and a group of Stanford University historians, we compiled a list of "mandatory topics" that should be included in a survey course in American history. Second, we selected a topic that would be taught in the fall semester, the time we had scheduled for the collection of data.

Teaching can be studied from myriad perspectives—in the same classroom different researchers can focus on the teacher's management strategies, students' response opportunities, the reciprocal communication of expectations between teachers and students, wait time, the use of visual aids, and students' time on task, to name just a few.[6] But until recently, few researchers carefully examined the *content* of instruction—the body of ideas, concepts, and facts that teachers try to teach and hope their students learn. What teachers actually know about the content they teach has been a neglected area of research (Shulman, 1986a, 1986b).

Our previous work has tried to address this lacuna. Time and again we discovered that subject-matter knowledge plays a central role in teaching (Grossman, Wilson, & Shulman, 1989; Gudmundsdottir, Carey, & Wilson, 1985; Gudmundsdottir & Shulman, 1987; Wilson, 1988; Wilson, Shulman, & Richert, 1987; Wilson & Wineburg, 1988; Wineburg, 1987). But while we have adopted a subject-matter perspective in our work, we do not assume that content, alone, lies at the heart of teaching. Rather, we use content as a window through which to examine teaching more generally, for we believe that the close examination of teachers' subject-matter knowledge yields keen insights about many aspects of the professional knowledge of teachers.

Data Collection

Eleven teachers participated in a series of extended interviews and classroom observations.[7] The first of the five interviews, an intellectual biography, provided critical background information on the teachers. We asked them about their previous education, their subject-matter preparation, their experiences in schools, their outside interests, and their motivations for entering teaching.

The second and third interviews elicited teachers' self-reports of their instructional practices during a unit on the American Revolution and the formation of government. First, we asked teachers to describe how they teach such a unit—the central concepts and characters they cover, and the scope and sequencing of their ideas and materials. In the third interview, we asked teachers to describe a single lesson from this unit, outlining its purposes, its connections to other lessons, and its accompanying assignments or assessments of student learning.

The last two interviews concentrated on the teachers' knowledge and use of documents related to teaching history. In the penultimate interview, we presented teachers with selections from five textbooks and asked them to evaluate their strengths and weaknesses.[8] In the final interview, we gave teachers a set of six primary sources from the Revolutionary period, including two eyewitness accounts of the Boston Massacre, Washington's Farewell Address, and *Federalist No. 84* (Hamilton's arguments against the Bill of Rights). We asked teachers about their past experiences using primary sources, and how they might use this particular set of documents in their teaching.

To complement the self-report data, we conducted a series of classroom observations. In most cases, we audiotaped the classes, but when this was impossible, we took ethnographic field notes.[9] We observed most teachers at least 6 times and we provided them with tape recorders so they could audiotape relevant lessons when we were not there. When schedules allowed, we conducted brief interviews before and after observations. Prior to observing, we asked teachers to describe the purposes and format of the lesson we were about to see. After observing, we asked teachers to reflect on the lesson and to comment on any changes in their plans, the relative success or failure of their goals, and how they might do things differently in the future. We also collected materials the teachers distributed during class, and made copies of lesson plans, lecture notes, and syllabi whenever available.

The Role of Subject-Matter Knowledge in Teaching American History

The role played by subject-matter knowledge in teaching is complicated: A teacher's knowledge of American history does not dictate in any algorithmic way what he or she chooses to teach. Teaching history melds subject-matter knowledge with a host of other understandings—knowledge of students, learning and teaching, schools, curriculum, and educational aims. Yet subject-matter knowledge does play a key role in pedagogy: What teachers know about U.S. history influences not only *what* they choose to teach but also *how* they choose to teach it. To illustrate, we describe two teachers engaged in the act of teaching about the American Revolution.

The Invisible Teacher

It is Monday morning in Elizabeth Jensen's[10] first-period American history class. As her students, a collage of white, black, Asian, and Hispanic faces, enter her classroom, they arrange their desks into three groups—on the left of the room sits a group of "rebels"; on the right, a group of "loyalists"; and in the front, a group of "judges." Off to the side, with a spiral notebook in lap and pencil in hand, sits Jensen, a short woman in her late thirties with a booming voice. But today her voice is silent as her eleventh-graders begin a debate on the legitimacy of British taxation in the American colonies. Written on the blackboard is this statement: *Resolved: The British government possesses the legitimate authority to tax the American colonies.*

The rebels' first speaker, a girl with curly blond hair and one dangling earring, takes a paper from her notebook and begins:

> England says she keeps troops here for our own protection. On face value, this seems reasonable enough, but there is really no substance to their claims. First of all, who do they think they are protecting us from? The French? Quoting from our friend Mr. Bailey[11] on page 54, "By the settlement in Paris in 1763, French power was thrown completely off the continent of North America." Clearly not the French then. Maybe they need to protect us from the Spanish? Yet the same war also subdued the Spanish, so they are no real worry either. In fact, the only threat to our order is the Indians. . . . but . . . we have a decent militia of our own. . . . So why are they putting troops here? The only possible reason is to keep us in line. With more and more troops coming over, soon every freedom we hold dear will be stripped away. The great irony is that Britain expects us to pay for these vicious troops, these British squelchers of colonial justice.

Another rebel, exuding self-confidence as he rises to speak, continues:

> Aside from the moral and practical issues involved there is another important fact to point out. The American colonies *already* tax themselves. When asked

what taxes his state already pays, Benjamin Franklin said, "Taxes on land; personal possessions; a poll tax; professions, trades, and businesses; a tax on wine, rum and other spirits; a duty of £10 on each Negro imported and other taxes." The questioner then asked what purposes the taxes served. Franklin answered, "To support the government and the military, to pay off the heavy debt run up during the French and Indian War."[12] The questioner asked if the taxes weren't easy to pay. Franklin responded, "No, the counties on the frontier have often been attacked by the enemy and had their property destroyed. They are poor and can pay little tax."[13] The colonies are clearly willing to pay taxes if they can be assured that the cause is just. This point was clearly demonstrated by the Virginia Legislature on May 30, 1765.[14] We were also willing to pay our share of the expenses necessary to keep peace in America. However, because we already have heavy taxes, our ability is limited. We will pay only if the method of raising taxes is decided by ourselves.

A tall black student with a Grace Jones haircut rises from his chair and moves to the center of the loyalist contingent. He begins the loyalists' response:

We moved here, we are paying less taxes than we did for two generations in England, and you complain. Let's look at why we're being taxed—the main reason is probably because England has a debt of £140,000,000 . . . This sounds a little greedy, I mean, what right do they have to take our money simply because they have the power over us. But did you know that over one-half of their debt was caused by defending us in the French and Indian War . . . Taxation without representation[15] isn't fair. Indeed, it's tyranny. Yet virtual representation makes this whining of yours an untruth. Every British citizen, whether he had a right to vote or not, is represented in Parliament. Why does this representation not extend to America . . . If it reaches over 300 miles to Manchester and Birmingham, why can it not [reach] 3000 miles to America? Are they not alike: British subjects and Englishmen? England proposed colonial representation in the House of Commons, but by 1765 Americans did nothing to signify their desire for this. England asked Benjamin Franklin, one of our strongest leaders, if the colonists wanted representation in Parliament. Yet he replied, "No, we do not." How can we complain about unfair representation when we do nothing to acquire what we are striving for? We might now cry that there is too much of a distance between England and America for representation in Parliament. Then why is there no problem with protection? The distance cannot be so overwhelming when troops from England can sufficiently protect the colonists in America.[16]

A rebel questions the loyalists about this last point:

Rebel: What benefits do *we* get out of paying taxes to the crown?
Loyalist: We benefit from the protection—
Rebel: (cutting in) Is that the only benefit you claim, protection?
Loyalist: Yes—and all the rights of an Englishman.

> Rebel: Okay, then what about the Intolerable Acts,[17] which deny all of us
>   these rights—acts to punish us, to punish us, for the actions of a few
>   Sons of Liberty[18] and the Boston Tea Party. The Intolerable Acts
>   denied us rights of British subjects. What about the rights we are
>   denied?
> Loyalist: The Sons of Liberty tarred and feathered people, pillaged homes—
>   they were definitely deserving of some sort of punishment.
> Rebel: So should all the colonies be punished for the acts of a few colonists?

A loyalist, dressed in purple sweat pants and ankle warmers, begins her line
of questioning:

> Loyalist: You're being a bit selfish in thinking it's alright to take what is given
>   and not offer, let alone obey, taxes that are levied. How can you justify
>   not having to pay taxes to England?
> Rebel: We're not saying we shouldn't have to pay taxes. We're saying that
>   we shouldn't have to pay taxes without being represented in
>   Parliament—paying taxes and not having a say in what's going—

Before she has a chance to finish her sentence, a chorus of loyalists shout
"cream, cream, cream" to signal that an alleged factual or conceptual error
has been made by the other side. Officially a "cream" was defined as (1) a serious
factual error, (2) stalling by the other side, (3) a contradiction by the other
side, (4) inability to answer the main question, or (5) an effective counterpunch
to a question or response by opponents.

The loyalists now have a brief moment to state their case before the judges.
Following that, the rebels have a chance to defend themselves. After both
statements have been made, the judges rule if the cream should be sustained.
The loyalist "creamer" begins:

> Loyalist: We *are* represented in Parliament—by *virtual representation*. We are
>   British citizens and are represented in Parliament. We had the
>   opportunity to send someone over to be *actually* represented in Britain
>   but you [pointing accusingly at the rebels] did not want to[19] ... Many
>   citizens in Britain have virtual representation, that's all they have so
>   its the sa—
> Rebel: (cutting in) No! They have *virtual* and *actual* representation.
> Loyalist: No! In the larger cities they have only virtual, so you are exactly the
>   same as many of the British citizens in England.

For a moment, the room is a cacophony of charges and countercharges.
"It's the same as in Birmingham," shouts a loyalist.[20] A rebel snorts
disparagingly, "Virtual representation is bull." Thirty-two students seem to be
talking at once, while the presiding judge, a thin student with horn rimmed

glasses, bangs his gavel. But his classmates—warring loyalists and rebels—ignore him. Jensen, still in the corner, still with spiral notebook in lap and pencil in hand, issues her singular command of the day: "Hold still!" she thunders. Order is restored instantly, and the judges uphold the loyalists' cream.

After opening statements by both sides, and a day and a half of cross examination, the debate concludes on the third day with closing statements by rebels and loyalists. The final speaker for the loyalists, with shoulder-length hair and a faded denim jacket with "Kiss" embroidered on it, stands to address his classmates:

> Does our country's government have the right to tax us? Of course. When the question is phrased in this manner, arguments to the contrary seem moronic. Yet our rash compatriots have taken to the idea that we should be exempt of this responsibility, that because of our seemingly unfair treatment . . . we should be liberated from our obligations. They have attempted to rationalize their positions, yet their logic seems to fall short. . . . They have said taxation without representation is tyranny. They are not given representation, they say, so why should they pay taxes? Simultaneously, they refused representation in Parliament. They say that virtual representation is nonexistent under the circumstances of the colonies and that actual representation would be meaningless because they would be constantly outvoted.
>
> What do they want? A representative force that equals over half of Parliament? Of course they will be outvoted if they try to do away with colonial taxation, as would any British district that attempted such a maneuver. It's preposterous to assume that they should get a humongous representative vote, so they say that the taxes themselves are a fraud. They need no protection seeing that Britain has taken care of France and Spain. They are quite secure in the fact that neither these nor any other countries will attack after the sound beating they received. But once ties are severed, America once again becomes a free-for-all for any nation capable . . . In view of these facts it should be painfully clear that paying taxes will produce much less strife for all of us than if we were to commence hostilities with Britain. So I put forth a resounding plea: Please be rational. Does our country have a right to tax us? Yes.

While we did not administer pre- and posttests to her students, we view statements such as this one as powerful evidence for the type of learning that goes on in Jensen's class. Note the care this student has taken in the construction of this statement, taking great pains to imitate the language of the eighteenth-century. It is through the commission of what linguists call a "mistake in register" (calling the rebels' request for representation "humongous") that we see how successful this student has been. He gracefully uses such phrases as "put forth a resounding plea," "commence hostilities," and "it's preposterous to assume" to capture the spirit of an age in which the style of one's message was as important as its meaning. Sixteen year-olds do not normally use phrases like "put forth a resounding plea." Under Jensen's guidance, this student has immersed himself in eighteenth-century primary documents and learned that, in addition to a history of events, there exists a rich history of language.

Making Visible the Invisible Hand

Throughout the debate, the judges have awarded "points" to the two sides. A maximum of ten points was awarded for the opening statements, a maximum of five points for the closing statements, and three points for each cream that was sustained. For the creams, each judge awarded a rating of one to ten, and the cream was sustained if the average totaled seven or above. While the judges tally up the points for the three days of the debate, a kind of nervous presence fills the room as students, eager to hear the judges' verdict, whisper about points not made that would have swayed the judges to their side. Even though the formal debate is over, students continue to discuss eighteenth-century conceptions of parliamentary representation. Meanwhile, the judges wade through three days of testimony, charged with reducing myriad points and counterpoints to a single decision: "Affirmed" or "Rejected."

For three days, Elizabeth Jensen has been an invisible presence in this classroom, nestled in the corner, scribbling notes on her pad. Sometimes, unable to contain her delight, she would flash a smile to a student after a particularly incisive point about Salutary Neglect or the imperatives of Natural Rights. But the only words she uttered (with the exception of "Hold still!") were to the judges, reminding them every so often to sound their gavels and maintain order. During these classes, Jensen did little that would conventionally be called "teaching"—she did not lecture; she did not present information; she did not write on the blackboard; she did not intercede when students became confused; she did not hand out a worksheet, a quiz, or a test. What accounts for this departure from the ordinary?

One might think, initially, that it is Jensen's students who allow her to sit back and, in her words, "play God." Perhaps with such seemingly self-motivated adolescents any teacher would sparkle. Yes, there is no denying that Jensen's students are motivated. As self-selected honors students, they chose this class knowing that it required extra work. But Jensen's students, nearly a third of them black and Hispanic, are not dramatically different in background from other students in other large urban high schools. Even the comprehensive high school they attend has the same dismal look as these other schools—the familiar cracked paint, the same exposed pipes, the scattered graffiti marking the stalls of the restrooms.

The impression that Jensen played a small role in this event is a testament to her artistry. For just as we do not see the choreographers of a Broadway musical standing on stage next to a group of dancers, neither do we see the hand of Elizabeth Jensen as her students shape ideas and craft arguments in a debate on the legitimacy of taxation. Choreographers work on and off stage with their dancers for months, helping them prepare for the moment when they are center stage, alone. In much the same way, during her years of experience with this activity, Jensen has learned how to help students prepare to be loyalists, rebels, and judges. For example, she knows that it is not easy for adolescents to transcend their narrow experiences to embrace the issues, emotions, and motivations of people whose world was vastly different from their own. What allows students to do so, in part, is knowing that the success of the activity is up to them: They know their teacher will not step in to save them if they flounder. Sometimes this means that Jensen has to restrain herself and let a wild goose chase go on longer than it should. But she knows that she cannot have it both ways:

> If I make substantive comments [students] are going to look to me for the substance. Until I help them debrief and get the issues out—if I enter with anything more than regulations to prevent it from becoming a shouting match or an arguing match or losing the structure—then they are going to look to me for all of it.

Jensen's approach here matches the implications of the laboratory research conducted by motivation researchers such as deCharms (1976) and Deci (1975; Deci & Ryan, 1980). Although Jensen is not familiar with these findings, she has reached the same conclusions after years of teaching. This is one instance in which the wisdom of practice matches the wisdom of the research literature.

But it is much more than a keen understanding of adolescents and her practical wisdom that allow Jensen to act as choreographer, arranging a learning experience to engage students in the search for cause and motive. Above all else, Jensen's debate rests on a *vision* of what it means to teach history, a vision that provides structure for classroom activities and infuses them with meaning.

For Jensen, history is held together by overarching ideas and themes, which lend it coherence and provide a way of understanding the rich texture of human experience. And so, Jensen begins the school year not with lists of explorers in an "Age of Discovery" unit, but with a conference on the "Nature of Man." Students read excerpts from the writings of philosophers (Hume, Locke, Plato, and Aristotle), leaders of state and revolutionaries (Jefferson, Gandhi, Mao Tse Tung), and tyrants (Hitler, Mussolini), presenting and advocating these views before their classmates. Students learn that theories of human nature undergird human choice, that some theories depict humans as sinister wretches a step above beasts while others depict them as enlightened beings who would manage ably without government. When it comes time to ratify the Constitution some months later, these now-familiar figures—Plato, Aristotle, Hume, Locke, Emma Goldman, Lenin—are reconvened to be courted by impassioned groups of Federalists and anti-Federalists. All of these activities exemplify the larger lesson Jensen wants to impart: that the making of history is a dynamic process in which people face real choices and rarely are those choices as simple as those presented in textbooks. What happened in the past was not fated or meant to be, but occurred because human actors shaped their destinies with the choices *they* made, just as people today shape their futures with the choices they make. And any choice of genuine significance demands reflection and deliberation, and usually can be viewed from multiple perspectives. Indeed, the notion of competing or multiple perspectives is central to what Jensen wanted her students to learn from the debate:

> I want them to understand that there were two points of view, that there was legitimacy to both sides—to understand the specifics of the mercantile system, the specifics of home rule, the problems of internal and external taxation. . . Basically we're not asking whether [the Americans] should've fought the war, or whether they should've won the war. We're asking about legitimate authority to tax.

Setting the Wheels in Motion

Many history teachers want students to be able to confront, grasp, and manipulate sophisticated ideas, but not all of them are able to translate their desires into practice. What makes Jensen different? How is she able to engage students in serious contemplation about these ideas? What type of knowledge does she have to possess in order to create a situation in which students zestfully debate Parliamentary notions of representation and the legitimacy of government?

Jensen's understanding of history is fundamental to how she captures the minds of her students. For Jensen, American history is more than particular dates, persons, or legislative acts. History is about themes like "authority," "freedom," and "representation," themes that bind past to present and provide a framework for organizing the welter of information in the eleventh-grade curriculum. These themes translate into curricular decisions that allow Jensen to foreshadow ideas months before her students confront them. Thus, when she introduces eighteenth-century views of man at the beginning of the year, she knows these same issues will resurface in discussions about the Constitution and the Bill of Rights, and in the debates about federalism. And long before students begin to prepare for the debate, Jensen has already laid the groundwork for them, introducing them to ideas that stimulate their thinking about the nature of authority.

She did this in several ways. Two weeks before the debate, she assigned selections from the "Student Handbook on Authority," a 72-page mimeographed booklet corresponding to the main units of this American history course, a kind of "nontextbook" textbook. Students first read a short story, "A Flogging at Sea," in which a ship captain beats a sailor under his command. Other selections included an excerpt from Emma Goldman's "The Case for Anarchism," and a short piece called "Two People Who Made Choices," which juxtaposes Josiah Quincy, a lawyer who defended British soldiers accused of murder in the Boston Massacre, with Rosa Parks, a black woman who 150 years later bucked public opinion and refused to move to the back of a Montgomery, Alabama bus.[21] As students read these selections, Jensen made the implicit explicit, bringing to the surface underlying issues, and in so doing, prepared students for the debate that would take place two weeks later. Discussions centered around questions like what is authority? What is freedom? What are the sources of authority and freedom? What are the costs and benefits of authority and freedom? What is the difference between authority and power? What is the scope of authority? Of freedom?

Jensen knows that abstract questions can intimidate even the brightest of high school students. To help students grasp complex ideas, she uses metaphors and analogies that allow her to build bridges between what students know and what she wants them to learn. When Jensen asked students to define the difference between power and authority, for example, many struggled, some of them falling into the same quandary as Socrates's Thrasymachus, who conceded to Socrates that those who possess power define authority, and consequently, what is just. Jensen asked students to imagine a 17-year-old boy still living in his father's household, eating his father's food and depending on his father for clothing and shelter. At 17, the son, strong and tall, outstrips his father in height and weight, and could, if he desired, overpower him physically. But as students quickly realized, the father, while no longer stronger than the son, still retains financial, legal, and moral *authority* over him. Connecting the abstract and the familiar, Jensen provided her students with an alternative way to frame the conflict between the Mother Country and her American colonies.[22]

Research Days

The four class sessions immediately preceding the debate are "research days" in which students working in small groups study the documents, books, and articles that Jensen has gathered to help them formulate their arguments. Students organized themselves into three groups—loyalists, rebels, and judges—with the loyalists and rebels further dividing into speakers and questioners, the former who prepared the opening and closing statements, with the latter responsible for asking questions and cross-examining the other side. Assigning students the role of rebel, loyalist, or judge was no easy task for Jensen. When she tried to draft volunteers for the loyalist side, 32 students stared at her in silence. Jensen broke the silence:

Jensen: If I ask you to take the position of the devil's advocate what does that mean?

Student: Yeh, like Phil Donahue?

Jensen: Yeh, like Phil Donahue, you take a side you don't necessarily believe in as an *intellectual* exercise. Sure, you can easily defend the side you believe in. *No problem.* But what on earth is the other guy going to say? That's a much better *intellectual* exercise.

The following morning Jensen had a dozen loyalists. During the ensuing days, the classroom bustled with activity—students, hunched over their desks, shuttled books back and forth, and mapped out their respective strategies. Jensen roved from group to group, acting as coach, trouble-shooter, and monitor—making sure that the topic of conversation was the Revolution and not the weekend dance. "The guy who's sitting there talking to his buddy . . . I'll ask him 'Where's your stuff?'" she explained during one observation. "'I'm doing it tonight,' he'll say, and I'll say, 'Well, *start it now!*'"

But making sure that students stay on task is only one part of Jensen's job. She is a walking encyclopedia, card catalogue, and archive, issuing page numbers, suggestions, and hints at a dizzying pace:[23] "Look at the Declaration of the Virginia Legislature on page 42"[24]; "Did you read what Bailey says about the Proclamation of 1763?"[25]; "Make sure you look at the chart for the real value in terms of a day's work of the different stamps in the Stamp Act"[26]; "Read the first chapter by Hofstader, he talks about it."[27] Jensen's knowledge of the historiography of the American Revolution is translated into sources and materials to hand her students. Never, though, is information delivered ready-made; instead, it is always conveyed as suggestions ("See what Bailey says about the British East India Company") or questions ("How does Hacker differ from Jameson on this?"[28]). This is particularly true when Jensen directs students to materials in the Student Handbook. Some sources are carefully excerpted and their meaning is clear. Others are less direct and students have to infer the relevance of, say, Parliamentary acts restricting the production of hats and pig iron in the colonies.[29] "The documents don't say 'this is a loyalist document,' 'this is a rebel document,'" Jensen reminded her students at the beginning of the research days, "Read *all* of them."

The questions that cropped up in the small groups ranged from the factual and conceptual to the mundane—from how long it took in 1770 to sail between Boston and London (about five weeks) to whether the opening statements had to be memorized (they did not). But every so often a student asked a question that could not be answered in a sentence. At the judges' table, where seven students studied selections on jurisprudence, a boy told Jensen that he feared he might be swayed, not by the persuasiveness of his peers' arguments, but by his loyalties to them as friends. Jensen stopped for a moment and thought. Judges, she gently explained, have never existed in a social vacuum. They have always had to rein in their emotions, striving to separate their prejudices from the merits of each case. As Jensen spoke, the students looked at her, nodding their heads. Detecting the spark of recognition, she moved on.

The Verdict

The judges' verdict at the conclusion of the debate was both beginning and end: The verdict ended the debate but began the process by which students made sense of what they had learned. Jensen's pad, her running commentary on students' confusions and insights, became the basis for a debriefing session the day after the debate. She reminded students, who by this time had become entrenched loyalists and rebels, that they were no longer partisans, but people who wanted to understand the complexity of historical choice. To do this, they had to understand all points of view and gain insight into the feelings, beliefs, and ideals that motivate human action. Revisiting the issues of the debate, Jensen clarified lingering misunderstandings and prepared students for the final assignment of the unit: a term paper on the legitimacy of British taxation in which students were to shape, summarize, and lend their own unique signatures to the material they had learned.

Broadly speaking, Elizabeth Jensen's classroom is an anomaly. The textbook does not drive instruction; teacher talk does not drown out student talk; and there are no worksheets. "Point of view" does not mean a canned exercise from the teacher's guide but a powerful psychological process wherein students embrace beliefs not their own and argue them with zest. By engaging in historical empathy, rather than just reading about it, students learned that Tories were not the villains depicted in textbooks, but ordinary people who saw their world differently from their rebel neighbors.[30] Sometimes one could even see this learning taking place—quizzical looks turning into "ahas" of recognition, perplexed brows becoming radiant smiles. At the end of the debate, one girl stared at the ceiling, dazed. Slowly, she begin to nod her head. "You know," she muttered to no one in particular, "we could've all been like Canada."

We interpret comments such as this one as powerful evidence of learning. According to Ference Marton and his colleagues, learning entails "a qualitative change in someone's conception of a phenomenon or of a certain aspect of reality. It is a distinct change in how that phenomenon is perceived, how it is understood and what meaning it carries for the learner" (Johansson, Marton, & Svensson, 1985, p. 235). The realization that, had the loyalists prevailed, Queen Elizabeth would appear on our stamps, as well as those of our northern neighbors, does not come easily to adolescents who grow up during an era when America, not Britain, is the dominant world power.

Often a dichotomy is posed between teaching for depth and teaching for breadth. At first glance, it might seem that spending two weeks preparing for, engaging in, and reflecting upon a debate about the legitimacy of taxation is an exceedingly long time given the material that must be covered in a U.S. history course. But the notion that students miss out on content if teachers choose to dig deeply rather than cast a wide net is false. Facts are learned in Jensen's class but in a way qualitatively different from that documented in studies of traditional social studies classes. The Tea Act, the Quebec Act, Salutary Neglect, the Nonimportation Agreements—these are not a list of acts and facts handed to students with the promise that they will be useful, someday. In Jensen's class, students first become *intrigued by a problem* and learn facts and concepts in the service of solving it.

The judges' decision at the end of the debate stunned the class. From no one being willing to take up the loyalists' cause, the debate ended in their victory: The American colonies did not sever ties to England, but reaffirmed them. Notions that students took for granted—that the colonists were oppressed by a government that wanted to rob them of their last shilling—were called into question. As students waited for the final seconds before the bell, the final speaker for the loyalists could not believe the judges' verdict. Puzzled, he turned to his teacher and asked: "Why is it that, like, in the seventh grade all you hear about is that all of these colonists all of a sudden were revolting and the British were running in mass terror. How come we're never told about this stuff?" Nodding her head as he spoke, Jensen said, "I'd like to know that too."

The Visible Teacher

In a high school about 20 minutes away from Jensen's, we enter another history class. The school looks much the same—similar graffiti, the same shabby exterior, a similar mixture of faces. John Price, a man in his early forties, paces between the blackboard, his students, and the center of a horseshoe formation of desks. He is in the middle of a discussion of the Intolerable Acts:[31]

> Price: In fact, these series of laws are called by Mr. Jordan[32] what?
> Jim: Intolerable Acts.
> Price: *Intolerable Acts! Intolerable*! We can't stand them! If you were to read an English history book, would they call these laws the *Intolerable* Acts?!
> Students: (In unison) No!
> Price: No! I don't know what they would call them but they might call them something like "The Laws Essential to Establishing Law and Order in Boston." You see? Because they see it differently. They see tea being lost. They see private property being destroyed and, in fact, what we are going to do today is look at the results of the Intolerable Acts.

The British *do* send soldiers. Sam Adams is *cheering* all this![33] He's *loving* it! Now the British are doing *exactly* what he wanted. We have already had the Boston Massacre, things calmed down, now they are heating up again thanks to mistakes made by the British and all we need now is an incident to set this whole thing off once again. Now, there was another *triggering* event[34] and I am going to have you read about what actually set it off. And the way that we are going to do this is that we are going to read two newspaper accounts that were written back in 1775. So let me pass them out to you. Take one and pass them along. Pass them quickly as you can, they're all the same . . . This is a newspaper account describing what happened in Lexington on the 19th of April, 1775. And because the language is old to our ears, 200 years old, I'm going to read with you the first paragraph to get you started on those. Listen to the sound of the language. "Last Wednesday, the 19th of April," says the reporter, "the troops of his Britannic majesty." Who is that?

Cindy:	The King.
Price:	The King. So what troops are we talking about?
Students:	British troops.
Price:	British troops. "Commenced hostilities upon the people of this province." What is this province?
Henry:	Boston.
Price:	Boston isn't the province.
Lawrence:	Lexington.
Price:	Lexington isn't the province.
Mark:	Massachusetts.
Price:	Massachusetts is a province. Alright now. "They commenced hostilities upon the people of Massachusetts attended with circumstances of cruelty, not less brutal than our venerable ancestors received from the vilest savages of the wilderness." That's a fancy way of saying that's—what did the British troops do?
Isabel:	They treated them as badly as the Indians had treated them.
Price:	Treated their ancestors on the frontier. In other words, they behaved like savages. "The particulars," that is, the details, "relative to this interesting event, by which we are involved in all the horrors of a civil war, we have tried, endeavored to collect as well as the present confused state of affairs will admit." That's quite a mouthful but in essence what he is saying is, "all hell has broken loose in Lexington, it's like a civil war." What's a civil war?
Susie:	A war inside one place.
Price:	Alright. Brothers fighting brothers. It's a war between people of the same country. And, in this case, he is talking about a war between Englishmen, between Englishmen from England and Englishmen who have been transplanted here. What we call Americans. Now, as you read this, I would like you to look first, before you start the article now, on the front board. And before we begin this, I want

to make sure that you understand the difference between a *fact* and an *opinion*. It is a very important skill for you to develop when you are reading something and trying to decide whether it is the truth or not. So I'd like anyone in here to make any kind of statement of fact that comes to mind. Well, if you want you can make it the American Revolution, the colonies. What *facts* do we know about the American colonies. Give me any fact.

The exchange between Price and his students takes fewer than five minutes. He dominates the conversation, uttering 770 words compared to the 26 words that a subset of his students contribute. Indeed, he has said more in these five minutes than Jensen did during the entire three days of debate. A casual observer peering into Price's classroom door might claim to have seen what Goodlad and other researchers have observed—teacher dominated whole-group instruction, with activities centered on the teacher's questions and explanations.

But there is something that makes this class different from those described by researchers. There is electricity in the air. Students lean forward in their seats, ask thoughtful and stimulating questions, and stay in the room to continue discussions after the bell has rung. Price is pure energy—laughing, pacing the room, bantering with students, gesturing excitedly. No ordinary teacher, John Price is a master performer who has seized the collective imagination of 35 adolescents, and led them on an expedition into the past.

As this journey continues, the students' voices emerge, although Price's remains dominant:

Price: Give me any fact.
Jerry: There were 13 of them.
Price: There were 13 colonies. That is a *factual* statement.
Tom: They were British citizens.
Price: They were former Englishmen a lot of them. And if we could do a study and find out how many people had come from England, how many were enslaved Africans, how many came from France, we could find out, couldn't we? It's a *factual* statement. What's another factual statement? Our town has a population of 100,000 and it is less in the summertime. Could we go out and measure and find out whether that fact was true?
Tom: Yes.
Price: Then that's a factual statement. You see? Now, I may have my facts wrong but look at the difference. The college students who aren't here in the summertime should not be allowed to vote in elections in our city.
Jenny: Opinion.
Price: It's an opinion, isn't it? And my reason would be because they don't live here all year round, they are only here to study, they shouldn't

be voting on the schools here and all the things that affect people who live here all year round and have families here and so forth. But it's an opinion, isn't it? And the tip-off is the word "should." If anyone ever says to you, uses the word "should," you know they're expressing an opinion. Here's another one. "A civil war is occurring in South Africa." Fact or opinion?

Terry: Fact.

Price: Fact. We'd have to define civil war, and if we used the definition we just used here, there is a civil war going on and every night on TV you can usually see an example of a Black South African fighting a Black South African or a Black South African fighting a White South African police officer. But there is no doubt that there is a kind of civil war going on there. Factual statement. Now, try this one. Americans should not invest in companies that do business in South Africa.

Students: (In unison) Opinion!

Price: Opinion and the "should" tipped you off. Now, what if I put it this way though. It is wrong for Americans to buy any products made in South Africa.

Students: (In unison) Opinion!

Price: Opinion, but the word should isn't in there but it's implied, isn't it? I might as well have said should because I am saying it's wrong. So statements having to do with whether it's right or wrong are matters of opinion. Statements that can be verified by doing some research and calculating are more what we call factual statements. So, as you read this article, which is a newspaper report back in 1775 of what happened in Lexington, I want you to write down any statements of opinion that you find in the article.

After this introductory discussion, Price directs students to read the first newspaper account. While they read, they are to look for evidence to answer the questions he has put on the board:

1. List statements of opinion.
2. Give examples of how the British troops are portrayed.
3. How could this story influence the Revolution?
4. Is this an English or American newspaper?

Students work quietly, independently or with a partner, while Price walks around the room answering questions. After 10 minutes, the class resumes when Jenny asks, "Who wrote this?":

Price: Well, who does it look like wrote this?

Jenny: A colonist.

Price: Looks like its an American newspaper, doesn't it? Because it looks like wherever you read here, you've got the British are the bad, evil *savages*, comparing them with the Indians, right? And the Americans, how are *they* described?

Jenny: Sweet.

Price: Anything else?

Jenny: Courageous.

Price: *Heroic.* They're *courageous*, standing fast. In fact, isn't there a phrase there somewhere about how they are *defenders* of *liberty*?! Have you come across that one? So, I think we can conclude that this is an American reporter. . .

Mark: (Interrupting) So, half of this is going to be opinion!

Price: Well, *where* is it though?

Mark: Well, they make a statement, any statement about the British is going to be opinion.

Price: Okay, but if they say the British. . . "In Lexington, the enemy set fire to Deacon Joseph Loring's house and barn. They also set fire to part of Mrs. B's house and shop and Mr. Joshua Bond's house and shop which were . . . They also set fire to several houses." Those are all factual statements . . . By the way, you are doing something that a lot of colonists couldn't do, namely, read an article. See, what would happen is when a newspaper was written, people couldn't read, and there were lots of them, [they] would gather in a public meeting house, often it was a tavern where they would serve liquor, in fact, [the] guys who end up shooting at the British soldiers were in such a meetinghouse.[35] In fact, there were a lot of meetings going on when the British closed down Boston and groups were formed that would come together, very suddenly.

The discussion continues for another four minutes. Price then moves the discussion toward the issue of motive:

Price: See how carefully this is written to create a mood? And so, how would *you* respond then to the third question here? How could this news story influence the Revolution? Who was going to read it?

Mark: It could make them all hyped up.

Price: It was going to hype people up. It's adding gasoline to the fire. It's making it worse. Can you imagine that this guy was maybe the friend of someone or himself was a member of the Sons of Liberty? Trying to sway those people who are sitting on the fence and don't want to get involved?

The conversation lasts a while longer but ventually Price directs students to the second part of the assignment, which involves reading another newspaper account and responding to a similar set of questions. This second account comes from *The London Gazette*, and after another close reading of the text,

Price discusses with his students how the author's point of view influenced this second, vastly different characterization of the Battle of Lexington and Concord.

Examining the Visible Teacher

Teaching has sometimes been compared to acting, and John Price is an actor *par excellence*—simultaneously sensitive to his audience and a master at using his body to communicate. He is keenly aware of his audience, asking them questions they can answer, relating the day's lesson to what they already know, pushing them to look for evidence to support their claims. Price knows that his manner of teaching grabs students' attention—he even calls it his "lion-taming act":

> I am always saying to myself that part of why I became really adept at lecturing and doing this stuff was that I had a lion-taming act back in the late 60s, in the early days of integration. You either got the whole group's attention and you kept them interested in something or you had [fighting] going on constantly. The fighting was . . . difficult to control . . . So the way I did it was just bowl them over with interesting stuff so that they are sitting there with their mouths open and they don't have time to be clawing away at each other. And that was a survival technique that I developed. Over the years, of course, I have loosened it up.

Though Price may be an actor, he writes and delivers his own lines. He has no formal script, and he does not plan meticulously. Although Price no longer spends much time preparing for his classes, he recounts that, as a young teacher, he spent long hours planning for his classes. When asked what advice he would offer a new teacher, he replied, "If you haven't thought it through, it's going to be a mess." Elaborating on this, he explained:

> Well, first of all, I would tell him that planning is everything. The game is won or lost by the time you go into the classroom. I mean, it's over if you just walk in there cold . . . Now the reason why I can get away with a lot of what I do is that the planning is in there (pointing to his head). It's programmed in the memory.

Nor does Price use the textbook as a guide. Although several researchers (e.g, Wiley & Race, 1977) have found that textbooks exert tremendous influence on the enacted curriculum, Price treats the textbook as Jensen does—it is but one of several resources students draw upon. Class time is often devoted to the "gaps" in textbooks: "I like to devote *class* time to discussing, and really getting into the nuances and the interesting aspects of history—some of the stuff that Jordan has to leave out." Although they do not rely heavily on textbooks as sources of information, both Price and Jensen use other sources in their teaching and thinking, as evidenced in the plethora of documents Jensen provided her students for their debate. Price carries with him a notebook filled with tidbits of information he has collected over time—how many British were injured and killed at Lexington and Concord; what Mao Tse Tung most admired about George Washington; notes about Tom Paine's father, a corsetmaker. Prior to the beginning of class, Price skims his notes, reminding himself of important details he wants to tell his students.

When the bell rings and Price begins talking, he is on stage—responding to student questions and concerns, using analogies and examples spontaneously generated to illustrate his points. While discussing the nature of civil war, he reminded students of events in South Africa, using graphic examples of the violence students hear about in the news to demonstrate the horror of war. Although examples and analogies such as these appear to be spontaneous choices dependent on serendipitous events (such as the newspaper Price read the previous evening or a student's comment), in some important ways there is nothing at all spontaneous about his selections. Like Jensen, Price has a clear sense of where he is headed:

> I have in mind pretty much where I'm going . . . If I'm going to lecture, of course, I have pretty much the timing down—I know how much time I want to devote to the Navigation Act. I have the basic concepts I want to get across with a reminder to me of some of the examples . . . All those things I deliberately do; I know what's coming in the future. Those things are thought out, they are not spontaneous because I know I'm going to draw on them later. But *when* they come up, I'm not sure. I couldn't tell you what day they're going to come up.

Price, like Jensen, has a sense of where he is taking his class. Just as Jensen laid the groundwork for the ratification of the Constitution by introducing her students to eighteenth-century views of man in the year's first unit, Price introduces organizing frameworks and concepts early on in the school year, thus enabling his students to cull through the information presented to them in class and in texts, and sort the wheat from the chaff.

Setting the Stage

While his students did not engage in "research days" like Jensen's students did, Price has spent as much time setting the stage for this class as Jensen did in hers. To talk about the Intolerable Acts, he had to introduce the Townshend Acts,[36] as well as the Gaspee incident,[37] Sam Adams, and the Committees of Correspondence.[38] He also introduced an adapted model of revolution that he has taken from the work of Crane Brinton:[39]

> The way I want students to see it, so they'll remember it, is I want them to approach it from the standpoint of certain elements of revolution that are necessarily present in all revolutions. So that when they come across revolutions in the future, they'll have some signposts to look for. And so I took Crane Brinton's model for revolution and applied it. We spent a great deal of time looking at the complaints that the colonists had regarding England: enforcement of the Navigation Acts, searches and seizures, the taxation issue, and so forth. And those I labelled "grievances." So that all the time we're studying the Revolution, they are listing these complaints, and it's a term that I began with in Bacon's Rebellion[40]—grievances—they know what that word means. The second thing they look for is the presence of leaders so that when I start talking about Sam Adams or they're reading about John Hancock or the others, the Sons of Liberty and so forth, that's another signpost. You have to have someone to organize, someone to express the grievances. The third thing I have them look for is hope for success. Are there enough colonists really convinced that something's going to come of all of this? Because they're not going to put their rear ends out on the line unless they think there is a real chance for change.

Once he introduced Brinton's model and its terminology, Price used it to organize new material he presented, as in the case of describing Lexington and Concord as a "triggering event." Price uses models like Brinton's for several reasons: He wants students to organize the material they encounter in some coherent framework; he wants to help students read for understanding and he believes that models and frames help guide their reading of text; and he wants students to see connections between events and individuals, searching for motive and causation, and observing how history "unfolds." His goals reflect his vision of teaching, learning, and subject matter: Teachers need to help students organize the material they encounter; learning history requires more than a superficial reading of the text; and history as a subject to be studied is an intricate web of people and events held together by cause and motive.

But the lesson about Lexington and Concord did not simply build on groundwork Price had already laid; it is in itself new groundwork for a concept he considers critical to the study of American history—point of view:

> The purpose is for them to take some time and look at one of the sparks that struck the American Revolution, which involved the first shots fired. Like the Boston Massacre, there's a question of what really happened, and who started it, and all that sort of thing. One of my secondary purposes is for them to have some understanding of the difference between a factual statement and a statement of opinion. I am also introducing the concept of point of view.

History As Interpretation

Price's students were no more surprised by his questions about the differences between fact and opinion than they were about his use of the term "triggering event." Since the beginning of the semester, Price has pushed students to look for values, opinions, interpretations: "We always start with values. We start with the values and opinions of the authors of the textbook, or the notion, I should say, that they have values that influence what they say and do." This emphasis is based on Price's well-articulated conception of history:

> I want them to know what history really is. That it's not what Mr. Jordan has here in this [text]—that's not history. A collection of human experiences means that it's too complicated for there to be one pat explanation as to what happened. It's his version of it. And there may be a differing version. And that's what makes history so exciting.

Clearly, Price and Jensen hold similar views of the nature of historical knowledge.[41] More importantly, they believe that teaching history means teaching students about the nature of history as a discipline and a way of knowing, as well as acquainting them with the narratives that historians have generated to explain America's past. Price did not begin the year with a conference on the "Nature of Man," but he used other activities to introduce students to the idea that history consists, in large part, of interpretation. Early in the first semester of the school year, Price engaged his students in a series of activities involving the Salem witch trials.[42] Beginning the first class of this unit with a close examination of the textbook's account of the trials, Price used the opportunity to point out to students that their textbook was simply "a set of conclusions drawn by three people regarding what they think must have happened." The rest of the period was spent discussing alternative and quite divergent explanations of the witch trials. With this activity and others, Price reinforced the notion that history involves problem solving, and that historians are "always on the lookout for clues and for motive and for causation." And just as Jensen engaged her students in debate over the legitimacy of taxation, so Price uses the notion of multiple causation—"the complexities of why people do things"—to convey to students "the excitement of what history really is— I don't believe they understand what history really is."

Price is always on the lookout for strategies to help students develop an appreciation for history, particularly a sensitivity to the issue of interpretation. One by-product of our work with Price was how he translated one of the wisdom of practice interviews, the textbook evaluation interview, into a classroom activity. Price described an activity he developed for his class shortly after our textbook interview:

> I decided to have my U.S. history class utilize three different textbooks. I have a group of people and they did research on the authors and found out as much about them as they could. Then, when we look at the Boston Massacre, I'll say, "Alright, I want a brief report from you people, you Boorstin people. What does

he have to say about it? What happened there at the Boston Massacre? Then we'll look at what Jordan says. Then we'll look at another and compare. I think it's important for them to understand that history is not what is in between the covers of those books . . . The nice thing about having the three textbooks, and having me give my version, is that we have this better grasp of what history really is. Where did he get his evidence for that I wonder? And how come this version is so different from this one? And then you get into the values of the author. What are their experiences? What are their ages?

For Price, as for Jensen, motivating students is essential to their work—and both teachers use the *subject matter* to stimulate student thinking and engagement with the material.

While Price wants his students to appreciate and recognize the interpretative nature of history, he is not interested in making his students "little historians." He acknowledges that the school expects that he will teach his students a certain amount of factual information, information he values because it provides his students with a sense of rootedness. Price is well aware of the fact that in a survey course he cannot do justice to both the content of history and the processes used by historians to reconstruct it:

> When I say that I don't want to make them little historians, what I mean is that I don't think we can overemphasize the process that historians go through. In other words, I'm seeking a balance between their understanding of the potential excitement of how historians do their work, and on the other hand, I fully understand where history is as a priority [in this school]. So *I've got to get to the exciting conclusions.* . . . My mission . . . is to really get them excited about some of the characters along the way so that they have some interest in the past. Second, for them to realize that there is a real excitement in how this information was discovered . . . Those are the two things I constantly have in mind.

Examining the Exciting Conclusions

Like Jensen, Price is known as a "hard teacher," one who pushes students harder than they have been pushed before. Unlike Jensen's class, this class is not an honors section; instead, it consists of students who have opted to enroll in Price's U.S. history class because of his reputation as a fine teacher. Students know that they are expected to work hard and that U.S. history is serious business:

> I think that the students have a sense that I don't want to waste their time and that, therefore, they are important. And that we're there to do a job and it's going to be done right. That I will not deal with interruptions and the students look and say, "Wow! Every minute counts in here."

But pushing in this class is not equivalent to the memorization of names, dates, and events that characterizes so many other history classes. True, conversations during class periods are replete with names and events, but the people Price introduces are not the lifeless figures of textbooks—they are living, breathing, feeling human beings complete with idiosyncrasies and foibles. Sam Adams, while a brilliant propagandist and the "Penman of the Revolution," was a shabby dresser who had a new suit bought for him by the Sons of Liberty before he had to visit another colony to represent their concerns. John Hancock resented the Tea Act not so much because it violated his rights as a British citizen but because it threatened his livelihood as a merchant who traded tea. Men and women in Price's history class had motives—some personal, some political—and history must be viewed through the prism of such motives.

By making the characters in his class real, Price engages his students in thinking about the actions of those characters: Once he has introduced them to the people in the story, his students are anxious to hear the tale of how those individuals made history. But the stories Price tells are not finished; they are not closed books with beginnings, middles, and ends. Price emphasizes that historians present *accounts* of events, not the events themselves. Students learn about the battles of Lexington and Concord but they see them from both the British and the American perspective. They learn about the Salem witch trials but they also find out that recent historiography has produced interpretations that differ from those presented by the authors of their textbook. They learn that, from the British point of view, the Intolerable Acts were not "intolerable" but quite reasonable. Conclusions *are* exciting in Price's class, for history is not a dusty and dated collection of people and places. Instead, history is an anthology of stories, told by people with differing values and commitments, many of whom cannot even agree on the story line.

INVISIBLE AND VISIBLE TEACHING: DIFFERENCES AND SIMILARITIES

The juxtaposition of Price and Jensen offers a study in contrasts. Watching Price, we see what Cuban (1982) has called "persistent instruction"—whole group recitation with teacher at the center, leading discussions, calling on students, and writing key phrases on the blackboard. Jensen's classroom, on the other hand, departs from the traditional—cooperative small groups replace frontal teaching; student debate and presentation overshadow teacher recitation; and the teacher's voice, issuing instructions and dispensing information, is, for the most part, mute.

But while both of these teachers have markedly different styles and systems of classroom organization, this variation seemed to affect students in ways more similar than different. In both classrooms, the issues of history spilled over neat 50-minute time blocks and continued to dominate discussions well after bells had rung. As students put away their books and left for their next class, we heard them comment not about the Friday night dance or basketball game, but about virtual representation and triggering events. In both rooms, the atmosphere sizzled with ideas.

What must Jensen and Price know in order to create such environments? Clearly both teachers are skilled at organizing classrooms and conveying clear goals to students. But beyond that, these two teachers are masters in their subject matter. Bacon's Rebellion, James Otis, Sam Adams, George Grenville, the Navigation Acts, the Quartering Act—these and countless other bits of information form tightly organized networks of facts stored in each teacher's mind. Both are also deeply familiar with the broader conceptual and theoretical issues of the period. They can talk at length about virtual representation, the difference between internal and external taxation, mercantilism, salutary neglect, natural rights, and so on. But in order to make sense of this information, each teacher possesses a more general body of knowledge that lends structure to this information and makes it cohere. So, for example, Price makes comparisons between colonial America and contemporary South Africa drawing on a theoretical model of revolution borrowed from Crane Brinton. Jensen makes sense of the complex and often contradictory evidence of the colonial period by her acquaintance with its historiography—the interpretations of Beard, Jameson, Hacker, Namier, and others. For both teachers, these broader and more general interpretive frameworks infuse detail with meaning. To them, history is not an endless parade of names and dates, but an intriguing story filled with discernible patterns and trends.

A Vision of History

There are striking similarities in the orientation of each teacher to the subject matter they teach. Both teachers see history as a human construction, an enterprise in which people try to solve a puzzle to which some pieces are faded, others distorted beyond recognition, and still others lost forever to the dust of time. We can know certain facts about people, events, and deeds, Jensen and Price assure their students, but the moment we turn to questions of significance—of why something happened versus the mere fact of its happening—history becomes an act of judgment. And in this process, the prior commitments historians bring to their evidence often loom as large as the evidence itself.

These commitments guide the act of interpretation. That the British passed a series of laws closing the Port of Boston and quartering troops in private homes can be established from several sources. But whether we regard these laws as "intolerable," as Price tells his students, or "as measures essential to establishing law and order in Boston" rests on something evidence alone cannot disclose. Similarly, as Jensen explains, whether we see virtual representation as an enterprise whereby lawmakers transcend narrow interests to embrace the interests of the commonweal, or whether we view it as an apology for disenfranchising entire populations, depends on how we read the evidence, which in turn rests on our commitments, convictions, and beliefs.

In many history classrooms, the textbook arbitrates such questions, sifting the evidence for students, never alluding that interpretation has come into play. While American history textbooks have come under increasing criticism of late (FitzGerald, 1979; Larkins, Hawkins, & Gilmore, 1987; Sewall, 1988), these complaints reiterate points made by Schrag (1967, p. 74) more than 20 years ago:

> History textbooks are bad, not because they are too biased, but because their biases are concealed by the tone. History texts are written as if their authors did not exist at all, as if they were simply the instruments of a heavenly intelligence transcribing official truths. The tone of the textbook is the tone of a disembodied voice speaking in passive sentences; it fosters the widespread confusion that the text *is* history, not simply a human construct composed of selected data, interpretations, and opinions.

Crismore (1984) provided empirical documentation of Schrag's characterization. In a study comparing history textbooks to academic and popular historical writing, she found that "metadiscourse," or indications of judgment, emphasis, and uncertainty, were frequently used in historical writing but virtually absent in conventional textbooks.

But textbooks in these two classrooms filled a far different role. Sometimes Bailey and Kennedy's (1983) *American Pageant* and Winthrop Jordan's (1985) *The Americans* entered the fray of conflicting interpretations; at other times, they acted as foils to teachers' favored interpretations; and at other times, they served as resources to help students grasp the story line of history. As "accounts" rather than facsimiles of the past, textbooks enriched but did not determine students' understanding.

The Representation of Subject Matter

Working within their visions of history and teaching, Jensen and Price rendered their knowledge into forms accessible to a diverse group of adolescents. In transforming their knowledge for teaching, Jensen and Price created a wide variety of representations of subject matter—examples, analogies, demonstrations, simulations, stories, role plays, and debates. Though diverse, all of these representations shared one feature: Each attempted to build a bridge between the sophisticated understanding of the teacher and the developing understanding of the student.

Creating a representation is an act of pedagogical reasoning. Teachers must first turn inward to comprehend and ponder the key ideas, events, concepts, and interpretations of their discipline. But in fashioning representations, teachers must also turn outward. They must try, as it were, to think themselves into the minds of students who lack the depth of understanding they, as teachers, possess. Martin Buber (1965, p. 100) has called this the "process of inclusion."

An instructional representation emerges as the product of these two processes—the comprehension of content and the understanding of the needs, motivations, and abilities of learners. The difficulty of this process is evident from the many ways it can fail. At one extreme, teachers always risk *misrepresenting* content by simplifying it to the point where it bears little resemblance to its disciplinary referent. At the other extreme, overly ambitious representations may add new layers of complexity to already troublesome topics. The goal for Jensen and Price, as well as for all teachers, is to craft representations that allow students to glimpse the complexity of subject matter without becoming overwhelmed by it.

When we look carefully at the representations used in these two classrooms, we see that they take different forms and serve different purposes. One way to think about instructional representations[43] is to classify them into two types. *Epistemological representations* model the ways of knowing in a given domain, exemplifying how knowledge is constructed and inquiry pursued. While specific content is always used in crafting epistemological representations, their implications extend beyond the particularities of content and bear on the issues pertinent to the entire discipline. *Contextual representations*, on the other hand, are narrower in scope. They represent specific concepts, ideas, and events that, while bearing on other contexts, are rooted in a specific time and place. We should note, though, that the designation of a representation as epistemological or contextual is not mutually exclusive. Indeed, some of the most powerful representations alternate between both levels simultaneously.[44]

Price's lesson on historical perspective at the Battle of Lexington offers a prime example of an epistemological representation. In selecting two contradictory newspaper reports of the conflict, one appearing in the *London Gazette* and the other in a Boston weekly, Price devoted about 15 minutes of class time to reading less than a page of text. In the process, he helped students see how words create images and how language, never neutral, subtly influences our understanding of history. The colonists' portrayal of their treatment by the British as "not less brutal than our venerable ancestors received from the vilest savages of the wilderness" is not merely a report on the events at Lexington, but an account designed to stir passions and sway opinions.

In cognitively modeling the close analysis of texts, Price represents a style of reading that lies at the heart of historical inquiry. As Willcox (1966, p. 25) has noted, we know history through witnesses and their documents, and are "as dependent on their eyes and emotions as we are on their pens." Willcox does not mean we must embrace the bias of historical documents, but explains that in order to account for bias we must first understand it. To do this, readers must place documents on the witness stand, extorting from them information they have withheld or slanted to their advantage. This way of reading forces students to consider words not merely as conveyors of information but as tools with polemical and rhetorical intent. While relevant to the particular context of Lexington, Price's lesson extends far beyond it, for all texts have subtexts. To take documents at face value, to read them without considering their larger, if less visible, social purposes is often to miss what is most important about them.

We should note that this representation functions at a contextual level as well. Price chooses to represent the close reading of texts not with any documents, but with texts describing the opening volley of the American Revolution, the famed "shot heard round the world" of Emerson's poem. Price culled documents from an extensive body of primary and secondary source materials on Lexington and Concord (French, 1925; Murdock, 1925; Tourtellot, 1963), and his final selection was not random but carefully designed to show students that their understanding of April 19, 1775, is very much a function of the perspective they adopt. After sifting through the accounts of the battle, most historians reach the same conclusion as Charles Beard and Mary Beard (1930, p. 43): "Whose hand kindled the flame is to this hour one of the mysteries of military romance." Also, we should note that this representation serves a second epistemological function. While the particular documents chosen by Price represent the limitations of our knowledge about Lexington, they also represent the fundamental indeterminacy of historical knowledge. Historians can amass data to support their interpretations of Lexington, but certainty, in this and countless other instances, remains elusive.

Jensen's debate on the legitimacy of taxation is an epistemological representation modeling the discourse of historiography. On one hand, loyalists read a set of documents favorable to the "imperial school" of historians, which locates the North American conflict within the larger context of British imperial policy.[45] Rebels, on the other hand, base their arguments on documents reflecting the "traditionalist" or "Whig" thread in American historiography, which casts the Revolution as a reaction to the tyranny of an oppressive British monarch.[46] Through this activity, students learn about the actual circumstances of the American Revolution as they learn to interpret and impute meaning to those circumstances.

Had Jensen's debate ended with the judges' decision, it would have been an impoverished representation of the language and spirit of historiography. However, the judges' verdict was but a way station to the finale of the unit: an integrative essay in which all students—loyalist, rebel, and judge—sifted through and synthesized the many perspectives they encountered. In so doing, Jensen's students pursued what many prominent historians see as the essence of historical work: "The attempt to make a general synthesis of all major factors

. . . is peculiar to historical studies. . . . The conscientious historian . . . never permits himself to forget the final goal, namely, comprehensive synthesis" (Second Committee on History of the Social Science Research Council, cited in Mink, 1987, p. 40).

Jensen's debate functions as a contextual representation as well. The attitude displayed by Jensen's students at the beginning of the research days is not uncommon—the loyalist position was ridiculed (recall that Jensen had to cajole her students into taking the role of loyalist), and students failed to see how any rational person could have resisted the rebels' call to arms. By studying documents favorable to the Tory position, students came to see that both sides had merit and that the issues were anything but simple. Through this complicated and finely orchestrated representation of subject matter, students learned to appreciate the deep divisions in the colonial population on the eve of the Revolution. Loyalists came to be viewed not as cowards or reactionaries but as "good Americans," much in the same way that Wallace Brown (1969) has portrayed them in his classic study of the American Tory.

The History Teacher and the Historian

In suggesting that a central activity for Jensen and Price is the representation of subject matter, we are also suggesting that the goals of the history teacher differ from those of the historian. The lodestar for historians is the discipline of history. As professionals, they seek to broaden that discipline through the creation and discovery of new knowledge, through the formulation of novel interpretations or the refutation of old ones. Teachers of history pursue other goals. Their aim is not to create new knowledge in the discipline but to create new understanding in the minds of learners. Unlike the historian, who only has to face inward toward the discipline, the teacher of history must face inward *and* outward, being at once deeply familiar with the content of the discipline while never forgetting that the goal of this understanding is to foster it in others. These different perspectives become abundantly clear when we consider how the historian and the history teacher view the raw material of historical inquiry, documentary evidence.

When historians designate a particular document as "good," that adjective refers to the intrinsic qualities of the document as a piece of evidence—its authenticity, the degree to which it corroborates other documents or reveals new information, and the direction in which it pushes research. But when we asked Jensen and Price about "good documents," these issues became background to other considerations: Is the language accessible to adolescents? Is the subject vivid and memorable? Is there "human interest" in the document? Can the document be excerpted without distorting its meaning? Can it be related to topics already covered in the curriculum? In neither class did teachers send students to ferret out documents from an archive or teach them to engage in "external criticism" (the process of ascertaining the authenticity of documents), two activities essential to the working historian. Indeed, the documents students confronted had already been carefully selected, excerpted, and in some cases, edited by their teachers.[47] For the history teacher, then, the question of a document's goodness relates both to its qualities as historical artifact and to its qualities as a tool for teaching history. It is precisely in this meeting of subject matter and pedagogy, an interface Shulman (1986b) has called *pedagogical content knowledge*, that we see the expertise of these teachers most clearly.

EXPERTISE IN THE TEACHING OF HISTORY

In pondering the nature of expertise in the teaching of history, we recognize that this chapter marks the beginning of that enterprise, not the end. There is much yet to understand. What expert teachers know and believe about history, what they know and believe about teaching, and what they know and believe about learners are but pieces of a complex set of understandings that comprise the professional knowledge base of teaching. But we have not been completely forthcoming in our rendering of these accounts of Jensen and Price, for we failed to mention several details we see as essential to our characterization of them as expert. In focusing on Jensen's debate and on Price's discussions of Lexington and Concord, we chose not to talk about other classes in which we observed these teachers. We have not described a classroom recitation by Jensen, who, with her thundering voice, seizes hold of students' attention and keeps them spellbound for 50 minutes. Likewise, we have not described Price's government class, run entirely by students who engage in a six-month simulation of Congress, each student playing the role of a legislator, proposing bills and making cloakroom deals, while Price remains invisible.

So we end this chapter with a cautionary note: Knowledge of subject matter is central to teaching but expert knowledge of content is not the singular determinant of good teaching. Just as the history they teach is not static and dull, so Jensen and Price are not unidimensional pedagogues who have learned to do one thing well. Both teachers possess rich and deep understandings of many things, understandings that manifest themselves in the ability to draw from a broad range of pedagogical possibilities. In fact, it may be their very ability to alternate between different modes of teaching that earns them the designation "wise practitioner."

EPILOGUE: COMMENTARY BY PRICE AND JENSEN

All too often the researcher gets the last word: blessing or condemning the teaching observed. But this work is intended to begin a conversation—among researchers *and* teachers—about the nature of professional knowledge in teaching, the role of subject-matter knowledge, and the nature of pedagogical expertise, and any attempts we make to provide closure on these questions might prematurely terminate that conversation. Thus, we end on another note by re-introducing the voices of Jensen and Price as they reflect on and respond to the claims we have made here.

Notes from Elizabeth Jensen

Rarely are public school teachers given the careful scrutiny and evaluation as has been afforded me in this study. I was both privileged and proud to be asked to participate, but the self-knowledge and professional growth I have been able to achieve as a result were most unexpected and rewarding. Frankly, I never believed so much was operating concurrently in my classroom, and for a while I had a hard time accepting that there really was all that met my researcher's eyes.

Perfunctory evaluations performed by an administrator, usually not competent in the subject area, do not serve me in any way. But the experience I gained by daily observation by a competent professional over an entire unit forced me to operate on many levels of consciousness (which are usually unconscious). Why was I doing what I was doing? Why did I respond in that way? What purpose was this question or action serving? How was I dealing with the sleeping student in the corner, the one doing his math homework? Was I conscious of the levels of my questioning strategies? I knew the researcher was going to be concerned about these in a few moments. I felt both exhilarated and exhausted!

My course works for many reasons: careful attention to detail; continuous reevaluation and revision over almost 20 years; dedication to the open-ended scientific mode of inquiry that demands high-level critical thinking—even before it became a buzz-word of the 1980s—and forces students to create their own interpretations of historical events based on their personal evaluations of the best evidence; a conceptual approach; and exciting and involving strategies. It has also been my great fortune to work with a department of experienced, dedicated master teachers who continually collaborate and restructure the courses we teach in light of current student needs and the changing times. This, in my opinion, has been invaluable in maintaining my continued integrity in the classroom.

Notes from John Price

First, the opportunity to look into a mirror and see what is happening in some of my classes was just plain fun. A great deal of what I do is spontaneous in the sense that I have a repertoire of facts, anecdotes, and so on, that I draw upon, but I am never sure when they will come out. Often the choices are triggered by student questions. Sometimes I will move in a particular direction simply because of what I have recently read, which somehow I have related in my mind to my previous knowledge of a particular historical event or person. While for the most part I do not say to myself, "Now here is something that I can relate in such and such a way," the information is filed away. And the connection is made whenever I need to discuss the event or person in class.

This process is somewhat like that used by Hal Holbrook when he did his one man show, *Mark Twain Tonight*. He had memorized whole bodies of material, but when he came out on stage, he was not entirely sure of the perfect order for delivering the lines. When in San Francisco during the awful days of the Vietnam War, he discovered quickly one evening that the audience was very receptive to the anti-war material in his head. He went on to make much more use of these lines than he had originally intended.

While I certainly employ this kind of flexibility, my choices are related less to the way in which the material is "playing" to that particular class, and more to student questions that trigger a train of thought that I continuously modify and update. This leads me to a clarification of your comments on my preparation. The statements are accurate, but the impression may be left that I continue to rely on the same old lines, examples, and so forth.

In reality, one of the great joys of teaching history is that as I continue to learn more through my own reading and through seminars and forums, the script changes. While it may not be a formal script, a seriousness is attached to the final determination of what I will present as being my version of what happened. I wrestle continually with the awareness that I may not be completely accurate, and I am constantly seeking new sources and testing the version of history that I am relating to my students. Incidentally, I make my students fully aware of this concern. I might say to them, for example, "I used to go along with a number of historians and most of my colleagues on this floor in portraying President Eisenhower as a relatively uninspiring, detached, mediocre intellect who cared more about reading western novels and playing golf than the hard work of active presidential leadership. I now believe that when I taught about Eisenhower that way, I was quite wrong. Let's look at the work of Professor Fred Greenstein who found some remarkable things about Ike in writing a book called *Hidden Hand Presidency*."

My efforts to improve accuracy have been increased and enhanced, particularly since my involvement in university projects aimed at developing the pedagogical and subject-matter knowledge of high school history teachers. Despite the efforts of such projects, I maintain that the demands of time in the teaching of history at the secondary level make it very much the art of simplifying just to the point that the integrity of the subject matter is not jeopardized.

Some of the most exciting insights that have come to me have occurred during class when I am responding to questions or seeking to present material in a different way because it is clear that my initial approach has not worked. Much of this never makes it into my notebook, which only suggests to me my starting point. One of my measures of success for a particular lesson is the number of new ways that emerged during the lesson to convey the basic points outlined in the notebook. Sometimes the dynamics between students or between a student and me will cause me to leap to a whole new approach in making transitions to anticipated lessons or units.

This, of course, does not happen with every lesson, and the maddening thing for purposes of understanding what is going on is that I can never completely replicate it with another class. However, I am convinced that these successes and insights are stored away and come out in different ways in future classes. An important point here is that, for me, creativity is driven by knowledge of— and my quest for further knowledge of—the subject matter.

Finally, I need to acknowledge that teaching in the way I do exacts a price on me emotionally and physically. Habits that are formed as a part of my acting style reinforce personality characteristics that are an asset in the classroom, but can become irritating at home or among adults outside of school. Sometimes it is hard to turn off school and leave the stage. The process is exhausting. After twenty years of teaching, I've almost concluded that doing it my way is rather like a tennis player who uses far too much wrist in his shots and finds great success in winning. He finds people complimenting him on his game and he gets better and better and better at it. Then one day he comes up with a sore wrist and the doctor forces him to hit the ball in a more orthodox way so that his wrist does not pay such a heavy price. I still hit with too much topspin in my survey history courses, but for two periods during the day and for two-thirds of each semester, I am very much the invisible teacher. Your remarks at the conclusion are therefore important to emphasize and perhaps even to amplify.

ACKNOWLEDGMENTS

Preparation of this chapter was supported by the Teacher Assessment Project, School of Education, Stanford University and by the National Center for Research on Teacher Education, Michigan State University. The Teacher Assessment Project is funded primarily by the Carnegie Corporation of New York. The National Center for Research on Teacher Education is funded by the Office of Educational Research and Improvement, United States Department of Education. The opinions expressed herein are those of the authors and do not necessarily reflect the position, policy, or endorsement of our funding agencies. The authors thank Louette McGraw for her help in data collection for this study.

NOTES

1.   Throughout this chapter we use the terms "history" and "social studies" interchangeably, although we acknowledge that history is only one part of the high school social studies curriculum. We concentrate on American history because it is the mainstay of most high school social studies departments.

2.   The language here is drawn from Todd and Curti (1982), a widely used American history textbook.

3.   We use the term "expert" carefully. Berliner (1986, p. 9) discussed some of the difficulties with discussing expertise in teaching, focusing primarily on the confounding of experience and expertise:

> The problems of studying expertise in pedagogy are harder than in other fields because of the widespread belief that we need to separate expertise from experience and to study how experience changes people without necessarily turning them into experts. This is not easy. Thus the terms "experienced" and "expert" are used throughout this discussion as if they were interchangeable. We know that they are not, but cannot yet untangle them, so we must ask for patience in resolving this situation.

In addition to the confounding of experience and expertise that Berliner notes, one of us (Wilson, 1988) has noted other problems in defining expertise in teaching. Because teaching is complex and multifaceted, teachers can possess expertise along a number of dimensions. One teacher may be a gifted algebra teacher but only a run-of-the-mill geometry teacher. Another may be skilled at teaching children in Palo Alto, but not in New York City. Teaching is a contextualized activity, defined by boundaries of communities and curriculum, subject matter and students. We believe that expert teachers exist, but that their expertise is bounded and situated in the contexts which define teaching.

4.   Furthermore, teachers can be identified as experts for a variety of reasons, including the gain scores of their students, their participation in school life, and their visibility in the community. The relationships between those factors and expertise in instruction are not clear. In our search for expert teachers, we chose to follow a strategy similar to that used by Berliner and his colleagues at the University of Arizona. We elicited nominations from teachers, administrators, and other professionals who had contact with the social studies teachers of the San Francisco Bay area. If teachers were nominated by multiple sources, they were recruited for the study. As with Berliner's work, we too encountered difficulties in pursuit of expert teachers. Wilson (1988) explores some of the problems inherent in such a search.

5.   A parallel set of studies was conducted with a group of elementary teachers. These studies focused on teaching the equivalence of fractions at the elementary school level.

6.   The variety of perspectives from which to view teaching is evident in the intriguing collection of papers by Morine-Dershimer, Rosenshine, Shuy, Eisner, Delamont, Bennett, and Peterson, Kromrey, Micerri, and Smith in a special issue of *Teaching & Teacher Education* (1987).

7.   The data for the history wisdom of practice research were collected by a group of researchers at Stanford University including Deborah Kerdeman, Louette McGraw, Lawrence Hyink, and the authors.

8.   The textbook selections, all relating to the American Revolution, were drawn from Bailey and Kennedy's (1983) *American Pageant*, Todd and Curti's (1982) *Rise of the American Nation*. Norton et al.'s (1986) *A People and a Nation*, Abraham and Pfeffer's (1984) *Enjoying American History*, and Boorstin and Kelley's (1983) *A History of the United States*. The five different books represent a wide range of different historical and pedagogical approaches.

9.   We also took ethnographic field notes to augment the audiotape data, noting such features as the layout of the classroom and the nonverbal interaction patterns between teachers and students.

10. This and all subsequent proper names are pseudonyms.

11. This student quotes from the textbook used in Jensen's class, Bailey and Kennedy (1983).

12. The French and Indian War was the American counterpart of the Seven Years' War in Europe, the fourth and decisive war between England and France for mastery of commercial and colonial supremacy. Hostilities in North America officially began in 1754 when colonists clashed with French forces over territory and control in the Ohio Valley. Although the French were initially victorious, the British eventually prevailed, and the Treaty of Paris (1763) marked the removal of France as a significant colonial power in North America.

13. The speaker quotes Franklin from a document included in the "Student Handbook on Authority," a mimeographed booklet of primary sources that Jensen, with the help of her colleagues, has compiled.

14. On May 30, 1765, the House of Burgesses in Virginia passed a resolution stating that, while recognizing the need to pay taxes to the Crown, they themselves would decide upon the appropriate methods for levying them.

15. Virtual representation, according to Edmund Burke, its most vigorous proponent, was the belief that all Englishmen were represented in Parliament whether they voted for its members or not (most Englishmen, in fact, did not vote). "Parliament," declared Burke, "is a *deliberate* assembly of *one* nation, with *one* interest, that of the whole, where, not local purposes, not local prejudices ought to guide, but the general good, resulting from the general reason of the whole" (cited in Gross, 1976, p. 36). Thomas Whately, an assistant to the British Chancellor of the Exchequer, wrote a pamphlet in which he argued that the colonists were represented in Parliament in the same way as most Englishmen, who could not vote because of property qualifications or because they resided in boroughs that sent no member to Parliament. See Morgan (1956, pp. 18-21) and Wood (1969, pp. 173-180).

16. Both opening statements are excerpts from statements approximately four times in length.

17. In response to the Boston Tea Party, Parliament passed four measures dubbed the "Intolerable Acts" by the colonists. The Boston Port Act closed the port of Boston until retribution was made to the British East India Company for the tea that had been destroyed. The Massachusetts Government Act revised the charter of that province so that the king appointed the governor's council (which was also the upper house of the legislature). Although this practice was already in place in other royal colonies, Massachusetts had been virtually self-governing since its inception. The Administration of Justice Act allowed for government officials, such as customs agents, charged with committing violence or other disturbances to be tried in England rather than face an American jury. The fourth "Intolerable Act" was the Quartering Act which required local officials to provide housing for British troops in towns where there were no barracks.

18. The Sons of Liberty were groups of colonial patriots—laborers, small businessmen, artisans—who initially formed to resist the Stamp Act in cities like New York and Boston. Although they began as secret organizations, they eventually became more public, openly demonstrating against British actions.

19. A few prominent colonists such as James Otis believed that Americans ought to have *actual* representation in Parliament, but Otis's was a minority opinion. Most American leaders recognized that the few representatives allotted to the colonists would be soundly defeated by the rest of Parliament, and their presence would serve to justify whatever acts Parliament passed. With this in mind, the Stamp Act Congress passed the following resolution: "That the People of these Colonies are not, and from their local Circumstances cannot be, represented in the House of Commons in Great Britain." See Morgan (1956, p. 25).

20. The Loyalists are correct here. Only a tenth of the population of Great Britain possessed the franchise, and many of the larger cities, including Birmingham and Manchester, sent no representative to Parliament. This fact was often used by British officials in the war of words with the colonists over representation: "If representation can travel three hundred miles, why not three thousand? If it can jump over rivers and mountains, why cannot it sail over the ocean? If

the towns of Manchester and Birmingham, sending no representatives to Parliament are notwithstanding there represented, why are not the cities of *Albany* and *Boston* equally represented in that assembly? Are they not alike British subjects? Are they Englishmen?" asked Soame Jenyns in his tract, "The Objections to the Taxation of our American Colonies by the Legislature of Great Britain, Briefly Consider'd" (originally published in London, 1765; cited in Wood, 1969, p. 174).

21.   These materials were drawn from an article on teaching the American Revolution that appeared in volume 38 of *Social Education*, 1974.

22.   The familial metaphor was a common one in the colonial world. Gross (1976) notes that colonial magistrates were often referred to as "father" and England as a "tender parent." In his pamphlet, *Common Sense*, Thomas Paine turned this metaphor on its head:

> But Britain is the parent country, say some. Then the more shame upon her conduct. Even brutes do not devour their young . . . the phrase "parent" or "mother country" has been jesuitically adopted by the king and his parasites with a low papistical design of gaining an unfair bias on the credulous weakness of our minds. Europe, and not England, is the parent country of America (Paine, 1776/1953, p. 21).

23.   Jensen has brought many of these reference books from the school's curriculum library and her own personal library. Most of these pamphlets and paperback books are dog-eared after years of use; others from Jensen's own library are new, like the titles she purchased for a summer enrichment course on Constitutional Law. Many of the titles are classics, such as Richard Hofstadter's (1971) *America at 1750* and Edmund Morgan's (1965) anthology, *The American Revolution: Two Centuries of Interpretation*. There are also anthologies of primary sources, like Vaughan's (1967) *America Before the Revolution 1725-1775*; as well as material specifically geared to high school juniors, like a mimeographed pamphlet titled *What Were the Causes of the American Revolution?*

24.   See note 14.

25.   Bailey refers to Bailey and Kennedy's (1983) textbook, *The American Pageant*. The Proclamation of 1763 was an attempt by Britain to limit colonial expansion to western lands.

26.   This suggestion refers to a chart in the Student Handbook on the value of money in colonial times, listing for instance that a half day's work was equivalent to a shilling in wages, which could buy two pounds of butter, or pay the price of the "Stamp Tax" on a deck of cards.

27.   Here Jensen is referring to Hofstader's (1971) *America at 1750: A Social Portrait*.

28.   Louis M. Hacker and J. Franklin Jameson were two important historians of the American Revolution and are representatives of two different historical schools in Jensen's class. Hacker saw the revolution as an economic movement, while Jameson cast it as chiefly a social movement. Articles by Hacker (1935) and Jameson (1956) were required reading for Jensen's students.

29.   To enforce its policy of mercantilism in the colonies, Parliament passed a series of acts restricting the manufacture of certain goods in America. The Hat Making Act (June 1, 1732) claimed that Americans were using low-paid apprentices to undercut the prices of British hats in other markets. This act made it a crime for "hats or felts, dyed or undyed, finished or unfinished" to be exported from the colonies. Likewise, the Pig Iron Act (April 12, 1750) declared that no factory in American that could "roll, slit, or forge pig iron" would be allowed to operate. For copies of these documents see Commager (1973).

30.   In this way, students come to understand what historians such as Wallace Brown (1969) have argued in *The Good American: The Loyalist in the American Revolution*.

31.   See note 17.

32.   Jordan is the first author of the textbook used in Price's class (Jordan, Greenblatt, & Bowes, 1985). Students and teacher alike refer to Jordan frequently in their discussions, as if they knew him personally.

33.   During class on the previous day, Price discussed Sam Adams and his role as "Penman

of the Revolution." At that time, students discussed the frustrations Adams must have felt after the British backed down as a result of the furor over the Townshend Acts. With approximately a third of the population supporting Britain and a third supporting the rebel cause, the Sons of Liberty hoped that Parliamentary measures like the Townshend Acts would sway more colonists to their side. When the British repealed the acts, the "fencesitters," as Price called them, remained undecided, and Adams instigated the creation of the Committees of Correspondence to keep the flame of revolution alive.

34.   The term "triggering event" is drawn from Crane Brinton's (1952) model for revolution, a framework Price introduced early in the year to help students organize the events leading to the American Revolution.

35.   Here Price refers to the fact that the minutemen first assembled on Lexington Green at about 2 a.m. They waited in the cold for several hours before deciding to go to Buckman Tavern for a warming glass of rum. It was not until daybreak that the British troops marched into Lexington. See Gross (1976) and Tourtellot (1959).

36.   The Townshend Acts (June 29, 1767) imposed a series of taxes on glass, lead, paint, tea, and paper imported to the colonies. The purpose of these taxes was to create £40,000 of new revenue, in part to pay the salaries of colonial governors. These taxes stimulated non-importation measures in many of the colonies, and within a year British exports were cut in half.

37.   The Gaspee was a British warship lent to the customs service to help suppress smuggling in the New England colonies. Reportedly, the ship's captain harassed fishermen in Narragansett Bay. While pursuing a smuggler, the ship went aground and a mob of angry colonists took advantage of the captain's plight by boarding the ship and burning it in retaliation. Rumors circulated that suspects in the affair were to be sent to England for trial.

38.   Founded in Boston by Sam Adams in 1772, the Committees of Correspondence were the outgrowth of the Sons of Liberty. Like the Sons, the Committees were secret organizations for coordinating colonial agitation, and also for facilitating communication between the colonies. In Virginia, Thomas Jefferson and Patrick Henry organized similar committees.

39.   See Brinton (1952).

40.   Bacon's Rebellion was one of the earliest protests against authority in the American colonies. In 1676, seventy years after the founding of Virginia, Nathaniel Bacon led an unauthorized attack against the Susquehannock Indians of Virginia, against the wishes of Governor William Berkeley. This action led to a crisis of leadership and Virginia was split into factions, with most of the poorer frontier farmers supporting Bacon and the more wealthy tidewater farmers supporting Berkeley. Bacon marched into Jamestown to demand that the government protect them from the Indians, and the governor promised changes. But when nothing happened, Bacon marched again, and this time burned Jamestown to the ground. Eleven hundred troops sailed from England to suppress the rebellion, but by the time they arrived, Bacon had died of fever. Without its leader, the rebellion collapsed. For a brief overview, see Cullen (1968).

41.   We do not mean to suggest that there is consensus about "the" nature of historical knowledge, for we agree with Schwab (1961/1978, p. 243) who states:

> Who *knows* the structures of the disciplines? The answer is, *Nobody* . . . First, we must face the fact that, with the possible exception of physics, most disciplines have *several* structures, not one.

42.   Twenty-five people were burned as witches in Salem, Massachusetts in 1692. The early histories of the trials, such as Thomas Hutchinson's in 1750, argued that the accused suffered from physical ailments that affected their imaginations. Modern accounts have interpreted the trials in terms of mass hysteria and collective psychosis (for a summary, see Davidson & Lytle, 1982). The events of Salem have also been interpreted as a control mechanism to suppress women (Demos, 1970). Finally, Boyer and Nissenbaum (1974), in a reexamination of the original

demographic records of Salem, showed that those accused as witches and their accusers lived on the opposite sides of town, and the alleged witches, living far from Salem's center, had threatened to create their own church and hire their own minister. Boyer and Nissenbaum's interpretations, based on these new facts about Salem's dwelling patterns, emphasizes the role of internal village politics and communal strife in accounting for Salem's witch trials.

43.   The word "representation" has been used in a variety of ways both in cognitive psychology and in research on teaching. The term "instructional representation" refers not to mental constructs but to the actual examples, explanations, activities, and demonstrations that teachers use to represent subject matter in their classrooms. For a brief discussion, see Wilson (1988).

44.   Wilson (1988) makes a similar distinction in her discussion of "epistemological" and "informational" aspects of representations.

45.   A short and classic statement of this position can be found in Andrews (1926).

46.   This line of interpretation goes back to the great historians of the nineteenth century. For a concise statement of this position see the excerpt from Bancroft's *History of the United States from the Discovery of the Continent* reprinted in Billias (1965). For an excellent overview of the historiography of the American Revolution, see Wood's (1966) now-classic essay, "Rhetoric and Reality in the American Revolution."

47.   The process of excerpting a primary source document was the focus of a case study emerging from our wisdom of practice research (Kerdeman, 1988). Some of the eighteenth-century documents appearing in Jensen's Student Handbook have been edited to modernize spelling and punctuation.

REFERENCES

Abraham, H., & Pfeffer, I. (1984). *Enjoying American history.* New York: Amsco.

Andrews, C. M. (1926). The American Revolution: An interpretation. *American Historical Review, 31,* 218-232.

Bailey, T. A., & Kennedy, D. M. (1983). *The American pageant: A history of the republic* (7th ed.). Lexington, MA: Heath.

Baxter, M. G., Ferrell, R. H., & Wiltz, J. E. (1964). *The teaching of American history in high schools.* Bloomington, IN: Indiana University Press.

Beard, C. A., & Beard, M. R. (1930). *Rise of the American civilization.* New York: Macmillan.

Berliner, D. C. (1986). In pursuit of the expert pedagogue. *Educational Researcher, 15,* 5-13.

Billias, G. A. (1965). *The American Revolution: How revolutionary was it?* New York: Holt, Rinehart, and Winston.

Boorstin, D. J., & Kelley, B. M. (1983). *A history of the United States.* Lexington, MA: Ginn.

Boyer, P., & Nissenbaum, S. (1974). *Salem possessed: The social origins of witchcraft.* Cambridge, MA: Harvard University Press.

Brinton, C. C. (1952). *The anatomy of a revolution.* Englewood Cliffs, NJ: Prentice-Hall.

Brown, W. (1969). *The good American: The loyalist in the American Revolution.* New York: W. Morrow.

Buber, M. (1965). *Between man and man.* New York: Macmillan.

Christopoulos, J. P., Rohwer, W. D., & Thomas, J. W. (1987). Grade level differences in students' study activities as a function of course characteristics. *Contemporary Educational Psychology, 12,* 303-323.

Clandinin, D. J. (1985). Personal practical knowledge: A study on teachers' classroom images. *Curriculum Inquiry, 15,* 361-385.

Commager, H. S. (1973). *Documents of American history* (9th ed.). New York: Appleton-Century-Crofts.

Connelly, F. M., & Clandinin, D. J. (1985). Personal practical knowledge and the modes of knowing: Relevance for teaching and learning. *Learning and teaching the ways of knowing* (84th Yearbook of the National Society for the Study of Education, pp. 174-198). Chicago: University of Chicago Press.

Crismore, A. (1984). The rhetoric of textbooks: Metadiscourse. *Journal of Curriculum Studies, 16*, 279-296.

Cuban, L. (1982). Persistent instruction: The high school classroom 1900-1980. *Phi Delta Kappan, 64*, 113-118.

Cullen, J. P. (1968). Bacon's rebellion. In R.J. Maddox (Ed.), *Readings in American History* (4th ed., pp. 15-20). Guilford, CT: Dushkin.

Davidson, J. W., & Lytle, M. H. (1982). *After the fact: The art of historical detection* (Vol. 1). New York: Knopf.

deCharms, R. (1976). *Enhancing motivation: Change in the classroom*. New York: Irvington.

Deci, E. L. (1975). *Intrinsic motivation*. New York: Plenum.

Deci, E. L., & Ryan, R. M. (1980). The empirical exploration of intrinsic motivational processes. In L. Berkowitz (Ed.), *Advances in experimental social psychology* (Vol. 13). New York: Academic Press.

Demos, J. (1970). Underlying themes in the witchcraft of seventeenth-century New England. *American Historical Review, 75*, 1311-1326.

Elbaz, F. (1983). *Teacher thinking: A study of practical knowledge*. New York: Nichols.

FitzGerald, F. (1979). *America revised*. Boston: Atlantic Monthly Press.

French, A. (1925). *The day of Concord and Lexington*. Boston: Little, Brown.

Goodlad, J. (1985). *A place called school*. New York: McGraw-Hill.

Gross, R.A. (1976). *The minutemen and their world*. New York: Hill and Wang.

Grossman, P. L., Wilson, S. M., & Shulman, L. S. (1989). Subject matter knowledge of beginning teachers. In M. Reynolds (Ed.), *The knowledge base for beginning teachers*. Washington, DC: American Association of Colleges of Teacher Education.

Gudmundsdottir, S. , Carey, N. C., & Wilson, S. M. (1985). *Role of prior subject matter knowledge in learning to teach social studies* (Knowledge Growth in a Profession Publication Series). Stanford, CA: Stanford University, School of Education.

Gudmundsdottir, S., & Shulman, L. S. (1987). Pedagogical content knowledge in social studies. *Scandinavian Journal of Educational Research, 31*, 59-70.

Hacker, L. M. (1935). The first American Revolution. *Columbia University Quarterly, 27*, 14-29.

Hofstadter, R. (1971). *America at 1750: A social portrait*. New York: Knopf.

Howard, J., & Mendenhall, T. (1982). *Making history come alive*. Washington, DC: Council for Basic Education.

Jameson, J. F. (1956). *The American Revolution considered as a social movement*. Boston: Beacon Press.

Johansson B., Marton, F., & Svensson, L. (1985). An approach to describing learning as change between qualitatively different conceptions. In L. H. T. West and A. L. Pines (Eds.), *Cognitive structure and conceptual change* (pp. 233-257). Orlando, FL: Academic.

Jordan, W. D., Greenblatt, M., & Bowes, J. S. (1985). *The Americans: The history of a people and a nation*. Evanston, IL: McDougal, Littell, & Co.

Kerdeman, D. (1988). *Lessons from the wisdom of practice: Excerpting documentary evidence*. (Teacher Assessment Project Tech. Rep.). Stanford, CA: Stanford University, School of Education.

Larkins, A. G., Hawkins, M. L., & Gilmore, A. (1987). Trivial and noninformative content of elementary social studies: A review of primary texts in four series. *Theory and Research in Social Education, 15*, 299-311.

Merton, R. K. (1947). The self-fulfilling prophecy. *Antioch Review, 34*, 193-210.

Mink, L. O. (1987). The autonomy of historical understanding. In B. Fay, E.O. Golob, & R. T. Vann (Eds.), *Historical imagination*. Ithaca, NY: Cornell University Press.

Morgan, E. S. (1956). *The birth of the republic 1763-1789*. Chicago: University of Chicago Press.

Morgan, E. S. (1965). *The American Revolution: Two centuries of interpretation*. Englewood Cliffs, NJ: Prentice-Hall.

Murdock, H. (1925). *The nineteenth of April 1775*. Boston: Houghton Mifflin.

Norton, M. B., Katzman, D. M., Escott, P. D., Chudacoff, H. P., Paterson, T. G., & Tuttle, W. M., Jr. (1986). *A people and a nation*. Boston, MA: Houghton Mifflin.

Paine, T. (1776/1953). Common sense. In N. F. Adams (Ed.), *Common sense and other political writings*. New York: Liberal Arts Press.

Ravitch, D., & Finn, C. (1987). *What do our 17-year-olds know?* New York: Harper and Row.

Schrag, P. (1967, January 21). The emasculated voice of the textbook. *Saturday Review*, p. 74.

Schwab, J. J. (1961/1978). Education and the structure of the disciplines. In I. Westbury & N. J. Wilkof (Eds.), *Science, curriculum, and liberal education* (pp. 229-272). Chicago: University of Chicago Press.

Sewell, G. T. (1988). American history textbooks: A literary disaster. *Organization of American Historians Newsletter, 16*(3), 20.

Shaver, J. P., Davis, O. L., & Helburn, S. M. (1979). *An interpretative report on the status of pre-college social studies education based on three NSF-funded studies*. New York: National Council for the Social Studies.

Shulman, L. S. (1983). Autonomy and obligation: The remote control of teaching. In L. S. Shulman & G. Sykes (Eds.), *Handbook of teaching and policy* (pp. 484-504). New York: Longman.

Shulman, L. S. (1986a). Paradigms and research programs in the study of teaching: A contemporary perspective. In M. C. Wittrock (Ed.), *Handbook of research on teaching* (3rd ed., pp. 3-36). New York: Macmillan.

Shulman, L. S. (1986b). Those who understand: Knowledge growth in teaching. *Educational Researcher, 15*, 4-14.

Shulman, L. S. (1987a). Assessment for teaching: An initiative for the profession. *Phi Delta Kappan, 69*, 38-44.

Shulman, L. S. (1987b). Knowledge and teaching: Foundations of the new reform. *Harvard Educational Review, 57*, 1-22.

Shulman, L. S., Haertel, E. H., & Bird, T. (1988). *Toward alternative assessments of teaching: A report of work in progress* (Teacher Assessment Project Publication Series). Stanford, CA: Stanford University, School of Education.

Teaching & Teacher Education. (1987). [Special issue]. *2*(4).

Todd, L. P., & Curti, M. (1982). *Rise of the American nation*. New York: Harcourt Brace Jovanovich.

Tourtellot, A. B. (1959). *Lexington and Concord: The beginning of the war of the American Revolution*. New York: Norton.

Vaughan, A. T. (1967). *America before the Revolution 1725-1775*. Englewood Cliffs, NJ: Prentice-Hall.

Wiley, K. B., & Race, J. (1977). *The status of pre-college science, mathematics, and social science education: 1955-1975, Vol. 3: Social science education*. Boulder, CO: Social Science Education Consortium.

Willcox, W. B. (1966). An historian looks at social change. In A.S. Eisenstadt (Ed.), *The craft of American history* (pp. 16-33). New York: Harper and Row.

Wilson, S. M. (1988). *Understanding historical understanding: Subject matter knowledge and the teaching of U. S. history*. Unpublished doctoral dissertation, Stanford University, CA.

Wilson, S. M., Shulman, L. S., & Richert, A. E. (1987). "150 different ways" of knowing: Representations of knowledge in teaching. In J. Calderhead (Ed.), *Exploring teachers' thinking* (pp. 104-124). London: Cassell.

Wilson, S. M., & Wineburg, S. S. (1988). Peering at history through different lenses: The role of disciplinary perspectives in teaching history. *Teachers College Record, 89,* 525-539.

Wineburg, S. S. (1987). *From fieldwork to classwork–Cathy: A case study of a beginning social studies teacher* (Knowledge Growth in a Profession Publication Series). Stanford, CA: Stanford University, School of Education.

Wood, G. S. (1966). Rhetoric and reality in the American Revolution. *William and Mary Quarterly, 23,* 3-32.

Wood, G. S. (1969). *Creation of the American republic, 1776-1787.* New York: Norton.

CONCLUSION

Jere Brophy

The contributions to this second volume in the *Advances in Research on Teaching* series represent the state of the art of studying teachers' subject-matter knowledge and beliefs as they relate to their instructional practices. They substantially advance our understanding of the mental lives of teachers by describing key aspects of teachers' professional pedagogical knowledge as it is developed in the context of teaching particular subject matter and showing linkages between this knowledge and (1) other pedagogical knowledge or beliefs held by the same teachers, (2) how the teachers taught their subjects in the classroom, and (3) (in some cases) the effects of this on student outcomes. Developed through improvements in conceptualization and research methodology, these findings and others like them have replaced earlier counterintuitive and unrewarding findings of research on teachers' subject-matter knowledge (as indexed by test scores or course grades) with exciting information about the development and effects of teachers' pedagogical content knowledge and beliefs.

The contributors to this volume studied a variety of school subjects taught at a range of grade levels. Even so, their findings replicate or complement one another in most of their comparable aspects. Thus, when taken together and considered as a set, they establish the beginnings of a useful knowledge base

Advances in Research on Teaching, Volume 2, pages 349-364.
Copyright © 1991 by JAI Press Inc.
All rights of reproduction in any form reserved.
ISBN: 1-55938-034-9

concerning aspects of teachers' pedagogical content knowledge that generalize across school subjects in addition to aspects that apply within individual subjects. Key elements of this knowledge base are as follows.

POINTS OF AGREEMENT

Except in the most basic sense that teachers cannot teach what they do not know, teachers' *subject-matter knowledge* does not directly determine the nature or quality of their instruction. Instead, how teachers teach particular topics is determined by the *pedagogical content knowledge* that they develop through experience in teaching those topics to particular types of students. Guided at least implicitly by the goals that they seek to accomplish with the students, teachers draw on their pedagogical content knowledge to decide what aspects of a topic to teach, how to represent these to the students, and how to develop the intended understandings using a combination of instruction, activities, assignments, and evaluation devices. Thus, pedagogical content knowledge "represents the blending of content and pedagogy into an understanding of how particular topics, problems, or issues are organized, represented, and adapted to the diverse interests and abilities of learners, and presented for instruction" (Shulman, 1987, p. 8). The contributions to this volume demonstrate quite clearly that how teachers teach particular content is determined in part by their pedagogical content knowledge (along with related orientations and beliefs).

Like practical knowledge in other professions, teachers' pedagogical content knowledge is organized not just in the form of general principles but also in the form of context-specific case knowledge that is easily accessed for application when the same or similar teaching situations (cases) are encountered in the future. Thus, this knowledge is organized around what teachers have learned about how to teach particular topics to particular types of students. Teachers develop networks of pedagogical content knowledge of how to teach multiplication of fractions in mathematics, how to teach the American Revolution in history, how to teach *King Lear* in literature, how to teach photosynthesis in science, and so on. Unlike nonteachers or novice teachers who may have equal or better knowledge of the subject matter, experienced teachers have well-developed and readily accessible "scripts" for teaching it. To the extent that such scripts have been honed to maximal effectiveness with the types of students to be taught, they greatly increase teachers' efficiency in teaching particular topics because they minimize preparation time and allow the teacher to lead the class smoothly through planned series of activities with a clear sense of direction and minimal confusion.

Ideally, these gains in efficiency will be achieved without losses in flexibility and openness to nonroutine student responses. This implies that scripts will be adopted consciously as means for accomplishing particular ends, monitored for effectiveness, and changed or temporarily suspended whenever the teacher needs to fashion an adaptive response to unanticipated events (as opposed to being conditioned as habits learned with minimal awareness and implemented rigidly as if they were ends in themselves).

Pedagogical content knowledge includes information about students' interests and activity preferences, but ideally it is organized to facilitate accomplishment of curricular goals, not just to maximize student affect. It includes ideas about what is worthwhile to teach and how to represent this to students, not just knowledge about what students like or respond well to. Thus, effective pedagogical content knowledge focuses on scripts for building subject-matter understanding in students.

The curricular goals that teachers choose to pursue and the models that they develop to help them select, represent, and teach academic content to their students are determined not only by the amounts of subject-matter knowledge that they possess but also by their general orientations to the subject and the particular types of knowledge that they have developed about it. Teachers' orientations toward particular subjects include their beliefs about why the subjects are important and why they are taught in the schools. Often these subject-specific orientations are subsumed within more general orientations concerning the nature and purposes of schooling and the roles of teachers. Kliebard (1987), for example, has suggested that many of the differences in observed approaches to curriculum and instruction in academic subjects can be understood as differences in the relative importance assigned to four potential purposes for K-12 education: (1) communicating historically important and influential knowledge, especially the knowledge represented in the academic disciplines, (2) capitalizing on and assisting normal processes of human development by keying content to the interests and learning needs associated with particular ages and stages, (3) meeting society's needs by preparing children for the roles that they will be expected to play as adults, and (4) seeking to combat social injustice and promote social change by developing values, critical thinking, and related citizen action dispositions.

Thus, to understand how teachers' subject-matter knowledge affects their teaching, one needs to ask not only what a teacher knows about a subject, but also what is the teacher's orientation toward the subject and the implications of this orientation for teaching goals and methods. These more general orientations toward academic subjects frame teachers' representations of what the underlying disciplines are and how one "does" them, not just their representations of concepts or other more specific content. Thus, depending on their teachers' orientations, some students may learn that mathematics is an organized body of knowledge to be understood whereas other students might learn that mathematics is a collection of procedures to be memorized, and some students might learn that history is a vast collection of mostly unrelated facts whereas other students might learn that history is disciplined interpretation that attempts to identify and explain the significant events and trends that occurred at particular times and places. Similarly, teachers' orientations toward and representations of school subjects will affect the degree to which students come to realize that science offers principles and methods that they can apply in their lives outside of school or that knowledge developed in English literature courses can increase their enjoyment and deepen their appreciation of the books that they read.

Teachers' representations of concepts or other more specific content are important too. As illustrated in several chapters in this volume and also in Lampert's (1989) chapter in the first volume of this series, different representations of particular content are needed to accomplish different instructional purposes. Also, examples or other representations differ in the degree to which they are familiar to the students, the degree to which they are typical or atypical of the concepts or principles they represent, the degree to which they are concrete and observable versus more abstract, and so on. Skilled teachers have a repertoire of such representations available for use when needed to elaborate their instruction in response to student comments or questions or to provide alternative explanations for students who were unable to follow the initial instruction and thus are in need of remediation.

Teachers' subject-matter knowledge and pedagogical content knowledge differ within as well as across subjects. Where their knowledge is more explicit, better connected, and more integrated, they will tend to teach the subject more dynamically, represent it in more varied ways, and encourage and respond more fully to student comments and questions. Where their knowledge is limited, they will tend to depend on the text for content, deemphasize interactive discourse in favor of seatwork assignments, and in general, portray the subject as a collection of static factual knowledge.

Besides reflecting their knowledge of and orientations toward subject matter, teachers' choices of goals, methods, and activities reflect their beliefs about how students learn, both in general and in particular subjects. The contributors to this volume share a theory of learning that is informed by the information-processing approach to human cognition, with its view of knowledge development as requiring the learner's own schema construction accomplished through active information processing and sense-making efforts. This implies that students must be able to integrate new input with existing knowledge that they already understand, a process that in turn is supported by forms of classroom discourse in which teachers draw out students' ideas and encourage them to explain them. Thus, when teaching for understanding, teachers not only will ask students to supply relevant facts, but also will ask them to suggest solutions to problems, to offer explanations, to articulate and defend positions on issues, or in other ways to engage in sustained and critical thinking about the subject.

Teachers' pedagogical knowledge, beliefs, and orientations are organized into networks that not only support but also limit what they do and how open they are to change in particular directions. Once such networks become well established, those who wish to induce significant change in teachers' classroom behavior may have to develop comprehensive inservice programs that address the entire networks, not just provide training in desired instructional methods. Many teachers may need to be resocialized to new beliefs about and orientations toward the subject before they can fully understand and appreciate the recommended changes in instructional methods, and many will also need additional subject-matter knowledge and increased support via better curriculum materials and more complete teachers' manuals.

Given their beliefs about the scope and depth of professional practical knowledge that teachers must have available in ready-to-use form in order to be able to teach well, most of the contributors to this volume are cautious or even pessimistic regarding the prospects for educating teachers to the point that most of them will be able to teach most topics well. Even teachers whose general orientation emphasizes teaching for understanding (i.e., not just for memorization) may be hampered by limited domain-specific knowledge about many of the particular topics that they teach, so that they often will recognize that their handling of these topics is less than ideal but will not know how to improve it. Change will be a gradual process in which teachers will use hybrid compromises or will alternate newer with older methods until they develop sufficient subject-matter knowledge and pedagogical content knowledge about the topic to enable them to teach it consistently in the new way.

Several of the contributors implied that programs for changing teachers would embody several of the features that are also emphasized as important when teaching school subjects for student understanding. One common theme was an emphasis on conceptual change, not only with respect to what is involved in teaching particular topics well but also with respect to general beliefs and orientations about the nature and purposes of schooling, the classroom conditions that foster development of student understanding, and the role of the teacher. Another was the value of working with teachers in groups and eliciting sustained critical discourse about instructional guidelines, as well as using journal writing assignments and other encoding and communication activities. There was also emphasis on the idea that in addition to exposure to generic principles and socialization activities, teachers need detailed information about how to teach particular topics (case knowledge).

To the extent that their chapters touch on them, the contributors to this volume appear to agree on the conclusions and implications summarized in this section. There is also a shorter list of issues on which they appear to disagree, summarized in the following section.

POINTS OF DISAGREEMENT

The authors appear to differ in their orientations concerning the purposes and goals of schooling and the primary sources for curriculum development. Some, especially those who focus on the secondary grades, look mostly to the academic disciplines for ideas about what to teach and how to represent it to the students. Others, especially those who focus on the elementary grades, look to other criteria in addition to the current structuring of knowledge within the academic disciplines. In particular, some would make content selection and representation decisions so as to emphasize content that links with students' current knowledge or beliefs about the topic or is applicable to their lives outside of school. These differences are aspects of the ongoing struggles among supporters of the competing curriculum sources described by Kliebard (1987).

Other disagreements center around the nature and depth of student subject-matter knowledge that various contributors would accept as evidence of accomplishment of worthwhile curricular goals. All of the contributors would like to see fact memorization and relatively isolated skills practice be replaced with the teaching of integrated networks of content for understanding and application. However, the envisioned networks differ in scope and depth and the envisioned applications vary in level of complexity and degree of resemblance to traditional school tasks. Thus, the intended outcomes implied by some of the contributors could be accomplished through important yet relatively modest changes in current practice (primarily, teaching fewer topics in more depth and with more emphasis on applications), whereas those of other contributors could be accomplished only through sweeping changes in schooling as we know it.

The contributors also appear to disagree concerning the level of specificity and detail of information that teachers will need in order to be able to teach effectively. For example, some contributors believe that generic models and guidelines include much of what is important about teaching any subject effectively, but others believe that the applicability of such generic models and guidelines is severely limited, so that they must be supplemented substantially with subject-specific (and in some cases, even topic-specific) models and guidelines. Disagreement along this dimension also occurs with reference to teachers' knowledge of what students know about a topic. Some contributors believe that teachers can accomplish most of what they need to do by working from experience-based knowledge of what typical students in the class are likely to know or think about the topic and by addressing most of their instruction to the class as a group, but others appear to believe that teachers will need to find out what each of their individual students is thinking and will need to conduct a good deal of tutorial instruction.

Finally, the contributors differ in their ideas about how to use their findings in teacher education programs. In particular, they differ in ideas about how specific to be in telling teachers what and how to teach. Some would state goals, make content selection and representation choices, and train teachers in specific instructional methods (sometimes backed by specially prepared curriculum materials), but others would present information and guide critical discussion but leave it up to individual teachers to decide whether and how to change their teaching.

LINKAGES WITH OTHER RESEARCH ON TEACHING

Having identified some points of agreement and disagreement among contributors to this volume, I will now offer some thoughts about how the information they have developed may relate to the findings developed in other branches of research on teaching. I will then conclude the volume with some discussion of design and methodology issues and some suggestions about needed next steps in research on teachers' subject-related knowledge, beliefs, and orientations.

One way that the research described here can be linked with other research on teaching is through investigation of developmental trends in the content and organization of teachers' pedagogical content knowledge as novice teachers begin to accumulate practical experience. Some such investigation was done in the early stages of the work by Shulman and his colleagues at Stanford. More recently, Roehler, Duffy, Herrmann, Conley, and Johnson (1988) have addressed this question in their studies of preservice teachers' developing "knowledge structures" relating to the teaching of reading. They have studied these structures using an "ordered tree" technique in which the preservice teachers are asked to state the concepts that they use in thinking about and planning for the teaching of reading and to show how these concepts relate to one another by developing graphic illustrations of their conceptual networks. Roehler and her colleagues have traced developmental patterns in these knowledge structures by beginning to collect data on them before preservice teachers began courses in reading instruction or had opportunities to practice it in the classroom and then repeating the data collection periodically thereafter. Their data indicate that interesting nonlinear patterns developed in the complexity and coherence of these knowledge structures as the preservice teachers gained knowledge and experience.

Prior to their coursework and teaching experience, the student teachers' knowledge structures relating to the teaching of reading were low in both complexity (number of concepts included) and coherence (degree to which concepts were related to one another within clusters that in turn were embedded within larger networks). As the teachers began to take courses in reading instruction, their knowledge structures gradually became more complex. However, at first this complexity was not matched by comparable increases in coherence (the structures got bigger but not better organized). Eventually, in fact, they became too complex. Over the course of a semester, for example, the preservice teachers' knowledge structures became "progressively overburdened with cluttered and unorganized declarative knowledge by the end of the course, rather than reflecting the simplicity and organization assumed to be associated with expert teachers' ability to access knowledge and make instructional decisions (Roehler et al., 1988, p. 163).

Later, however, as the preservice teachers continued to gain knowledge and experience, their knowledge structures became both less cluttered and better organized. In the language used in this volume, these novice teachers had selected, organized, and transformed a variety of types of knowledge (about reading, about teaching, about students, etc.) into pedagogical content knowledge that could be accessed and used to guide their instruction. The functional role of these knowledge structures was suggested by observational data indicating that student teachers with more coherent knowledge structures taught more coherent lessons than student teachers with less coherent knowledge structures.

Analyses parallel to those of Roehler et al. (1988) that used the "ordered tree" technique or other techniques for tracing developmental patterns in novice teachers' pedagogical content knowledge would be instructive. So would similar analyses of changes in the pedagogical content knowledge of experienced teachers who were involved in reeducation efforts designed to increase their emphasis on teaching for understanding and higher order applications of academic content.

Along with some of the work reported here, the work on knowledge structures raises interesting questions about possible nonlinear relationships between teachers' subject-matter knowledge and their pedagogical content knowledge. Perhaps there is an optimal breadth and depth of subject-matter knowledge for teachers working at any particular grade level, such that additional subject-matter knowledge beyond this optimal level would be counterproductive because (1) it would never be needed for teaching the content that this teacher teaches, and (2) by adding nonfunctional complexity to relevant knowledge networks, it would make it more difficult for the teacher to select appropriate content to teach to students and to transform it into pedagogical content knowledge. Research on these issues might not only shed light on interesting theoretical questions, but also provide data that would inform policy decisions about how much subject-matter preparation teachers need and whether their courses should be the same as or different from those taken by disciplinary majors.

The work presented in this volume can also be related to research on teachers' expectations (reviewed in Brophy, 1983, & Dusek, 1985). That work indicates that teachers' decisions about how much and how thoroughly to teach particular content to students are shaped by their expectations concerning what the students are capable of accomplishing in the available time. Most of this work has focused on teachers' differential expectations concerning the probable achievement of individual students, with emphasis on how initially inaccurate expectations, if not soon corrected by the teacher, can solidify and begin to exert self-fulfilling prophecy effects on student achievement via mediating effects on teachers' instructional decisions and actions. Reviews of such research indicate that such self-fulfilling prophecy effects of teachers' expectations are minor or nonexistent in most teachers' classrooms, but play a significant role in the classrooms of the minority of teachers whose expectations are both inaccurate and rigidly held and who thus do a poor job of meeting the needs of many of their students.

With hindsight, we are coming to realize that it may have been unfortunate that so much of the teacher expectation research was focused on teachers' expectations concerning individual students. Both logical analysis and a few empirical findings suggest that teachers' differential expectations for the achievement of individual students are merely elaborations on more basic themes established by their expectations for the class as a whole (Good & Brophy, 1991). To the extent that this is true, between-teacher differences in expectations for achievement by comparable classes of students would have the potential to affect student achievement in more powerful and widespread ways than within-teacher differences in expectations for achievement by individual students (Brophy, 1983).

The tie-in with the work presented in this volume is that teachers' expectations concerning achievement by the class are part of the network of professional pedagogical knowledge that they develop through experience. So far, the contributors to this volume have looked at teachers' goals and instructional agendas primarily with respect to the teachers' subject-matter orientations and content selection and representation decisions. It should also be profitable to look at these same aspects of teachers' pedagogical content knowledge with an eye toward the nature and accuracy of the beliefs about their students that they use to make decisions about appropriate content, activities, and assignments. To the extent that such decisions are based on uncorrected inaccurate information or invalid logic, they would provide the potential for self-fulfilling prophecy effects on student achievement and other manifestations of mismatch between instruction and students' learning needs.

A larger issue here is the validity of the pedagogical content knowledge that teachers develop. The very term "knowledge" implies that the teacher's thinking is valid and verifiable against the relevant facts. Actually, however, not only teachers' subject-matter orientations and beliefs but also their pedagogical content knowledge is subjectively constructed and thus open to distortion because of misinformation acquired from others, misperception or misinterpretation of classroom experience, the operation of defense mechanisms, and other factors. Perhaps we should refer to pedagogical content *beliefs* rather than to pedagogical content *knowledge*.

In any case, more explicit recognition that pedagogical content knowledge varies not only in complexity and coherence but also in accuracy would add a new perspective to this line of work and also provide a basis for relating it to several different sets of findings. For example, Doyle (1983) and others have noted that the curriculum as enacted in the classroom often tends to be lower in cognitive level and less focused on understanding and higher order applications than the ostensibly intended curriculum. Doyle interprets this discrepancy as resulting from fear of ambiguity and risk that causes students to exert pressures on teachers, who then "bargain" with the students by simplifying demands in exchange for good cooperation. However, some of the contributors to this volume, along with several other investigators (see Brophy, 1989, & Newmann, 1988) have shown that expert teachers sustain their focus on understanding and higher order applications and thus impose corresponding expectations and agendas on their students, yet elicit positive affective as well as cognitive responses from the students (i.e., the students find their classes demanding but nevertheless look forward to them because they also find them valuable and interesting). Such findings suggest that at least part of the reason why poor subject-matter teaching occurs in many classrooms is that the teacher is weak in pedagogical content knowledge or lacks a clear orientation toward teaching the subject.

The concepts of conceptual change teaching and confronting and correcting student misconceptions have, so far, received significant attention in studies of teachers' pedagogical content knowledge only in science. These ideas could be incorporated into the research in other subject areas as well, once more information becomes available about what knowledge and misconceptions about a topic are likely to be common among students at particular grade levels (science, and to a lesser extent mathematics, have been ahead of the other subjects in developing such information). In mathematics, for example, conceptual change ideas would be useful in studying teachers' thoughts and actions relating to the misconceptions that can occur when a shortcut is taught before the full procedure is understood or when content representations are misleading. Conceptual change thinking would also apply in social studies, such as when designing instruction about American history or government to include correction of childish beliefs that American presidents are both much more powerful and much more benevolent than they really are. In general, much more research is needed in all subject areas about the content-related knowledge and beliefs of students at different grade levels and their implications for teacher knowledge and action.

Comparisons of findings in different subject areas can be made by interpreting the research using concepts that describe alternative teaching goals or contexts. For example, many scholars have distinguished between the scientific disciplines and the interpretive disciplines. This distinction might be useful in stimulating such questions as, for example, whether the pedagogical models developed by Gudmundsdottir to describe teachers' approaches to teaching literature and history (primarily interpretive disciplines) would also apply to teachers' approaches to teaching mathematics or science. It also may prove useful to distinguish among (1) the teaching of processes or procedures, (2) the teaching of concepts or generalizations, and (3) the teaching of explanations or other interpretations. Such distinctions might be useful in studying, for example, the degree to which the criteria put forth by Leinhardt, Putnam, Stein, and Baxter concerning good explanations and useful representations apply across subjects (rather than being specific to math) or across teaching situations (rather than being specific to the teaching of processes or procedural knowledge).

Concepts from the literature on curriculum sources and goals also can be helpful for sharpening comparisons and making judgments about what different teachers are trying to accomplish. Kliebard's (1987) scheme mentioned earlier serves as a reminder that teachers may pursue other goals besides the teaching of discipline-based knowledge, that content is supposed to be selected as a means to accomplish curricular goals rather than treated as an end in itself, and that a demonstration that students at a particular grade level *can* be taught some discipline-based content is not by itself an argument that they *should* be. These considerations imply the need for research on pedagogical content knowledge surrounding types of content other than those drawn rather directly from the disciplines. They also suggest the value of seriously entertaining the possibility that networks of content can be elaborated to the level of *too much* depth and breadth for a given grade level, not just *not enough*.

These considerations also serve as a reminder that value differences are necessarily involved in any attempt to draw conclusions about teachers' general subject-matter orientations or teaching goals. Grossman's descriptions of Colleen (text orientation) and Martha (reader orientation), for example, suggest that they are both effective but teach different literature courses. The same is true of the two history teachers described by Wineburg and Wilson. This underscores the need for multidimensionality in thinking about teaching, especially good teaching. It may be that the best teachers are outstanding not because they do the same things in the same ways, but because they do a well-articulated subset of worthwhile things well, whereas poor teachers do not do anything well.

Finally, the contributions presented in this volume raise a host of questions about teacher education. I have already mentioned questions about how much and what kind of subject-matter preparation teachers will need and whether their subject-matter courses should be the same as or different from those taken by disciplinary majors. Other teacher education questions are: (1) Can we find ways to educate teachers to do good subject-matter teaching without requiring them to complete years of work in each subject taught? (2) Can we teach general principles in ways that will enable teachers to access and apply them efficiently in particular situations, or will teachers need years of case knowledge and experience? (3) How much will it help to provide teachers with much better teachers' manuals that include detailed information about intended student outcomes, rationales for content selection and representation, probable student beliefs and misconceptions, and methods for teaching for understanding and higher order applications? (4) Given that value-based decisions must be made in adopting general orientations toward subject-matter teaching, to what extent should we socialize teachers to adopt particular orientations versus leaving it up to them to decide for themselves?

DESIGN AND METHODOLOGY ISSUES

Compared to most of the studies of teachers' knowledge and thinking that had been done up until just a few years ago (reviewed in Clark & Peterson, 1986), the work described in this volume embodied several methodological advances. In particular: It focused data collection around naturally occurring teaching situations rather than contrived experimental situations; it provided for thick description of the thinking and actions that teachers invested in curriculum units or lessons; it considered teachers' pedagogical content knowledge rather than just their subject-matter knowledge; it developed detailed information about teachers' content goals, selection, and representation; and it explored relationships between teachers' subject-matter knowledge, orientations, and beliefs and their instructional actions. However, only a few of these lines of investigation have so far included attempts to assess the effects of instruction on student outcomes. It is important that other lines of investigation in this area be extended to include assessment of effects of observed instruction on student outcomes, because this is the only way to know for sure whether assumptions about the effectiveness of particular approaches to teaching particular content are valid.

Ideally, studies would be designed to ensure that each teacher's students were assessed to determine the degree to which they had acquired the outcomes that the unit or lesson was designed to develop. If comparisons were to be made between teachers who differed in their intended outcomes, the assessment package would include the full range of outcomes so as to be fair to each teacher and to generate data to inform a sophisticated analysis of the trade-offs involved in the various approaches (as opposed to a misguided "horse race" model designed to declare a "winner" by treating outcome measures as unidimensional). The outcome measures might include individual interviews, work samples, or various higher order application tasks instead of or in addition to traditional tests; the key characteristic of assessment devices would not be their format but their appropriateness as ways to measure student progress toward the teacher's intended outcomes.

Investigators can address student outcomes indirectly (as several contributors to this volume did) by imposing sample selection criteria to recruit subsamples of teachers who differ in known ways. I have several comments on this approach. First, although there is value in comparing novices with experienced teachers as part of a larger effort to understand how teachers' content-related knowledge and beliefs grow and change with experience, it should be kept in mind that experience is not the same as expertise or effectiveness. Thus, in order to draw inferences about appropriate or effective beliefs and practices, it will be necessary to identify teachers who are not merely experienced by demonstrably effective (at minimum, effective in accomplishing their stated goals; preferably, effective as indexed by a range of criteria including reputation and documented effects on cognitive and affective measures of student outcome). Second, once such outstanding teachers are identified, they can be compared most instructively not with novices, but instead with other experienced teachers who are equally effective in managing their classrooms and keeping their students consistently engaged in academic activities but who are mediocre rather than outstanding in their effects on student outcomes.

Such comparisons of outstanding teachers with similarly experienced but mediocre teachers would yield fewer and subtler differences than comparisons of outstanding teachers with novices or experienced but highly ineffective teachers would. However, information about these relatively subtle differences would be very important because it would help us to sharpen our conceptualizations of key qualitative characteristics of the best teaching. Also, it would provide thick description of "success models" for analysis and imitation. Comparisons of teachers who shared the same goals (e.g., conceptual change teaching of photosynthesis) would be especially instructive in this regard. Finally, it strikes me that the method of making within-teacher comparisons of thoughts and actions associated with the teaching of high-knowledge content with thoughts and actions associated with the teaching of low-knowledge content (see Carlsen's chapter, this volume, pp. 115-143) is a useful supplement to the between-teachers comparison method for addressing some of these issues.

There is need for extension of these lines of investigation to different contexts, especially different grade levels, preferably by the same investigators studying teaching on the same topics. Especially if it included assessment of student outcomes, such work would help to develop much-needed information about the nature of and reasons for differences in what constitute appropriate goals, content selection, content representation, and instructional activities and assignments in different contexts.

Mention of activities and assignments raises one last point that I wish to emphasize: Most of the work reported in the first two volumes of this series, and more generally most of the content-related work in all of research on teaching, has focused on teachers' content explanations and on the teacher-student and student-student discourse that occurs during group lessons, without much attention to follow-up activities and assignments. I believe that systematic research attention to the topic of classroom activities and assignments is badly needed, beginning with fundamental questions such as the following: (1) What kinds of activities and assignments are used at different grade levels in different subjects? (2) What is the rationale for their inclusion (i.e., what intended outcomes are they expected to produce)? (3) What are the trade-offs involved in using different kinds of activities and assignments? (4) For a given type of activity or assignment, what are desirable and undesirable features? (5) How should teachers introduce various types of activities and assignments to their students, monitor progress and provide feedback while the students are working on them, and handle accountability and grading issues? The forthcoming third volume of the *Advances in Research on Teaching* series will address these questions.

CONCLUSION

Having raised a range of methodological issues and speculated about ways in which the lines of work represented in this volume could be expanded to link with other kinds of research on teaching, I will conclude by returning to consideration of what has been accomplished in research on teachers' subject-matter knowledge and related beliefs. The progress represented by the contributions to this volume provides cause for enthusiasm about research on teachers' subject-matter knowledge and beliefs, but it also represents just the beginnings of what ultimately must become a much larger and more differentiated yet better integrated knowledge base. Much needs to be done even on issues of basic conceptual clarity and definition (How might the concept of teachers' pedagogical content knowledge best be defined and differentiated from related concepts? How might basic philosophical issues surrounding the distinction between knowledge and belief be resolved most sensibly?), and of course there is a need for much more empirical work. Ultimately, information about teachers' pedagogical content knowledge and related knowledge and beliefs will be needed about each major topic taught in school, along with information about students' prior knowledge and misconceptions relating to the topic and information about appropriate methods for teaching it. Viewed from this perspective, the contributions to this volume may be seen as just the first few steps beginning a very long journey.

Still, these steps provide cause for celebration, because they represent real progress. By developing better ways of conceptualizing and measuring teachers' subject-matter knowledge and beliefs, investigators doing the kinds of research represented in this volume have moved us well beyond the counter-intuitive and uninformative findings of early research on these topics. First, they have shown that teachers' subject-matter knowledge and beliefs do make a difference after all: Contrary to the impression given in early research on the topic, we now know that both what teachers teach about a topic and how they teach it will be affected by the extent and nature of their knowledge about the topic and by their beliefs and orientations concerning what is involved in teaching and learning it. Furthermore, we now know something about what the important dimensions of teachers' subject-matter knowledge, beliefs, and orientations are, about contrasts along these dimensions between teachers who differ in levels of experience or expertise, and about how teachers change along these dimensions as they acquire experience or expertise. This information is important for understanding why teachers do what they do, as well as for broadening our perspectives on what will need to be included in effective teacher education and professional development programs.

In conclusion, it can be said that although there is a long way to go, the field of research on teachers' subject-matter knowledge, beliefs, and orientations is now firmly established as a productive scientific enterprise. It has already developed a useful knowledge base, and several different but complementary lines of work are under way that should further increase our understanding of teachers' subject-matter knowledge, beliefs, and orientations and their relationships to teacher behavior and student outcomes. Studies by the contributors to this volume are among the most important components of this emerging knowledge base.

REFERENCES

Brophy, J. (1983). Research on the self-fulfilling prophecy and teacher expectations. *Journal of Educational Psychology, 75,* 631-661.

Brophy, J. (Ed.). (1989). *Advances in research on teaching, Vol. 1.* Greenwich, CT: JAI Press.

Clark, C., & Peterson, P. (1986). Teachers' thought processes. In M.C. Wittrock (Ed.), *Handbook of research on teaching* (3rd ed., pp. 255-296). New York: Macmillan.

Doyle, W. (1983). Academic work. *Review of Educational Research, 53,* 159-199.

Dusek, J. (Ed.). (1985). *Teacher expectations.* Hillsdale, NJ: Erlbaum.

Good, T., & Brophy, J. (1991). *Looking in classrooms* (5th ed.). New York: Harper & Row.

Kliebard, H. (1987). *The struggle for the American curriculum 1893-1958.* New York: Routledge & Kegan-Paul.

Lampert, M. (1989). Choosing and using mathematical tools in classroom discourse. In J. Brophy (Ed.), *Advances in research on teaching, Vol. 1* (pp. 223-264). Greenwich, CT: JAI Press.

Newmann, F. (Ed.). (1988). *Higher order thinking in high school social studies: An analysis of classrooms, teachers, students, and leadership.* Madison: University of Wisconsin, National Center on Effective Secondary Schools.

Roehler, L., Duffy, G., Herrmann, B., Conley, M., & Johnson, J. (1988). Knowledge structures as evidence of the 'personal': Bridging the gap from thought to practice. *Journal of Curriculum Studies, 20,* 159-165.

Shulman, L. (1987). Knowledge and teaching: Foundations of the new reform. *Harvard Educational Review, 57,* 1-22.

Advances in Research on Teaching

Edited by **Jere Brophy,** *College of Education, Michigan State University*

The *Advances in Research on Teaching* series has been established in the hope that it will make important contributions to the further development of this knowledge base, both by documenting advances in our understanding of particular topics and by stimulating further work on those topics. Toward that end, each volume in the series will be planned with an eye toward pulling together and providing visibility to emerging trends in research on classroom teaching that appear to be spawning important contributions likely to have lasting value. Scholars who have made programmatic contributions to the emerging literature on the selected topic will be invited to prepare chapters in which they not only describe their work but synthesize it, place it into the context of the larger body of research and scholarship on the topic, and give their current views of its meanings and implications. Topic selection for the volumes will emphasize conceptualization and analysis of the processes of teaching (including not only the behaviors that can be observed in the classroom, but also the planning, thinking, and decision making that occur before, during, and after interaction with students). Especially likely to be selected are topics that involve linking information about teaching processes with information about presage variables (especially teacher knowledge and beliefs), context variablesm, or student variables.

To further enhance the cohesiveness of each volume, authors will be invited to raise questions or make comments on one another's work, and to reply to these questions or comments in crosstalk sections that follow their chapters. The first two volumes in the series focus on aspects of the teaching of academic content. The first volume is on teaching for meaningful understanding and self-regulated learning, and the second volume will be on teachers' pedagogical knowledge of content and their planning and teaching of lessons based on that content.

Volume 1, l989, 375 pp. $63.50
ISBN 0-89232-845-2

J A I P R E S S

JAI PRESS INC.
55 Old Post Road - No. 2
P.O. Box 1678
Greenwich, Connecticut 06836-1678
Tel: 203-661-7602